W9-CNC-368

PSYCHOTHERAPY OF THE DISORDERS OF THE SELF

The Masterson Approach

Edited by

James F. Masterson, M.D.
and Ralph Klein, M.D.

 BRUNNER/MAZEL, *Publishers* • New York

Library of Congress Cataloging-in-Publication Data

Psychotherapy of the Disorders of the self.

Includes bibliographies and index.
1. Personality disorders—Treatment.   2. Object
relations (Psychoanalysis) 3. Self.   I. Masterson,
James F.   II. Klein, Ralph.   [DNLM: 1. Ego.
2. Personality Disorders.   3. Psychoanalytic Therapy.
WM 460.5.E3 P974]
RC554.P79 1988   616.89   88-19341
ISBN 87630-533-8

Copyright © 1989 by Brunner/Mazel, Inc.

Published by
BRUNNER/MAZEL, INC.
19 Union Square
New York, New York 10003

MANUFACTURED IN THE UNITED STATES OF AMERICA

10 9 8 7 6 5 4 3 2

Contents

Preface

The Masterson Approach has evolved from 32 years of scientific inquiry, including four formal research projects, nine books, and 75 papers. It found expression first through my own clinical work, and then after many years of training, through the work of my associates in New York and California. It also led to a postgraduate training institute, as well as a nationwide society. Through a unified view of the growth of self and object relations, the Masterson Approach provides a unique window of observation on all the clinical vicissitudes of developmental disorders of the self. This book then elaborates on and extends the work presented in *The Real Self.*

Scientific theory about the human psyche does not rise from static, set observations and formulas. The Masterson Approach evolved from a constantly adapting capacity to observe, empathize, and speculate while clinically responding to the problems of adolescents and adults. It also required the ability to integrate newly emerging psychoanalytic theories of the development of object relations and the self with child observation research that put these theories to the test of comparison with actual parent-child interaction.

The Masterson Approach did not appear in a flash of "revealed knowledge"—it did not spring forth full-grown, like Athena from the head of Zeus. It emerged from a long, slow, often laborious struggle, which required that I grapple with professional challenges, and the personal conflicts these challenges produced.

Out of this crucible of professional experience, observation, and personal insight, I developed a dynamic theoretical and clinical psychotherapeutic approach which, I believe, has two major advantages: (1) it integrates developmental theory with both object relations theory and a psychology of the self, and (2) it provides its own self-corrective tools. It allows the formation of clinical hypotheses whose validity can then be tested in the clinical arena. Beyond that, it both widens and deepens the practitioner's area of observation and reflection, immersing one still deeper in the clinical endeavor, and

vii

equipping one to explore these complex, subterranean themes with confidence and optimism.

For me, this volume marks an important stage in a professional journey that has had many turnings. Clinical concern and theoretical introspection evoke a wish to share, which led to writing and teaching. The deepening of this need to build a continuing community of ideas has impelled me to invite those who have learned from me to join me. This book represents their commitment and contribution to the Masterson Approach. It demonstrates how this approach has stimulated their thinking, broadened their clinical perspective, and enabled each to add his or her own unique contribution.

James F. Masterson, M.D.

The Authors

THE MASTERSON INSTITUTE FACULTY

James F. Masterson, M.D., Director
Ralph Klein, M.D., Clinical Director
Karla Clark, Ph.D., Associate
Richard Fischer, Ph.D., Associate
Karen Dean Fritts, Ph.D., Associate
S. Barlas Nagel, Ph.D., Associate
Candace Orcutt, Ph.D., Associate

The authors consist of two groups from two different areas: New York and California.

THE NEW YORK GROUP

The founding of the institute and the establishment of a training program has begun a vigorous program of instruction in these ideas in New York City. The faculty of the institute have worked with me in the Masterson Group in close association for many years. At the top of the list is Ralph Klein, M.D., a psychiatrist who was a Chief Resident of the Adolescent Unit back in the early 1970s, finished his training, had a personal psychoanalysis, and for years was head of the Outpatient Department at the North Shore Hospital division of the Cornell University Medical College, where he supervised treatment and training.

He returned to see me after leaving that position, at which point we started to work together. He later became the Clinical Director of the Masterson Institute.

Next in sequence was Candace Orcutt, Ph.D., who at the time she joined the Group had an M.S.W., and also had worked at the Payne Whitney Clinic. In addition, for six years she had supervised the psychiatric outpatient clinic at St. Joseph's Medical Center in Paterson,

New Jersey. She had the persistence to get her Ph.D. in social work, as well as a certificate in psychoanalysis after nine years of study.

The last member to join was Richard Fischer, Ph.D., who trained at the State University of New York at Buffalo, and who had several years of postgraduate training at the Westchester Division of the New York Hospital before joining the Masterson Group and Institute.

THE CALIFORNIA GROUP

In 1979 I began to make yearly trips to California to lecture—in the beginning for other groups, but after 1980 through my own organization. In the course of these trips I came across a number of therapists who were dissatisfied with their understanding and treatment of the personality disorders, and who requested supervision. With many misgivings I began group phone supervision.

I found, to my surprise, that it was extraordinarily successful, and shortly after I started individual phone supervision with Karen Fritts, Ph.D., followed shortly after by Karla Clark, Ph.D., in San Francisco, and finally by Shelley Nagel, Ph.D., in San Francisco. These supervisory sessions led to additional conferences with them when I was in California. They began to present their work at our organization's conferences and have become integrated into the associate faculty of the Masterson Institute.

Each of these professionals has learned and digested the theory, and is able to apply it clinically as well as to teach, but each of them also has added his or her own very important individual contribution to enrich the Masterson Approach.

Prologue: Evolution

James F. Masterson, M.D.

The pathway to the Masterson Approach began after my psychiatric training and can be divided into four stages, each of which had a central preoccupation, which was expressed in clinical research and resulted in a book. There was a progressive development of the point of view in each stage, each making its own contribution to the final perspective presented here as the Masterson Approach.

FIRST STAGE: PSYCHIATRIC DILEMMA OF ADOLESCENCE (1956–1968)

I was looking for a subject for a required research project during my residency. I began to notice at case conferences that whenever an adolescent was presented, someone would inevitably say that one had to be careful about diagnosis because "he may well grow out of it." I checked the literature for research on adolescents who had "grown

out of it" and found next to nothing. Thus began a central preoccupation about "what happens" that was to dominate my professional life
for 20 years and involve three follow-up studies. During my last year as
a resident and a postgraduate year as chief resident, I finished and
published a follow-up study on what happens to hospitalized
adolescents.

At the same time, dissatisfied with the methodological limitations of
retrospective in-patient follow-up study, I wanted to do a prospective
study that would eliminate as many of those methodological loopholes
as possible. What I did not realize at the time was that (a) I was now
flirting with becoming a methodological researcher and relegating the
intrapsychic and psychodynamic to the background as a means of
dealing with my own intrapsychic problems; (b) I had made a decision
to undertake a project from which it would take me 12 years (from
1956 to 1968) to extricate myself, and (c) when I emerged, the
temptation to use work as a resistance to understanding my own
intrapsychic problems would have been resolved with the crystalliza-
tion of a unified, harmonious perspective on both the inner and the
outer, on my self and on my work.

Those years entailed an ongoing struggle as to what perspective I
would adopt on clinical material as well as, inferentially, on my own
emotional problems and, consequently, as to what direction my career
would eventually take. I had obtained a large research grant for the
follow-up study, which provided two complete research staffs. The size
and the momentum of the research accelerated like a snowball rolling
downhill. Not yet familiar with the defense of denial, I only now
began to wonder if my reach had exceeded my grasp. It became
necessary to drop my clinical duties in order to accommodate the
research.

This was the post-Sputnik time in science. The physical sciences,
spurred on by the Russians' initial success with Sputnik, were
beginning their ascendancy. Psychiatrists were beginning to feel that
their research methodology was inadequate compared to that of the
physical sciences. At this point the social scientists came to the fore
with a so-called objective research methodology focusing on such
matters as defining variables, validity, reliability, and statistical
analyses.

I came under the influence at that time of an extraordinarily
talented social psychiatrist researcher by the name of Alex Leighton,
M.D., who was engaged in what is now the well-known Sterling
County and Midtown Mental Health studies of the prevalence of

psychiatric illness. He made his methodology and his statisticians available to us as consultants. Caught up in the same enthusiasm for methodology, I buried my reservations as to how appropriate this approach might be to clinical work and plunged in.

A conflict began to grow in me between the social science methodological point of view, and the clinical point of view, which emphasizes the importance of considering all variables at one time and sees clinical judgment as the only final instrument of observation and decision. At the same time, in my personal analysis I was delving deeper and deeper into my own psyche. I would spend three hours a day at the clinic trying to refine methodology—for example, conducting reliability studies or considering various statistical approaches to clinical material—and then go to an analytic session that would repeatedly demonstrate how often these activities served as well to reinforce my resistance to facing my own emotional problems.

This conflict was finally resolved. It happened at a conference with both staffs and all statistical advisors and consultants. The entire assemblage sat around all day listening to the statisticians debate various microscopically different statistical ways of approaching clinical material. I became so impatient and exasperated that after that day the matter, for me, was settled in favor of the clinical point of view. At the same time my use of work as a resistance to my own intrapsychic problems diminished dramatically.

The findings of this project were published in a book in 1967 entitled *The Psychiatric Dilemma of Adolescence*. We found the adolescent did not "grow out of it." Five years after evaluation more than 50% of the adolescents were severely impaired. At that time we called the impairments personality disorders rather than borderline conditions, and we found on review of the treatment records that if the patients and their parents were treated once a week over a course of a year, their symptoms (such as anxiety, depression, and acting out) did indeed diminish. But what was giving them so much trouble five years later, their pathological character traits, had not been touched upon in the treatment at all.

I began to ponder how to pursue further the questions the study had raised. What are these pathological character traits? Where do they come from? How can we identify them, and how can we devise better methods of treatment? At that time I was invited to take charge of the adolescent inpatients at the Payne Whitney Clinic, as the adolescents in the last six months had kicked out fifty door panels.

This was a serendipitous opportunity to pursue these questions in an inpatient setting over the long term where we would have a chance to carefully monitor and correlate the interviews with the adolescents' behavior.

STAGE TWO: TREATMENT OF THE BORDERLINE ADOLESCENT—A DEVELOPMENTAL APPROACH (1968–1974)

I designed a research unit for the intensive psychoanalytic psychotherapy of personality disorders in adolescents. I received the necessary commitments for a staff and residents from the chairman of psychiatry, who was willing to do almost anything within reason to get the adolescent problem contained. He agreed to allow patients to stay at least a year and the resident to remain on the service for that period of time. Those next six years were extraordinarily fruitful for the development of my own thinking and, in retrospect, provided the bedrock of what later became the Masterson Approach.

The adolescents who were admitted had such behavioral difficulties as truancy, taking drugs, and other forms of socially unacceptable behavior. The principal clinical symptom was acting out. In order for the unit to survive we realized we had to find means to set limits to this acting out. Having to deal with acting-out adolescents in a structured setting presented an absolutely unparalleled opportunity to learn how to understand and manage this defense mechanism.

The adolescents were forever putting the residents', and often my own, "feet to the fire" to test our competence and trustworthiness. Successfully surviving these adolescents' "trials by fire" taught us the therapeutic management of acting out. I also received much education on how to control adolescent acting out from Willard Hendrickson, M.D., who had already been in charge of the University of Michigan adolescent unit for a number of years.

Today, in supervision, as I see the problems most therapists have in understanding and managing acting out, I wish that they could have had that experience in that unique crucible. Only after we had become professionals at setting limits in order to survive did we learn that it had a far more important and profound psychodynamic effect. We saw adolescents become depressed as they controlled their behavior—i.e., the first link between affect and defense.

It was now clear to us that the acting out was a defense against the depression. However, the source of the depression remained unclear. We speculated it might have to do with adolescent conflicts over emancipation. In trying to puzzle it out, I had exhausted all known resources, including the writings of Anna Freud, Peter Blos, E. H. Erikson, and P. Greenacre. The breakthrough in understanding the sources of the depression came while I was browsing through journals in the library and ran across an article by Margaret Mahler on her study of psychotic children entitled "Autism and Symbiosis: Two Disturbances in the Sense of Entity and Identity." This article led me to investigate further her reports of her child observation studies of the development of the normal self through the stages of separation-individuation.

I immediately sensed that her work resonated with my own, and I was on the track she outlined like a bloodhound, following her work closely. At the same time that I was studying her work our depressed adolescents began talking not about conflicts with their parents in the present or in the here and now, but about earlier and earlier separation experiences and finally the mother's inability to acknowledge their emerging self.

It dawned on me that again serendipitously I was in the midst of two complementary research experiments. In other words, Mahler's work educated me about the early development of the normal self while my own adolescent patients were describing and demonstrating dramatically the failures of that normal process, the developmental arrest of the self of the borderline personality disorder.

I put the two together, which led to the view that the borderline personality disorder was a developmental problem—a failure in separation-individuation or in development of the self.

This opened for me the doors to some of the mysteries of the borderline personality disorder: the concept of maternal unavailability for acknowledgment of the self, the resultant abandonment depression, and the developmental arrest of the ego. It also led to an emphasis on a therapeutic technique—confrontation—that was integrated into the design of a treatment to deal with this developmental failure: confrontation of the adolescent's defenses against his abandonment depression led to the working through of the depression, which attenuated or removed the anchor from his developing, activating self and allowed it to resume its development.

These findings were published in 1972 in a book entitled *Treatment of the Borderline Adolescent: A Developmental Approach*. This book, in retrospect, must have been way ahead of its time, as its appearance was greeted with thundering silence. I felt as if it had been dropped down a bottomless well. It was only after the second book, *Psychother-*

apy of the Borderline Adult, was published that the first book attracted considerable attention.

STAGE THREE: PSYCHOTHERAPY OF THE BORDERLINE ADULT—A DEVELOPMENTAL OBJECT RELATIONS APPROACH (1974–)

A key question remained: What was the link between maternal libidinal unavailability and the developmental arrest? Object relations theory supplied the link that I had been looking for and was an enormous catalyst to my own thoughts about the role of maternal acknowledgment in the development of the self and of intrapsychic structure.

During part of this time I had corresponded with Donald Rinsley, M.D., in what, in retrospect, seems to have been an unusual congruence of mind. I taught him about normal separation-individuation theory and the role of maternal libidinal unavailability in the borderline personality disorder, and he taught me the finer points of object relations theory.

After the adolescent book was published, I was asked to present a paper on the treatment of the borderline adolescent at a symposium in Philadelphia honoring Margaret Mahler, M.D. I suggested presenting another paper I was working on, integrating object relations theory with separation-individuation developmental theory. In the paper I combined four ideas: (1) the developmental point of view about separation-individuation and maternal libidinal availability and acknowledgment, (2) object relations theory of the development of intrapsychic structure, (3) a very early paper of Freud's on the two principles of mental functioning, and (4) my own clinical observation that as borderline adolescents improved and became more adaptive— as they separated and individuated—they felt worse, not better—in other words, more depressed. These four ideas were combined in a paper entitled, "The Maternal Role in the Genesis and Psychic Structure of the Borderline Personality Disorder." The day I presented the paper at the meeting I felt confident that I had made a breakthrough, at least for myself, and that a whole new perceptual world lay before me. I realized also that I would have to move out of adolescent psychiatry and into the broader world of the psychoanalytic developmental object relations approach to the character disorders. After giving the paper at the meeting, I sent it to Dr. Rinsley, who responded with great enthusiasm and suggested that he might be able to integrate it better with Fairbairn's views on object relations. I agreed, and he became co-author.

I was already applying these new ideas to adults in my own private practice. This work with adults was presented in a book entitled *Psychotherapy of the Borderline Adult: A Developmental Approach* (1976). This book changed, crystallized, and consolidated my developmental object relations point of view of the borderline as well as my image of myself, which changed from that of an adolescent psychiatrist to one of a psychoanalytic psychiatrist with an interest in the developmental object relations approach to the character disorders in adolescents and adults.

This change, of course, led to another identity crisis. It was one thing for me to feel inside that not only was I no longer primarily an adolescent psychiatrist, but that I was now an expert on psychoanalytic psychotherapy of character disorders. It was quite another to get my peers in the field to accept this change.

I sent the book on the adult to my publisher with some misgivings, knowing full well that the adolescent book had not yet done that well. The editor sent the book out for review and several very, very long months later called me in for what was the briefest and most depressing interview of my life.

He turned the book down flat, quoting his reviewer as saying, "People interested in development read Mahler and there is much written on the borderline. There is no place for your book." I left dismayed and despondent. I had anticipated trouble but not so much trouble. Nevertheless, my conviction about the value of the work itself was not in the least shaken.

Luckily, through the good offices of another publisher, I was referred to Brunner/Mazel, which accepted the book immediately. One hurdle accomplished, I now had to await the book's reception. While the book was being prepared for publication a good sign occurred: It was accepted as a selection by most of the psychiatric book clubs. But my doubts remained. I couldn't help remembering the awful silence that followed publication of *Treatment of the Borderline Adolescent.*

A good sale of a featured book for a psychiatric book club is several thousand copies. Several months after the book was published (1976), I found a note my secretary had left on my desk. It read simply, "Psychiatric Book Club—13,000." I knew immediately that the comma had been misplaced and that the figure was 1,300, not 13,000. And that wasn't too bad. As I brought the error to my secretary's attention she assured me I was wrong; she had checked carefully. The number was 13,000. I cannot adequately describe the feelings of both relief and fulfillment that flooded me at the realization that the identity crisis was over. My own inner image of my self was now being accepted and reinforced by my peers.

That book had and continues to have an extraordinary record. It opened a whole new and exciting world for me. I received spontaneous letters from numerous therapists across the country describing how exactly it explained their problems with the treatment of the borderline patient and how helpful it had been. I also received any number of similar letters from borderline patients themselves. I was inundated with requests for lectures from all over the country. The lectures were crowded with enthusiastic and responsive audiences. Concurrently, I found that my own integration of this developmental object relations point of view had greatly expanded my own grasp and perception of clinical problems as well as my ability to manage them.

This development also helped me to decide to leave Cornell, which had been my professional home ever since I became a psychiatrist. I set up my own organizations, The Masterson Group for the treatment of personality disorders, and the Masterson Institute, a nonprofit organization for teaching and research. This decision expanded my teaching from one institute to many institutions. The Masterson Group had its inaugural public conference in October 1977 at Hunter College in New York on the borderline, and we had planned for several hundred people. We were inundated by over two thousand.

In 1976 I received a call from a young woman, Jacinta Lu Costello, finishing her Ph.D. studies at Smith College, who wanted to know if I would allow her to use the adolescents from our unit to do a follow-up study. I was astonished that anybody would think I would turn over these "jewels" to anyone else, since I had long planned to do the follow-up myself. We met, and it turned out that she was sound in every respect. We ended up doing a joint follow-up study of the borderline adolescents treated in our unit, which was published in 1980 as *From Borderline Adolescent to Functioning Adult: The Test of Time*. This study demonstrated the effectiveness of the treatment, an effectiveness that could be predicted by the degree to which the patients' treatment course followed the hypothetical model.

I then extended the clinical application of the theory in two other books, *The Narcissistic and Borderline Disorders: A Developmental Approach* (1981) and *Countertransference and Psychotherapeutic Technique* (1983).

In these books a developmental object relations approach to narcissism and the narcissistic personality disorder was spelled out, and the concept of the underlying etiology of the borderline personality disorder was extended as follows: There are three inputs into etiology—nature, nurture, and fate—and the therapist must make a clinical decision as to how much each has contributed to his patient's disorder. Nature consists of organic problems or constitutional or genetic defects. Nurture refers to maternal libidinal unavailability for support of the emerging self, regardless of the cause. And fate refers to those accidents of life that can affect either track of the two-track separation-individuation process—i.e., any event that diminishes the mother's libidinal availability or interferes with the child's individuation in the first three years of life.

STAGE FOUR: THE REAL SELF

By 1983, with the publication of the countertransference book, I felt that my writing days might be over. However, I felt that the developmental object relations theory as outlined still did not give adequate consideration to the self, and the concepts of the self offered by others seemed to lack something. I found myself without intention or plan focusing more and more in my work with my patients on the patient's self, to the point of spontaneously developing a symbol (S) for when the patient was activating his real self in the session, and (O) for his relationship with objects. I began thinking and talking more and more in terms of a real and defensive self as it became clearer and clearer in the clinical material. Only after I had been using this concept of the self in psychotherapy for several years did I finally decide I had to think it through further, organize it, and write it up, if only to become clearer about it myself and to get it out of my system. This material became *The Real Self: A Developmental, Self, and Object Relations Approach.*

This theory of the self now seems to bring the developmental self and object relations approach to a kind of fullness or completeness appropriate to the demands of the clinical material. At least it is probably as full or complete as I can make it. It is this comprehensive perspective that I call the Masterson Approach.

It has been extremely exciting and gratifying to have been fortunate enough to be involved in the veritable explosion of knowledge that has taken place in this field in the last thirty years, to see the gaps being filled and the pieces of the puzzle beginning to fit together. I had worked with borderline and narcissistic patients for years without being able to help them enough with their struggles. To finally have the tools to do the job with many patients as well as to teach others to do the job, to have mastered this task—to the limit of my ability—has provided the ultimate fulfillment and satisfaction in the work.

This volume takes the work into a fifth stage: its faithful transmission to others who can deepen and extend it. The authors presented here have all been trained by me, and all are actively engaged in teaching others through the Masterson Institute. The institute conducts a three-year, part-time postgraduate training program in New York City, as well as study groups; individual supervision and conferences for therapists are offered throughout the country and abroad.

PART I

The Masterson Approach

The Masterson Approach challenges some of the major arguments for, and tenets of, descriptive psychiatry in its approach to classification and diagnosis of the personality disorders. The descriptive approach was epitomized by DSM-III and DSM-III-R. In the period since the publication of these manuals, dissatisfaction with the limitation of a descriptive approach has become increasingly evident.

For those working in the field of psychotherapy of the personality disorders, descriptive psychiatry has always been only a stepping-off point. The advances in the treatment of the personality disorders in the past several decades has proceeded so far and so fruitfully because of the expanding knowledge and understanding of intrapsychic structure provided by developmental, object relations, and self theory.

Success in the psychotherapeutic treatment of the personality disorders has been the result of extensive clinical experience, not refinements in research design.

In Chapter 1, I integrate the formulations of object relations theory into a clinically useful dimensional model for the classification of the personality disorders that uses the descriptive categories of DSM-III-R as a starting point. The dimensional model integrates knowledge of intrapsychic structure with manifest symptomatology along a spectrum of adaptive functioning.

In Chapter 2 Dr. Klein presents a developmental, self, and object relations approach to the diagnosis of the personality disorders. Thereafter, the differential diagnosis of psychoses, neuroses, and personality disorders is systematically reviewed and its clinical application demonstrated.

My integration of developmental, self, and object relations theory with descriptive psychiatry culminated in my concept of the real self. This concept is reviewed in Klein's discussion, in Chapter 3, of the impaired self and the disorders of the self, which emphasizes the contribution of this integrated approach to

3

understanding the psychopathology and the treatment of the personality disorders.

The material contained in this introductory section establishes a common ground for understanding the language used throughout the chapters of this book, as well as providing an understanding of the criteria used to arrive at diagnosis and treatment decisions.

J.F.M.

Chapter 1

Application to the Personality Disorders (DSM-III-R)

James F. Masterson, M.D.

The advantage of the *DSM-III-R* approach to the personality disorders is that the system is descriptive and focuses on the most readily identifiable and most easily replicated phenomena: symptoms. In addition, since it is free of any theoretical bias, it can be used as a basis to study any number of theories.

However, the Masterson Approach to an understanding of the personality disorders views this diagnostic approach as having a number of limitations. Symptomatology is the most episodic and transitional of personality disorder phenomena. In point of fact, for a long time our emphasis on symptoms prevented us from getting to the essence of these developmental disorders.

The great advantage of the Masterson Approach to diagnosis is that it is developmental and psychodynamic and focuses on the least episodic, the most enduring of all personality disorder phenomena—

the intrapsychic structure: self and object representations, ego defenses, and ego functions.

The clinical application of this perspective, or this way of arranging the diagnostic categories, illustrates the guiding principle of the Masterson Approach. We can reorganize the eleven categories of *DSM-III-R* from the perspective of the Masterson Approach using an object relations framework derived from many years of clinical experience, and so transcend the present limits of formal research.

The eleven categories of *DSM-III-R* could be divided into four, as follows:

1. Borderline Personality Disorder
   a.   Histrionic
   b.   Avoidant
   c.   Dependent
   d.   Passive-aggressive
   e.   Compulsive
2. Narcissistic Personality Disorder
   a.   Exhibitionistic
   b.   Closet
3. Antisocial Personality Disorder
4. Paranoid and Schizoid Personality Disorders
   a.   Paranoid
   b.   Schizoid
   c.   Schizotypal

Thus, the four basic diagnostic categories are: Borderline, Narcissistic, Antisocial, and Schizoid. Within the borderline diagnosis there are a number of subcategories, which reflect the same basic borderline conflict although with different styles of defense against the abandonment depression. The passive-aggressive emphasizes passivity, the dependent dependency, and so forth. Underlying the different defensive structures is the abandonment depression and the same basis intrapsychic structure.

Within the diagnosis of the narcissistic personality disorder there are two subtypes, the exhibitionistic and the closet. The exhibitionistic exhibits his grandiosity, whereas one with the closet narcissistic disorder hides his grandiosity and idealizes the object (or other person).

The schizoid type comprises three subcategories: schizoid, schizotypal, and paranoid. Whether the schizotypal category belongs within the personality disorders or within the schizophrenia disease spectrum is not clear at this time.

A principal difference among these categories is the way in which the self relates to the object. In the borderline personality the self clings to or distances from the object. In the narcissistic disorder the self co-opts the object; in the psychopathic, antisocial disorders the self is totally emotionally detached or uninvolved with the object. In the schizoid disorders the self relates to the object by distancing, and in the paranoid there is major use of projection. Crucial diagnostic and treatment implications arise from the determination as to whether the self clings to the object, co-ops the object, detaches from the object, or distances from and projects on the object.

This view integrates diagnosis, the clinical picture, psychodynamics, and the indicated therapeutic strategy. Additionally, the Masterson Approach takes a broad, inclusive view that there is a very wide spectrum within each of these diagnostic categories from lower-level, poorly functioning patients to higher-level, better functioning patients.

The importance of this concept is illustrated by the story about three hunters lost in a jungle so dense and dark they have to feel their way. They encounter a large animal. One attempts to put his arms around the animal and says that it is thick and like a tree. The second, taking hold differently, says that it is thin and supple like a snake, while the third exclaims that it is very long and hard, like a spear. They are grabbing the leg, tail, and tusk of the same elephant, but their perspective is so limited that they perceive a part as the whole. This story is applicable not only to subcategories within the diagnostic types but also to levels of functioning.

Many therapists working only in hospital outpatient clinics view the diagnosis of borderline personality disorder, for example, as denoting patients who have separation psychoses and feelings of unreality and depersonalization—in other words, only lower-level borderline patients. This view is reinforced by the fact that particularly with the borderline personality disorder, the symptomatic criteria seem to have been derived from the study of hospital and clinic outpatient populations and are unduly weighted toward the lower-level borderline patient.

Similarly, many therapists in private practice who do not work with patients in hospitals tend to think that only the upper level is borderline and those who are lower level are probably psychotic. In fact, many of the patients in my private practice would not qualify for the diagnosis of borderline personality disorder using only *DSM-III-R*.

Among the narcissistic personality disorders, both the exhibitionistic or closet types can be either higher or lower level. The antisocial, too, may function along a spectrum from higher level—the "successful" psychopath—to the lower level—the criminal. The schizoid spectrum, too, shows a range from those who demonstrate pervasive pathology, the schizotypal, to those with higher-functioning schizoid disorders, who may function at high levels in terms of work but nevertheless have substantial difficulty with object relations.

The advantage of this multidimensional—developmental, object relations based—approach is that it simplifies and integrates clinical material while pointing the way to the application of specific therapeutic techniques.

Chapter 2

Application to Differential Diagnosis

Ralph Klein, M.D.

AREAS OF OBSERVATION

The process of differential diagnosis is dependent on many levels of observation, each one reinforcing the others to build a composite picture—a framework of diagnosis. The areas critical for making a diagnosis are: (1) the presenting picture of the false, defensive self; (2) review of current ego/self functions and impairments; (3) developmental history; (4) medical history; (5) family history; (6) assessment of intrapsychic structures; and (7) nature of the therapeutic relationship.

I will review briefly each area before presenting for differential diagnosis the cases of five young men.

Presenting Picture of the False, Defensive Self

The starting point for differential diagnosis is, and should be, the criteria put forth by *DSM-III* and *DSM-III-R*. A working knowledge of the range of psychopathology described by both Axis I and Axis II is a requirement that must be constantly updated and improved upon. Especially in the assessment of possible personality disorders, the DSM forces the therapist to ask: "Am I seeing the false self of a dependent, fearful, passive patient, or am I seeing the impersonal manifestation of a major mood disorder—or am I seeing both in the same patient?" The therapist must ask: "Am I seeing the false self of a grandiose, manipulative, narcissistic individual, or am I seeing the impersonal manifestation of the manic phase of a bipolar mood disorder—or am I seeing both in the same patient?"

Differential diagnosis includes a systematic assessment of static, impersonal, nonconflictual illness processes (diseases) as well as personal, conflictual, fluctuating illness processes (the personality disorders).

Once this assessment is made, differential diagnosis within the spectrum of personality disorders can utilize the descriptive criteria of *DSM-III-R* as a rough guidepost—at least to the more extreme examples within a diagnostic category, such as an exhibitionistic narcissistic disorder or an unsuccessful, lower-level antisocial disorder.

Beyond this, the clinician must now move to the other levels of observation in order to clarify unanswered diagnostic questions, whether between Axis I and Axis II or among the personality disorders themselves.

Review of Current Ego/Self Functioning

The personality disorders will present with defects and impairments in many, if not most, of the following areas of functioning: separation reactions, infantile or immature attachments, stunted efforts at individuation or creativity, and failures of self-regulating, autonomous capacities. The internal turmoil experienced by the individual with a personality disorder which is created by these impairments often manifests itself:

• at work, with poor, inconsistent performance or performance clearly below the patient's capabilities
• in the nuclear family, with a pattern of interaction marked by stress and conflict, particularly around issues of separation and autonomy

- in relationships more generally, with marked difficulties in forming mutually gratifying and lasting relationships and with relationships characterized by considerable dependency, clinging, distancing, manipulation, or detachment
- in self identity, with marked identity diffusion and/or difficulties in self-activation, assertion, and self-esteem regulation

The assessment of overall ego/self functions and impairments can establish the nature of impairments in the real self as well as the severity of such impairments.

Developmental History

In reviewing the history, the therapist should look for patterns of depersonification. Did parent and child (now adult) collude in regressive, dependent modes of relating which reflected how painful and conflict laden the separation process was for both? Was the emotional (and physical) milieu one of deprivation, devaluation, and danger, which is characteristic of the early experience of the schizoid or antisocial individual? Was the patient the receptacle of the parents' unrealistic and idealizing projections, or, conversely, were the parents unavailable as the objects of the child's need for idealization of and by the object, as is often the case in narcissistic disorders?

In reviewing the developmental course, "nature" and "fate" must take a place along side of "nurture" as etiological factors. The constitutional, including temperamental, characteristics of the child, the "goodness" or "poorness" of fit between child and caretakers, and accidents of fate must all be evaluated for their contribution to personality development.

Medical History

Although depression and anxiety are, for example, common manifestations of an underlying abandonment depression, the clinician must not forget that such dysphoric affects may also be presenting features of underlying primary medical illnesses as well as the secondary reactions to medical illness. Further complicating the process of differential diagnosis is the fact that any medical illness or disease process, from pancreatic carcinoma to panic disorder, can coexist with personality disorders as separate, comorbid entities. Therefore, a careful review of a patient's medical—as well as "psychiatric"—history must be undertaken.

Family History

A comprehensive review of the family history includes both psychological and biological family antecedents. The personality structure of the parents, as well as the psychiatric and medical illnesses present in the extended family, may further provide invaluable clues to aid in diagnosis of the current identified patient. The usefulness of such data, however, may be limited when it is second hand. This is especially true either when forming hypotheses about personality structure (as seen through the eyes of the patient), or in accepting previous psychiatric diagnoses—since diagnostic practices change over time and from place to place (a problem *DSM-III-R* resolves to some extent).

Intrapsychic Structure

Each personality disorder has a unique intrapsychic structure, which the therapist should be able to map out. This internal, representational world consists of a host of internalized objects—both self and object representations—as well as the relationships between and among these objects—internalized object relationships. The therapist must understand the patient's ideas and fantasies about what the patient is like and what he contains (self representations) as well as his ideas and fantasies about what people are like (object representations). The relationship between the self and object representations involves the crucial assessment of whether the self attempts to cling to the object, control and co-opt the object, distance from the object, or detach from the object. Although these ways of relating self to object are not mutually exclusive, one or another tends to predominate as a final common pathway for many etiological, motivational, pathways—nature, nurture, and fate.

Nature of the Therapeutic Relationship

The therapeutic relationship is a window into the intrapsychic structure of the patient. The manner in which the patient relates to the therapist affords a testing ground on which to evaluate and confirm or disprove the body of accumulated data and observations. Further, the therapist can use the patient's response to therapeutic strategies and interventions—confrontation, interpretation, mirroring, and communicative matching—to further validate his diagnostic decision.

We can put this diagnostic framework to use in examining the process of differential diagnosis of five young men, all of whom presented at a similar age (18 to 23) and faced—at least on the surface—similar life challenges consistent with that age. Despite these apparent similarities, all five eventually emerged as having quite different diagnoses.

MR. B

Mr. B was referred to me after a three-week hospitalization, during which he had been placed on lithium after having been diagnosed as manic-depressive. He was 22 and had graduated from college one year previously. Since graduation he had remained at home. There were intermittent brief attempts to work, return to school, or live away from home. However, each attempt precipitated depression, paranoid ideation, and feelings of paralysis (depersonalization), which led to increased drug use and sexual acting out, so that he was unable to continue whatever he had begun. Instead, he would end up at home, usually back in bed. In addition, he had frequent violent-hysterical outbursts, during which he would destroy furniture in the house and verbally attack or threaten to physically assault his parents and sister. He had seen several psychiatrists during the past year, and had been receiving neuroleptic medication (for paranoid schizophrenia) prior to the current treatment with lithium. It was as a consequence of one of his outbursts that he had been hospitalized.

Given this initial presenting history, the diagnostic possibilities were numerous. The severe symptomatology present during this past year was consistent with a psychotic illness (schizophrenia or manic depression), drug-induced and sustained illness, or a severe personality disorder (most likely borderline or antisocial).

I hoped that a more general review of his current ego strengths, impairments in the real self, and defenses would help sort out the possibilities. In fact, his psychopathology not only was severe but involved every area of his life: self-management, work, family, and relationships. For example, he insisted that he could not deal with his feelings without external support, usually from drugs or alcohol. In his life, clinging and acting out seemed the most usual substitutes for impulse control. He insisted that he was incapable of planning for the future, and wished only to feel better quickly; he insisted there was nothing wrong in wanting to feel good, while refusing to see the enormous cost to himself. He admitted, however, that he was unable to attract friends or women except by acting like a helpless boy. He would then cling tenaciously and indiscriminately to any man or woman who took an interest in him. This would leave him feeling momentarily good (not alone) but usually was followed by increased feelings of emptiness and aloneness, from which he would escape with drugs and alcohol. His self-image was admittedly that of a foolish, incompetent, "crazy" person.

This recounting of his current functioning began to narrow the differential diagnosis. Although he showed faulty reality perception, especially in his judgment, he maintained good reality testing. A persistent theme was emerging that the acting-out behavior was a defense against depression—not psychosis or neurotic anxiety. Further, his extensive drug use did not seem to be in the form of a primary addiction but, rather, seemed to be in the service of defense against depression. The absence of antisocial behavior in the history as well as the absence of hostile projections, haughtiness, grandiosity, or devaluation militated against a diagnosis of antisocial personality. At this point, the differential diagnosis was narrowed down to either borderline personality or major depressive illness without melancholia but with drug abuse. I looked now to the developmental history for further clarification.

Mr. B had been adopted at birth. He had attended private schools throughout his youth, always achieving above average grades. He described being unhappy a great deal of the time, especially after the birth of a younger sibling when the patient was 4. He recalled the conscious fear that his parents would "get rid of him" if he was not obedient and good. During adolescence, he had experimented heavily with drugs and promiscuous sex—behaviors that made him feel good and were either ignored by, or unknown to, his family. He still managed to maintain above average grades, a "network of acquaintances," and one close friendship despite spending most of his senior year of college "in an alcoholic haze."

The history seemed to support the differential diagnostic decisions I had already made. Arguing against a schizophrenic illness was the fact that, despite considerable substance abuse, there was no evidence of progressive deterioration in functioning. Also, in schizophrenia, it is the loss of structure, not the anticipated loss of structure, that leads to overwhelming anxiety and fragmentation. Mr. B, however, was manifesting separation anxiety increasingly throughout adolescence, culminating in massive acting out during college. The use of drugs and alcohol as a defense against depression was apparent. Importantly, the presence of depression (or unhappiness) was reported from early in life, leading one to think of a "characterological" depression rather than a "major affective illness." This was further supported by the absence of a family history for affective illness or alcoholism.

The history was consistent with a diagnosis of borderline personality. The history of abandonment fears, separation stress becoming symptomatic in adolescence and intensifying in college, and the acting-out defense against depression made the diagnosis of borderline personality disorder most likely.

Inferences drawn from the patient's reporting of the past can often be supported or, conversely, refuted by direct observation of the parents. In speaking with Mr. B's parents, I was struck by the degree to which they seemed clearly overwhelmed by, and consistently infantilizing of, their son. They seemed to use him as a receptacle for their projections. The father seemed to clearly derive satisfaction from his son's acting out; he promoted and even encouraged it. For example, despite his son's enormous difficulty with drugs, he would often pay him to come to work with him at his place of business—he owned a pharmacy. It was here that the patient got both drugs and money from the cash register with which to buy drugs (this was the only antisocial behavior).

His mother seemed to use Mr. B as a substitute for her husband, with whom she had a poor relationship. She was much less distressed by his being at home and, in fact, was "resigned" to his living there forever. She seemed depressed, and it was she who most consistently referred to her son as "crazy."

Though this pattern of family interaction is by no means pathognomonic of borderline pathology (in fact, many of the features of the interaction can be found particularly as reactive, or secondary, coping, patterns in schizophrenic families), certainly the pattern of interaction seen here is consistent with that which can produce the characteristic intrapsychic structure of the borderline patient: the split object relations part units (RORU and WORU) and the borderline triad.

In fact, in the very first interview, Mr. B's description of his present and past behavior seemed to demonstrate the split object relations units of the borderline in his belief that to maintain approval and "supplies" from parents and any significant other he had to be passive, helpless, infantile, and regressed. Efforts at separation, individuation, and self-regulation precipitated feelings of being paralyzed, empty, and alone (abandoned). He further mentioned that his behavior caused his parents much distress and was an appropriate revenge upon them for their not loving him. (This is example of the borderline patient's talionic impulse—the wish to get even at whatever cost to the self.)

The nature of Mr. B's relationship to me in the treatment provided the important final piece to the diagnostic puzzle. If Mr. B was borderline, the nature of the transference should support and reinforce the picture I had formulated of the intrapsychic structure. Indeed, for the most part Mr. B initially could relate to me only through either the RORU or the WORU projections. The alternating projection of these transference-like structures resulted in his alternately clinging and distancing. For example, he would state at times that I, like his parents, thought he was crazy and a spoiled brat. At other times, he felt that he had to remain ill to keep me interested in him.

The unique split part object relations units of the borderline patient demonstrated so consistently by Mr. B—in both his interpersonal and internalized object relationships, and both within and outside the treatment—are in sharp contrast to the intrapsychic picture found in either the schizophrenic or the antisocial personality, the two other personality organizations initially considered in the differential diagnosis. Simply stated, in the schizophrenic patient one finds not split object relations units but, rather, a fused self and object to varying degrees. And, unlike the undernourished, underinflated self representation of the borderline patient within the framework of a state of defense, one finds in the antisocial personality a fundamental grandiose or overinflated self representation within the framework of a state of siege.

Last, if the patient is borderline, the nature of his response to confrontation should confirm the existence of the "borderline triad." During the first sessions when I confronted Mr. B about his lack of success in managing his life and how self-destructive it was to handle his anger through revenge, he would pause, look sad, and admit that maybe he had "gone too far." He went on to describe being buffeted by his feelings, which often seemed out of control. Then, before I had the opportunity to further confront him (i.e., "Why do you think you can't manage these feelings?"), he blurted out that his moods just descended upon him unpredictably. That was what the doctors in the hospital had told him, and that was why he was taking lithium. This brief interaction demonstrated for the first time something that would be demonstrated time after time in the treatment—the operation of the borderline triad: separation-individuation leads to depression, which leads to defense, which leads to the need for further confrontation.

The nature of the patient's typical response to confrontation was a valuable additional differential diagnostic tool. While, characteristically, confrontation of the borderline patient results in containment of acting out and, hence, depression, confrontation of the schizophrenic patient often produces greater anxiety and frank disorganization. The antisocial patient will typically respond with distancing and controlling defenses: projection, hostility, suspicion, and rage.

The answer to the diagnostic question posed by Mr. B could now be given: Mr. B was borderline.

MR. E

Mr. E was 19 when he first appeared for treatment. He had been in therapy for two years but had stopped one year previously, when he had moved away from home to go to college. Away from home he had found himself increasingly "confused," unable to concentrate, anxious, and lonely. He felt increasingly unable to function, and without finishing the school year had dropped out, moved back to an apartment near home, where he was financially supported by his parents, and decided to resume treatment.

Since being back, he had enrolled at a local college for summer courses—all of which he was failing—and was working part time. He described having lost touch with his few friends since going to college, having had difficulty making new friends at school, and of having no past or present female friends or heterosexual relationships. An area of strength was his talent as an artist, basically a solitary activity, however, and one that he had decided to put aside since going away to school because he felt it was a distraction from the more important goals of getting an education and making friends. Finally, he alluded in the initial interview to an enormously conflicted and long-time unstable relationship with his parents.

At this point, I felt the differential diagnosis was between borderline personality, schizoid personality, schizophrenia, and possibly a severe depressive neurosis exacerbated by a superimposed major depressive episode. The diagnosis of major depressive episode would be necessary to explain the pervasive influence of his pathology across the spectrum of his ego functioning.

During the initial evaluation period, he described his problems as being "classically borderline" and as characterized by his refusal to grow up and take charge of his life. He stated he had never been allowed to grow up due to the influence of an overprotective mother and a narcissistic father, both of whom had tried to completely control and dominate him in different ways. There had been a period during adolescence of increasingly violent verbal and finally physical altercation, with the father pushing and shoving the patient until finally, on several occasions, they threw punches at each other and the mother had had to call the police.

By age 15, the patient had developed obsessive thoughts of killing his parents, and he decided that he could avoid this outcome only if he stopped speaking to his parents unless spoken to, which he proceeded to do. He stated that the focus of his initial treatment—begun when he was 15—had been separation, and he had been encouraged in his decision to have minimal interaction with his parents. However, his difficulty with making relationships had extended beyond the family, and his adolescence had been basically isolated.

The history, combined with the present illness, continued to be consistent with the diagnosis of borderline personality—albeit a lower-level, primarily distancing borderline patient with prominent engulfment fears. However, the striking paucity of manifest clinging and attachment behaviors throughout the history seemed even more consistent with the diagnosis of schizoid personality. The chronicity of the illness, combined with a mixture of dysphoric emotions and the absence of vegetative or melancholic signs or symptoms, weighed against a primary affective illness, whether severe depressive psychoneurosis or major depressive illness. The diagnosis of a more malignant schizophrenic illness was also still possible, and was given support by the history of paranoid schizophrenia in the paternal grandfather.

I began to focus on clarifying the nature of the intrapsychic structure, and gradually over the ensuing weeks I was able to map it out. He increasingly reported that he was unable to distinguish what was "real" about himself. This depersonalization reached a more malignant extreme when he felt at times that he was in pieces, fragmented and unable to "hold himself together." These feelings were transient but accompanied by extreme panic. They had continued to worsen over the past several months. At times he was no longer sure who he was, and particularly whether his thoughts were his own or his parents'. There were also feelings that he had actually become his father or his mother or other people around him. When speaking to a person standing next to a mirror, he did not know whether to speak to the mirror image of the person or the person—he was not sure which one was real. He was, as he put it, "unclear where [he] ended and the world began."

Was the diagnosis of borderline personality or schizoid personality still possible? Was there evidence of split object relations units along side of self and object separation or clear differentiation? Certainly not. Was there overriding evidence of the borderline triad (as in the borderline patient) or of cautious avoidance of engulfment, on the one hand, and annihilation on the other (as in the schizoid patient)? Again, no. There *was* instead the loss of body boundaries, creating confusion and an inability to discern the source and ongoing location of feelings, ideas, or even body parts, which is characteristic of the autistic process. This inability to maintain the separateness of ideas and identity contained within the mental structure of, and the definition of, the self from actions and identities outside the self—external events and people—is part of the malignant depolarization that is the quality defining the autistic transformation of the personality in schizophrenia.

Would it not be possible for a severe personality disorder, especially a borderline patient, to manifest transient psychotic episodes secondary to stress outside the treatment, and transference psychosis secondary to stress within the treatment that could account for the psychotic features described in this patient?

Almost certainly not.

The transference psychosis in the borderline patient manifests itself within the session by a blurring of the distinction between the therapist and other significant people in the patient's life—most commonly, for example, a blurring of therapist with "mother" or her part object symbolic representation as "attacker." This kind of delusional misidentification or paranoid delusion is quite different from the autistic breakdown between self and object that occurs in the schizophrenic process.

Psychotic features as part of circumscribed or transient or prolonged psychotic episodes outside of the treatment may be bizarre, delusional, and hallucinatory but will not violate the distinction between the psychotic and the autistic process. In fact, there is much growing evidence to suggest that such psychotic episodes are not "real" and secondary to separation stress but, rather, "factitious" and represent a conscious or unconscious attempt at defense or at manipulation for secondary gain. The singular situation in which manifestations of the autistic process may occur outside the framework of schizophrenia occurs as a consequence of acute drug intoxication through use of the hallucinogens or phencyclidine; however, when drugs are the underlying cause, the situation will be acute, not chronic.

For the schizophrenic patient like Mr. E, the relationship between therapist and patient requires the therapist's willingness to function as an auxiliary ego in areas of ego functioning that have undergone regressive and malignant alteration, such as reality testing, problem solving, judgment, and limit setting. Confrontation with the schizophrenic patient increases the demands on an ego structure that is already damaged and fragile. In fact, confronting Mr. E during the evaluation period would dramatically increase his anxiety, with resultant disorganization and fragmentation of existing ego functions before my eyes in the session. In confronting Mr. E, I was asking him to do something he could not do and, consequently, I was increasing his anxiety to the point of overwhelming him—because, as I had come to discover, Mr. E was schizophrenic.

MR. H

Mr. H was referred at the age of 20 by his mother, a psychologist, who had ignored for some time her son's disturbing behavior. This behavior had included some evidence of drug use, mood lability, lying, and, more recently, poor academic performance. Suddenly, however, the boy's situation had worsened. He had been caught cheating at school and had been suspended for a semester. When seen initially, the patient appeared relatively calm—this was before the suspension. When seen on the second occasion—after the suspension—he appeared distraught, stating that he was enraged and homicidal and, at the same time, empty and suicidal.

At this point, the diagnostic picture was totally unclear. I could rule nothing out for sure: the insidious onset of a schizophrenic illness; a "cry for help" in a borderline adolescent; the rage and humiliation of a narcissistic patient; or even an acute symptomatic attempt at defense or conflict resolution in a basically neurotic adolescent, with the picture again complicated by possible drug use.

Examination of his current and past functioning helped sort out the various possibilities. His behavior had startled both his parents as well as his teachers. To them, the behavior was of recent onset and totally out of character. The patient had always been an above average student—a position he had maintained despite doing very little work. He preferred, as he told me, to "make his mark" socially, which was manifested in his extensive social network and his involvement in a continuous series of short-lived, intense, and at times sexual relationships with girls whom he would initially idealize but soon find disappointing or unable to fulfill his needs.

After I had seen him for a few weeks, I felt that the stability and persistence of a good level of social functioning, combined with the absence of any schizophrenic signs or symptoms, enabled me to eliminate that possibility. The differential diagnosis was narrowed to that of a higher functioning personality disorder—either borderline or narcissistic—or a psychoneurosis.

The explanation for the acute acting out behavior remained unclear, because I was unable at first to identify any clear precipitating stress—specifically a separation stress, which might have pointed more toward a borderline disorder.

I began to look to the developmental history to help further with the differential diagnosis. The history revealed that Mr. H was an only child whose parents had divorced when he was 3. He had continued to live with his mother although he maintained close contact with his father, who lived nearby. The mother, whom I met, was a strikingly narcissistic woman, infantile and seductive, who used our meeting to describe in tearful and forceful detail the frustration of *her* needs as a consequence of her unfulfilled relationship with her son. She insistently showered her son with a host of depersonifying, yet idealizing projections. Rather than permitting him to grow, she seemed to consistently and clearly expect him now, as she always had, to be her emotional anchor, to listen and respond to her needs and to be her special man. Mr. H's father had long dealt with his own depression and guilt by, among a host of defenses, gratifying his son's wishes or demands. The boy seemed in no way threatened by or competitive with his father.

The family dynamic was making the picture look less and less borderline; the patterns of depersonification seemed to demonstrate mirroring and idealizing projections rather than regressive projections. Among the personality disorders, such a pattern is most consistent with the developmental course of a narcissistic disorder. However, such a history is not incompatible with a basic psychoneurotic disorder, albeit one with a marked disturbance in the capacity for self-esteem regulation, i.e., a narcissistic disturbance. I was struck, nonetheless, with the fact that the conflict in the family seemed dyadic, not triadic; in other words, the conflicts were between mother and son on the one hand, and father and son on the other, with little real conflict among all three, or their mental representations in the patient's intrapsychic structure.

I began to focus my attention on the nature of the self and object representations and the relationship between the two. In session after session it became clear that Mr. H's self-image was basically inflated and, for the most part, consistently activated. He had a clear idea of what he deserved and was entitled to and what his parents and the world owed him. This, of course, is in striking contrast to the borderline patient who (rather than seeking acknowledgment for what he feels he deserves) is satisfied to seek acknowledgment for his existence and for his need for essential supplies. It is in striking contrast to the psychoneurotic patient, too, who is often struggling to integrate the conflicting demands and nature of reality as well as the wishes and needs of others into his own self-identity.

With regard to object relationships, Mr. H maintained a few highly idealized relationships with important figures at school. In addition, there was need-fulfilling mirroring provided by his parents and a series of submissive female relationships. The superficiality of his social relationships, with both men and women, was striking. He was rarely able to convey a clear picture of the relationships, especially with girls, who occupied him so intensely. His interactions were marked by splitting, idealization, and devaluation, as they are for the borderline patient. In addition, however, the dominant themes were envy, humiliation, rage, and the wish for omnipotent control—characteristic of the narcissistic patient.

He would explain to me, for example, how control—more accurately, his fantasy of omnipotent control—over a relationship was more important than the relationship itself. What was important, he stated, was to be dominant so that he could get what he needed and deserved—the woman's undivided attention and caring: "My feelings are not for the person, but for the control. I think I frown on people who don't have control. I envy those who do have control of their friends." I asked whether he envied the control or the friendships. He replied, "The control."

Unlike the superficial relationships of the narcissistic patient, characterized and maintained by primitive defenses, manipulation, and control, the relationships of the borderline patient are often intense, chaotic, and characteristically dependent. Relationships for the neurotic are characterized by a range of higher- and lower-level defenses and can be empathic and gratifying even when difficult to achieve and requiring great effort to maintain.

By this time the diagnosis of narcissistic personality disorder seemed clear. In Mr. H, as in all those with narcissistic disorders, there was a false, defensive self manifested in the almost continuous, pervasive projection of a single grandiose self–omnipotent object fused object relations unit, which for the most part effectively concealed from view the underlying aggressive, empty fused part object relations unit. This contrasts with the borderline patient's split and separate rewarding and withdrawing part object relations units, which are alternately projected and which account for the alternating clinical picture of clinging and withdrawal. Both intrapsychic structures contrast sharply with that of the neurotic, whose whole self and whole object representations are much more realistic and are maintained despite frustrations.

Along with the diagnosis of Mr. H came understanding of the presenting picture. His most recent trouble had surfaced not at a time of increasing separation stress, which is typical for the borderline patient, but at a time when his ability to control omnipotently and successfully had come under pressure on all fronts. At school there were increasing expectations to work and to perform. He had essentially refused to put out more work and, hence, he was getting worse grades—a narcissistic blow. Outside of school, his narcissistic supply lines had dried up: both parents were in treatment and had begun to act more appropriately toward their son, and, additionally, Mr. H had almost literally run out of girls in his school to be involved with. Without the constant reinforcement of narcissistic wishes and the gratification of his feelings of entitlement, he was rapidly exposed to enormous underlying feelings of emptiness, assault, shame, and rage directed at those whom he considered mediocre, average, ungratifying, and inferior.

The nature of Mr. H's relationship to me provided the final piece of the diagnostic puzzle. He would react to my pointing out the self-defeating aspects of his behavior as if it were a mild attack. His face would cloud over and he would become irritated when he perceived even a slight lapse in my empathy, support, and understanding. He was unable to view confrontation as a constructive therapeutic effort. Rather, to work effectively with him, it was necessary for me to replace confrontation with interpretation, point out the aspects of reality that he was avoiding and denying, devaluing, or controlling, create a "consensus" that the way he had been acting was not the way for him to get what he felt he needed and deserved, and help him to discover more and more actual ways of affecting external reality.

MR. D

The patient was 25 years old when he first came for consultation as the result of a bribe from his parents. Essentially, he could remain at home (with all rights, privileges, and allowance intact) only if he was in treatment. The reason for this action was that Mr. D. had repeatedly threatened to kill his mother. He was frequently verbally abusive to both parents and physically threatening, especially toward his mother. He had always stopped short of direct violence (toward his mother; he had struck several girls he had dated). Both parents felt that maternally directed violence was growing more likely. Typically Mr. D's outburst occurred over a parental attempt either to set limits or to say no to one of his demands. The most recent outburst was a result of the mother's efforts to link the patient's financial support to certain "conditions" of behavior in the home.

Such a presenting picture of violence immediately aroused several diagnostic possibilities and eliminated others. Certainly the possibility of a psychotic illness or of drug-induced violence had to be ruled out. With regard to the underlying personality organization, such violence could be consistent either with an antisocial personality or possibly with a lower-level borderline disorder in which the talionic impulse was intense. In these instances, however, the history will usually reveal evidence of real, not just imagined or "felt," trauma that is often physical, not just emotional.

An assessment of the patient's overall functioning revealed that he was, according to himself and his parents, "brilliant, arrogant, unable to submit to any authority, hostile, charming, a real con artist, explosive, and lazy." He had dropped out of college during his sophomore year and had lived at home since. He was frequently using drugs, primarily "pot," Quaaludes, and cocaine. He had no good friends, only acquaintances. No friend was worth going out of one's way for, except as a source of drugs. No girl he dated meant anything to him. If they contradicted or criticized him, they would likely "get smacked." This brief overview of his current life cast an immediate pall over the prognosis. There was little evidence indicating features of a psychotic disorder: delusions, hallucinations, illogical or incoherent thought or speech, mania, or depression. While drug use was admitted, it seemed insufficient as an explanation for the pervasiveness of the psychological and social defects. Further, there was no evidence of a rewarding unit part object relations unit. Rather than needing others, he seemed barely to acknowledge their existence, and then only if they were need gratifying.

Although the diagnosis of antisocial personality was rapidly taking center stage, I looked to the developmental and family history to further confirm such a bleak diagnosis. In fact, the parents described many of these behaviors and characteristics as present from his early childhood. Again, this contrasts with the antisocial behavior of the borderline patient, which usually begins in adolescence and represents efforts at object-relatedness, whether by maintaining the patient in a dependent, regressive position within the family or by enabling him to become part of a peer pressure group. In both cases, infantile dependency or acceptance is the goal.

In contrast, Mr. D's childhood and adolescence were a tale of aggressiveness and defiance toward parents and teachers. The parents reported episodes of stealing and truancy beginning in latency. The patient reported that a teacher who called forth his hostility would likely find his or her tires slashed the next day. The patient stated that he particularly hated his mother, whom he described as a "cold, detached, narcissistic bitch." He blamed her for most of his problems: "She's never there when I need her." Mr. D spoke of his father as generally "benign" but under the domination of his mother. There were intimations that his father manifested an antisocial disorder himself.

In the relatively brief time I saw this patient, I was struck by the pervasive attacking and dangerous nature of his internal object representations. His internal world seemed a picture of a core unmodified grandiose self within the framework of a state of siege. His defenses operated to maintain this precarious and fragile state of affairs, and the most common defense appeared to be object detachment. This detachment was reinforced through social isolation and, most prominently, drug use. In response to a question about his immediate goals and plans, he stated that he needed to think of a way to get enough money to support his drug habit and that he was considering a kidnapping. At this point I felt uneasy and threatened. When I asked him about his future, he replied: "By 30 I will either be rich, dead, or in jail."

Unlike the individual with a "successful" narcissistic disorder, for Mr. D the need for idealization of and by the object gave way to, and was largely replaced by, detachment from the object. It seemed to me that any experience or person who attempted to penetrate this isolated, self-contained grandiose self structure, including the therapist, must be perceived as potentially dangerous and therefore must be either fled from, controlled, or destroyed.

Based on the understanding of Mr. D's intrapsychic structure, it could be predicted that he would demonstrate one of only two possible relationships to the therapist: either no relationship, manifested by persistent distancing or manipulation, or a mirroring relationship in which the sole purpose of the therapist is to mirror the patient's grandiosity. I asked Mr. D after the first few sessions if he could see any reason to continue to see me, aside from the wish to use me to remain at home. He replied, "It's something to do when I get bored. Anyhow, you're not an idiot like a lot of the psychiatrists I have seen. You're smart enough to realize how smart I am."

In summary, Mr. D demonstrated an antisocial personality disorder. Such a diagnosis always has serious treatment implications. Treatment failure is not a self-fulfilling prophecy on the part of the therapist; rather, the difficulties in treating the antisocial patient reflect the very difficulties in growth and development that are seen in the clinical experience with these patients.

MR. A

Mr. A was an 18-year-old high school senior when he was referred for evaluation for increasingly infantile and explosive behavior—as well as possible drug abuse—which seemed to be threatening the patient's immediate plans to go away to college.

Mr. A had suffered from moderately severe asthma since age 13; the frequency of attacks as well as their severity had increased during his senior year and were correlated with the behavioral changes: increasingly hostile communication with his parents, especially his father; admitted experimentation with marijuana and cocaine; and increasingly negativistic and passive-aggressive acting out at home and in his dealings with his internist, as well as in the management of his illness. This behavior had culminated in a recent hospitalization for what the internist had described as a relatively minor attack of asthma, but for which the patient had demanded hospitalization.

Based on the presenting clinical picture, the diagnostic possibilities were numerous, and an overall evaluation of his current functioning was necessary to narrow the possibilities.

In referring the patient, the internist raised his strong suspicion of "separation anxiety" and stated his belief that Mr. A's anxiety about leaving home and his attacks were directly related. In fact, the patient was now considering applying to a local community college and living at home.

Assessment of his current ego functioning revealed that he was an above average student who had been accepted at an above average college. He spoke of having a small but extremely close group of friends—all somewhat sexually and socially immature and inexperienced—from whom he gathered great support and about whom he anticipated intense feelings of loss when they would go their separate ways after graduation. He acknowledged having used marijuana infrequently and having tried cocaine on one occasion. He emphasized that he wished to take more control over the management of his illness—an issue that had always been a struggle, first with his mother, who had insisted for many years on administering his medication to him, and now with his internist, who refused to let him adjust his medication on his own.

At this point the diagnostic possibilities were narrowing down to a few. The more ominous diagnoses suggested by the aggressiveness, primitiveness, and age at onset of the presenting symptomatology were essentially ruled out—these included, respectively, an antisocial disorder, a lower-level personality disorder more generally (either borderline, narcissistic, or schizoid), and an incipient schizophrenic illness. Rather, the acute symptomatic picture of acting out could more appropriately be seen within the framework of either a higher-level personality disorder (either borderline or narcissistic) or a psychoneurosis. The distinction here can be made on several levels, but perhaps the single most important is whether one can more adequately track the patient's difficulties back to a core oedipal, and hence triadic, conflict or a core preoedipal, and hence dyadic, conflict. Stated alternately, would the history of this patient demonstrate a failure in separation-individuation or a failure in resolving his oedipal relationship, which was reemerging around the issue of emancipation? While the issue of the extent of drug use was not completely resolved in my mind, the preservation of his functioning scholastically and socially argued against drug dependence or abuse.

A review of his developmental history was further revealing. He spoke of relatively successful efforts to achieve age-appropriate social competence and task mastery during his school years. There had always been a tension, as he called it, between his mother and himself, primarily around efforts at individuation. He described his mother as always having been overprotective and overly concerned about his coping with new experiences: beginning school, going to sleepaway camp, and so forth. But he was able to persist and insist on doing phase-appropriate behaviors with his friends. What concerned him most, and what he spoke about spontaneously, were his conflicts and fears, primarily regarding sexual thoughts, feelings, and behaviors. He described a great deal of anxiety, shame, and guilt (remembered) from early adolescence with resulting almost total inhibition of sexual behavior. He had always had active sexual (masturbatory) fantasies involving domination either of or by a female. He felt fearful of, intimidated by, and enraged at his male schoolmates consciously (and his father, more or less unconsciously), with whom he felt he could not compete successfully.

He was consciously aware of increasing despair and hopelessness over his ability to overcome these difficulties. This had led to his brief experimentation with drugs. But he was not aware that he was defending against the anxiety associated with neurotic conflict by acting out his rage and fear through his temper tantrums and through his passive-submissive plans to now remain at home and attend a local community college.

Thus, despite the presenting difficulty with "separation stress," which was manifesting itself in acting-out infantile, clinging, and explosive behavior, evaluation of the patient's history showed many areas of ego strength and previous management of separation experiences and of age-appropriate tasks generally.

There was no other evidence of medical illness or of a family history of mental illness.

His internalized object representations were for the most part whole and realistic. His internalized self representation was also integrated—except in the area of his "body"-self image—around his belief that good work and hard study would permit him to find a comfortable professional identity and need-gratifying companionship. In other words, his internalized object relationships were clearly triadic, not dyadic, in nature. Conflict centering around wish and fear, desire and prohibition, action and inhibition, castration and moral anxiety was clearly center stage.

The diagnostic impression of a psychoneurosis was further confirmed in the therapeutic relationship. From the very first session he spoke with a minimum of prodding and in a spontaneous and open manner. He clearly viewed me as someone who could be potentially helpful to him. There was always the sense of working together on "the problem" rather than the sense of the problem as existing between the two of us. In short, a therapeutic alliance was present very early in the treatment.

Both in form (triadic) and content (the oedipal conflict), the diagnosis of psychoneurosis, hysterical type, could now be made.

MR. X

Mr. X is the next patient who presents himself for evaluation and treatment to you. What is his diagnosis? The answer to this question will be yours to determine and may make all the difference in that patient's life. Without correct diagnosis there can be no correct treatment. Without correct treatment, the patient's problems will continue.

Chapter 3

Introduction to the Disorders of the Self

Ralph Klein, M.D.

This chapter examines the clinical relationships between the impaired "real self," and the defensive false self which is pivotal for both theory and clinical practice. The concept both develops and helps to integrate the contributions of structural theory, developmental object relations theory, and self psychology to the understanding of personality disorders.

The Real Self Develops and Integrates Previous Models

Freud wrote little about the nature of "character" formation. He was interested in symptom formation and neurotic conflict generally. The essential construct of structural theory—the tripartite organization of the mental apparatus—accepted a priori the existence of a stable, cohesive, functional self-identity or self-structure upon which was superimposed, in psychopathological states, an array of neurotic defenses and conflicts which would clinically manifest themselves as symptoms, inhibitions, and psychoneuroses. The nature of the ego, or "I," of structural theory, therefore, was built upon the foundation of an intact and functional self.

The understanding of the development of personality disorders accepts, or rests upon, no such a priori structure. In fact, it is the failure to develop a stable, cohesive, separate, and individuated self that defines for object relations theorists and self theorists alike the core defect in the personality disorders.

Margaret Mahler defined the concept of separation-individuation as the principal organizer of preoedipal personality development, and identified two distinct but interrelated developmental tracks. The first focuses attention on the evolution of the self as separating from the object. This process begins with a stage of primary identification (symbiosis or merger) and evolves through subsequent stages of separation and internalization (by incorporation, introjection, and identification) until a final stage of object relationship is achieved. This stage is characterized by the individual's having a full differentiated self (separate) as well as the full capacity for sharing, empathy, intimacy, commitment, and the ability to recognize the individuative ideas, wishes, and needs of others (mature attachment). The "significant other" to whom the differentiated self is maturely attached is conceived as separate, whole, and consistent over time and varying emotional valences—in other words, libidinal object constancy has been achieved. Self theorists define a similar process when they describe the individual's task of building and rebuilding a network of "selfobjects."

In general, however, object relations theorists have focused on the ways in which the self is differentiated from and maturely attached to the object on the way to mature object representations and libidinal object constancy. The self theorists have focused on the ways in which the self becomes individuated and autonomous on the way to mature self-object relationships and libidinal self constancy. These perspectives, viewed from a developmental object relations vantage, are simply opposite sides of the same coin.

Although the study of the child's progress on the way to libidinal object constancy was at the center of Mahler's clinical contribution, it was the study of the individual's progress on the way to libidinal self constancy that was at the center of Kohut's clinical contribution. It was Kohut who primarily was responsible for "flipping the coin," and in so doing turning attention to the development of the self-regulating, autonomous functions and capacities of the self and away from the primacy of the capacities for object love and hate. For Kohut, interest lay primarily in the origins and evolution of the capacities for self-soothing, self-acknowledgment, self-activation, self-assertion, creativity, and self-esteem regulation. More generally, self psychology has focused on the entire experience of the self as stable, predictable, autonomous and continuous over time and shifting emotional valences—in other words, on the achievement of libidinal self constancy.

In this brief review, I am not implying that Freud was unaware of the importance of the individual's earliest experiences, that Mahler was unaware of the importance of the object's role in the self's developing capacity as self-acknowledging and regulating, or that Kohut was unaware of the importance of the separate "other," object relationships in their own right, and the capacity to acknowledge the legitimate needs, feelings, and wishes of others. I am suggesting, however, that all were focusing their clinical microscopes on different areas (or sides) of personality development. In contrast, the Masterson Approach attempts to integrate these constructs into a cohesive theory of the development and treatment of the personality disorders.

Masterson's concept of the "real self" denotes basically healthy personality development and structure. It encompasses the capacities for mature separation, attachment, individuation, and autonomy—the experience of the self with and without others—and the integration of these capacities into the overall personality structure. It is the entire area of the individual's identity that Masterson is putting under the clinical microscope and examining (Figure 1).

Masterson's real self has been erroneously equated with Winnicott's "true self," but the concept of the real self is in fact more widely clinically applicable, both in clinical examination and in therapeutic interventions. Essentially, Winnicott's concept of the true self refers to the subjective experience of the individual's capacity to acknowledge and give appropriate weight to his own individuative needs, wishes, and actions separate from the needs, wishes, and actions of others—people or society more generally. Masterson's real self incorporates this concept into an integrated theory that specifies the developmental tasks to be met and mastered on the way to libidinal object and self constancy. In this inclusive model, the real self—or healthy personality foundation—relates to the world through the successful alliance with a healthy, reality-based ego structure. Clinically, the individual feels a sense of continuity, stability, and mutuality in the experience of self

Figure 1. The Real Self: Structure and Functions

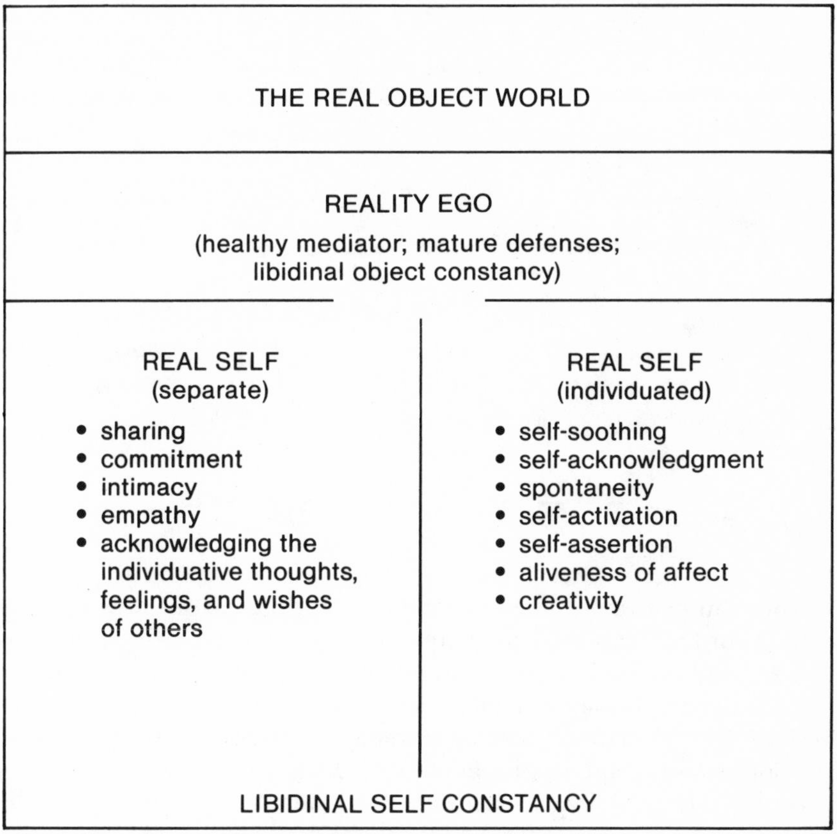

THE REAL OBJECT WORLD

REALITY EGO (healthy mediator; mature defenses; libidinal object constancy)

REAL SELF (separate)	REAL SELF (individuated)

• sharing
• commitment
• intimacy
• empathy
• acknowledging the
  individuative thoughts,
  feelings, and wishes
  of others
	• self-soothing
	• self-acknowledgment
	• spontaneity
	• self-activation
	• self-assertion
	• aliveness of affect
	• creativity

LIBIDINAL SELF CONSTANCY

with and without others, both maturely attached and comfortably self-regulating.

Impairments in the real self (Figure 2) will then manifest themselves in difficulties in the exercise of those functions and capacities associated with mature separation or mature individuation. The individual will complain of problems in intimacy, empathy, and sharing (or may be unaware of difficulties in these areas). The individual may manifest, on the other hand, difficulties in acknowledging and appropriately asserting his own individuated thoughts, feelings, and wishes in reality. The spontaneous gesture or act will be lacking and the capacity for self-soothing often painfully absent.

Figure 2. The Impaired Real Self and Disorders of the Self

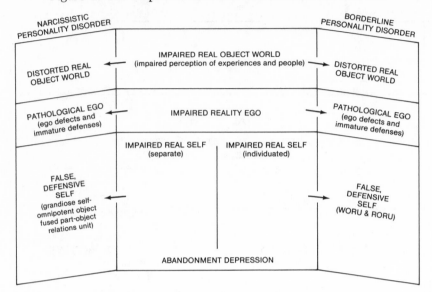

These impairments in vital functions and capacities are a consequence of the abandonment depression against which the individual
must defend. The false, defensive self of the borderline and narcissistic
disorders, and the personality disorders more generally, therefore
represents the pathological adjustments—defenses, distortions, and
deceptions—necessitated by failures in development in these crucial
areas. The false, defensive self of the personality disorder, unlike the
real self, relates to the real world through a pathological alliance with a
maladaptive ego structure. The patient experiences this as a sense of
discontinuity, fragility, or unstable self-identity; as distortions in the
normal balance of investment in self and others (Winnicott's false self
in the narrow sense); and as gross distortions between fantasies of what
one contains and what people are like with the reality of what one
contains and what people are really like.

Although Figure 2 highlights the false, defensive self of the
borderline and narcissistic disorders, all individuals with personality
disorders demonstrate, and suffer from, the impairments in the
development of the real self to some extent.

In the borderline patient, the failure to build a foundation of a real
self is manifested clinically in impairments in functions and capacities

associated almost equally with mature separation and individuation. This is most evident in lower-level borderline disorders, where the impairments are both pervasive and severe.

In the narcissistic personality disorders, the failures in the self in achieving mature separation with the associated difficulties in sharing, empathy, and acknowledging the thoughts, feelings, and needs of others are most manifest; the failures in the self as individuated (self-activating and self-assertive) are often concealed and latent and become manifest only during periods of acute narcissistic disappointment or trauma or later in life when narcissistic supply lines and defenses dry up, wither, and fail.

The antisocial personality disorder manifests the most obvious and profound defects or impairments in the capacity for mature separation and attachment (hence, Selma Fraiberg's accurate definition of sociopathy as a "disease of nonattachment"). Moreover, self-activation and self-assertion to achieve legitimate, healthy, adaptive, and individuative goals undergo an arrest and a pathological transformation into object control and object manipulation as the only pathway to pleasure and gratification. The problems are of equal scope and chronicity in all antisocial disorders but may be more or less severe and manifest depending on whether the individual is an unsuccessful sociopath (criminal) or demonstrates a more socially successful disorder.

The schizoid spectrum disorders (schizoid, paranoid, schizotypal) demonstrate fearful avoidance and withdrawal in approaching and managing object relationships. They perceive relationships as invariably depriving, enslaving, or dangerous. The degree of difficulty in initiating and maintaining individuative, self-regulating functions will vary depending on whether the patient occupies the higher (or schizoid) end or the lower (or schizotypal) end of the spectrum. The schizoid patient often has developed the capacity for self-sufficiency to a marked degree. Self-reliance has substituted for the fear of reliance upon others. The schizotypal patient, however, like most with lower-level personality disorders, manifests very real and multiple difficulties in daily living.

THE REAL SELF HAS IMPORTANT
THERAPEUTIC APPLICATIONS

The following case examples demonstrate the varied clinical manifestations of the impaired real self and the defensive, false self as seen in various borderline and narcissistic personality disorders. The usefulness of the concept of the real self as a diagnostic tool and as a therapeutic "beacon of orientation" for the therapist's interventions will be highlighted by examination of specific clinical material.

The Borderline Personality Disorder

The borderline patient characteristically feels that the caretaking ministrations of a significant "primary other" are crucial to his functioning and to his survival. The leitmotif of his life is the conviction (conscious or unconscious) that his very existence is dependent ultimately upon the presence of need-gratifying and life-sustaining others.

Implicit in this description are characteristic impairments in the real self: excessive dependency upon others and the perceived inability to manage one's own life in an active, adaptive, and healthy manner. Further, the capacity of the self to demonstrate mature separation, attachment, individuation, and autonomy is not found in the border-line patient. Rather, infantile dependence and failures in self-activation and management prevail.

In order to deal with these defects and the powerful, painful, and intense abandonment depression that accompanies and underlies them, the borderline patient turns to a false, defensive self structure. The false, defensive self representations of the borderline patient—infantile, primitive, and based mostly on fantasy and distortion rather than on reality—consist of two coexisting, alternately activated, and equally unrealistic self-images: a helpless, compliant, dependent child who is rewarded for this behavior and an inadequate, bad, worthless person who causes others to withdraw emotional support at any hint of real self-activation or self-assertion. Thus one can see how the distorted internal representational world of the borderline patient is mirrored in the distortions in the patient's perception of the object (real, external) world.

The psychopathology of the borderline patient is best understood by linking this description of the external and internal world of object relations to the concept of the borderline triad: efforts at separation-individuation (or building a real self) precipitate the abandonment depression, which then sets the false, defensive self (defense) into motion. The borderline patient, therefore, is almost always in a state of defense or, stated in another way, identified more or less completely with the false, defensive self.

The following cases exemplify the great variation in the clinical appearance of the false, defensive self of the borderline personality disorder, ranging from the subtle to the obvious. Despite these differences the underlying motif and the necessary therapeutic intervention remain the same.

Whatever the presenting picture, the therapist must differentiate between the false self, which has as its purpose defense, and the underlying impairment in the real self—which represents a real developmental failure. In work with the borderline patient, both of these areas must be addressed by the therapist, whether one is doing confrontive or intensive psychotherapy. However, whether one is doing confrontive or intensive therapy will determine how one addresses these two distinct problems.

In confrontive psychotherapy the containment or giving up of the false, defensive self that is brought about by confrontation brings to the patient's awareness the existence of the abandonment depression and the impairments in the development of the real self. The patient is then encouraged to deal with these by developing more adaptive and healthy defenses—a process of ego repair that strengthens the impaired real self but leaves the patient vulnerable to separation stress and abandonment depression.

In intensive therapy, containment or giving up of the false, defensive self again brings the impairments in the real self and the underlying abandonment depression to center stage, where the process of working through (employing primarily interpretation and communicative matching rather than confrontation) serves to effect optimal structural development and rehabilitation of the impaired real self. The end point is the full development of the capacities of the real self and freedom from separation stress and abandonment depression.

The case of M.A. M.A. was a 22-year-old woman who presented with the chief complaint of chronic and pervasive unhappiness and a vague sense of having something wrong with her. Her description of a false, defensive self was conveyed by her self-depiction as a chameleon and a "walking collage." She reported that she felt that she was made up of parts of all of those people—men and women—whom she met, and that she could evoke whatever part she needed, depending on the wishes and needs of whomever she was with at the time. She had no stable or continuous sense of which parts, part, or combination of parts represented who she "really was."

Initially she presented this material with a sense of pride—attempting to make a virtue of necessity. However, confrontation made this false, defensive self less ego syntonic. She grew increasingly angry and depressed when she would recognize she had "automatically" resorted to this kind of behavior.

About six months into treatment she reported a dream in which she was a contestant on an old television show that she had watched as a child called "To Tell the Truth." At some point in the show the announcer would ask the "real" contestant to stand up (there were three people all claiming to be the mystery guest). In the dream when the announcer asked the real M.A. to stand up, she could not decide which was the "real M.A." and all three stood up. She reported the dream by saying, "I did not know which was the real me and which were the imposters."

As confrontation continued to impede the operation of the patient's false, defensive self, a therapeutic alliance began to emerge. With this, the underlying impairments in the development of the patient's real self began to take center stage. She noted that whenever she attempted to respond spontaneously, or to assert her own feelings or wishes rather than cueing into the expectations of others, she would become depressed and anxious. Further, she was unable to soothe or activate herself.

Confrontations at this point are directed both at the manifestations of the false, defensive self:

> Why do you feel you must rely on someone else to make decisions for you?

and at the manifestations of the impairments in the development of the real self:

> Why do you feel you are not entitled to express your own feelings or wishes?

Such confrontations helped to focus the patient's attention on the developmental impairments in the real self, and to encourage her exploration into the origins of the developmental failures.

Over time, many memories emerged that helped her to understand the link between environmental failure, the underlying abandonment depression, the subsequent impairments in the development of the real self, and the resultant attempt at compensation by the erection of a false, defensive self.

Thus, she related with a mixture of depression, rage, and guilt how both parents would routinely stop talking to her for periods of time (ranging from days to weeks) since she was 6 years old, to punish her "defiance" or "disobedience." The punishment would continue despite her desperate pleas and promises to be good and obedient. This memory became central to her understanding of her failed efforts to build a real self structure.

Awareness of the destructiveness of the false, defensive self, as well as awareness of the impairments in the real self, are the necessary primary building blocks in the development of a real self. During treatment, unique aspects of the individual emerge and become focal points for the structure of the real self. For M.A., the ability to acknowledge and soothe herself was built upon her emerging interest in writing. With wonderment she reported that the hours she spent writing in her journal helped her contain and control her acting out and also identify her thoughts, feelings, and wishes.

Therapeutic work with M.A., as with all borderline patients, followed the circular process of the borderline triad. Efforts at building a real self would precipitate painful feelings associated with the abandonment depression. These in turn would provide an opening for the false, defensive self to be activated. Confrontation of the false, defensive self was then necessary again to get the patient back on the track of repairing the impairments of the real self.

The case of D.B. At the time he sought treatment, D.B. was in his forties and divorced from his second wife, following a series of extramarital affairs. For as long as he could remember, D.B. reported, he had had the fantasy that he contained concealed within himself "a naked, abandoned child." This was at odds with the image he projected to the world—that of a successful and competent professional and father of four.

The internal self-image of the "naked, abandoned child" had been associated with a recurrent dream from his childhood. In the dream he had been able to find solace and safety only by hiding in the folds of his mother's skirt. In this description, the naked child can be seen as representing the patient's awareness of the impairments in the real self while the false, defensive self was identified with the helpless child needing his mother's protection.

The reality of D.B.'s life contained countless examples of impairments in the real self and of the false, defensive self. The impairments in the real self were pervasive, though not obvious to the casual observer or to the patient himself in many instances. For example, he lacked the capacity to soothe himself or to acknowledge, activate, and assert himself to his potential, for although he was moderately successful he had failed to live up to great promise and for most of his adult professional life had shunned the relationship of peers for fear of being exposed as inadequate and incompetent. He was unable to appropriately express his expectations for and of others except through inappropriate temper tantrums. His conscious experience of the impairments in the real self was found in his feelings of shame, passivity, anxiety, and emptiness whenever he tried to assert himself socially or professionally. His defensive, false self would then be activated and he would flee from these painful affects to misalliances with a succession of "mothering" figures.

He would often be involved in several sexual relationships simultaneously. When he first entered treatment he had had a series of especially troublesome and anxiety-provoking experiences, and was carrying on affairs with four women—none of whom knew about the others. He stated that he could see me only once a week because of the huge financial drain of maintaining four lovers at the same time. Hoping to immediately make his false, defensive self less ego syntonic by emphasizing the "cost" involved in its maintenance, I remarked that it seemed to me that he needed one session a week for every affair—therefore my recommendation was for four sessions per week, not one. After a stunned silence, and some further discussion, he agreed to three sessions per week along with the promise to immediately terminate at least one of the current affairs.

During the initial period of treatment, confrontations revolved almost continuously around these relationships, to which he clung so tenaciously and which represented the constant activation of his false, defensive self. In fact, as he began to strip one after another of these relationships from the reality of his life and terminate their role in the maintenance of the false self, he became increasingly consciously aware of the manifestations of the impairments in the real self—an awareness that had been elusive for much of his life.

As he contained the tendency to act out the false self, he became interested in exploring the origins of the developmental failure to build the real self. Since he was in intensive psychoanalytic therapy, this exploration was promoted by confrontation and interpretation of all resistances against continued exploration. He recalled in great detail the relationship with his mother, and he became aware, for the first time, of the pathological nature of their interaction and how this created and maintained the condition preventing the development of his real self.

As an example, he recalled particularly a time during his young adulthood when he would visit his mother, who was dying of cancer. He realized that he could make his mother happy and receive praise if he "put on a little boy act"—even dressing and talking like a little boy. He added:

> For a long time I didn't realize what I had been doing. It seemed to be so natural, like it was really me. But at times I saw fleetingly what I was doing and that I wanted to change it. But I realized that if I acted my age [in other words, gave up his false, defensive self], my mother's face would cloud over, and she would become cold and detached. It was nothing dramatic. If you were standing there you would probably not have noticed a thing. But it was clear to me. It was more than that I was simply disappointing her. It was as if I was hastening her death, and, in a strange way, my own.

For D.B. every autonomous, self-assertive act, whether in his life or in memories recalled and feelings relived, became a vital component in the building of the structure of his real self. The emerging real self also manifested itself in previously untapped skills and talents and personal qualities. As an example in the area of self-soothing, D.B. was able to begin to derive genuine pleasure from artistic activities. In addition, he became able to engage in professional and paternal activities, in contrast to his previous passivity. Finally, he was able to find one compatible partner whom he felt he wanted to be with rather than needed to be with, and thus he was able for the first time to enter into a mutually committed and intimate relationship.

The Narcissistic Personality Disorder

In contrast to the presenting picture in the patient with a borderline personality disorder, who staggers from one rapprochement crisis to another through life, the narcissistic personality disorder presents with a comparatively stable clinical picture and self-structure. The relative stability of both stems from the almost continuous projection of the internalized, affectively fused omnipotent object–grandiose self object relations part unit. The capacity to deny depression and to devalue environmental traumas (disagreements, criticism, contradictions—essentially anything that frustrates the need for constant perfect mirroring) permits the narcissistic disorder to perpetuate the illusion of stability. The denial of reality—especially the individuative and separate wishes and needs of others—supports and maintains this self-contained state.

How, then, does the therapist working with the narcissistic personality disorder distinguish or identify the false, defensive self when the cost of the false, defensive self, unlike that in the borderline disorder, may not be painfully obvious to either therapist or patient?

In these patients, the pathological quality of the false, defensive self is revealed clinically by its content, methods, and rigidity, and by the denial or devaluation of reality that is required—first in the realm of object relationships and secondarily in the realm of genuine autonomous self-activation and self-esteem regulation.

The content of the false, defensive self revolves around the pathological inflation of the self's capacities as a result of fantasies of perfection and omnipotence. The method involves the endless search for perfect mirroring or for the perfect mirrorer—in other words, the idealized, perfect object. The rigidity of the narcissistic structure is revealed by the acute and intense and immediate feelings of depression, disappointment, and defensiveness whenever there are failures in perfect mirroring or in the perfect mirrorer. In this regard, the narcissistic disorder is like the proverbial tree that will not bend and therefore must break. At such times, the narcissistic disorder's good feeling is likely to explode into nothingness like an inflated balloon being pricked. However, this dysphoria usually is short-lived, because the patient is usually able to repair the damage and deny reality by reinflation through self-aggrandizement, projection of self-damage into others, or devaluation of the offending other or situation.

The pathological qualities of the false, defensive self become ego dystonic when the narcissistic individual is forced by life or by treatment to step out of his narcissistic cocoon and to function autonomously or empathically over time. At this point, defects in self-esteem regulation and self-activation, as well as defects in object relations (especially commitment, intimacy, and sharing), become apparent.

In the examples that follow, the patients had no awareness at the beginning of treatment that they were operating with a false, defensive self and that there were severe impairments in the capacity for attachment and autonomy. As each attempted to build a real self structure in the course of treatment, each became increasingly aware of the defensive nature of the false (grandiose) self. In each instance, efforts to mobilize the real self uncovered the deep and pervasive underlying abandonment depression.

The case of A.C. Now in her late fifties, A.C., the daughter of two highly successful narcissistic parents—one a model, the other a successful physician—had always managed to coerce her environment into resonating with her grandiose self-omnipotent object affectively fused object relations part unit. She thus was able to refuel the grandiose self and perpetuate the illusion of its stability and cohesion.

A.C. was a highly successful lawyer and moderately successful politician. She had other narcissistic supply lines, ranging from having her picture on the cover of a national magazine to having the mirroring and idealization provided by her narcissistic husband and by her three children. She lived, in short, within a seemingly impenetrable narcissistic bubble.

At least twice in her life, however, she had suffered acute narcissistic traumas that revealed the nature (and fragility) of her narcissistic structure. The first arose from an unsuccessful political campaign, which had precipitated weeks of despair. She had been able to deal with her loss primarily through denial and devaluation of the office she was seeking, her opponent, and the electorate.

The second injury stemmed from her divorce after twenty years of marriage. This time denial, projection, and devaluation did not work, and she had experienced months of mind-body-self fragmentation characterized by severe depression, shame, emptiness, somatic preoccupations, and transient periods of depersonalization and derealization. She eventually recovered from the divorce and managed to maintain her false, defensive (grandiose) self through her fantasy of being a perfect and powerful "Mother Earth–type wellspring" of advice, strength, and resourcefulness to her children, clients, and constituents. She was, as she later said, the mountain—and others had to come to her.

Over a period of a couple of years, however, her narcissistic balloon began to deflate as her children left for college or careers, and several friends either died or moved away. At this point, the mountain stood alone, and the impairments in the real self became increasingly obvious. Passivity, and at times almost total paralysis, set in, and A.C. both refused and genuinely seemed unable to activate herself to manage her affairs, maintain her career, find new friends, or soothe painful affects without resorting to alcohol.

When she first presented for treatment (for depression) this symptomatic picture was accompanied by her refusal to acknowledge the reality of her situation. The continuous activation of the false, defensive grandiose self of the perfect, powerful mother kept from her the awareness of the impairments in the real self. This was reinforced by increasingly severe alcohol abuse.

Gradually in treatment (three and then four times weekly) the nature of the false, defensive self became clarified, primarily through careful and repeated interpretation of small and large disappointments and vulnerabilities to narcissistic injury. As the false, defensive grandiose self receded from center stage, the impairments in the real self and the associated abandonment depression emerged, and the patient reported feeling "small, bewildered, hopeless, cold, empty, insecure, and full of panic and dread." The patient was able to stay in touch with the abandonment depression, to trace its origins, and to relive it in memory and with affect. This permitted the gradual emergence and consolidation of her real self.

The false, defensive self of the narcissistic disorder appears in varied forms, as does the false, defensive self of the borderline personality. The common denominator is the illusion of perfection, which may take strange forms. Consider the following example.

The case of D.R. At the time of the initial consultation, D.R. was in his mid-forties and three times divorced. He presented as depressed, and with the consciously expressed wish to find a magical, omnipotent therapist/mentor who could help him to overcome all of life's obstacles.

This wished-for idealizing transference quickly developed. This transference, however, failed to stabilize the patient's self-esteem. Despite his professed belief that he had found the perfect therapist, he continued to seem depressed and despairing and to feel "miserable."

Careful exploration of this feeling state over time revealed that the false, defensive grandiose self of the patient was organized around the self-image of a "modern-day Job . . . the Perfect Martyr . . . St. Sebastian full of arrows." The patient was almost totally identified with this self-image, which was accompanied by feelings of entitlement to the ministrations and admiration of others for the way he bore his suffering.

I made D.R. aware of the operation of this fantasy associated with the false, defensive self through clarification and interpretation of his narcissistic vulnerability to disappointment at my failure to mirror, and admire, his perfect martyrdom. As the pathologically inflated grandiose self–omnipotent object object relations part unit began to "shrink" (and correspond more closely to reality), the patient became aware of impairments in the capacity to mobilize a real self. He reported his perception of the impaired real self when he stated, "I feel like a nobody, a derelict." Increasingly this type of perception was no longer accompanied by an affect of "contented despair" but rather by early childhood memories of emptiness, fear, and dread. The image of the derelict was especially painful and was associated with the period, starting at age 5, when his father would take him to his factory on weekends. As they would leave after taking care of whatever business had to be done, they would exit by the rear door, where there were usually derelicts loitering. The young boy was terrified by these men.

His father had died of a heart attack when the patient was 8 years old, and the image of the derelicts became for him the symbol of his dashed hopes, disappointment in both parents, and his own vulnerability.

The dismantling of D.R.'s false, defensive self and gradual reassembling of the component parts of his self into the structure of a real self was a slow and painstaking process, involving every thought, feeling, and wish. Well along in treatment the patient could report and contrast two different perspectives associated with meeting women, one from the vantage of the false (martyr) self and the other from the vantage of the impaired (but developing) real self:

> When I felt like the martyr, I thought that all I had to do was walk down the street and someone would come up to me and express their admiration for me, realize how truly special I was, and then whisk me away to a life of ease and comfort. Now when I have to go out to meet a woman, I feel scared. I'm terrified of exposing myself. I say, "Who am I? and what am I? and why would they be interested in me?" . . . When I'm into my martyr self I feel that no one is really good enough for me; no one can really appreciate my suffering. But when I drop that and try to just be myself, I feel that it's me that won't measure up.

Both A.C. and D.R. illustrate the nature of the false, defensive self of the narcissistic personality disorder, especially the relentless pursuit of perfection and of narcissistic supplies. Underlying this pursuit in all instances is the abandonment depression and the profound impairments in the capacities and functions of the real self.

SUMMARY

This chapter has demonstrated the theoretical importance and the practical application of the concept of the real self for the diagnosis and treatment of the personality disorders, in particular the borderline and narcissistic personality disorders. This concept integrates previous models of the mind into a single supraordinate construct that highlights the whole rather than the parts. Clinically, use of this construct can serve to deemphasize debate and controversy regarding competing systems of classification. It stresses instead a systematic evaluation of those functions and capacities that form the core of personality development.

An understanding of the specific nature of the false, defensive self organization then helps to guide the therapist's interventions. Knowledge of the functions and capacities associated with optimal mature separation, attachment, individuation, and autonomy helps to guide the therapist to identify and accomplish the goals of treatment.

PART II

The Scope of Psychotherapy

The clinical evidence for the developmental self and object relations theory is derived from intensive psychoanalytic psychotherapy with personality disorder patients. Since this is the source, some therapists believe that the only use of the theory is with patients in intensive analytic work.

This section on psychotherapy demonstrates how widely the theory applies to therapeutic contacts with personality disorder patients. The extraordinarily wide ranging therapeutic activities presented all spring from the same developmental theoretical source and illustrate its scope and flexibility.

In Chapter 4 Dr. Clark, focusing on the psychotherapy of a patient with borderline personality disorder, dissects the difference between the experiencing of the abandonment depression and the "bad feelings" associated with the need to defend against experiencing the depression. In Chapter 5, Dr. Fischer describes and illustrates in detail the therapeutic management of the narcissistic personality disorder. Shorter-term psychotherapy of both the borderline and narcissistic personality disorders is described by Dr. Klein in Chapter 6. He clearly illustrates the goals of shorter-term treatment, which are far more ambitious than was thought possible years ago, as well as the different therapeutic techniques necessary in shorter-term work with the two disorders.

In Chapter 7, Dr. Orcutt abundantly illustrates the point that therapeutic technique changes as the patient's ego and object relations mature. In Chapter 8, Dr. Klein gives extensive consideration to diagnosis and treatment of those borderline patients who occupy the lower level of the borderline range and who are frequently found in the inpatient ward and the outpatient clinic. This subject, which has occupied us a great deal clinically, has not previously been reported on in such a systematic and thorough manner. In her work with a wide range of borderline personality disorders, Dr. Clark details in Chapter 9 the clinical evidence for self-activation or separation-individuation

49

*and in so doing provides rich clinical examples of what is meant
by separation-individuation.*

*The question is often raised as to whether the Masterson
Approach can be applied to psychotherapy with adolescents. In
fact, it was in the area of the identification and treatment of the
borderline disorder in adolescence that my clinical work had its
beginnings. Dr. Orcutt in Chapter 10 demonstrates the
application of the work to the psychotherapy of a borderline
adolescent. In Chapter 11, Dr. Orcutt and I expand the
application of the therapy to the marital treatment of a couple,
each of whom has a narcissistic personality disorder.*

*From shorter-term to longer-term psychotherapy, whether upper-
or lower-level borderline personality disorder or upper- or lower-
level narcissistic personality disorder, in work with adolescents
and couples, through the making of difficult but crucial clinical
distinctions, the theory ranges widely to form a solid, reliable
base for both evaluation and therapeutic action with a variety of
personality disorders.*

J.F.M.

Chapter 4

Psychotherapy of the Borderline Personality Disorder

Karla Clark, Ph.D.

This chapter describes how the projection and acting out of the withdrawing part unit, and the depressive affects associated with it, serve to defend against the activation of the real self and the associated emergence of the abandonment depression. The split intrapsychic structure of the borderline patient is characterized by a rewarding and withdrawing object relations part unit, each with its component self and object representation. Both units reflect specific internal responses by the individual to the developmental task of separation-individuation, and both work against further separation-individuation and the activation and development of the real self.

In the rewarding self and object relations part unit (the RORU), the intrapsychic representation of the part object is powerful and "protective," approving of and rewarding regressive behavior. There is a corresponding part self representation of being a good and compliant child. These part self and object representations are linked with affects of feeling good. This produces a false self representation which leads the person to behave in regressive and self-destructive ways and see himself as a good person when so doing.

The withdrawing self and object relations part unit (the WORU) consists of a part object representation which attacks and/or withdraws at signs of separation-individuation, linked to a part self representation which is bad, evil, and disgusting. These part self and part object representations are linked to affects of feeling defective, worthless, and loathsome. The false representation of this part unit is of a defective, bad person.

In the following case, the WORU/pathological ego alliance was projected and acted out in the form of a false, defensive self, which both hid the actual impaired real self from the view of the patient and the therapist, and prevented the real self from fully developing. A major task of the psychotherapy was to identify this false defensive self, and help the patient to understand its functions, in order to give it up and work through the resulting abandonment depression.

The progression from (1) identifying and working with the affects of the false defensive self to (2) challenging the patient to give up the false defensive self to (3) the subsequent emergence of the affects of the abandonment depression is a common, expectable clinical sequence. However, in the case to be presented (as in many others that have come to my attention), the normal task of working with the set of depressive affects associated with the WORU/pathological ego alliance as prelude to working through the abandonment depression was complicated by the ease with which the affects associated with the one could be confused with those of the other. This occurred because the patient experienced and described both sets of affects as "depression" and failed to distinguish between them.

Such confusion may lead to failure to manage the defensive depression adequately, which in turn leads to treatment complications and failures as the abandonment depression itself, then, fails to emerge in a clearly identifiable form. In the case to be discussed, the crucial point for the psychotherapy was to identify and distinguish one of these forms of depression from the other.

In order to address the questions of (1) the identification and management of the WORU/pathological ego alliance, (2) its projection and acting out expressed as a false defensive self, and (3) distinguishing it from the underlying abandonment depression, one must first consider the defensive function of splitting and the effect of such splitting on the development of the real self.

Splitting is used defensively in order to maintain and protect "good" images of self and other from being overwhelmed by "bad" images, which the individual fears would threaten and destroy the good (Kernberg, 1975, p. 25). When splitting leads to the development of a false defensive self, the implications for the individual's development of his real self are far reaching and grave:

> In the borderline personality disorder . . . those impaired by this disorder are unable to use the real self to react to reality challenges with supportive realistic self-assertion, but run instead to a false defensive self—a product of the alliances between the pathological ego, the rewarding unit relations part unit and the withdrawing object relations part unit. This leads to avoidance, passivity, denial, and preoccupation with fantasy, thus further feeding their lack of self-esteem.
>
> Their defensive self representations—based mostly on fantasy rather than reality—consist of two equally unrealistic fantasy images: that of a helpless child who is loved or rewarded for not asserting himself and an inadequate, evil, bad self which impels the mother to withdraw. (Masterson, 1985, pp. 31–32)

It is perhaps easy enough to see why a borderline individual would fail to consciously question a compliant, clinging, and non-self-activating false self representation, when by so representing himself he feels "good" in both an absolute and a moral sense. But why would an individual embrace a false, defensive self representation that is based upon his feeling that he is "bad"?

Fairbairn makes the point that, having initially internalized bad objects, an individual may also defend himself from knowing about their existence by seeing himself as bad. Fairbairn believes that the patient does this because he prefers to see himself as a bad person in an essentially good universe rather than as an essentially bad person in a bad and malignant universe (Fairbairn, 1986, pp. 109–110).

To extend Fairbairn's premise, seeing oneself as bad in a bad universe is felt as preferable by some borderline individuals to repudiating the bad introject altogether, thereby loosening one's defensive affective investment and experiencing the feelings of loss of the abandonment depression. The projection and acting out of the WORU/pathological ego alliance (henceforth to be referred to as the WORU defense) thus forms a barrier to the even more painful feelings that lie beneath it. The patient sees himself as being bad and disgusting. Frequently, he will describe this self experience as "being depressed," and in fact he may be acting or feeling depressed: tearful, lethargic, subdued, or flagrantly suicidal. He then compounds this by resisting any challenge to this view of himself because of his unwillingness to face the abandonment depression beneath.

Experiencing oneself as bad and malignant in a bad and malignant universe, and behaving badly in order to justify the feeling, are therefore two levels of defense against calling the entire self representation into question. One can think of the very existence of the WORU false, defensive self representation as the most basic, primary defensive configuration in these cases. The defenses against seeing that the WORU self representation is a false self representation are a secondary defensive maneuver. These secondary defenses must often be worked through before the primary defense is either identifiable or workable.

The first key to distinguishing all of the affects associated with the withdrawing part self and part object relations unit from those of the abandonment depression proper is the quality of moral badness, or self loathing, associated with the WORU defense. This quality can be easily distinguished from the affects associated with working through the abandonment depression. The latter includes feelings of helplessness and hopelessness, emptiness and void, separation anxiety, depression, rage, and guilt over separating (Masterson, 1976, p. 39). All of the latter affects share the quality of feeling abandoned and alone but lack the feeling of moral badness and defectiveness of the WORU false self depression.

The second key to the distinction between the depression of the WORU defense and the working through of the abandonment depression is to be found in whether the patient is focusing, through his depression, on keeping the relationship with the old internal objects alive or trying to give them up. When the abandonment depression proper is at the center of the patient's awareness, the relationship to the old part objects is absent or subordinate. In contrast, affects attached to a false defensive self refer to an internal relationship between the part self (or selves) and still dominant internal objects, the self being subordinate. In the latter case, the WORU defense depression, for example, is characterized by affects of feeling bad, worthless, and otherwise invalid vis-à-vis an internal object who is attacking or withdrawing. The depressive affects experienced in this context are reactive rather than active, i.e., "I am bad because 'it' thinks I am. This makes me feel awful." Clinically these depressive affects are a barrier to (defense against) self-activation and *maximally* interfere with adaptation and function. These affects must be distinguished from the abandonment depression itself, which is associated with *loss* of the object, not the *threat* of loss, in consequence of one's own attempts to take the initiative to separate and individuate, i.e., "I feel hopeless of ever receiving support for separating from the object and must give up and go on. This makes me feel empty, terrified, guilty, etc." The affects associated with the abandonment depression refer to the individual's efforts to give up the old ties to destructive part object representations. Thus they are active rather than reactive. Clinically they are the result of self-activation and minimally interfere with adaptation and function.

Once the clinician can distinguish between the WORU defense and the underlying abandonment depression, the question arises as to how to manage or work through the WORU defense. The defensive expressions of the false defensive self (or selves) are managed in precisely the same manner as are other defenses of the borderline: through confrontation.

The technical principle is the same for confronting secondary defensive manifestations of either the RORU or the WORU. The patient must learn to identify their presence and view their projection and acting out as antithetical to his best interests, and therefore learn to control them. When confronted, a patient may be able to control his impulse to act in such a way as to verify his internal view of himself as wrong and bad. He may thus learn to call into question the *thought* that he is wrong and bad before ceasing to experience the *feeling* of being bad.

A variety of options open at that point. The patient may stop there, saying that he knows that he feels like a bad person (especially when experiencing separation stress) and that that feels awful to him, but that he knows that these feelings do not reflect a true picture of what he is like, and that he is not going to allow the feelings to stop him from functioning.

If, however, the patient then goes on in therapy to repair the split by working through the abandonment depression, the following three stages unfold: (1) The hope of support for separation-individuation from the objects is given up and is replaced by self-acknowledgment. (2) For this group of patients, this leads to withdrawal from the internal objects and increased attention to the self, with subsequent abandonment depression and separation anxiety. (3) Finally, after the tie to the internal object has been given up, the personality is reconsolidated based upon whole self and object representations.

The case presentation that follows will illustrate this process.

CASE ILLUSTRATION: MR. E

Presenting Complaints

Mr. E is a single man in his early forties.[1] He entered therapy with complaints of depression, low self-esteem, and feelings of social isolation. He had recently changed careers (from recreational program director to lawyer) and was having problems on the job. He felt that the job itself was poor, and that the administration of the firm was unprofessional and inadequate. He was in trouble with his immediate supervisor, a woman, whom he felt unfairly criticized his work.

Mr. E had other difficulties in managing his daily life. He reported a good deal of past and present drug and alcohol abuse. He suffered from financial problems. He had no permanent living arrangement, because he had constant fights with his roommates. He saw himself as exploited and victimized, the other as selfish, abusive, and exploitative. He would move on, only to repeat the process elsewhere. He seemed to have no friends.

He had had five years of weekly individual psychotherapy with a male therapist. He complained, however, that he still felt depressed— perhaps more so than ever. More important, for him, he had been unable to develop any lasting relationship with a woman. He wanted to marry and to have children and hoped that seeing a woman therapist would help him to achieve this.

As we began treatment once a week, I noticed several things about him that appeared problematic to me, but of which he was unaware. Certainly, these traits interfered with his stated goal of meeting and marrying a woman. He had allowed himself to become noticeably overweight (although not truly obese). He dressed in unkempt, ill-matched clothing. Often he appeared for sessions in dirty denim overalls and a smelly tee shirt. His long hair was frequently dirty and uncombed, and he often had a powerful body odor. His expression was chronically angry, aloof, and disconnected.

There were contradictions and inconsistencies in this picture of Mr. E, some of which were apparent at once and some of which did not appear for some time. These contradictions and inconsistencies were

---

[1] Countertransference with this patient is presented in Chapter 19 in this volume.

signs that the picture he presented was a false, defensive self. I happened to know from other sources that he had a reputation as a highly creative and innovative recreational program director. His story of the way he left his job, in contrast, left out his achievements and job satisfactions and emphasized his quarrels with fellow staff. He presented himself as little better than a bum, certainly as though he were incapable of achievement or taking himself seriously. In contrast, he had graduated from a good college, had some graduate training in art history, and had now finished law school, where, as he revealed when I inquired, he had done quite well scholastically. Additionally, Mr. E was an artist of considerable talent, who had achieved some recognition for his work. He revealed this in such an offhand way that it was almost impossible not to discount this important information.

There were similar discrepancies between his reports of his social relations and what one could gather concerning the objective facts of the matter. Despite his representation of himself as alone and friendless, he had several friendships that had endured since childhood. He also referred in passing to social contacts with people whom he had met at law school and work and whom he obviously continued to see. Furthermore, despite his appearance, when he made overtures to women, he apparently had no difficulty in getting dates. In a highly competitive job market, with many lawyers unable to find employment, he had managed to secure a job as a clerk, with the promise of employment after he passed the bar exam. All of this indicated two things: (1) that he did not always present himself to others (at least initially) in the same way that he presented himself to me, and (2) that there was more to him than he appeared.

At the beginning of therapy, the inconsistencies were far from obvious. Rather, they were fleeting moments of contrast buried in a sea of overall impressions of his "defectiveness." What was occurring was that he was steadily acting out the WORU. He was representing himself to me, and usually saw himself, as a worthless, loathsome individual. He hid his many virtues and talents or, after making an initially good impression, rapidly buried it under his flagrant, provocatively unattractive behavior.

History

Mr. E is the oldest of three brothers, from an intact middle-class family. The father had a business of his own, which was quite successful and to which he devoted almost all of his time when Mr. E was very young.

When Mr. E was 18 months old, his father became ill with a chronic, painful, and debilitating disease. He did not immediately stop work, but it is possible to speculate that both parents became preoccupied with the father's worsening condition and the prospects for the family that it implied.

When Mr. E was 6, his father, in considerable pain, underwent surgery that left him crippled and did not (as had been hoped) control his pain. He sold his business and stayed at home. He made no attempt to cope with his crippled condition adaptively by finding meaningful work that he could manage, or by socializing with other people. Instead, he stayed at home, drinking more and more heavily, praying, and either slumped in apathy or attacking his wife and children.

As the oldest son, Mr. E was given much responsibility around the house and, as he grew older, for his father's physical care. He bathed his father, toileted and dressed him, and took him for drives. His father characteristically was extremely critical of Mr. E, reviling him and insulting him. The father ignored, discounted, and devalued his son's efforts to help. These attacks intensified as Mr. E got older, becoming physical as well as verbally abusive, to the point where they were vicious, paranoid, and virtually continuous.

Mr. E's mother did nothing to protect her son from attack by his father. She tended to side with the father or to remain passive. His dominant overall impression of her (a projection of his introjected bad object which combined some of her features with those of his father) was of a person who was incapable of recognizing his separateness or ability, ignored his achievements, and was herself vicious and attacking.

A vivid memory from his eighth year serves as a metaphor for his predominant internal experience of his mother. He had become encopretic, and he recalls that his mother took a pair of his soiled underpants and rubbed his nose in the excrement. In this memory, until late in therapy, Mr. E saw himself as the helpless victim of a heartless ogre. Retrospectively, it is possible to identify the encopresis as an early acting out of the WORU, in which he provoked his mother's intense involvement with him by acting in a disgusting manner, since he felt that he had failed to engage her through his achievements.

There was evidence of early efforts by Mr. E to activate and develop his real self, as well as abandonment of those efforts when discouraged. For example, throughout school he was to intermittently excel academically, artistically, and in sports, only to undercut himself and collapse into periods of laziness and boredom. This behavior gradually grew worse the further along he went in school. The alternating attempted activation of the impaired real self and defensive collapse into provocative "bad" behavior was to be the dominant pattern of his life up until treatment.

In the years prior to his first course of psychotherapy, he managed to physically leave his home and get a new job in an innovative program in recreational counseling, which went extremely well. He began to paint and draw consistently. At this point, because he was not acting out in a massive and global fashion, he began to experience feelings of abandonment depression. He felt increasingly anxious and empty. He defended against these feelings by activating the WORU and became what he called "depressed," meaning that he experienced himself as worthless and disgusting. He projected and acted out, quarreling with friends and work associates. He sought psychotherapy. During this first effort at treatment, he did not question this self representation. Rather, he acted out. He decided that he was "burnt out" on recreational work. He stopped painting. He decided to go to law school. While in law school, he terminated psychotherapy and acted out by beginning a painful and humiliating love affair, which ended with mutual recriminations and bitterness.

He completed law school and, during the period of preparation for the bar exam, took the job that he held when his present treatment began. He hated his work and really had no interest in the law. He was broke, socially and emotionally extremely isolated, and felt terrible about himself. His life was in a shambles. He had succeeded in all but destroying everything of real worth that he had built for himself since leaving home.

Psychotherapy

At the beginning, Mr. E continued to act out globally, drinking heavily, fighting with people, antagonizing his employers, and taking drugs. He used projection and projective identification as major defenses to support his acting out. He denied his provocative and self-destructive behaviors and saw himself as a victim of others. Confrontation began around the consequences of his behaviors: that he hurt himself when he got drunk, took drugs, or acted provocatively with other people. Slowly, these behaviors came under control.

As he contained the earlier forms of acting out, he began transference acting out, alternately projecting onto me aspects of both the RORU and the WORU. He began to talk, during this phase, about how much he resented my pointing out to him how destructive his behaviors were. When I confronted him, he saw me as berating him, as cold and contemptuous. He gave this experience of me the name of the Bad Nun (WORU part object). He then would quickly defend against his feelings of rage and resentment toward me by becoming compliant and dutiful (RORU part self). He labeled this part self representation the Good Catholic Boy and filled his treatment hours with content that seemed meaningful, but that was without affect and did not lead to change.[2]

Mr. E then began to identify the self representation attached to the Bad Nun. This came about in the following manner. At the time, Mr. E. had begun to prepare to take the bar examination. He discussed the possibility of falsifying certain information required by the bar association. This behavior was vigorously confronted in psychotherapy, in terms of both the self-destructive nature of his behavior and its essential dishonesty. Mr. E responded to the confrontation by acknowledging how often his style was to take the easy or dishonest way out when faced with an issue in his life, when trying to get by with things. He saw that this led him in turn to be constantly afraid of being found out. He described this as "living on a banana peel," and used the word to describe himself which subsequently became his nickname for the WORU false self: he said that he acted like a "sleaze." He saw that he undercut his self-esteem whenever he acted out of his wish to get away with things or, as he put it, "scam." Recognizing how destructive this was to him, he began to make more active efforts to control himself. Mr. E took and passed the bar examination honestly. He was promoted at work to a position commensurate with his new status as an attorney.

Despite his promotion, however, he constantly did sloppy work, refused to ask for help when he needed it, and provoked fellow employees, acting the Sleaze. His therapy, which was now twice weekly, was also not going well. He would come in and provocatively present himself as having fouled up again, waiting for me to point it out. If I did so, he would clean up his behavior, experiencing me as berating him, squelching his resentment of me, but not, in any sense, growing in his capacity to control himself. He noticed this himself and tried to control his efforts to provoke me into confronting him

---

[2]At this time he had no name for a WORU part self representation, having named only the part object (i.e., the Bad Nun). Earlier I referred to the intensity of absorption in the part object that is characteristic of WORU defensive depression as opposed to abandonment depression. This inability to even recognize a part self representation attached to the part object representation is an example of the dominance of preoccupation with the part object.

unnecessarily. The static quality of the hours did not, however, change much.

As I tried to identify what was going on, I noted that for some time I had had the nagging thought that Mr. E was wasting his time trying to be a lawyer. He appeared temperamentally unsuited to the work and essentially miserable in it. I experienced great difficulty, however, with the idea of speaking to him about this. I knew how much he had invested in his career change. I experienced myself as judgmental and cold at the idea of calling it into question, and felt reluctant to do so. Recognizing and controlling my countertransference, I decided that the static quality in his psychotherapy probably resulted from his massively acting out the Sleaze through a career choice which so completely ignored the qualities that seemed to reflect his real self (i.e., his abilities as a recreational worker and as a painter). I decided to confront him with the question of his career choice.

He had begun bringing in samples of his drawing and painting. He obviously adored art and did it extremely well, but he was developing it solely as a hobby. One day he discussed his art and an associated memory of creativity from his old job with obvious pleasure and longing. Then, he turned to more incidents of continuing humiliation and poor performance at work. I asked him why he became a lawyer, when it was clear that his heart was in his painting and his recreational work with children. Initially, he felt shocked, and immediately defended. He saw me as joining his bosses as seeing him as a failure and a loser. When I pointed out to him the obvious contrast between the way he spoke of law and of recreational work and painting, however, he was able to begin to consider the question without defensively dismissing it out of hand.

The whole false self defense, which had had its strongest and most entrenched life in his maladaptive career choice, was being called into question. He became intrigued with the possibility of leaving the law, but was badly frightened by what he saw as the financial insecurity of giving up his job and starting over again as a recreational worker. He was doing so poorly at law that his financial worries about giving it up were far from well founded. Rather, his fear was the fear of giving up his false self (the Sleaze) and pursuing the activities and interest of the real self. Separation anxiety was being projected onto the issue of finances, so that he feared his ability to "survive" if he gave up the law. The unrealistic nature of his financial worries was confronted, and Mr. E decided to quit and go back to recreational work.

He did this, however, by creating a situation in which his behavior was so intolerable that his boss had to fire him. He therefore could leave the firm without separating: i.e., undoing the acting-out defense of the Sleaze. This time, however, he himself questioned why he had needed to act this way. For the first time, Mr. E was beginning to question the accuracy of his WORU self representation.

After a number of months, Mr. E found work in a recreational program. He completely stopped using alcohol. He began to dress more appropriately. When taking out a loan to help tide him through, he at first lied about his debts, and saw that this had a corrosive effect upon his self-esteem. He experienced the tendency to "scam," to slough off and bluff his way through things. Instead, he controlled himself. He went back to the loan officer and told him the truth.

Again, a static quality to the treatment interaction alerted me that, despite the assumption of more responsibility for his life, he was still in a defensive impasse. Hour after hour, he would rage about one or another aspect of his parents' treatment of him, but the anger had a ritual quality; it never led to deeper insight or to the production of new memories. Samples of the artwork he brought into the therapy during this period were labored, flat, and melodramatic (despite his obvious talent), also indicating the continuing serious impairment of the real self and the presence of destructive defense.

He was acting out with women, having a series of disastrous and destructive encounters with them. Over a number of months, this behavior slowly yielded to confrontation. Eventually, he questioned his motives for wanting a relationship and the effect this was having on him. He decided that it would be better for him if he stopped trying to date for a while and concentrated on his work, his painting, and his therapy. He therefore once more controlled his defensive acting out.

He had secured a permanent job in a recreational program for inner city children. He realized that he loved the work and was happy with it. His painting efforts had, however, been going badly. In order to defend against the affects stimulated by efforts to activate this probably deepest expression of his real self, he had again activated the WORU. Feelings of tremendous tiredness and lethargy would come over him whenever the time came to paint. He described this as feeling depressed. He intensified his transference acting out. He began to consistently provoke me to remonstrate with him about his "laziness." When he identified this, he revealed that he was not sure whether he was painting for himself or resisting painting to provoke me. He recalled the ways in which, as a child, he had complied with his father's excessive demands upon him to work and make money, all the while provoking his father by behaving in ways that the father would see as lazy and irresponsible. He linked these to his own father's presentation of himself as a mule, somebody who worked without joy or vitality, in an endless and dogged way. He did not want to paint, he said, if he was going to "mule" it like his father. He felt it necessary to stop painting until he was certain that he was not using it to act out.

Meanwhile, his life was assuming more order and continuity. He was not dating, but he had friendships that were increasingly valuable to him. He had an apartment. He liked the town in which he lived and was increasingly coming to see it as his home. He began to address the problem of why despite all of this he felt so dull and flat (abandonment depression).

By this time, Mr. E had increased his frequency of sessions to three times a week, with the stated goal of working things out so that he could be free of his past constraints. He now reflected back on the "horror" of his years as a lawyer. He reviewed my part in helping him see how off base that career choice had been. At first, he expressed gratitude to me for helping him to see this. Then, rather than address the defense—how he had gotten himself in that jam in the first place— he turned on me, once more transference projecting and acting out the WORU defense. There was a major eruption as, more than a year after I finally had called into question his choice of the law as a career, he called me to account. Why had I not confronted him about this sooner? I must have known! Why had I waited so long to bring it to his attention? I acknowledged my error and the cost to him but pointed out that, in fact, I *had* eventually brought it to his attention, with constructive results.

The attacks temporarily diminished as he recognized the reality that I had indeed demonstrated my ability to face and learn from my mistakes to his benefit. He picked up his efforts to work effectively and began to paint again, this time with renewed interest and vigor. He was, for the first time, consciously facing the abandonment depression in a consistent manner. He began to actively mourn the years of wasted opportunity, and contrast his prior functioning with the shape his life was taking now. For the most part, his hours at this time contained meaningful childhood memories as he worked on his feelings of not having been acknowledged for his needs as a child. Having temporarily gained control of the WORU defense, he was now working through aspects of the abandonment depression.

It had been sufficient at the time to acknowledge my errors for the work of treatment to proceed. Because the defense itself had not been thoroughly worked through, however, it would return. It did so when the therapeutic pressure mounted once more. This came about because he turned specifically to the issue of his inability to love himself. This issue directly challenged the false self representation of the Sleaze, and he defended as he had before, by employing secondary defenses in which the Sleaze was externalized. Rather than attack me for past, major errors (since he had been discouraged from employing that particular content), he attacked me for present minor ones.

Minute problems in my phrasing, times when I kept him waiting for a moment or two, moments in which my attention or understanding was imperfect, became the focus of his attacks. I wondered whether I was dealing with a full-fledged narcissistic defense (Masterson, 1981), and began mirroring him and interpreting his sensitivity. Although this would mollify him, I noticed that once more the treatment became static. I therefore began to question my mirroring and interpretive interventions. I identified the pattern of attack. Unlike a narcissistic personality, or a borderline personality using a narcissistic defense, it was not true that he was intolerant of my every error. Rather, his attacks on me would always follow sessions in which he had been trying to challenge the self representation of the Sleaze—i.e., to love himself. I therefore acknowledged the accuracy of his criticisms of me as before, but went on to point out how these attacks interrupted the flow of his material. I questioned: Why all of the attention to me and to my errors at those particular times? Did he notice when the wishes to attack me came up? After all, things were not going badly— on the contrary, they were going exceedingly well. Why did my minute errors throw him so easily? In response, his hypercritical behavior toward me diminished. He began to talk about *wanting* to attack me rather than *doing* so. He began, for the first time with real affect, to explore spontaneously the constant devaluation and under-cutting of others that was indulged in by his whole family. He had known for some time how he felt as the victim of such attacks. Now he faced the fact that he also made them, not only on other people, but on himself.

He recalled many instances of undercutting and contempt. Memo-ries of his relationship with his father came flooding out at this point. In recounting these memories, Mr. E had now, however, moved away from simply, repetitively raging at his father. He was exploring the effects of this childhood climate of brutal psychological and physical abuse upon himself. He was turning his attention from the part object to the self representation. He was once more working through the abandonment depression.

He again began to call into question the family view of him as a sluggard and a lazy wastrel (the Sleaze). He knew that there were many times when he had been lazy, dirty, and provocative. He commented, however, that as a child he had often also been creative and vital. He remembered his love of sports, his feeling of freedom when with his friends. He noted that he had had many interests at school. He remarked that he had always tried to please his father by working hard, had never rebelled and become a major delinquent, school dropout, or crazy person. He had, in his way, tried to express his love and be a good son. Grieving, he recalled many times when he had felt and expressed his love for his tortured father and dealt with feelings of helplessness concerning his inability to help him or ease his pain. Sadly, Mr. E reflected that he had not been the bad kid or emotional basket case that he thought he had been, and he began to turn his attention to his parents' inability to parent, and his own subsequent refusal to assume responsibility for parenting himself. Why, he asked, when I am doing all of these good things, do I not see myself as good? He knew that his self perception simply did not match his outward behavior. He was not acting like a Sleaze, but his feeling about himself, he observed, did not enduringly change.

As he controlled the externalization of the Sleaze, he began to express more internalized defenses. He complained once again of exhaustion. He was unaware that, although he had stopped acting out the WORU with other people, he was enacting the self representation of the Sleaze to himself, reinforcing it with the defense of avoidance. Slowly, through confrontation, the reality of his exhaustion was called into question and he began to control himself so that he did not give in to it. As his behavior improved, he alternated between what he saw clearly as periods of great pleasure and fulfillment with his painting and work, WORU feelings of terrible worthlessness and badness, and feelings of sadness associated with the abandonment depression. He said, "The real issue here in treatment, the bottom line, is that I learn to love myself. My parents aren't in it. I have to learn to love myself."

He once again defended. He was increasing his attacks on himself, expressed in attacks on his own body. He somatized. Prior chronic physical complaints became exacerbated. He developed an infection that would not go away. The attack allowed him to partially external-ize the underlying feeling of severe panic associated with dying (i.e., that affects of the abandonment depression), which was being brought up by his challenge of the reality of the self representation of the Sleaze. He would experience brief panic attacks and, rather than calling them into question or exploring them, defend by becoming preoccupied with his health, ascribing his choking feeling and panic to a chest ailment.

He fought against these feelings, slowly acknowledging the need not to give in to his illnesses and acknowledging the psychological rather than physical nature of his exhaustion. Bad feelings surfaced about himself, which he once again called into question, contrasting them with the reality of his life. The calling into question of the WORU defense again brought up the threat of separation with its attendant anxiety, which he defended against time and time again by invoking the false self: becoming exhausted and ill. He called this feeling depression. Hours began with his announcement that he felt depressed, awful. Gradually, he began to distinguish "depressed" and "awful" into two groups of feelings. There were feelings, he said, of badness and worthlessness, of being a "banana slug." There were other feelings, more fleeting, which seemed much worse to him. These were feelings that he was dying, feelings of panic and emptiness. He observed that sometimes he defended against his second group of feelings (the abandonment depression) by becoming the banana slug (i.e., the Sleaze).

As of this writing, Mr. E is calling his whole pattern of fatigue and hypochondriacal preoccupation into question, which supports the giving up of the false defensive self of the WORU and the concomitant reaching of the bottom of the abandonment depression. He recently said, "Yesterday may have been the best day of my life. I just said to myself, if you eat, watch TV, lay down, you are killing yourself. No bull, that is what it is. I see a vision of my father, destroyed, lying in his bed. As I start to get out of it, I get clear that it is not me. I am lively and energetic. That other is not me, and I have to fight it.

"Yesterday, I said, that's *it*. There was such an intensity of feeling. I must have cried four or five times during the day. It was . . . titanic. I have never been so vigilant, constantly. I went to bed crying. I am a good person. I refused the Sleaze. I simply did not let it in." Here, he began to explore the abandonment depression proper. He went on to say that when he doesn't let the Sleaze in, he feels empty, becomes panicky and afraid that he is going to die: "A choking feeling. A death." He indicates his knowledge of how he then defends: "There is so much emphasis in my whole life of just doing a little and then stopping." He noted that when he challenges that dead feeling, empty feelings emerge and with them feelings of hopelessness concerning his ability to fix parental figures. This brings to his attention the need to relinquish that wish. "Then I feel hopeless. It's a choking thing. I just feel completely anxious. But I haven't given in once. It is like going through rapids, sometimes you just have to get through." This illustrates how, as the "depression" associated with the withdrawing unit is confronted and exposed (the feelings of badness and worthlessness), the affects of the abandonment depression emerge (as, for example, feelings of emptiness, hopelessness, and separation anxiety).

Mr. E is turning his attention actively to the issue of the relinquishment of the archaic internal part self and part object representations. He is aided in this effort by the development of the functions of the real self, which are expressed in his art work and his vocation. The activation of the real self provides Mr. E with a source of strength, allowing him to challenge the older introjects and endure the affects associated with their loss. Although the final outcome of his struggle lies ahead, one has every reason to believe that he will be successful in his efforts.

SUMMARY

In this case discussion, one is able to trace the extraordinary tenacity of the projection and acting out of the WORU as a defense against the recognition and relinquishment of the underlying abandonment depression. At first the WORU defense presented itself as an almost airtight, global self representation. The patient acted in such a way that he appeared to "be" bad, thus avoiding having to call his feelings of badness into question. Defenses such as acting out the wish for reunion, projection, projective identification, and avoidance all were put into play in support of the primary, false self representation. As these secondary defenses came under control, the most embracing manifestation of the Sleaze became visible: Mr. E's choice of an inappropriate career. The giving-up of that career and the substitution of career interests that actively supported and helped him to continue to develop his dormant real self, raised the threatening possibility for Mr. E that his WORU part self representation was false. This led to his return to secondary defensive use of the WORU, in which he employed projection, acting out, transference acting out, and projective identification in order to externalize parts of the false self and give them credence. The persistence of this defense is a vivid demonstration of how tenaciously false defensive self representations are defended (even when they seem so distasteful to an observer), because of the individual's greater fear of the affects beneath.

A period of intense transference acting out followed. When the defense was fully confronted and worked through, the patient began to actively and vigorously develop his real self and work on his own behalf to challenge and relinquish the false defensive self. At this point, the difference between the depressive affects associated with that false self (badness, loathsomeness, deadness, and fatigue) became distinguishable from the abandonment depression and separation anxiety brought on by his efforts to relinquish it.

The entire outcome of this case depended upon the patient's capacity to first identify, then control, and finally call into question the false self representation. In this sense, he is not unique. It is always vital to the successful treatment of the borderline that he gain control of false self representations. Only when this occurs does the struggling real self have the ego as an ally in support of its development.

REFERENCES

Clark, K. (1988). Clinical manifestations of separation-individuation (this volume).

Fairbairn, W.R.D. (1986). The repression and the return of bad objects (with special reference to the war neuroses). In P. Buckley (Ed.), *Essential papers on object relations.* New York: New York University Press.

Kernberg, 0. (1975). *Borderline conditions and pathological narcissism.* New York: Jason Aronson.

Masterson, J. (1976). *The psychotherapy of the borderline adult: A developmental approach.* New York: Brunner/Mazel.

Masterson, J. (1981). *The narcissistic and borderline disorders: An integrated developmental approach.* New York: Brunner/Mazel.

Masterson, J. (1985). *The real self: A development, self, and object relations approach.* New York: Brunner/Mazel.

Chapter 5

Psychotherapy of the Narcissistic Personality Disorder

Richard Fischer, Ph.D.

The individual with the classical narcissistic personality disorder presents with a façade of grandiosity, self preoccupation, and the constant pursuit of admiration. He or she is perfectionistic in striving for money, power, wealth, and fame, shows an extreme sense of entitlement, and lacks empathy and concern for others. The narcissist exploits others to mirror and admire the false defensive grandiose self. Beneath this seemingly impenetrable façade, there exists a fragmented self manifested in intense envy, rage, feelings of worthlessness and rejection, and a pervasive sense of impotence and inadequacy. The grandiose façade of the narcissist can break down dramatically under relatively minor exposure to criticism, rejection, or even lack of acknowledgment.

The surface adaptation and the lack of anxiety and depression that many narcissists exhibit can be most misleading, and is often incorrectly seen as healthy or as evidence of personality integration and maturation.

Another group of narcissistic patients presents with a dramatically different façade and symptoms. The closet narcissist does not display overt exhibitionistic behavior and may even present as humble, anxious, inhibited, or shy. It is only later, as many of the defenses against manifest grandiosity are interpreted and resolved, that the false defensive grandiose self and its manifest need for mirroring and idealization become apparent. This group of latent narcissists may not resemble the *DSM-III* diagnostic picture, but the intrapsychic structural organization is very similar to that in the classical overt narcissistic personality disorder.

The structural organization of the narcissistic patient dictates the treatment interventions. The narcissist has a fused object relations unit that is markedly different from the split object relations unit of the borderline patient.

The manifest unit is a grandiose self-object, which is superior and elite with an affect of being special or unique. The omnipotent object is perfect and powerful and necessary for idealization and mirroring. The manifest (or classical) narcissist continually activates this structure with its need for grandiose exhibition.

The hidden structural organization is the aggressive or empty object relations unit, which is the other fused self-object representation. It consists of an object that is harsh, punitive and attacking, and a self representation that is humiliated, shamed, and empty. This extreme sensitivity to feeling criticized or attacked forces the therapist to rely on therapeutic interventions other than confrontation.

The developmental histories of narcissistic patients reveal arrests during the separation-individuation phase similar to those that have been documented with borderline patients. Two kinds of memories are often reported by the narcissistic patient. The most typical report is of having been the recipient of the mother's idealizing projections—i.e., her mirroring and admiration, which bordered on the mother's being obsessed with the particular patient. Closer examination, which occurs only later in the treatment, reveals the mother to have been cold and exploitive—unable to acknowledge, confirm, and support her child's real self, and instead treating the child as an extension of her own frustrated grandiose needs.

This patient's grandiose self is continuously mirrored and confirmed so long as he maintains a merged relationship with his idealized object, but his real self is devalued and unacknowledged and remains impaired. This preoccupation with maintaining the mother's idealization preserves the grandiose self and helps avoid awareness of the real self and the mother's empathic failures and depersonification of her child. These patients as adults even confuse the grandiose self with the real self, and have a most difficult time during the initial stages of treatment in differentiating these psychic structures.

The second type of patient is more able to recall memories of being attacked, devalued, and disparaged as a child. The first type of patient, with a prolonged idealizing-mirroring history, has a more rigid grandiose self that is less vulnerable to minor failures of empathy. The second type is more prone to narcissistic vulnerability and injury, as well as being more cognizant of the impaired self.

All too often, the therapist observes an exterior of cool confidence, surface adaptation, and career success as evidence of psychological growth, rather than as a defensive false self that conceals an impotent and enraged impaired self.

The dramatic differences in technical interventions with the narcissistic personality disorder, as compared to the borderline personality, have been described elsewhere. Confrontation, which is typically a powerful tool that facilitates ego repair and improves adaptation in the borderline patient, is usually perceived as an attack by the narcissistic patient, who then mobilizes his grandiose defenses and becomes arrogant, contemptuous, and devaluing of the therapist.

The usually recommended treatment of choice for the narcissistic patient is long-term intensive psychoanalytic psychotherapy, with a minimum frequency of three times a week. Therapeutic technique should emphasize the interpretation of the patient's almost microscopic vulnerability to narcissistic injury and the disappointment of his need for perfect mirroring of his grandiose self. These failures of empathy will be inevitable during the course of treatment. This results in the systematic analysis, through the use of interpretation, of the need for perfect mirroring, the deep sense of worthlessness, and the connection between the false defensive grandiose self and the extremely vulnerable impaired real self.

The first section of this chapter describes how long-term work with the narcissistic personality disorder requires the therapist to shift from clarifying and interpreting the false defensive grandiose self to empathizing with the impaired real self. During the initial stage of treatment, the defenses of distancing and detachment of affect keep the patient from acknowledging the impaired real self. In fact, most of these patients have accepted the false defensive grandiose self as a competent substitute for the real self. As interpretations focus on the defenses against the impaired real self, it emerges tentatively and cautiously. At the same time, the defensive function of the grandiose self becomes clear. (The therapist must focus on the relationship between these two structural representations of the self, and on fears that accompany the activation of the impaired real self.)

This process is further complicated by the inhibitions of the external expression of grandiosity by the patient. Interpretations that focus on the painful affects of fear, shame, humiliation, and attack allow the patient to acknowledge the grandiose self defense and its need for perfect mirroring. In contrast, confrontation usually produces further distancing, withdrawal, or devaluation, which forces the therapist to rely on interpretation as the primary therapeutic intervention with this patient.

This chapter will consider two treatment modalities with the narcissistic personality disorder: (1) long-term psychoanalytic psychotherapy and (2) short-term psychotherapy.

LONG-TERM TREATMENT

The working through of the false defensive grandiose self is the primary goal of long-term treatment. The following case illustrates this therapeutic process in greater detail.

Case Illustration: Mr. T

Identifying data. The patient is a 53-year-old married Catholic man who lives in Westchester, New York, with his wife and three daughters. Mr. T is a successful businessman with his own clothing design firm.

Chief complaint. Mr. T contacted the Masterson Group when his wife threatened to dissolve their marriage unless he sought treatment. Mr. T recognized that his self-centered and distant behavior was placing a drain on his family. He had recently expanded his business and felt unable to manage the responsibilities that developed from this venture. He also felt incapable of being alone and constantly sought a frenetic schedule to cope with this anxiety.

History of present illness. Mr. T was feeling considerable pressure from his recent business expansion, which required more involvement on his part. Simultaneously, his wife was enraged at his inability to have any emotional involvement with his family. He claimed that he was "always running from involvement and the demands of others." He reported needing other people and using them to supply emotional nourishment.

He was always caught in a dilemma of trying to get "love, attention, and admiration from others" without "being involved and burdened by responsibilities and demands from others." He felt unable to distinguish other people's needs from his own and was extremely sensitive to any criticism. He felt terrified of asking for things directly, for this would only lead to disappointment, shame, and humiliation.

Mr. T complained of living in a fantasy world dominated by magical thinking and the fantasy of being special, adored, and recognized. He felt that any real involvement would lead to his being attacked, which he believed would make him disintegrate.

His brother had been chronically psychotic, which he thought was due to his brother's lack of emotional distance from his family. He said, "I walked a fine line between being special and being dysfunctional." His marriage of twenty years had been troubled by extramarital affairs, emotional distance, and a refusal to pay attention to the needs of his wife. He said, "I've been running all my life from diffuse anxiety."

Relevant past history and family history. Mr. T felt that his parents had been emotionally negligent. His parents wanted him to be a model child, and he ran from these unreasonable demands. At a very early stage, he decided to use his family as a fueling station. He avoided all contact and used his family for food and shelter. He said that his father was responsive until Mr. T developed a personality and a will of his own. His mother was attentive so long as he became an extension of her wishes.

Neither parent was able to recognize his needs as distinct and separate. His brother was "a model kid" who became a chronic schizophrenic. Mr. T said his brother stayed and got crushed, and he ran to survive. He had friends and was a good athlete, but he gave up easily when things required practice and effort. All his life he tried to seduce others into providing what he wanted. He felt impotent and unable to act on his own needs. He always struggled to survive emotionally.

School was characterized by poor grades and periodic discipline problems. He felt shy as an adolescent, unable to approach girls directly for fear of being turned down. He nurtured a fantasy of turning a "Liza Doolittle" into a "princess" who would adore him.

His work history was characterized by an inability to cooperate with others, which forced him to open his own business. He got married when his wife gave him an ultimatum. He views all decisions in his life as being externally motivated by his strong need for approval. He became the father of three girls, but continuously maintained emotional distance from his family and took no part in decision making. He was continually trying to get soothing and caring while shunning responsibilities.

Treatment. A treatment contract was established according to which the patient would be seen three times a week. The patient began by telling me that he had heard that the Masterson Group was known for confrontation and that we were a "bunch of headknockers." He said that he would fight back, and that even though his wife wanted him to get spanked he was not going to tolerate it.

The patient was immediately telling me about his sensitivity to confrontation, which I missed at this point. He went on to say that he wanted unilateral support and love from his family but he was unable to give anything in return. He used his family as a gas station. He would "fill up on food and emotional supplies" and then run out and did whatever he wanted to.

I began by confronting the destructiveness of his exploitive distancing behavior, and told him that this was working against his goal of improved familial relationships. He reacted with outrage, hurt, and retaliatory devaluation. He called me "a clone of the headknockers." He said his previous therapists were more insightful, and my lack of intelligence would interfere with his therapeutic progress. His extreme sensitivity and negative reaction to confrontation became apparent to me.

Initially, I thought he was a borderline personality with a distancing defense. In fact, the patient was a closet narcissistic personality with an inhibited, inadequate front. He kept his grandiose fantasies from the observer for fear of being disappointed. This is not an unusual façade for many narcissists. Although he had a strong need to exhibit his grandiose self and produce perfect mirroring, this fear of disappointment led to depleted self-esteem, withdrawal, and rage. Thus, the initial stage of treatment was characterized by testing to see if I would be able to respond properly and empathically to his need for mirroring and confirmation of his self representation.

I apologized for that intervention and focused on his extreme sensitivity with his wife and with me. He said that he felt like a child when criticized, and so would overreact. Criticism felt like an attack, and he would distance himself as soon as he perceived it. He began to speak of his childhood and how his needs were never recognized by either parent.

He insisted on recreating his childhood dissatisfaction by trying to force his family to respond to him (i.e., mirror him). I did my best at this point to resist further confrontation in order to allow the false defensive grandiose self to emerge more clearly. He said, "I want to be seen as a beautiful boy who can do whatever he wants. I want people to admire me and love me and see me as a beautiful cherub. I want unconditional love and I hate to work for it." This was a clear expression of the defensive grandiose self with its need for perfect mirroring, which was able to surface only after he tested me.

The patient spent many sessions focusing on various somatic symptoms and self-conscious preoccupations. I became bored at times and felt myself drifting off. Then one day he handed me a brochure that he had written for his work. I looked at it quickly and handed it back to him. His somatic preoccupations increased, and he became more distant and exploitive with his family. His wife began to criticize his insensitivity and noninvolvement, and he spoke of his need to find "a special place and a special haven where needs aren't frustrated."

I told him that his distance had seemed to increase since he shared his work with me. I wondered whether he was disappointed in my response and therefore felt an increased need to emotionally distance himself. He said that he was hurt because I did not spend most of the session reviewing his paper, and since I showed no interest in him he would do his usual distancing.

I told him that although he had handed me his paper, he never asked that I take the time to read it during his session. He said, "I would never ask directly for your attention (i.e., mirroring)—it would be too disappointing to be turned down. I would feel crushed at that point." He spoke about his approach to get things from people without asking by seducing them into his corner. He felt that directly acting on his needs was potentially shameful and humiliating.

I told him that his extreme sensitivity to potential disappointment forced him to cut himself off from people and potentially gratifying experiences. He confirmed this interpretation, and spoke about his need to be an Apache warrior and deny pain or any needs. He said, "If you triumph over need for people, you can never be hurt or humiliated—the world is loveless and you will never get what you want." I told him that it was easier for him to write off the world and his therapist and to distance himself than to face his extreme sensitivity to the disappointment of his needs.

The patient said, "My parents saw my soft vulnerable child self and they stepped on it. It can only happen again." This response shows the dual defensive sides of this patient. Either he was to be mirrored perfectly and his grandiose self would flourish, or he would be attacked and shamed. Real involvement, with its risk of normal disappointments and frustrations, had to be shunned because of its potential for narcissistic injury. Rather than face such a risk the patient would distance himself, seduce others into providing for him, or force others into being an extension of his needs (i.e., using his home and therapy as a gas station to provide needed emotional supplies). The patient was unable to share his needs in any intimate relationship for fear of narcissistic injury. This patient's continual citation of reality disappointments was used to justify distancing in the transference. My interpretations were used to focus on his need for perfect response and empathy, which resulted in his need for defensive retreat.

The patient began to speak of his defensive maneuvers in a more ego-dystonic tone. He spoke about the "unfulfilled potential" in his life, and realized that he never persisted with his goals. He would make a quick impression, receive his accolades and admiration, and would then drop the task rather than go through with the work required for mastery. He realized that he was never truly involved with work or people because it would leave him feeling vulnerable. He spoke about his need to view life as magical where needs were met automatically with no effort. He felt reality was harsh and disappointing. He said he never had developed a real self because he would never expose it to injury. He said that if he did not live in a world of magic and automatic gratification, he would be crushed like his brother. The only difference between him and his brother was that he kept his real feelings and desires hidden.

He began to complain about the realistic burdens of marriage, his work, and his family. He then focused his complaints on treatment, saying that it took too long. He wanted hypnosis, or something that required little work on his part. I interpreted his wish that treatment be like magic so he would feel provided for and not have to work and risk disappointment. He spoke about his need to build up his self-esteem, and began to question his extreme sensitivity and his need for perfect mirroring. He said life is not really heavenly and perfect, nor is it a nightmare—"Why do I refuse to see it in realistic terms?"

This interaction marked the beginning of a therapeutic alliance with the patient. He began to see the compromises that were made by his real self and saw the grandiose self as a defense against involvement and potential injury.

In the prior ten years, Mr. T had had several extramarital affairs and infatuations in which he felt "adored by a special girl." He said, "I feel impotent with women—like a cherub with no penis—but I thrive on being able to seduce a goddess who can warm me and motivate me by her specialness." This narcissistic enmeshment with the highly idealized female was used to counteract the harsh attacking image of his marital relationship. He said, "My wife and marriage are reality—it smells, it stagnates—it is the dying old man."

As his treatment progressed, he began to discover the futility of his extramarital relationships, and the narcissistic glow began to fade. He first complained that his girlfriends no longer seemed so special. They had defects: pimples, body odor, and imperfect intellects. He began to cry when he realized this, saying that his childhood dream of a "magical woman" to counteract his emptiness and depression was no longer available to him. Reality still seemed harsh, but it was becoming something that needed to be addressed.

The gradual diminution of the idealized object set the stage for his increased involvement with others, self-activation, and the gradual tentative expression of his very vulnerable but real self. These expressions were met by interpretations of his fears of rejection and disappointment, and of his reactive retreat from further expression. His exquisite sensitivity to my failures of perfect empathy were consistently clarified during this period. In turn, the patient began to identify with this therapeutic attitude and also questioned his sensitivity and this enormous need to distance himself from reality.

During one session he noticed his distortions in a very clear way: "I used to see people as cruel and savage animals—and then it would justify my retreat—or I had to become the perfect angelic cherub [grandiose self]. Now I realize it is not a savage world. The problem is my fear of rejection and this need to be loved, admired, and seen as special. I don't operate in business and gave up my marriage and family for this need—what a tragedy." Indeed, the patient had now seen the tragedy of his life. He had submerged his real self and was constantly seeking the expression of the grandiose self and its need for perfect mirroring.

This patient demonstrated many manifestations of the impaired real self. He was unable to be involved with his family. His chronic distancing and withdrawal was a defense against his fear of being attacked, depersonified, and used by someone else. His fear of involvement at work resulted in an inability to monitor his employees and difficulties in asserting himself. He maintained a magical fantasy of things being taken care of without his asking for it. His needs were to be provided for by others' recognizing them and acting on them. He continually tried to seduce others into caring for him.

The patient also had pronounced problems with self-management and self-entitlement. He showed an inability to be by himself and used others for emotional sustenance and replenishment. He felt inherently bad and not worthy of obtaining gratification or pleasure for himself. He felt impotent, was unable to act on his own, and never developed a sense of an autonomous self. There was an urgency to his needs that had to be denied or acted on impulsively. There was no acknowledgment as to their legitimate expression. In addition, his creative self was thwarted. He showed some potential as a writer, but never completed a work because he was terrified of criticism and ridicule. His speech at times was characterized by inaudible mumbling, because he feared disinterest and lack of recognition by others.

The patient's awareness was followed by behavioral changes. He became more involved at work and challenged some practices of his employees that he had chosen to ignore in the past. He felt that if he asserted his real self, he would no longer be mirrored. Each negative reaction was met with sensitivity and feelings of humiliation.

He recalled memories of his childhood. When he would create something artistically, his parents would ignore him, but they would praise him if he was the model kid. He had dreams of going back to his hometown and facing his childhood realities without being a special child.

He began to feel that I no longer cared about him, found him boring, and preferred my other patients. I told him that he saw me as like his parents, who only loved a phony façade and had no interest in the real thing. He picked up on this and said, "It really doesn't matter if you see me as special."

Similarly, he became more involved with his wife and children. His wife was a very critical and angry woman who demanded constant attention. In the past, he would make deals with her, supplying some of her needs, and would then distance himself. This way he could be mirrored without working. He began to assert himself with his wife, stood up against her assaults, and recognized that her anger was related to her problems and not necessarily to his behavior. He opened communication with his children, risked their defensive rejection, and continued in his efforts. He expressed remorse about their growing up without him.

He began to feel more vulnerable, and expressed this somatically. He became preoccupied with his aging bodily processes and various aches and pains. He said that his body was more vulnerable since he was middle aged. I told him that he was *feeling* more vulnerable because of his increased involvement, and that he was translating this into a physical fear. This interpretation helped reduce his somatic preoccupation.

During this period, he began to see me as stronger and as a possible identificatory model. Periodically, he would insult and devalue me to see if I could withstand the assault. He said, "You are not like some of my *other* brilliant, insight-oriented therapists who did not prepare me for reality." These deprecatory comments were responded to by my saying that he needed to test me to see if I could back my words up with action and was strong enough to tolerate his criticisms.

This patient has much more work to do to consolidate his real self. When feeling threatened, he still retreats to a distant or detached position or leans on the grandiose self as protection. At other times, he will externalize his conflict and act as if reality is the problem forcing him to defend himself.

When working with the narcissistic personality, the therapist must continuously focus on the vulnerability of the impaired real self, its hypersensitive stance, and the need for the false defensive grandiose self. First, the resistances against the emergence of the grandiose self must be interpreted. Confrontation will only encourage further defense with the narcissist. Second, the protection of the real self must be explored. Countertransference responses must be monitored, because the sensitivity of this patient will otherwise quickly result in a stalemate of the treatment process. The therapist must be able to empathize with the fears, disappointments, and vulnerability of this patient, and understand his defensive need for the false defensive grandiose self and perfect mirroring and its relationship to the impaired real self.

SHORT-TERM TREATMENT

Although long-term treatment directed toward changing intra-psychic structure is extremely useful for some patients, many are unable to engage in such a prolonged treatment process, for a variety of reasons including cost, availability of treatment, age or motivation of the patient, and the capacity of the patient to undergo intrapsychic change.

Short-term treatment approaches have emphasized a reduction in acute symptomatology and improved functioning with a minimal working through of the abandonment depression and the separation-individuation failure. Confrontive psychotherapy with the borderline patient is tailor-made for these treatment goals.

The question remains as to what, if anything, is a useful short-term treatment approach for the narcissistic personality disorder. It has often been noted that a therapist can restore narcissistic defenses crumbling from an acute separation stress by supplying appropriate mirroring responses or sometimes by just listening.

Many clinicians have a guilty sense of being unemployed by the narcissist as he uses the therapist to restore a narcissistic equilibrium. Although most of this work is experimental, many narcissistic patients do modify their behavior, reduce symptoms, contain destructive acting out and disruptive affect, and become able to function in a more adaptive manner after once-a-week psychotherapy for one to two years.

Although interpretation of narcissistic vulnerability is a crucial treatment intervention, other variables such as providing mirroring, giving responses encouraging an idealization of the therapist, allowing the patient to use the therapist as a self-object, and even using confrontation, when it is to promote an aggrandizement of the therapist and pave the way for an idealizing transference (i.e., in working with adolescents), can be extremely effective in catalyzing behavioral change and symptomatic improvement. In order to do treatment effectively, the therapist must be comfortable in negotiating with the narcissist, and must avoid moralistic attitudes that interfere with the formulation of a therapeutic relationship. The clinician must be willing to accept modifications of behavior rather than structural change, or the therapist and the patient will experience mutual disappointment. The following cases will help illustrate some of these approaches.

Case Illustration: Danny

Danny was a 15-year-old from an upper-class family in New York when his parents sought treatment. His father was an extremely successful businessman, and his mother came from an aristocratic European family.

History of present illness: His parents sought treatment because of his poor motivation in school and his dismissal from several boarding schools. Danny had a history of learning disabilities, got poor grades, and had been disciplined in several schools for drinking, pot smoking, and theft. Danny was described as a good-looking social charmer who got by on style. Danny's parents were concerned about his "Napoleonic complex," as he often spoke about getting even with authority and of being the dictator and leader of a chosen group of children. He often referred to his special destiny and voiced his contempt for ordinary people.

Past history. During the initial consultation, Danny's parents gave a frank account of their idealization of Danny and their consistent difficulty with providing appropriate limits for his behavior. The parents had been married in their forties and had adopted Danny and his younger brother. Danny's father was often absent from the family for long periods because of the demands of his business. Both parents described him as a "beautiful toy," and were unable to provide limits or interfere with any of his demands. They described him as a precocious infant who was perfect in every way.

His father said there was "nothing that I wanted to change about him. He was gregarious, outgoing, and confident—everything that I wasn't." His mother gave a similar description but added that he was distractible, had a short attention span, and had temper tantrums when he was not gratified immediately. Danny's mother reported being depressed by her husband's long absences, and of clinging to Danny to relieve some of her depression. Danny's father, on the other hand, was oblivious to the family's problems, claiming that he thought he had a perfect family. He was shocked and concerned to discover Danny was having school-related problems. Both parents said that "whatever Danny wanted, we did."

Danny was manipulative with his parents. When his father would try to spank him for transgressions, he would say, "If you were my real father, you wouldn't be this mean to me." These tactics would always disarm his parents. Both parents came from wealthy families that were cold, rejecting, and disinterested. They both admitted to using Danny to feel better about themselves and were proud of his casual, easy-going confidence. Despite this idealization of Danny, both sets of grandparents were rejecting toward Danny because he was not from an aristocratic bloodline.

Course of psychotherapy. Danny came into his initial visit by knocking on all the doors in the waiting room and shouting, "Where the hell is this Dr. Fischer?" Dr. Masterson came out of his office and told him to sit in the waiting area until I was ready for him. When

Danny came into my office he immediately took off his shoes, sank into the couch, closed his eyes, and said, "One more boring shrink to put up with."

He told me that his problem was that teachers and other adults were not as smart as he was, and that he was able to con the best of them. He went on to tell me that shrinks must love spoiled rich kids like himself to help pay the bills, and that I had better do as he said because he gave the orders, and could cut off his parents' purse strings if I was not obedient to his wishes.

After 15 minutes of his contempt and devaluation, I began to recover. I asked him what his present allowance was. He told me that the amount was not important, because he could charm his parents into giving him any amount of money he wanted. He went on to tell me that obviously someday he was going to be president of the country and that the masses needed him. I laughed and told him that from what his parents told me, it sounded like he was unable to cross the street by himself. I then told him to put on his shoes and get his feet off my couch. Danny sneered at me and said, "I call the shots with shrinks." I said, "You don't understand your parents. Since I told them that you are a wise ass punk, they have now decided to listen to someone far brighter than you."

He said, "Who the hell do you think you are?" I told him that he was looking at his new boss. He said, "We'll see about that." I told him, "Don't press your luck or I'll make sure that you become the poorest kid on the block." He began to protest, and I told him to leave my office and to be on time for our next session. As he walked out he said, "Holy shit! I really got myself into a fix this time."

Although confrontation is usually not the intervention of choice with the narcissistic personality disorder, it was deliberately employed with Danny. I felt that the lack of parental authority was responsible for his grandiose acting out and arrogant contempt. In order to become effective as a therapist with Danny, I had to first release myself from a position of contempt and possibly unleash some underlying idealizing needs for an object who could help him contain his behavior and affect. If such an idealizing relationship developed, then a therapist could become a valuable source of mirroring supplies.

During the next session, Danny was on time and was very careful with my couch. He told me that he told his friends that this shrink was a crazy drill sergeant. He then began to tell me that at times he was worried about his behavior and felt that his parents were scared of him. I told him that he felt reassured knowing that someone was now able to see through his front.

Danny spoke about acting like Superman but was really concerned about not doing well in school, and not being able to live up to his parents' expectations. He said that "most people are unable to see through my front and need me to be a big shot." He went on to say, "You are a cool dude. My other shrinks were old fogeys. I think you can understand me."

This marked the beginning of an idealizing transference through which Danny was able to uncover his impaired real self. These transactions were addressed with interpretive interventions that would relate the grandiose self and its need to conceal an impaired real self.

The next session Danny came late with his pants unzipped. He said, "Sorry, dude, but I was getting laid." He then asked me to give him "skin" (a reference to being soul mates or a request for mirroring). He told me that if women didn't give him sexual gratification, then he would physically abuse them. I told him that, although he acted like a man, it was nothing more than a façade because only weak boys had to be abusive to girls.

He then spoke in great detail about feelings of worthlessness, linking these to his adoption. He wondered if he came from an inferior genetic line. I interpreted his need to show off as being related to these other feelings, and told him that his sensitivity to rejection had to be dealt with in a more appropriate way. Danny needed confrontation of his grandiose acting out as well as interpretation of the defensive grandiose self and its relationship to the impaired real self. These interventions paved the way for idealization and the use of "conditional mirroring," which is most useful in the short-term treatment of narcissistic personality disorder.

Several months into the treatment Danny called me in a state of panic. He had had a dream in which everyone was admiring his beautiful bronzed body. He looked like a Greek statute on display. All of a sudden his body began to decay and fall apart. His limbs were weak and broken, and all his admirers left him. I interpreted the fear that without his front (grandiose self) he would be worthless and unacknowledged. He told me that I was a very wise man and that he felt better. Usually, I do not conduct treatment on the telephone. This deviation of the frame is permissible in short-term treatment, however, because the therapist does not attempt to work through the grandiose self or promote separation or autonomy. The therapist must become an appropriate self-object or extension of the patient's self by providing appropriate gratifications and mirroring responses in order to create a narcissistic equilibrium and to help the patient defend against painful self-esteem fluctuations, affective instability, and fragmentation of the self. With Danny, the idealization of the therapist was not interpreted or disrupted, because it became a necessary vehicle and catalyst for change. This treatment typically was conducted on a once-a-week basis, but there were long breaks in the treatment when the patient's family took extensive vacations, which enabled the patient to deal with separation experiences and promoted self-containment.

As treatment progressed, Danny's behavior began to improve. His school grades were better, he put in more hours working, he accepted the limits that his parents had required of him, and he stopped abusing drugs and alcohol. He would come in talking about his accomplishments. I would smile and give appropriate positive remarks. He said, "I like to make you proud of me. Your opinion is important to me." This need to be mirrored for constructive behavioral change was gratified in the treatment and not confronted or interpreted. Periodically Danny's defensive grandiose behavior would return and the necessary confrontations and interpretations were given during those episodes, resulting in improved containment of behavior, and symptomatic improvement.

Danny was graduating from high school and going away to college. During his last sessions, his idealization of me intensified. He told me that I must be the *best* therapist in the world, as I was able to help him. He brought in a camera and took a picture of me to keep with him when "things got rough." Danny wanted to become an actor, and during his initial consultation he had spoken about success without having to work for it—a clear expression of narcissistic entitlement. He now told me that someday after *years of hard work* he was going to be in the movies. He said, "You'll enjoy seeing your patient in the movies." I said, "Yes, I will." Danny and I parted with the understanding that he could call during times of stress and might return for treatment if necessary in the future. When Danny left, he said that he felt much better about himself, but that he still had trouble with girls. He felt that he sexualized relationships because he had a problem with genuine feeling. He ended by saying, "What the hell. You can't be perfect. Besides, I'm a teenager and don't have to worry about marriage for awhile. I'll call you then for a major valve job."

Throughout the course of treatment, Danny's parents were seen by another therapist to help them manage his grandiose acting-out behavior, and to supply appropriate limits. These were seen on a twice-a-month frequency.

The closing phase of treatment was characterized by a number of treatment strategies. The need to incorporate the therapist (idealized object) through the picture taking was permitted and not interpreted. This intensification of defense was supported to help him tolerate separation stress. It was important that the patient leave feeling appreciated and important to me—that I was as invested in him as he was in me; thus, the need for the final mirroring response. Danny left with a beautiful description of short-term treatment goals. Separation was denied, and our relationship would continue at some point. There was an improved capacity to work without working through. Finally, the false defensive grandiose self was left intact with modifications and improved containment of affect and limiting of self-destructive acting out, but the capacity for intimacy was not developed.

The following case illustration is another example of technical interventions used in the short term treatment of narcissistic personality disorder.

Case Illustration: Mr. Smith

History of present illness. Mr. Smith was a 38-year-old salesman who was referred by an employee assistance program for poor job performance, selling cocaine to an employee, and a recent obesity problem. Initially, Mr. Smith denied any problem, and said that people had always envied his intellectual strength and physical prowess. He was always skilled at getting people to admire him, and they looked up to him as a physically powerful person. He dismissed the drug sales as an attempt to respond to a friend's needs. His supervisor at work was his high school football coach, who was always a source of inspiration. When Mr. Smith was passed over for promotion, he felt enraged and his job performance deteriorated. He said, "I was no longer interested in being his shining star."

Past history. Mr. Smith was the son of immigrant parents. His father was described as authoritarian and dominating, with high expectations for his son. His mother was a passive and relatively distant woman. Mr. Smith always wanted to be like his father, who was "admired and respected." Throughout his childhood he felt "important and superior" to others. At the age of 5, he was bedridden for a year with rheumatic fever. He remembered this as the most humiliating time of his life, during which he was passive and lacked control. Mr. Smith said that he was always in charge of his life, had to control others, and sometimes would mismanage things when his arrogance became unchallenged. He was married with two children and denied any family or marital problems.

Course of psychotherapy. When I first met Mr. Smith I was struck by his awesome physical presence. He weighed more than 350 pounds and was unable to fit in a chair. He looked embarrassed and moved to the couch. He told me that people did not realize that he was in control of his life and could change whatever he wanted to change. He said that throughout his life he had a superior physical presence, that people admired him, and this was due to his enviable physical stature. He felt that maybe there was some problem since nobody was capable of supervising him.

I told him that it was unfortunate that a man of such talent and capability was running into so much trouble. It was obvious that the patient objected to my speaking. He needed complete control of the interview and felt threatened when someone else became a separate and distinct person who might not mirror him. He also had a "sliding meaning" defense, manifested by many narcissists, by which he would reinterpret every deficit and make it into a virtue. Thus, obesity would become physical prowess and exploitation of others would be concern. I slowly became a self-object for Mr. Smith, or an extension of his false-defensive grandiose self. I would sit and listen, allow him to control the interview, and would periodically clarify what he had already verbalized. This enabled him to avoid feeling the impaired real self with its vulnerability to injury. Furthermore, by taking control of the interview, he could take further control of his life in a more constructive and less defense-ridden way. This process requires that the therapist endure periods of boredom and detachment, because he is being depersonified and used as a self-object by the patient to recreate a narcissistic equilibrium.

As the sessions progressed, the patient said that he was using therapy to put him on the right track. He said, "Therapy is not a humiliating or passive experience. It allows your potential to come to fruition." He wondered if his anger at his boss was motivating his self-defeating behavior, and for the first time spoke about his life being out of control. He said, "I really have a weight problem, and I think we should make this an area of focus." He continued by saying, "I want you to keep an eye on me so the train doesn't go off the track."

I told him that he now felt comfortable enough to allow me to be part of his life, and that he wanted some guidance, but that all along he feared intrusion. This interpretation brought up painful memories of his rheumatic fever, being passive and bedridden, and feeling humiliated by his heart problem. "I felt that either you are an invalid or omnipotent," he said. He also realized that he was never able to cope with supervision because of his fear of passivity. These memories clearly connected the false defensive grandiose self to the impaired real self.

The patient's sense of control during the interview (which was felt as dominating the object in the transference) enabled him to let go of this defense in the external world and to appraise his life more realistically. Mr. Smith joined a weight control program and lost 160 pounds in the course of a year and a half. His job performance improved dramatically, and his employer was startled by his recovery. I was somewhat doubtful about his rapid recovery, but one year after termination all symptomatic improvement remained intact. Upon termination, Mr. Smith (like Danny) denied separation, saying that he always had to keep track of his life and would call me if he needed another pair of eyes.

Both of these cases illustrate some of the principles and interventions in the short-term treatment of narcissistic personality disorder. The goals of this treatment must be carefully clarified: containment of the false defensive grandiose self, self limiting of destructive acting out, symptomatic improvement, and changes in adaptive functioning.

No attempt should be made to work through the false defensive grandiose self, to promote genuine autonomy, or promote intimacy. The therapist must be satisfied with improvements in the work function rather than working through. Symptomatic improvement and adaptive change can be of enormous benefit to the narcissistic patient.

While working with this type of patient, the therapist must be willing to suspend moralistic judgments and not try to make this patient "more object related" rather than self centered. The narcissist's world revolves around power, fame, money, and status. These supplies should not be devalued by the therapist, but should become the focus of treatment insofar as the patient misuses them to sabotage his or her own goals. The work with the narcissistic patient requires a much greater use of the transference than the work with the borderline patient.

The need for idealization, mirroring, or merging gives the therapist a powerful group of supplies that can be used during the treatment. Whereas these needs are analyzed during the course of long-term treatment, they become the resources for change in short-term treatment.

Those patients who are unable to move from a position of contempt or devaluation will not be accessible to a short-term treatment approach, because idealizing and mirroring needs can never be utilized during the course of the therapy. The therapist must be comfortable in becoming an ally of the grandiose self—opposing its direction, but modulating its momentum. Countertransference responses of anger, envy, and boredom can be mobilized as residues of the therapist's grandiosity stimulated by the patient. If these reactions are addressed by the therapist, then enormous benefits can be gained by the patient during a relatively brief course of treatment.

OVERALL TREATMENT STRATEGIES

This chapter delineates the various treatment strategies that can be used with the narcissistic personality disorder.

In order to be effective with the narcissistic patient, the therapist must be cognizant of the continuously activated fused grandiose self–omnipotent object structure. This requires a technical shift from confrontation of external acting-out behavior, to interpretation of the patient's microscopic vulnerability to the narcissistic disappointment of his grandiosity that develops as the inevitable failures of empathy occur during the course of treatment. The defensive grandiose self with its need for mirroring, exhibition, and idealization must be related to the impaired self with its sense of injury and vulnerability.

The real self, which has been defensively hidden by fears of shame, humiliation, worthlessness, and inadequacy, can emerge only through a transference relationship that consistently interprets the patient's exquisite sensitivity and defensive reactions.

The therapist works more closely with the narcissistic transference and does not confront external acting-out behavior as he would with the borderline patient. Thus confrontation, the main treatment tool for short-term ego repair and improved adaptation, is not utilized with this patient.

This radical technical shift with the narcissistic patient forces the therapist to move his focus from the behavioral acting-out dimension to the phenomenological affective sphere. The continuous activation of the false defensive grandiose self forces the narcissistic patient to deny, devalue, or avoid any stimuli that interfere with idealizing and mirroring supplies, and thus restores a narcissistic equilibrium through defensive arrogance and contempt. This defensive constellation, coupled with the narcissist's vulnerability to wounds and intolerance for depression, results in a clinical situation in which confrontation usually mobilizes further distancing, defense, and sometimes therapeutic stalemate.

This therapeutic dilemma forces the therapist to rely almost exclusively on the interpretation of narcissistic vulnerability (as it emerges in the interview) and the activation of the false defensive grandiose self as a defense against injury. Through the repetitive explanation and analysis of disappointment and narcissistic rage (which are the results of the inevitable failures of empathy), the source of such vulnerability—the maternal failure to acknowledge and support the real self—becomes readily available for reconstructive working through.

The systematic use of interpretation to analyze the false defensive grandiose self and its idealizing and mirroring needs becomes the primary focus of a long-term intensive psychotherapy. The goal of such a treatment is the working through of the false defensive grandiose self and the slow emergence and development of the real self.

Short-term treatment approaches are less global in focus, and the goals and expectations are more circumscribed. First, the therapist does not attempt to work through the false defensive grandiose self or the developmental arrest but, rather, tries to reduce symptoms, improve adaptive functioning, and restore a narcissistic equilibrium.

The primary approach for short-term treatment is the strengthening of the false defensive grandiose self through the provision of idealizing and mirroring supplies, or tolerating and encouraging the use of the therapist as an extension of the self. The therapist uses whatever techniques are necessary to facilitate the illusion of a dual omnipotent unity between patient and therapist. This has to be done with a thorough assessment of reality testing and a careful monitoring of self-destructive acting-out technique. If the therapist suspends moralistic judgment and empathically responds to the narcissistic vulnerability and its need for compensatory defenses, then the patient can restore a sense of self that was previously lost.

Chapter 6

Shorter-Term Psychotherapy of the Personality Disorders

Ralph Klein, M.D.

Many therapists in training are eager to help patients turn their lives and their intrapsychic structures around in a dramatic and all-encompassing way. This enthusiasm must often be redirected in treatment, however, because of factors simply beyond a patient's capacity to change and grow, or a therapist's ability to promote change and growth. Practical matters such as time, money, institutional constraints, or the lack of patient motivation may become determining factors in setting treatment goals.

In fact, these very constraints are so often present that therapists since and including Freud have found it necessary to assume a more circumscribed role by turning to the theories and practices of briefer, time-limited and goal-limited dynamic psychotherapy.

Many therapists have found that brief therapy can be useful in helping patients work through focal current conflicts and acute symptoms. The value of brief dynamic therapy for revising core personality structures is less clear. I have found that when such changes do occur, they appear to reflect changes in more "neurotic" personality structures, with, for example, strengthening of the ego's sublimatory capacities and modifications in an overly harsh, punitive, or perfectionistic superego.

A diagnosis of personality disorder—and especially borderline personality disorder—is generally viewed as a contraindication for shorter-term therapy unless the treatment focus is on a particular stressful event or a particular symptomatic situation. Although this might suggest that shorter-term treatment is of limited usefulness when working with a patient with a personality disorder, this is in fact not the case.

This chapter examines the efficacy of shorter-term treatment of borderline and narcissistic disorders.

THE BORDERLINE PERSONALITY

The Masterson Approach is often misperceived as requiring long-term intensive psychotherapy. In fact, the treatment model lends itself to shorter-term work, should this be indicated. Although structural, intrapsychic change can generally be accomplished only through long-term, intensive psychotherapy, shorter-term treatment can be used in the borderline personality disorder to achieve other worthwhile goals.

For the average patient with a borderline disorder, shorter-term treatment—once weekly for six months to two years—can achieve the following: improved functioning, decrease in focal symptoms, correction of delimited irrational and fantasy beliefs revolving around a patient's self-image, and creation of a model for a new object relations unit that can anchor future relationships and, in general, aid the patient in establishing a more adaptive life course.

Criteria for Selection of Cases for Shorter-Term Treatment

External circumstances often dictate which borderline patients receive shorter-term treatment. Limitations involving time or money have already been mentioned. In addition, the therapist's availability can also be a limiting factor for those who practice in clinic or agency settings where the caseloads limit or preclude intensive psychotherapy.

Aside from practical considerations, a patient's motivation for change carries great weight in predicting those patients for whom relatively shorter-term therapy can be successful. Whereas the capacity for intrapsychic change and growth is predictive of and crucial for the success of intensive, long-term therapy, in shorter-term therapy this factor is secondary to the patient's motivation to change his behavior. When the patient is motivated by painful affects or circumstances to behave in a more adaptive and realistic manner, his condition meshes with a focal point of shorter-term treatment: adaptation to reality.

The motivation for change is of such importance that it is generally more predictive of successful outcome in shorter-term treatment than any other single factor, including the level of personality organization (higher level versus lower level). For example, a patient with a lower-level borderline personality disorder who presents for treatment with ego-dystonic maladaptive or destructive behavior with an acute awareness of painful feelings (usually depression or anxiety) is much more likely to have a successful course of shorter-term treatment than a higher-functioning patient who presents with ego-syntonic acting out. In these latter instances, a time-consuming first step in treatment must be to make the symptoms dystonic, and this makes the patient a poor candidate for shorter-term treatment.

Goals and Objectives

The treatment goals for the borderline personality disorder in shorter-term psychotherapy are threefold: containment, learning, and adaptation. These three objectives are not achieved in consecutive linear stages in treatment; rather, they are components of a circular ongoing process of psychotherapy:

1. Containment—the patient must recognize, control, self-limit, and contain the tendency to act out
2. Learning—the patient must learn that the emerging affects (component parts of the abandonment depression) uncovered by the stripping away of defenses can and must be verbalized in treatment rather than acted out
3. Adaptation—the patient must channel the energies associated with these affects into adaptive and sublimated expressions and behaviors, thus promoting a more reality-based and healthy lifestyle

Treatment Techniques

Shorter-term treatment technique follows the Masterson treatment model with two modifications: the frequency of sessions is limited, and confrontation is virtually the sole therapeutic technique utilized.

Shorter-term treatment necessitates the limiting of the number of treatment sessions to once, or at most twice, a week. More frequent sessions involve the patient more deeply in the transference and promote the emergence of fantasies, memories, free associations, and dreams—all of which deepen the abandonment depression when the goal of the treatment is not the working through of the depression. In shorter-term treatment, the day-to-day problems of adaptation and healthy defense should remain the focus of attention.

Occasionally, an increase in the number of weekly sessions may be necessitated when more frequent confrontation is needed to help the patient to contain and limit severe acting out. Once such acting out is controlled, the frequency of sessions should be immediately reduced.

Confrontation is the key therapeutic technique throughout the course of shorter-term treatment. It is the crucial intervention that initiates and maintains the therapeutic focus on containment, learning, and adaptation. Clarification, interpretation, and communicative matching all play a far more secondary role in shorter-term treatment. These interventions are increasingly used and necessary in intensive therapy, where they help to maintain the focus on the process of working through the abandonment depression. The following case examples illustrate the use of shorter-term treatment with borderline personality disorders.

THE CASE OF W.L.

W.L. is a high-level borderline patient who came to weekly sessions for one year. A 31-year-old divorced accountant, she presented with the following chief complaints: (1) fear that her continued chronic abuse of cocaine was seriously affecting her mood and her mind, (2) a history of unsatisfactory relationships with men, and (3) pervasive feelings of depression, emptiness, and boredom.

The patient had used cocaine for several years but had only recently become concerned about this usage, as she began to connect it with severe mood fluctuations as well as difficulties with memory and feelings of derealization and depersonalization. Since her work as an accountant was the sole anchor of her identity (otherwise there was marked identity diffusion), her difficulties in concentration were particularly disturbing to her.

Her unhappy relationships were a secondary, but still important, motivation to seek treatment. Although she recognized that she had severe problems with interpersonal relationships, she had no insight into the nature of these problems. She was especially upset, though, by the failure of her marriage one year previously. She had been married for only two years, and she described with dismay the "change" that had taken place in her husband from a totally care-taking, need-gratifying suitor to a verbally, and finally physically, abusive husband.

Her description of the people in her life, women as well as men, was remarkably superficial and lifeless. For example, though she stated that a current problem was deciding which of three current boyfriends was the right one for her, she in no way connected this dilemma to her more generally perceived dissatisfaction with relationships even though, by my calculations, the average distance between her and these men was 3,300 miles—one lived in California, one in Mexico, and one in Germany. Also, in describing the qualities that she looked for in a man, she stated first that she could never become involved with a man who was not powerful and who did not drive a red Porsche.

She had pervasive feelings of emptiness, depression, and boredom associated with a markedly impaired real self. She had failed to achieve a stable, cohesive identity; rather, she struggled constantly with the demands of her false, defensive self. Although she had finished school and received a degree in accounting and was now working as an accountant for a television production company, she was doubling as the unofficial "company escort." She stated that she felt like a professional businesswoman half of the time and like a prostitute the other half. What, she wondered, was the real her?

Finally, she stated that she had carefully calculated her finances and had put aside enough money for treatment once weekly for a year.

W.L. was a good candidate for shorter-term treatment because of her high motivation for change and because of the evidence in her past history and present functioning of sufficient ego strengths to effect and maintain adaptive changes in a relatively brief period.

Course in Treatment

W.L. began the initial interview by stating that she hoped I had experienced E.S.T. so that I would be able to understand her thoughts and feelings better. I quickly confronted this statement by wondering why she felt that she could not tell me how she felt but, rather, expected me to intuitively understand her through a "shared" experience. It seemed to me, I added, to be an unnecessary extra step.

She responded that she did not know how she felt most of the time, probably because the cocaine so confused and altered her ability to think and feel. I wondered why she would continue to use a drug that affected her so adversely. She stated that she did not know if she could give it up, since it played such an important role in her friendships and her social network more generally. Further, she had tried unsuccessfully to give it up before.

I reflected that she seemed to be feeling and acting helpless in the face of her own impulses and the wishes of others, and I wondered why she did this (already I was implicitly communicating my expectation that she could contain the impulse to act out and could behave more adaptively). She responded to my question with the explanation that she felt happy if she made other people happy. I pointed out that clearly her formula for happiness was not working, since she had just stated a few minutes earlier that she was increasingly unhappy and upset with her life.

She acknowledged the confrontation by stating that she wanted to try to stop taking the cocaine. She asked, however, if I would continue to see her should she try but fail to stop the drug use (in other words, would I ally myself with her impaired real self or accept an alliance with her false, defensive self?). I told her that I thought cocaine and psychotherapy did not mix. She stated that she could continue the cocaine and just not tell me, as many of her friends did with their therapists. I told her that she could, indeed, do that but that she should know that she would be wasting her time and her money because there could be no effective treatment built on a foundation of drugs and deceit. Rather, it seemed to me that she had to decide whether she wished to get high or to get better—she could not do both.

Within three weeks she had completely stopped the cocaine use—evidence of her significant motivation for change.

At this point I began to confront her about her "second addiction" to her boyfriends, to whom she would turn, whenever she felt unhappy or frustrated, for a quick "fix." She argued that just because a man made her feel good, I had no right to call an affair an addiction. I replied that since these contacts substituted for sticking with and dealing with painful thoughts and feelings—and also substituted for the difficulties inherent in real relationships—I could correctly characterize them as addictions. Over a period of time she gradually integrated these confrontations, finally acknowledging, "I don't think I ever had a decent relationship."

As W.L. increasingly contained her tendency to act out, painful affect consistently began to emerge, and she would increasingly verbalize it in the sessions. She began to feel more in control—"Every day I feel less frantic, not grabbing at things"—yet this would be soon followed by depression—"Can't we hurry this process? I feel helpless and no good. This is difficult and I'm depressed." She gradually began to recognize the relationship between these two affective states. She saw that acknowledging and asserting her own individuative thoughts, feelings, and wishes precipitated depression, fear of aloneness, and panic, which she then tried to defend against by compliance, self-paralysis, and clinging to men (the false, defensive self). Stated dynamically, she was beginning to identify the operation of the borderline triad: separation-individuation, depression, and defense.

The following excerpt is from a session several months after treatment began. The patient, for the first time, made spontaneous reference to her early relationship with her parents:

> It's too hard to do anything, to change anything. I have never been in charge of my own life. If I am in control of my life, if I didn't give myself to others, if I'm not willing to lose myself, then I'm afraid I will be alone. I think I have felt this way from the time I was 11 or 12. That's when I first turned to drugs. I remember feeling that my parents were not parents, just people who used me and made me act the way they wanted me to act. They pretended to give me independence, and constantly took it back. They encouraged me to make my own decisions and then made me do what they wanted. My mother seemed to be afraid that she would lose me and my father was just sadistic, constantly teasing me and telling me I wasn't good enough. I felt like I lived in an orphanage.

Over the next month, a deepening of her depression corresponded to a shift from work on the borderline triad in the "here and now" to work on the borderline triad in the "there and then" of her childhood past. I was beginning to feel increasingly concerned that she was getting too deeply into the abandonment depression. In shorter-term treatment, the therapist must be constantly monitoring the patient's progress so that the experience, exploration, and understanding of emerging affects do not outstrip the patient's capacity to evolve adaptive defenses. When the emerging affects outdistance the evolving defense, this gap must be managed. In intensive treatment, it is the process of working through of the abandonment depression which "fills the gap." In shorter-term treatment, mature defenses and adaptive behaviors must "fill the gap." Therefore, the exploration of affect and the building of adaptive defensive structures must proceed in tandem, one keeping pace with the other.

When the therapist fails to monitor this process adequately in shorter-term treatment, then the patient is at risk of being overwhelmed by the emerging affects, which cannot be contained and managed. At this point in her treatment, W.L. began a session by reporting, "I get really scared. I won't have anybody. I'm paranoid about being alone. I get so insecure, so scared. I just want to shut down. Maybe I've gone too far. Will I end up going crazy?"

In the next session the patient stated, "It is hard to be out there in the world and at the same time into myself. It feels like my father will kill me if I change. I can't talk to my mother anymore, either." She went on to describe with intense anxiety and fear how she had thought that week that her father would break into the house and kill her. It was clear that she was struggling to reality test this fear; yet, at the same time, she was planning to get protective bars for all the windows in her house.

I realized at that point that I had allowed affect to overwhelm defense. This was my clue that the focus of the treatment had to be redirected to exploring the operation of the borderline triad in the "here and now," while helping the patient evolve more adaptive ways of dealing with the emerging affects associated with the abandonment depression.

During the final months of treatment, emphasis was placed on strengthening adaptive defenses that would help the patient get her life on track. This involved, in addition to confrontation, the use of communicative matching. Communicative matching functions, at this point in shorter-term treatment, as a kind of therapeutic "glue" that helps to cement adaptive defenses in place. For example, we would discuss the kinds of friends she wanted and how she could meet them. We discussed the kind of men she wanted to have a relationship with and how she could assess their qualities, both good and bad, without the interference of her splitting defenses or the pressure of her felt need for a "fix." She shared her thoughts about important career decisions and even the significance of the clothes she now chose to wear: "I went out to buy new clothes, good solid clothes, a little conservative, not seductive. Something between boring and sleazy. Something I can feel really good about."

This focus on the adaptive aspects of her life she named her "Operation Bootstraps," which she defined as follows: "I must see the reality of every thing. We can all have our fantasies as long as we live in reality. Reality [she added humorously] is for those who can't handle drugs."

Toward the end of treatment, she met and became involved with a man who was quite different from any of her previous boyfriends. This man lived nearby and was a long-haired struggling artist and carpenter. He didn't own a car, let alone a red Porsche. She felt ready to attempt to negotiate this relationship and her life on her own. She said, "It's so scary to go ahead with just wanting to be yourself. Yet at the same time, deep down, I'm happier than I have ever been in my life." The treatment concluded after the fifty-third session. She stated that she would be back if she ran into trouble. She has not been back.

At the time of termination, W.L. had achieved improved life adaptation. Since there was minimal working through of the abandonment depression, her changes remained primarily at the level of ego repair. For the borderline patient in shorter-term treatment, success involves the awareness that the battle to manage life in a healthy and realistic manner is an ongoing one. The patient summarized this struggle well when she stated, "Like the alcoholic, I have to begin each day by saying, 'I am borderline.'"

The therapeutic alliance had become a new relationship model which she could use as an alternative to the endless repetition of the split object relations part units (RORU and WORU). This new object relations unit offers the shorter-term patient the potential for greater resiliency in responding to stress without regression. However, the preexisting schematizations of self and other are not erased. They remain as latent models for organizing experiences, and are likely to be reactivated during a regressive response to separation stress. Therefore, it is not uncommon, or unexpected, for such patients to return to treatment periodically if life events create sufficiently severe difficulties.

The Case of A.H.

In the previous case, a high-level borderline personality disorder was treated by an experienced therapist. It might therefore not be particularly surprising to the reader that the patient made meaningful progress in shorter-term treatment. Indeed, it could be argued that given these nearly ideal circumstances, the role of the treatment model is secondary to the strengths of both the patient and the therapist.

The case of A.H. serves to highlight the efficacy of the shorter-term model in circumstances that are far from ideal. The case takes us out of the traditional outpatient office setting and into the patient's home. The patient has a lower-level borderline disorder. She does not come asking for help. In fact, the help goes to her in the form of a first-year social work student.

A.H. was referred to a social service agency for homemaking services by a hospital social worker. She was a battered wife, living in a welfare hotel with two small children, aged 1 and 3 years. There was concern on the part of the hospital worker that A.H. was overwhelmed and potentially unable to function, and that she was a possible risk to herself since at the time of referral she was about to be released from a psychiatric unit where she had been for two weeks following a suicide gesture. The homemaker's job was to assist the patient with the care of her children.

The patient had agreed to the referral for homemaker services because she feared that she might hurt one of the children. She was not asking for treatment, and had indicated no desire for treatment. In fact, she had no idea what treatment was about and was singularly unsophisticated in her view of herself and her problems.

A.H. was 25 years old. She had lived in a foster home for several years in early childhood for reasons that were unclear. During adolescence she had returned to live with her mother. However, when the mother remarried, the patient left home and school, took a job, and quickly entered a loveless marriage which was never consummated.

The marriage was short lived. It was followed at age 21 by her marriage to the children's father, who began to beat her. A.H. fled from her husband to New York, where she had spent the past year living in a welfare hotel.

The patient's main concerns reported at intake were: (1) to keep her husband from learning her whereabouts, (2) to find an alternative to living in the welfare hotel, and (3) to get assistance in managing her 3-year-old son, whose severe head banging and temper tantrums (lasting up to eight hours) had made her fear that she would lose control and harm him.

In addition to the homemaker, the agency assigned A.H. a first-year social work student, whose goal was to provide concrete services in response to the patient's stated concerns. The student was also asked to work to effect some improvement in A.H.'s adaptation and functioning. Specifically, the student was asked to address the patient's poor sense of self-esteem, competence, and ability to actively manage her life, and the patient's relationship to her son, whom she perceived and related to in a distorted, irrational, inconsistent, and angry way— in other words, through the screen of a withdrawing object relations unit projection.

The boy was the repository of most of the patient's aggressive and painful feelings associated with her abandonment depression. Splitting, projection, and projective identification were prominent in the relationship. She saw her son as willful, angry, hostile, destructive, manipulative, and bad—"Just like my husband." The 1-year-old daughter, on the other hand, was equally distorted as an idealized and rewarding object.

A.H.'s few relationships with adults were also characterized by a dramatic lack of object constancy. Others were either need gratifying (which was rare) or need frustrating (which was common). She seemed as fearful of engulfment as of abandonment. When she encountered a particularly empathic, sensitive person, she would become uneasy and end the relationship (with her children's pediatrician, for example, she displayed how she would react to closeness with the need to distance). The combination of her prominent aggressive impulses, her ability to relate only through the split object relations units, and her engulfment fears made it impossible for A.H. to have lasting friendships.

Her social isolation made her vulnerable to extreme separation stress. Her fears of abandonment and her inability to be alone made any separation from her children impossible. Thus, as things stood, her son could not get the help which would be most appropriate for him— a therapeutic nursery setting—since this would necessitate a three-hour-a-day separation.

Course in treatment. The patient was seen once weekly in her room by the social work student for the seven months of her field placement (a total of twenty-five sessions). The student was supervised by an experienced social worker who was receiving supervision from me.

In approaching the treatment, the student had three assets on which to build. First, although the patient was in no way motivated for "treatment," and despite the presence of rage as the dominant affect of her abandonment depression, A.H. was motivated to change by her wish to be a good mother to both children and her desire not to inflict on them the suffering she had endured while growing up. Second, the student had a basically intact personality structure herself, along with a good empathic capacity, which enabled her to manage the feelings that were evoked constantly by the patient's hostile, abusive, alternately idealizing, but usually devaluing attacks. Third, the student had a supervisor who was there to patch up her wounds each week and to encourage her to get back into the ring with the patient.

The student took to the challenge. Using her relationship to the needed (and perceived "good") homemaker, and the patient's wish to be a good mother, as her "foot in the door" (literally), the student quickly established the therapeutic frame. She insisted on establishing clear goals, regular appointment hours each week, a clean place to sit in the apartment, and the patient's responsibility to work actively along with the student in the effort to help the patient manage her life more effectively.

From the initial session, the student continually confronted the patient's splitting until the words "good and bad" and "black and white" were as common as "hello" and "how are you?" The patient's constant projection of the withdrawing unit was also constantly confronted. "Bad" perceptions of her son were confronted and redefined as "bad" feelings within herself, which would much better be handled by verbalizing them to the student than by "dumping" them on to her son and others.

The cost to A.H. and to her children of her continuing to act on her feelings rather than talking about them was pointed out time and again, and talking about feelings was always offered as a better alternative.

Evidence that a therapeutic alliance was beginning to take hold first emerged after four months of treatment. A.H. was becoming consciously aware of her tendency to see her son as all black and her daughter as all white, and herself as a helpless victim. She began to make efforts to remind herself that none of this was so. Along with some degree of containment of her enormous rage, she was able to show increased ability to nurture. For example, despite the difficulties involved, A.H. was able to prepare a birthday dinner for herself and her children (a combination of prepackaged stuffing and a barbecued chicken heated on a hot plate) and to find several small toys for both children.

As treatment continued, containment and verbalization seemed to lead to further gains. Her paralyzing fear that her husband would find her and attack her, which had kept her confined to the hotel, abated as her own rage abated. She showed an ability to relate positively to some of the other mothers in the welfare hotel (without indiscriminately labeling them all as "good-for-nothing whores," as she had previously done).

One episode revealed this dramatically. When a friend moved out, A.H. was first inclined to react to the separation stress defensively by seeing the friend as all bad and not having anything to do with her. But by the actual time of the move—two weeks after first learning about it, and after talking about her feelings in session—she was able to help her friend move out. She felt "upset and nervous," but not angry.

Increasingly, A.H. was able to actively redirect some of her energies into looking for a new home, which she was now able to find. It was a decent five-story walk-up in a decent neighborhood. Although it was not exactly what she had wanted (an insistence that had kept her mired down in the welfare hotel for over a year), she was now able to "compromise" her unrealistic expectations with more realistic and adaptive ones.

In the final sessions before the student left, there had been an ongoing confrontation over the patient's inability to part with her children so that her son could get the special treatment he required. Her separation stress was acknowledged, but her refusal to try to deal with it more adaptively was confronted as a serious obstacle to her son's welfare—and also her own. The issue remained unresolved at the time of termination.

When the student left, the patient said a simple thank you and goodbye. She refused the offer of further treatment with anyone else. The student left feeling somewhat satisfied over the progress, but frustrated by the obvious continued obstacles to greater adaptive functioning.

The supervising social worker had an opportunity to talk to the patient about six months later. The patient reported that she had resurrected on her own the referral to the special therapeutic nursery for her son. He would be attending the program five days a week. In addition, her daughter would be attending two days a week. A.H. further stated that she was looking forward to having two days a week without the children. Although there was no doubt that she still could not tolerate being alone, she seemed to have chosen to deal with this more adaptively by joining a local church, where she was now an active member and volunteer. Finally, she commented that such "service" was in preparation for eventually taking her high school equivalency test, attending college and, she hoped, going on to become a social worker.

She had called to say that she no longer needed homemaking services.

Clearly this borderline patient as well was able to benefit greatly from shorter-term psychotherapy. Containment of acting out and the novel (for her) alternative of verbalizing feelings in interaction with an empathic, healthy "other" seemed to open up for this patient alternate avenues for discharging energies that before had been totally committed to shoring up primitive defensive structures. The interaction with the student seemed to have provided her with a role model for a new object relationship that could be tried out with others. A degree of flexibility had been introduced into a previously rigid structure.

The student therapist had initiated this process. Armed only with her dedication, a belief in confrontation, and a supervisor versed in the Masterson Approach, she had been able to effect a significant change in the patient's life—change that clearly did not end with the end of the treatment.

THE NARCISSISTIC PERSONALITY DISORDER

The treatment of choice for the patient with a narcissistic personality disorder is generally long-term intensive psychotherapy, because structural, intrapsychic change can be accomplished only using this treatment modality. As with the borderline personality disorder, however, shorter-term treatment can be used in the narcissistic personality disorder to achieve other worthwhile goals. These goals are somewhat more limited for the narcissistic disorder than for the borderline disorder.

Criteria for the Selection of Cases

In assessing the narcissistic personality disorder for the suitability of shorter-term treatment, motivation plays a significant role. The patient with a narcissistic disorder who presents for treatment with relatively chronic, nonspecific, vague, or ego-syntonic symptoms will not be a candidate for shorter-term treatment. When problems are chronic and vague, the motivation for treatment is often highly ambivalent; goals are unclear and the acknowledgment that one is at least in part responsible for problems and, hence, responsible for the solution is, by definition, difficult for the narcissistic individual to accept. Narcissistic disorders often present with ego-syntonic problems in that such patients are often not self-referred; rather, they come as a response to the pleas, demands, or insistence of others because of behaviors or attitudes that others find intolerable. Under what circumstances would the individual with a narcissistic disorder be highly motivated for treatment and, therefore, be a good candidate for shorter-term treatment? Generally there are two situations:

1. When there have been acute interruptions of narcissistic "supply lines" (interpersonal rejection, career disappointment, etc.) resulting in acute narcissistic injury (humiliation, shame, rage, envy, etc.) necessitating the temporary opening up of a substitute "supply line." The therapist may fill the patient's need in a constructive time-limited fashion. Through the process of empathic mirroring, he helps the patient to stabilize a faltering self-esteem until such time as the patient is able to develop new supply lines in the real world or until old supply lines are repaired.

2. When a narcissistic injury makes conscious a more persistent vulnerability often felt as disappointment or depression, or experienced through somatic preoccupations. This patient is motivated to learn more successful ways of managing and manipulating his environment ("successful" essentially substitutes for "adaptive" when discussing the narcissistic disorder). Once the new behaviors are learned or "perfected," the patient terminates treatment. The patient to be described shortly falls in this category of narcissistic disorders.

Goals and Objectives

The goals of shorter-term treatment with the narcissistic disorder are not ego repair but, rather, making the narcissistic patient into one with a more successful (or adaptive) narcissistic disorder. Although some therapists might object to such an approach as being either potentially unethical (by improving the patient's skill at manipulation) or counterproductive (by making a potential patient into a nonpatient), it is more to the point that the therapist essentially has no other choice. One can hope that a successful mirroring and/or idealizing transference will increase the likelihood of the patient continuing treatment either now or in the future.

Specifically, the goals of shorter-term treatment of narcissistic disorders are:

1. Learning—the patient must learn to become aware of, and anticipate, the vulnerability to disappointment, injury, and shame.
2. Containment—the patient must develop the ability to contain the affects associated with the emergence of the empty/aggressive unit and the underlying abandonment depression, and verbalize them in treatment rather than act them out through defensive devaluation or withdrawal.
3. Adaptation ("success")—the patient should be able to behave in a more successful manner by consciously taking into account those aspects of reality that had previously been ignored and that had resulted in unwished for, and even destructive, consequences.

Treatment Technique

Confrontation is anathema to the narcissistic personality and to the successful treatment of the patient. Rather, interpretation of exquisite narcissistic disappointment and vulnerability, and clarification of the need for containment of defensive devaluation and/or withdrawal, are the cornerstones of the therapeutic process.

The following case illustrates a typical course of a six-month, shorter-term treatment with a narcissistic patient.

The Case of Mr. Black

Presenting picture. Mr. Black was a 23-year-old man with the chief complaint of difficulty in achieving a "complete, fully satisfying, and pleasurable sexual life," which had troubled him since mid-adolescence and for which he had often considered, but never undertaken, treatment.

He had seen many medical specialists, who found nothing wrong and had tried to reassure him. It seemed that no one, least of all his sexual partners, were aware of his difficulty since he was able to get an erection, perform, have an orgasm, and satisfy his partners. The problem, of which he alone was aware, was his feeling that his orgasm was not sufficiently pleasurable.

Because of this "problem," he would inevitably end his relationships. His goal for treatment was clear: he wanted his "problem" to be "taken care of" and would give me six months to see what I could do.

In this one encapsulated area, the patient was highly motivated to change.

The patient was a successful junior executive. He reported that at work he was demanding, intolerant, and perfectionistic. His attitude was condescending and devaluing when he spoke of business associates. He stated that he could not acknowledge his faults or errors in judgment, and when confronted with such behaviors he would subtly implicate or accuse others. He saw none of this behavior as a problem; in fact, he felt that his demeanor and behavior were necessary and desirable traits for success in business.

His relationships with women, however, did trouble him. He worried that he would never settle down or find the right woman because women were basically manipulative and out to "catch" him. He characterized them often as "vultures." He also saw relationships as a battle over who would control whom. With women he insisted that his wishes and needs had to come first before anything and anyone else. If a woman disappointed him, he would become coldly rejecting and abruptly terminate the relationship.

At the same time he was extremely self-critical. He would chastise himself constantly for not being better—a better businessman, lover, and so forth. This critical attitude toward himself paralleled his feelings of disappointment in others. The patient could not live up to his own grandiose self-expectations any more than others could live up to his need for them to function as receptacles for his idealizing projections.

Course in treatment. I accepted his time limit for treatment, telling him that we should both consider it a challenge. In addition, I allowed his definition of the problem to serve as a basis for treatment. I did this because I had decided that in order to have any therapeutic leverage I had to function as a temporary receptacle for his idealizing projections, as someone who might "magically" cure him in a brief time. The foot in the door of treatment was the rapid establishment of an idealizing transference.

The capacity of the narcissistic patient to establish spontaneously an idealizing transference, rather than a mirroring transference, is an important predictor of therapeutic success. The greater the idealizing transference, the greater the willingness of the patient to listen to the therapist's interventions. In the mirroring transference, in contrast, the patient's need to be listened to minimizes the therapist's therapeutic leverage.

As treatment began, however, I would unremittingly interpret either his narcissistic disappointment or vulnerability as being at the core of his difficulties, both with his sexual satisfaction and with his overall relationships with women. I used every opportunity to point out to him the maladaptive defenses he used to manage his vulnerability.

I interpreted his need for a "perfect orgasm" as comparable to his need for perfection more generally, and his disappointment with his orgasm as a mirror of his disappointment with himself. I compared his perception of himself as being essentially that of a sexual organ—his failure to achieve his hoped-for goals in any area of his life had become symbolized by his penis.

I further suggested, whenever the opportunity arose, that bringing into accord with reality his overinflated expectations of himself and others might allow him to bring the fantasies about the intensity of his orgasm more into accord with reality, too. Relationships with women, I told him, might soon follow a similar, beneficial course.

My constant acknowledgment of his narcissistic vulnerability further satisfied the needs of the mirroring transference, and the combination of acknowledgment (within the framework of the mirroring transference) and interpretation (within the idealizing transference) enabled him to contain the affects and to begin to verbalize feelings more in the sessions. He would acknowledge each of my interpretations by elaborating upon it. He stated that he realized that he felt only 80% accomplished in any area of his life. He began to ponder whether his problem truly rested in his penis or in the practice and conduct of his life: "Maybe my problem is not so much with orgasm as with an overinflated ego," he stated. I quickly agreed.

His concern and focus upon his orgasm quickly and dramatically moved to the periphery, and his self-image more generally began to occupy center stage. He began to increasingly acknowledge his sensitivity to criticism, his sense of injury, and his shame and embarrassment. This acknowledgment would immediately mobilize the omnipotent object–grandiose self defensive unit, and I would immediately clarify this defensive need to maintain an unrealistic view of others and himself as an unsuccessful and unnecessary defense.

By the third month of treatment, he was no longer concerned about his orgasm. He felt he had put the problem in its proper perspective. He was more concerned about a new woman he had met and that he "not make the same mistakes with her I have made with everyone else." The patient had shifted his focus to adaptation.

I consistently worked with him on bringing this new relationship into accord with reality. Whether the issue was the woman's sensitivity, her looks, or her behavior toward him, I would constantly point out any tendency to distort toward either idealization or devaluation ("the black and the white syndrome," as we agreed to call it). His willingness to deal in the realm of reality, I told him, would allow him the possibility of satisfying his needs; his continuing to live life in the black and white would seriously interfere with any sustained capacity for gratification.

Six months into the treatment, he announced his engagement to this woman, and at the same time announced that he was stopping treatment. He explained his actions in two ways. First, the time period was up. Second, he could not tell the woman that he was seeing a psychiatrist, because it would still be admitting to too great a weakness. He felt that the relationship was one in which he was trying to be honest and real and therefore he did not want to lie about seeing me. Since he also felt good enough about himself and relieved of the anxiety over which he had come for treatment, he felt it was time to stop. His stopping treatment at the time he chose, and for the reasons he stated, clearly showed that the results of treatment were based not on intrapsychic change but rather on his change in behavior. He was far more consciously aware in his relationship with women of his vulnerability, his defenses against vulnerability, and the harmful effects of both in terms of symptom formation, dissatisfaction, and loneliness.

He was able to effect a partial, circumscribed, and encapsulated improvement in functioning. Limited though this was in terms of intrapsychic change, it was effective in removing anxiety and loneliness. His personality structure otherwise remained unchanged.

CONCLUSION

There is little question as to the applicability of a shorter-term treatment model to work with personality disorders. Success with this type of therapeutic approach has been demonstrated time after time. It must be remembered, however, that the goals of shorter-term therapy center around adaptation to life's realistic demands and improvement in interpersonal behavior and relations. This contrasts with the more ambitious goals of intensive therapy: the emergence and consolidation of a stable and cohesive real self. That obviously is an ideal outcome of treatment.

For many, perhaps most, patients with personality disorders, the therapist can rightfully feel that therapy has been successful (for certainly the patient will), even if the patient falls far short of this ideal end point. When short-term therapy enables a nonfunctional patient to function, or improves a patient's overall capacity to work and to love, or assists a patient in attaining his or her own goals or ideals, the experienced therapist knows that these are difficult feats and is able to feel, along with the patient, a sense of accomplishment.

Chapter 7

Progressive Interventions Based on the Developmental Paradigm

Candace Orcutt, Ph.D.

Psychotherapy with the "narcissistic neuroses" has required a recasting of both classical theory and technique. This chapter outlines a progression of therapeutic interventions based upon the Masterson Approach, which utilizes Margaret Mahler's developmental theory (as well as other sources). It is a conceptualization that relies dynamically on the idea of developmental sequence, and arrest of that sequence. Mahler primarily offers a model of healthy emotional development, whereas Masterson describes the pathological "shadow" of healthy development: how the patient's inner world remains arrested as a frozen replica of the time when the mother-infant interaction failed to support psychic growth (the emerging self), and how this "moment" is repetitiously projected and reimposed on current significant relationships, effectively turning the present into the past. Masterson emphasized that this approach is designed for the personality disorders and is not appropriate for the schizophrenic. However, in describing how technique must shift in order to meet the maturational needs of the patient's developing ego and object relatedness, I shall borrow some aspects of the Masterson approach to apply to the schizophrenic patient.

I shall illustrate that, in psychotherapy with the preoedipal disorders, the interventions progress in a sequence that parallels the developmental progression.

A NOTE ON DEVELOPMENTAL THEORY

Freud's reconstruction of the psychic world of the child was inevitably followed by direct clinical observations of children themselves. Paramount among these observers was Winnicott, who declared that "there is no such thing as an infant" but, rather, a baby within a maternal environment (1958, p. 99). How early relationships impress themselves on the inner world of the child's psyche became the cornerstone of a new construct: developmental theory, pioneered by the work of Melanie Klein and transformed into an extensive body of knowledge by Anna Freud, Rene Spitz, John Bowlby, Jean Piaget, D. W. Winnicott, Erik Erikson, Margaret Mahler, and others. I have emphasized Mahler's concepts but at the same time must acknowledge there is no escaping the influence of the others on any statement about developmental thought. (Mahler herself freely synthesized the concepts of these others in her work.)

Masterson's application of developmental theory to clinical theory and treatment rests also on drive theory and its later offshoots (which often grew up to be autonomous schools of thought): ego psychology, object relations theory, and self psychology. This elaboration of his work retains the same conceptual frame.

THE SCHIZOPHRENIC PATIENT

The Developmental Model

Margaret Mahler borrowed Freud's metaphor of an egg "as a model of a closed psychological system," and used it to describe her concept of normal autism. She quoted Freud's description: "A neat example of a psychical system closed off from the stimuli of the external world, and able to satisfy even its nutritional requirements autistically . . . is afforded by a bird's egg with its food supply enclosed in its shell; for it, the care provided by its mother is limited to the provision of warmth" (Mahler, 1967, p. 78).

Mahler, still following Freud, makes the distinction between two subphases of primary narcissism. The first, which she calls "normal autism," is the more egglike and is "marked by the infant's lack of awareness of a mothering agent." The second, which she refers to as "the symbiotic stage proper (beginning around the third month)," is one in which "the infant begins dimly to perceive need satisfaction as coming from a need-satisfying part object" (1967, pp. 79–80). The shift from the first to second subphase is introduced by a "maturational crisis" that occurs at about three to four weeks of age. Mahler cites John Benjamin's findings here, describing how the infant begins to experience stimuli with such increased sensitivity that the mother is now required psychically as well as physically to shelter the infant's being. The "quasi-solid stimulus barrier . . . —this autistic shell, which kept external stimuli out—begins to crack." In its place, a "positively cathected stimulus shield begins to form and to envelop the symbiotic orbit of the mother-child dual unity" (1967, pp. 83-84). "The specific smiling response at the height of the symbiotic phase" acknowledges the new and unique mother-infant relatedness, and at five months "the symbiotic partner is no longer interchangeable" (1967, p. 82).

Mahler vividly characterizes the symbiotic relationship. It is "an omnipotent system—a dual unity within one common boundary" (1967, p. 78). She describes how the infant adapts by drawing the mother into his "internal milieu" (Hoffer), and how she reciprocates with "good-enough mothering" (Winnicott). Through her "holding behavior" (Winnicott), the mother intermediates between the inner and outer worlds and becomes the baby's "symbiotic organizer" (1966, p. 60; 1967, p. 81). Mahler quotes Spitz, saying that the symbiotic mother acts as a "protective living shield" against stimuli and functions as the infant's "(external) auxiliary executive ego" (1966, p. 60). The mother acts as "the beacon of orientation in the world of reality," while protectively maintaining the "'symbiotic membrane' of the mother-child dual unity" that mediates between the vulnerable infant and the outer world (1966, p. 62).

Within the protection of the dual unity, the infant's psyche begins to develop structure. Mahler says: "Only if symbiosis has been adequate, is [the infant] ready to enter the phase of gradual separation and individuation [and achieve] a stable image of the self" (Mahler & Gosliner, 1955, p. 111). Even at this stage, there is a "rudimentary ego" that has begun to mediate between "inner and outer perceptions," and a sense of "body self" centered on inner sensations and bounded by a sensory-perceptive acquaintance with outer reality (1967, p. 80). And even in these first months, Mahler (citing A. Freud) observes a critical shift in object relations: "Whereas, during the quasi-prehistoric phase of magic hallucinatory omnipotence, the breast or the bottle *belongs* to the self, toward the third month, the object begins to be perceived as an *unspecific, need-satisfying* part object" (1967, p. 81).

It is important to note that the tendency to perceive part objects begins in the first three months of life. According to Mahler, this perception takes the form of scattered "memory islands, containing imprints of 'pleasurable-good' or 'painful-bad' stimuli [which] are not yet allocated to the self or to the nonself" (Mahler & Gosliner, 1955, p. 112). "The confluence and primitive integration of the scattered 'good' and 'bad' memory islands into two large, good and bad part images of the self, as well as split good and bad part images of the mother," is a major developmental achievement, which will "not occur before the second year of life" (p. 114).

Finally, and especially important for the concept of developmental arrest, is the point Mahler makes that, as early as the first two months, "learning takes place through conditioning," and that "toward the third month . . . the existence of memory traces can be demonstrated experimentally" (1967, p. 81). In the symbiotic phase, memory as we understand it begins, and with it, the capacity for fixation and regression.

The Pathological Model

Prefatory note. This discussion is limited to the psychogenic aspect of schizophrenia. The nature versus nurture argument, which reduces this complex subject to an either-or matter with a "winner," divides the field and is an additional burden to patients and their families. A discussion of etiologic factors in schizophrenia goes beyond solely psychodynamic concepts or developmental paradigms. However, one can advance the hypothesis that, in the biopsychosocial etiology of schizophrenia, there are significant dynamic factors that contribute to the making and maintaining of this dysfunction.

Mahler provides a context that contains these variables when she describes the symbiotic psychotic child as "constitutionally vulnerable and predisposed toward the development of a psychosis." There is a "constitutional ego defect in the child that helps create the vicious cycle of the pathogenic mother-child relationship in ways that are deleterious to his attempts to separate and individuate." When the mother contributes her own pathogenic overanxiousness or overprotectiveness, the process is intensified (Mahler & Gosliner, 1955, p. 116).

Mahler's achievements include pioneering work in defining and treating childhood psychosis. She herself has drawn the parallel between normal symbiosis and the pathological disruption of symbiosis that leads to schizophrenia. I am following this model, with the following qualifications:

1. Mahler made a clear distinction between the *autistic* and *symbiotic* psychotic child. The autistic psychotic child, for whom the establishment of any interrelatedness is an achievement, shows "inherent lack of contact with the human environment" (1952, p. 138). The symbiotic psychotic child, however, begins to show some picture of regression to a point of ego fixation. These children "will use autism as a desperate means of warding off the fear of losing whatever minimal individual entity they may have succeeded in achieving" (p. 151). The present chapter is concerned with symbiotic psychosis.

2. I will be focusing on schizophrenia as it appears in adolescence and adulthood, where my clinical experience lies. This does not appear to distort Mahler's work, because she extrapolates from childhood to later-onset schizophrenia, noting "the essential differences between the syndrome of the psychotic child and the adult schizophrenic would seem to be due to the degree of structural differentiation [of the ego, superego and id]" (1952, p. 158).

Mahler describes the symbiotic psychotic child as in a state of regression "from the challenge of separate functioning at the onset or during the separation-individuation phase into a symbiotic-parasitic, panic-ridden state" (Mahler & Furer, 1960, p. 223). My assumption here is that the adolescent-adult schizophrenic experiences a similar regression under pressure of similar maturational challenges, especially around the emancipating ages of 16 and 21. The psyche's falling back on earlier resources at a later age, rather than in childhood, seems to depend on the kind and intensity of factors generally categorized by Masterson as "nature, nurture, and fate." Even a healthy psyche is capable of a transient defensive break with reality to preserve the self in the face of overwhelming stress. An immaturely structured psyche may regress when normal development threatens to increase individual responsibility while diminishing the auxiliary ego support of the family. Thus, as Mahler describes, when "no object image in the outside world can be depended upon," some individuals, at varying ages, will turn to a "regressive psychotic defense," a "reactive restitution" in which the ego attempts to illusively restore "the blissful oceanic feeling, the oneness with 'the object'" (Mahler & Gosliner, 1955, p. 129).

The pathological model. Drive theory stresses regression. When we shift to ego psychology, the fixations of the psyche—developmental arrests of the ego in particular—assume an equal importance. We are examining the structure of the psyche that supports the maturation of its functions and management of the drives.

From whichever point in time the psyche flees back to a symbiotic-psychotic defensive base, that foundation shows the same dynamic blueprint. In Mahler's words: "The mental representation of the mother remains, or is regressively *fused with*—that is to say, is *not* separated from the self. It participates in the delusion of omnipotence in the . . . patient" (1952, p. 139). Or, again: "In this need-satisfying period of object relationship, which coincides with the phase of normal symbiosis, the mother still participates in the omnipotent orbit of the mother-infant dual unity" (1965, p. 156).

Mahler describes the role of both regression and fixation in the predicament of the schizophrenic. She believes that symbiotic psychosis (at any age) represents "a functional failure of the controlling, steering, integrating part of the central nervous system—in other words, the 'ego'" (1965, p. 159). During this failure, the psyche loses its grip on the object world and seeks whatever rudimentary hold is left in the inner world. However disastrous the psychotic descent appears, however, it is still in the service of the ego: "Psychotic object relationships . . . are restitutional attempts of a rudimentary or fragmented ego which serve the purpose of survival, . . . as no human being can live in an objectless state" (Mahler & Furer, 1960, p. 192).

How does the developmental arrest take place? Mahler does not use this concept, but it is harmonious with her strongly ego-psychological bias and is focal to Masterson's application of her observations of childhood to the realm of the disturbed borderline adult. Mahler notes that, in half of her cases of infantile psychosis, there was a "good-enough mother" (Winnicott), and the cause was probably to be found in some "intrinsic vulnerability" in the child.

However, in the other half, she clearly delineates the pathological mother-infant interaction: "We often find . . . a debilitating emotional unavailability on the part of the mother because she has a depression. We also find, at the opposite pole, an interference with the infant's gratification-frustration experiences, a stifling of his budding ego, by a smothering disregard of his need to experience gratification and frustration at his own pace" (1965, p. 161). In addition, the mother's attitude is exacerbated as her infant attempts to separate and individuate (and the overlapping of developmental phases must always be kept in mind): "The pathogenic effect of the attitude of the symbiotically overanxious mother is particularly increased if that mother's hitherto doting attitude changes abruptly at the advent of the separation-individuation phase. . . . A complementary pathogenic factor is the well-known, parasitic, infantilizing mother who needs to continue her overprotection beyond the stage where it is beneficial" (Mahler & Gosliner, 1955, p. 116).

Whether the vicious cycle begins with a difficult child or a difficult mother, pathology begins when the interrelationship cannot regulate itself, when there is a breakdown in "the mutually reciprocal relationship which enables mother and infant to send out, and receive, each other's signals, a compatible predictable interreaction, as it were" (1961, p. 270).

The Clinical Picture

Theoretically, the schizophrenic patient presents clinically as someone desperately trying to establish a symbiotic bond to undo ego disintegration in the face of severe separation stress. The function of the therapist is to ally with the schizophrenic patient at the symbiotic level of functioning, and to strengthen this position so that higher levels of adaptation can be reclaimed or newly established.

The first goal, then, is to facilitate the formation of a symbiotic transference. This amounts to therapeutically meeting the transference acting out, which is the patient's repetitive response to the therapist from the outset of treatment. Transference acting out, as defined by Masterson for patients with a personality disorder, consists of the "activation and projection upon the therapist" of the patient's inner object world (1981, pp. 148–149).

Unlike the acting-out transference of the personality disorders, symbiotic transference acting out is a psychotic transference, in which the distinction between the patient's projections and the reality of the therapist (along with any other self and object differentiations) effectively disappears. In other words, there is only a trace of a working alliance, which must be painstakingly developed from a positive symbiotic transference, into which the negative is gradually integrated.[1]

---

[1]Does a "self," capable of making such an alliance, exist in the schizophrenic? In my experience, no one has a fiercer, more existential valuation of the self than the schizophrenic, because the sense of self *is* so tenuous. For the schizophrenic, madness and suicide are acceptable defenses against loss of "selfhood."

What are the components of this primitive transference? The internal world projected onto the therapist by the patient is a dedifferentiated one. There is no effective separation between self and other, nor is there a clear split between good and bad. The ego is a rudimentary body ego.

The patient who has regressed to this level of psychic organization (because of a fixation point that existed here all along) has been able to make an adaptive adjustment sufficient to superficially negotiate the subsequent maturational phases, especially when the family system has provided enough outer structure—auxiliary ego strength—to compensate for deficient inner formation.

Under separation stress (classically, when the adolescent is caught in the vise of internal pressures asserted by the drives, and external pressures imposed by expectations of emancipation), the self no longer can use enmeshment in the family as a defense, and is unable to find adequate sustaining self or object representations in its internal world to support autonomy. The symbiotic structure comes to the fore as the "defensive false self" collapses (Masterson, 1985, pp. 31–32). The remaining fragment of the patient's self makes a pathological alliance with the therapist in a symbiotic transference that defends against the sense of dissolution.

How is the symbiotic transference established? At first glance, this seems to be an easy step. The schizophrenic patient exerts a kind of interactional pull on the nondefensive therapist, a sort of readiness for reparative bonding that typically evokes feelings of curiosity and concern among those who come in contact with the patient (when such feelings—called up from such a primitive level—do not provoke a defensive antipathy).

However, this symbiotic bond, threatened by loss in the outer world, has its inner perceived dangers as well. As Mahler (speaking of treatment with children) observes, the aim of "restoration of the omnipotent oneness with the symbiotic mother" leads also to "a panicky fear of fusion and of dissolution of the self" (1965, p. 162). Consequently, the therapist walks a thin tightrope and, in Mahler's words, must remember that "it is important to let the [patient] test reality very gradually at his own pace" (1952, p. 152).

The goal of the symbiotic transference is to provide a curative therapeutic environment that will establish in the patient, for the first time, a truly secure sense of symbiosis. (Mahler's team, in working with children, was able to use the mother herself—with the therapist's help—to create a "corrective symbiotic experience" [1960, p. 224ff.].) With the lessening of anxiety, regression begins to reverse, and the developmental arrest attenuates as the psyche builds more stable intrapsychic structure. With the establishing of a healthy sense of symbiosis, the "islands" of good feeling cohere sufficiently to allow a similar coherence of "islands" of bad feeling, without evoking a fearful apprehension that the gathering sense of bad will overwhelm the good. Once this good and bad split inner world is established, the patient begins to renegotiate the pathological equivalent of the differentiation subphase of separation-individuation.

In conceptualizing theory and treatment of schizophrenia, I find it impossible to stray far from the monumental achievements of Searles and Spotnitz. The transference I am attempting to describe has already been set forth by Searles as "pre-ambivalent symbiosis" (1965, throughout), and by Spotnitz as the "narcissistic transference" (1969, throughout). Searles's works serve as an empathic guide, never allowing the clinician to lose touch with the human relatedness essential to the schizophrenic, no matter how divorced from the object world it may seem. His work is a guide mainly for advanced practitioners gifted in understanding the need for the schizophrenic to build a sense of self out of mutually contained introjections and projections in the therapeutic interaction. Spotnitz's works are more specific in providing exact technical detail.

It is the responsibility of the therapist to cultivate a therapeutic bond based on the symbiotic transference that is being acted out by the patient. The therapist must have the psychic tolerance to meet with the patient on the symbiotic level without becoming engulfed or seduced. The primary hazard for the therapist is a loss of the therapeutic self while engaged in the patient's regressive need for merger. As Searles points out, one danger is the therapist's failure to manage his own psychotic countertransference (1965, pp. 254ff.). Also, as Spotnitz cautions, the patient's (and, I think, also the therapist's) anxiety level must be titrated in order to achieve an optimum working situation (1969, pp. 892–893).

The symbiotic transference requires a therapeutic bonding between patient and therapist, who must, more than ever, call upon his intuitive capacities. To borrow from a patient of mine, the therapist must be willing to "hear with the left ear" (perceive with the right— intuitive—hemisphere). At the same time, of course, it is imperative that the therapist's ego remain firmly established in reality.

Schizophrenic patients react intensely to the therapist's intuitive failures, as has often been noted, but they will react equally strongly to

the therapist's failure to be realistic (which is often a countertransferential repetition of the mother's regressive interference with her
infant's maturational needs). Perhaps the element characteristic of the
Masterson Approach to the personality disorders that is most applicable to treatment of the schizophrenic patient is the belief that the
therapist can *and must* expect the patient to behave in as adaptive and
realistic manner as possible. When a therapist expects regression,
regression will ensue. If one expects containment or adaptation, one
will get it to whatever degree possible—and with schizophrenia,
degrees make all the difference.

Oscillating part units. The concept of oscillating part units is a
presupposition essential to the idea of progressive interventions. An
accelerating oscillation of "good" and "bad" part units marks the
gradual and eventual emergence of the sense of whole self and other,
and the degree and ease of oscillation is a diagnostic indicator in work
with patients whose developmental arrest replicates these primitive
states of self. The oscillation increases as one ascends the developmental continuum.

The division of the inner world into major "good" and "bad"
affective states, respectively uniting alternating partial representations
of "self" and "other," characterizes the separation-individuation
developmental stage and its pathological corollary, the personality
disorder. In the symbiotic stage (with consequences for the pathologically related schizophrenic state), the processing of the inner world
from one lacking differentiation into one with coherent areas of good
and bad is a major task, whose accomplishment marks the completion
of the phase and the achievement of a profound perceptual shift.
(Even with this shift, the good and bad feelings are still not attached to
clearly differentiated part objects.)

The symbiotic transference must be secure enough to allow this shift
in the inner worldview. At this stage in therapy, there should be a
minimal oscillation between the patient's perception of the self-and-
therapist as good or bad, because it is an achievement to accept that
two such universally different attitudes can exist at all.

In work with the schizophrenic patient, the therapist's presence
must provide a restitution of the stimulus barrier on the interpersonal
level. The therapist (like the early mother) substitutes a social agent for
a biological phenomenon, which permits safe working space for the
building of psychic structure.

Joining and mirroring techniques. "Joining" is the name Spotnitz gives to the technique of psychological reflection (1969, p. 40). This technique, closely related to mirroring, communicates agreement that resonates on both literal and subliminal levels. To quote Benjamin Margolis: ". . . Just as the patient's overt resistance communication is linked to subterranean emotional tendencies, so does the analyst gain access to these tendencies by allying himself with the overt resistance pattern. In other words, by joining the manifest resistance, the analyst is also speaking to the unconscious forces warded off behind it" (1986, p. 22).

Joining, although it uses words, essentially is a communication closer to feeling than thought and, as such, maintains an almost nonverbal quality. For the schizophrenic patient in a symbiotic transference, silence itself is a kind of joining, especially since words, no matter how empathically chosen, inevitably call attention to some lack of total congruence between therapist and patient. As Spotnitz observes: "*Motionless silence* communicates the message: I do not want to disturb you in any way" (1969, p. 178).

Besides the use of silence, the therapist's tone of voice and minimal and unintrusive activity are critical in working with the schizophrenic patient, who is forever warily balancing the need for bonding against a fear of engulfment. The therapist should be neutral in a way that is calm, not detached, and demonstrate appropriate (and carefully monitored) feelings without imposing them upon the patient. It is always a matter of therapeutic equilibrium—for, much as the schizophrenic patient fears being emotionally intruded upon, it has been my experience that he equally fears a mechanistic, dehumanized approach, and makes an uncanny discrimination between therapeutic neutrality and cold disinterest or defensive removal.

Margolis makes a distinction between joining and mirroring, saying that "in the case of mirroring, . . . agreement takes the form of communications in which the analyst presents his own condition or attitude in matching that of the patient" (1986, p. 23). In other words, mirroring is more differentiated than joining. Margolis (p. 24) gives examples of both joining:

P: My mother was more interested in having fun than in taking care of me.
A: She neglected you.

and mirroring:

P: I'm not doing so well in the analysis.
A: Perhaps I'm the one who's not doing so well.

From the point of view of the developmental paradigm, joining precedes mirroring as a technique. Mirroring responds to increased attempts at interpersonal differentiation on the patient's part. Joining is concerned with affectual congruence, and with the validation of sensations that come before the perception of a substantial distinction between self and other.

Because the therapist's presence alone begins to call the patient's attention to the existence of the object world, verbal interventions should be kept at a minimum (Spotnitz [1969, p. 65] recommends that such "verbal feedings" be limited to two to five per session). Interventions, however infrequent, lead inevitably to some disruption in the sense of oceanic merger, to anger on the patient's part, and to renewed joining by the therapist, who at the same time models a capacity to direct and neutralize aggressive impulses and to tolerate ambivalence.

Interventions are made at points of resistance, specifically, the patient's resistance to being in the session, or talking in the session, or to allowing the fostering of the symbiotic transference. Successful interventions, by helping the patient to resolve anxieties that interfere with verbalizing, limit the acting out of these resistances.

Initially, the patient derives a sense of safety from the therapist's joining sufficient to halt the regressive descent of his illness. As treatment continues, the patient begins to make a reconstitutive ascent, during which a tacit sense of alliance is added to the symbiotic transference and hints at the growth of an underlying interpersonal process. Differences of opinion are allowed (if not necessarily welcomed), and a sense of developing intrapsychic structure begins to emerge. Now the therapist must be alert to this shift in order to meet it constructively with a shift in interventions: from joining to mirroring to confrontation and other ego-supportive, self-acknowledging approaches, and here-and-now interpretations. This sequence will not be steady but, rather, will be interrupted by sporadic regressions, when joining will again be necessary.

Case Illustration

Ruth (a pseudonym) was referred to the Masterson Group at age 20. Following the familiar pattern, she had initially decompensated at age 16, had regained a semblance of adjustment within the family structure, and had regressed again when attempting to pursue studies away from home. During her recent hospitalization, she was described as having catatonic motor behavior, and on one occasion was found curled up inside a clothes dryer.

Home after discharge, Ruth refused to continue taking her medication and relied on her intelligence and obsessive-compulsive defenses to maintain a marginal degree of psychic integrity. Her parents also helped to support her, but the mother's anxiousness and both parents' overpermissiveness exacerbated her condition. The parents brought Ruth for outpatient treatment when her behavior became openly destructive—she smashed things, shouted obscenities, and left notes with such ominous messages as "kill you."

For the first few sessions, Ruth was brought in by her parents and remained mute, with her fingers stuck in her ears. She was upset at crossing the threshold—either entering or leaving. She hated coming, and seemed to hate going, but she did not attempt to run away during the sessions. Although she sometimes crawled into a corner mumbling and shouting, "It's a lie!" she would at times interpose encouraging injunctions such as "Listen to her! She's the doctor!"

Further, after the close of one session, she returned and knocked on my door. Completely articulate (but with eyes averted), she told me that I was not to take her actions personally—they were a "protest." I quietly responded that I was seeing the family because of her parents' concern, and that she was not obligated to speak to me. However, if she ever wished to do so, she could feel free to make her own appointment. Ruth's capacity to sometimes suspend her schizoid behavior was startling evidence of the role of regression in her case. My sense of her real, if embattled, self making choices was always present.

During this initial phase, Ruth acted as though I represented an attack on her autonomy. However, her impaired self was also attempting to have an effect on me. And, as she had returned after a session to let me clearly know, the battle was not between us literally, but in her psyche.

The acting out escalated, but now in the sessions, giving me the hope that Ruth was narrowing the focus of her pathology to the therapeutic environment. I had been treating the family as Ruth's extended self (a well-established family therapy technique), and relied on the parents to act as her auxiliary ego. It was the only prospect for maintaining her on an outpatient basis. I hoped that she would begin to perceive me as a continuation of the familial extended self, but with a clearer capacity for containment and limit setting.

Ruth refused to join the family sessions, but began to throw things in the waiting room. This was a clear message that she was demanding we respond to her as a person in crisis. I insisted her parents bring her into my office. For the next few sessions, Ruth was literally dragged in and out of therapy, while I waited for some decisive turning of the tide. I suspected that this was as much a testing as a protest, and that Ruth was listening to everything I said. Occasionally, I felt I was saying something helpful. For instance, when she let loose a string of obscenities, I remarked that this was simply "talk about growing up," and was rewarded by her momentary verbal and physical quietness. Were these remarks of mine adding up?

Ruth's parents showed impressive dedication during this period. I believe my persistence supported their capacity to set limits, and eventually satisfied Ruth's need to know that this was possible. Ruth reinforced the need for proof of limit setting by throwing her shoes at me. After instructing her father to contain her, I said (as evenly as possible under the circumstances) that Ruth had taken the matter past anybody's choice; she could not be seen on an outpatient basis and would have to seek in-patient treatment; and I called the process to an end.

Ruth responded by coming in, alone and composed, to individual sessions. Apparently the impasse had been broken when I acknowledged the full severity of the situation, thereby suggesting the possibility of hope for containment and understanding.

In her sessions, Ruth tensely followed a persistent, pressured line of thought. She was trying to puzzle out what was happening inside of her, especially to understand how she had "lost an important part of myself." As she described it, part of her was struggling for expression, while another part demanded a crushing conformity.

I could understand how she had internalized the child-parent contest over self-definition, but she rapidly defeated any attempts to define her struggle on that level of object relationship. She said that the embattled part of her was equally tyrannizing, demanding that she violate manners she considered essential to her being and that were associated with the idealized, outward part of her nature. Her dilemma made no sense in terms of whole self and other object relations but was clear in emotional terms: she was trapped between persecutory and idealized states (extreme, primitive states of good and bad), which fluctuated in their attachment to part self and object representations. The element of her that was "missing" was the capacity of the self to begin to organize these states into separate camps, with attachment to distinct self and other part representations. This was no problem to be solved by an appeal to advanced ego functions such as rationalization. Although Ruth tried endlessly to reason out her situation, my attempts to assist her reasoning (interpretation) created greater anxiety. She indicated an impulse to throw her purse at me. Mirroring, I said I thought I had disrupted the flow of the session, and she relaxed and continued her verbal puzzling over her dilemma.

I came to realize that she needed me to "join" the struggle itself—to sit with her in a mostly silent validation of the importance of her verbalizations. I believe that my congruence with her striving for meaning was more important than forcing my irrelevant logic upon her statements. Her obsessive persistence with definitions of right and wrong was essentially a side-product of her need to organize her perception of good and bad in the "world."

In the developmental paradigm, reparation through a good symbiosis is basic. As Mahler says: "A strong and adequate symbiotic phase is prerequisite for subsequent successful disengagement [in order to establish] a stable image of the self" (Mahler & Gosliner, 1955, p. 111). With a patient who has regressed to this level, the therapeutic point is not to exhort her to return to the rational state that has become secondary to her maturational struggle. The purpose is to accept the struggle itself and to provide a neutral place where the patient feels safe to work things out. Joining is an intervention directed primarily to feeling, not reason, and context rather than content. (The metaphor, used by Spotnitz among others, is that of feeding the hungry infant; explaining what hunger is about simply does not meet the situation.)

My goal, then, was not to explain to Ruth how she had regressed to a level where whole objects and differentiated affect states were no longer meaningful. It was to reflect the validity of her struggle with her feelings of persecution and idealization, and so to lower her anxiety level to the point where she could begin to get on with the work. In effect, this supported her real self on that "developmental" level, thus strengthening her belief in her capacity to manage what was going on there, and so feel confident enough to take on a further challenge.

(One has a glimpse, at such times, of the original mother's anxiety that she may not be good enough, and so needs to push the evolution of the infant's development in order to find confirmation of the adequacy of her mothering. In this case, I had the countertransference as a guide: the pressure I put upon myself to hasten Ruth toward rational understanding. And I also had first-hand observations of the mother's response: of this highly intelligent woman's excessive need to "help" her daughter.)

At this point, the important thing was to foster the symbiotic transference and, relying on the developmental paradigm, to assume that the patient's embattled self would find strength to grow and differentiate from there.

I knew that the symbiosis was taking hold when she clung to one of my pillows during the session, commented that it matched her dress, and asked, at the session's close, if she could take it home. I said, "Should I come home with you and bring my pillow?" She smiled, and was able to leave without the pillow; the separation had been bridged by words.

Within our symbiotic sphere, I began to introduce negative remarks about myself, trying to facilitate her differentiation of her anger. When she was silent, I reflected that I hadn't helped her to talk: "Perhaps the only helpful thing I have done is to let you hold my pillow." She laughed (the validating "consensus laugh" Masterson notes), and began to talk somewhat more freely about her anger. In this context, she said: "I'm trying to break away from part of myself— acting against part of myself that's restrictive." This highly symbiotic statement also represented her increasing willingness to differentiate.

As she relaxed, she began to tolerate more give and take and became interested in discussing more characterological issues, her perfectionism in particular. She discussed concepts of moderation and extreme and was interested in continuing our "scientific" talks. She began to show interest in me as a person, asking about my professional orientation (I told her). She began to allow me to be more responsive.

At this time, I received a note from her apologizing for "abusing" me "as a person and a therapist." She stated her belief that I had gained an understanding of how she had felt impelled to act out of a sense of being "trapped."

She had returned to school, and had allowed herself to feel happy about it (although this condition wavered). She remarked: "Everything doesn't have to be a labor that defines my being. You do what you do, and you have the feelings that accompany it." She noted that she needed to be more socially involved, but still worried that she was not "working with the essence." I agreed that there was a paradox here, and that she couldn't "understand the inner world without attending to the outer world, too." The fact that I could make a clarifying statement of that sort indicated how much she had allowed us to differentiate and to exchange opinions.

After eighteen months of treatment, Ruth had used the symbiotic transference to grow. She had returned to her previous level of functioning, and added that she was able to leave "more room for joy" in her life. She was also allowing herself moments of authentic depression. As she permitted herself increasing feeling, she said, "I almost feel good—closer to who I am." This achievement had not come primarily from insight into a puzzle (the outward form it took) but, rather, from a therapeutically supported step forward, based on the patient's need for a validating emotional unity with the therapist.

THE NARCISSISTIC PERSONALITY DISORDER

I have described in some detail the dynamics and treatment of the schizophrenic young person or adult from a developmental point of view. The Masterson Approach has not previously been directed to this deeply regressed area of psychic disturbance, so the attention it receives in this inquiry is, by necessity, disproportionate. The following considerations of narcissistic and borderline pathology will be briefer, because they need only summarize the work already done by Masterson—in the case of the borderline personality disorder, especially, work of profound originality, developed over several volumes.

The Developmental Model

Masterson (1981, p. 12) hypothesizes that the narcissistic personality disorder reflects a developmental arrest in the practicing subphase of the separation-individuation developmental phase described by Mahler.

As Mahler describes this subphase, the infant, now "hatched" from the symbiotic egg, enjoys an especially delightful period of maturation (7 to 15 months of age, generally speaking). This is a time when the sense of omnipotent merger with the mother still remains, but grandiose feelings are beginning to be appropriated to the self. The infant negotiates such heady challenges as standing, "coasting" (walking with support), and taking the first independent steps. These accomplishments are reinforced by a new interaction with the mother, as the infant moves out on his own (Mahler is emphatic that the child's first steps are *away* from the mother) but returns of necessity for "emotional refueling." "*Body differentiation* from the mother; the establishment of a *specific bond* with her [as opposed to the symbiotic one]; and the *growth and functioning of the autonomous ego apparatuses in close proximity to the mother"* define a time of exhilarating discovery free of the tariff of conflict. The infant, exulting in his own new accomplishments, still partakes of the sense of oneness with an omnipotent being, and must return to mother to renew his confidence. At the height of the practicing subphase, the "junior toddler," on the crest of a developmental wave, "seems intoxicated with his own faculties and with the greatness of his world." "Libidinal cathexis shifts substantially into the service of the growing autonomous ego and its functions," and, in his elation, the child is temporarily impervious "to knocks and falls and other frustrations" (Mahler, 1972a, pp. 123–127).

But at this phase, what Winnicott describes as the "not-me" space is growing. Mahler describes the child's sense of pleasure in responding to the mother from a physical distance, and the child's state of "low-keyedness" at times of physical separation, which seems to indicate an attempt to access an internalized image of the mother (1972a, p. 127). The transitional object appears at this time to bridge the growing sense of difference between self and other (or, more accurately, to ease the anxiety evoked by that perception). And play begins, as the conscious enough interpersonal bridge that supplants symbiosis (Mahler, 1984).

The Pathological Model

Masterson defines the intrapsychic structure of the adult narcissistic personality disorder as essentially arrested at the practicing subphase of separation-individuation. He sees this narcissistic inner world as composed of two object relations *fused* part units: the grandiose self–omnipotent object fused part unit, and an "underlying pathologic aggressive or empty object relations fused-unit [consisting] of a fused object representation that is harsh, punitive and attacking and a self-representation of being humiliated, attacked, empty, linked by the affect of the abandonment depression" (1981, p. 15). The pathologic ego allies itself with the grandiose unit and activates it almost continually, splitting off the punitive, empty unit to the point at which "the continuous, global projection of this defensive unit [allows the individual] to minimize the experience of depression" (p. 16).

The origin of the developmental arrest (aside from the influence of nature and fate) is to be found in the "mother's defective mirroring" of her exhilarated infant. For instance, the mother may not support her infant's attempts to refuel, nor delight in his increasingly autonomous moves away from her. Excessive idealized doting on the infant can have a similar effect. Too much too soon, too little too late, or inconsistent doses of both do the damage (pp. 21–24).

The Clinical Picture

The transference acting out of the narcissistic patient, like all preoedipal transference, is present from the initial session. The patient repeats with the therapist, as he repeats with all those around him, his need to see present relationships in past terms. The patient immediately (although without awareness) begins to shape the therapeutic relationship in terms of the old mother-child dyad; he especially strives to recreate the grandiose self–omnipotent other part unit, to reclaim a gratifying sense of mutual mirroring and idealization.

The inevitable "failure" of the therapist to fuse perfectly with the patient's grandiose/omnipotent part unit projection precipitates a dramatic response from the patient, who collapses emotionally into the aggressive/empty part unit. This momentary experience of the depressed, inadequate self is rapidly warded off as the pathologic ego projects the aggressive aspect of the aggressive/empty part unit onto the therapist.

The therapist is accused of having aggressively caused the upset in the vulnerable patient, who massively denies having played any part in the catastrophe. This devaluation continues relentlessly until the therapist is able to reinstate the grandiose/omnipotent part unit, and the treatment continues. Alternately, the patient succeeds in inducing the therapist to assume the empty self role, while the patient settles into the aggressive other role and is able to use this countertransference impasse to maintain a sense of righteousness; in this case the treatment may end or become stalemated.

Mirroring and interpretive techniques. Masterson describes the use of a combined technique of mirroring and interpretation in working with the narcissistic patient (1981, pp. 114–116). He writes that "therapeutic technique emphasizes interpretation of the patient's vulnerability to narcissistic disappointment of his grandiosity and need for perfection as seen in the transference acting-out" (1981, p. 31). I believe this kind of interpretation retains a quality of mirroring, because it is expressed in language syntonic to a patient who takes pride in being sensitively and perfectly perceptive.

This technique is akin to the family therapy concept of "reframing," which is derived from Milton Erickson's pioneering work with hypnosis (Watzlawick, 1978, pp. 139–144). An individual's use of language reveals a view of the world intrinsic to the sense of self, and so this type of interpretation *demonstrates* an alignment with the patient's self, and a capacity to perceive as he perceives, even while introducing a message that (because it implies a separate viewpoint) would usually be taken as attacking.

The nonverbal metamessage (conveyed by tone of voice and choice of language) reinforces the needed sense of fusion and, in a sense, delivers the message from "inside" the patient's extended self. Reframing is not humoring or parroting the patient (although the content may be the same as though this were so). It is a carefully thought out intervention in which emotional congruence titrates an undesirable anxiety level, and so improves the patient's receptivity to the educational content of the message.

Oscillating part units. Although the good-feeling and bad-feeling part units have been well established in the inner world of the narcissistic patient, the interchange of these part units is still minimal: their oscillation is still very difficult to tolerate and is accompanied by upset and a sense of dislocation. However, the momentary loss of the grandiose/omnipotent part unit may be felt as devastating, but the more realized self does not allow the same regressive descent as in schizophrenia. Instead, the aggressive/empty part unit is defensively manipulated, along with its associated fantasy of power and subjugation. The aggressive element is used to inflate an awesome false self (like the sight-and-sound show engineered by the Wizard of Oz, the "Great and Terrible"), while the sense of ineffectual emptiness is projected onto the therapist. Reality undergoes a severe distortion in the service of defense, but is not lost.

The role of the self. The degree of impairment of the self, as an observing, containing, and adaptive phenomenon, marks perhaps the most significant distinction between schizophrenia and the narcissistic personality disorder. In the schizophrenic state, there is little capacity for achieving distance from, containment of, or adaptive use of the object relations part units: it is a dynamic achievement to establish a perception of them. With the schizophrenic patient, the therapist must enter the patient's symbiotic orbit as an extended self to help the patient make a bridge to reality (the therapist must really be more than an auxiliary ego, because a sense of person is added along with the capacity for improved executive psychic functioning). The patient internalizes this experience and becomes less desperate over whether he "exists."

The narcissistic personality disorder, on the other hand, has begun to establish a real sense of self and other, although these are still fused and are subordinated to feeling states. Working with the narcissistic personality disorder, one has a definite sense of the presence of a real self that overarches both sides of the object relations split and is able to summon up each defensively.

I believe that this capacity of the self to manage the object relations split defensively (albeit with an intermittent loss of this capacity) indicates the beginning of the resolution of the split. The oscillation of part units is coming under conscious observation and control, eventually to become ego dystonic and discarded altogether as maladaptive to adult, consensus reality.

Because the narcissistic patient's self is better able to comprehend and adapt to reality, the need for fusion is less total than in schizophrenia. There is a marked qualitative difference in the use of reflective techniques when the patient suffers from a personality disorder. The narcissistic personality disorder does not seem to have the same degree of existential need for joining and mirroring as does the schizophrenic, and even shows a tendency to move away from it— the patient begins to provide his own interpretations and is increasingly willing to accept interpretation from the therapist.

The interaction has a feel that is reminiscent of the practicing subphase, where some degree of separation is actively sought and even playfully enjoyed. I find that a verbal playfulness is often possible with narcissistic patients, and that it provides a constructive discharge for the anxiety that builds during the therapeutic process. Play can add an element of pleasurable anticipation to the sessions as a counterbalance to the dread usually associated with the accessing of difficult feelings.

As the patient and the therapist repeatedly repair the patient's narcissistic "wounds," such occasions become less terrifying for the patient. The patient is able to allow the real presence of the therapist into his world without becoming as demoralized by the shock of separateness.

A therapeutic alliance is added to the positive transference (that has been reinforced by the patient's significant experience of the grandiose/omnipotent part unit together with the therapist). Once there is both positive transference and therapeutic alliance, the treatment has a figure-ground perception of difference to work with, and the observing ego can be encouraged to grow. The patient may be able to accept confrontation at this stage, although, as with interpretation, there will be intermittent alarms over "lost" empathy, which must be calmed by a return to mirroring.

In the abandonment depression experienced in the narcissistic personality disorder, separation anxiety is the predominating element and is a diagnostic indicator. The schizophrenic, with minimal anchorage in object relations, fears separateness as the equivalent of annihilation. The individual with a borderline personality disorder, whose object relatedness is becoming more constant, fears being left by the object to endure endless sadness. In the narcissistic personality disorder, somewhere between the other two, the beginning of autonomy is experienced as the loss of the object accompanied by profound damage to the self—the experience of the "fragmented self," as described by Kohut.

Case Illustration

William ("Captain") Gordon (a pseudonym) circled around the prospect of therapy for two years (two consults a year), and then waited another year to start. Devoted to both his marriage and his job, he still experienced a disturbing indecisiveness about his commitment to both. He was a highly successful management consultant married to a bright and talented woman who had similar difficulties with commitment. With a mixture of pride and irony, he referred to himself and his wife as "Superman" and "Wonder Woman." Typical of the narcissistic personality disorder, he bridled at having to "submit" to my "controlling" *his* therapeutic process, and subjected me to persistent devaluation around this issue. He early and frequently impressed on me the importance of his work, and somewhat threateningly indicated he would *not* be held to a "rigid" schedule, nor to payment for what he considered unavoidable absences. His work was indeed important and demanding, but his defensiveness seemed excessive. He responded favorably to my comments on the former, but not the latter, further indicating the narcissistic makeup of his personality. He made the initial commitment to treatment because his wife said he should "take a risk." This was exactly the right reframing of the situation for a man who defended against profound anxiety by hurling himself in a grandiose way into an unending series of "outward bound" experiences.

The patient maintained a close emotional tie (at a safe geographical distance) with a mother who continued to impose on and embarrass him. During his childhood, she had also been suffocatingly controlling and physically abusive. As a child, he had perceived his mother as "beautiful; like a goddess." Now he saw her as "crazy, frightened, and arrogant." As a child, he had been reckless in evading her edicts, plunging through city traffic on his skateboard when she forbade him to have a bicycle. As an adult, he continued this evasive pattern but felt too protective of her to let her go. His father had remained a passive background figure, although the patient tried to coach him into being someone he could idealize; just as he had begun to feel closer to his father, the father had died (the patient was 18 at the time). "Cap," an only child, was left to the mercy of the maternal dyad.

In his sessions, "Cap" recreated the watchful fusion he experienced with his mother. He showed a compliant—sometimes flattering— charm that can be characteristic of the type of patient described by Masterson as a "closet narcissist." This is a patient who has learned to idealize a narcissistic or schizophrenic mother in order to get the reciprocal mirroring necessary for psychic survival. But never far from this surface was intense anxiety. He said: "You'll get me to trust you, and then I'll say things that will embarrass me, and maybe it won't do any good, anyway." The grandiose self–omnipotent other fused part unit was precariously perched, like Humpty Dumpty.

However, as I mirrored his sense of professional competence and interpersonal vulnerability, be began to settle in. As he did so, he began to let me catch a glimpse of the impaired self behind the scenes, which was forever evading and testing.

One of the pleasurable aspects of the treatment was finding ways to encourage this "bad kid" self to find expression directly in the sessions (he perceived directness as definitely risky). He wondered whether any of my patients ever came in literally wearing a mask. When this idea (a fanciful description of himself) amused me, he then thought it would be fun to come to sessions dressed as a bear, and said he liked to bite people.

He began to recall childhood pranks, and enjoyed himself thoroughly. But the next session he came in feeling "humiliated" at having been such a "show-off." I responded with a here-and-now interpretation, saying he seemed to expect to be chastened for being entertaining. He responded by saying that he saw this as a pattern in himself, and in his relationship with his wife: his enthusiasm was persistently being snuffed out. Recently, he had been happily walking in the woods with her, and she had unexpectedly asked him whether he had discussed his "problem with intimacy" with me. He had felt anger, confusion, a sense of having been obliterated, and could not speak.

One can see the developmental paradigm in operation here. First, there is a clear picture of the repetition: the developmental arrest created by the mother's persistent failure to support her child's exuberance. Second, there is the patient's need, similar to the practicing child's, to have the adventures of the self validated and enjoyed by the therapist. He did not want compliments from me—he wanted a sense I was emotionally there with him, delighting as he delighted. The mirroring here feels qualitatively different from mirroring when done with a schizophrenic patient. There is a sense that the joining of feeling takes place *across an interpersonal distance*, and that the potentially negative reaction to this beginning separation may be offset by playfulness as a constructive emotional support.

So my patient would warn me he felt "paralyzed by disappointment when not understood," and then would eagerly test out my willingness to accept his usually covert rebelliousness. He threatened to leave a dead mouse in my drawer, and accused me of keeping a monster in my closet. Then he hesitated, and warily sought my reaction: "What *do* you keep in there [the closet]?" When I responded, "Your mother!" he laughed with surprise and relief, and became reflective. He said that his mother had told him, "Never be angry in front of me!" and beat him if he was.

As "Cap" felt more accepted, he required more of himself in the therapeutic process. He was still too anxious to make a consistent attempt to communicate more directly with his wife, so he began to practice self-assertion on his circle of card-playing buddies on the commuter train. I supported his autonomous experiments with increased interpretation. He encouraged interpretation, which brought a serious reflectiveness to the sessions and balanced the emotionally gratifying, but insightfully limited, mirroring interventions. Inevitably, at some point he would react to interpretation with a narcissistic recoil. He then warded off the intensity of his feelings by summoning up the aggressive empty fused part unit, and saw me as "rigid," "stuffed," "critical," an arch representative of the "Female Mafia." He denied his feelings, saying that he was "empty" and that, when he tried to understand what was going on inside him, his "thoughts were scrambled."

Having soothed his narcissistic wound by projecting his aggressive, attacking introject onto me, he would then try to reverse roles within this externalized conflict: my "power" would be devalued, while his perception of himself became inflated. He said I was not producing results quickly enough and was too concerned with "tactics," when a commanding "strategy" was required. He, on the other hand, had professional proof of his strategic mastery, and provided me with examples. Under the pressure of projective identification, I would begin to feel myself turning empty and ineffectual. I would search for a means to repair the therapeutic situation by mirroring.

One time, I hit upon a spaceship metaphor that seemed to magically restore the grandiose/omnipotent fused part unit. As he made another devaluing swipe at my authority, I said I was both impressed and concerned that he traveled so much at warp speed. He was pleased to be seen as Captain Kirk of the Starship Enterprise, and his critical attitude changed to an excited display of his knowledge of the technical definition of warp speed. Warp speed became our "consensus metaphor" (Masterson) for the headstrong bravado with which he maintained his embattled self.

And so the treatment continued in this pattern: accelerating to defensive warp speed, stalling sickeningly at moments of narcissistic crisis, repairing itself through mirroring, and resuming progress on a slightly more integrated and adaptive level.

After a year, there was a working alliance, and "Cap" felt more confident about approaching his wife directly about their problems without as much need to evade and bluster. With his better management of his feelings, his object relatedness seemed to mature. He now spoke about the marriage in a way that made it come to life in the sessions—I could now understand the intensity of his bond with his wife, where before I had wondered to myself why he stayed with her. He began to come to grips with old memories, as well, and asserted himself more with his mother in the present. He remarked ruefully that once he had been awed by his mother and had thought she had unimagined depths, but now he realized that she was shallow and needed others to maintain her façade (an accurate description of her need to be narcissistically mirrored). He felt sad for himself that, as a child, he had had to become devious in order to feel independent. And he was depressed that, as an adult, he was still evasive about getting close to others, and still needed to create risks and meet challenges in order to sustain his sense of self. He was beginning to acknowledge and contain his abandonment depression.

THE BORDERLINE PERSONALITY DISORDER

The dynamics and treatment of the borderline personality disorder are Masterson's unique territory. Among the many definitions of "borderline," I find more and more that his is the one that provides the missing piece to the puzzle, so that once it is grasped, a comprehensive view of progressive states of pathology can be attained, along with an evolving technique that follows the same paradigm. Because the main body of Masterson's work is on this subject, I will keep my review as brief as possible.

The Developmental Model

Masterson traces the origins of the borderline personality disorder to a developmental arrest in the critical rapprochement subphase of Mahler's separation-individuation phase of childhood development. This subphase occurs roughly from 15 to 22 months of age, and precedes the final subphase of "on the way to object constancy"— although, as Mahler says, the task of separation-individuation *"as is the case with any intrapsychic process, . . . reverberates throughout the life cycle. It is never finished"* (1972a, p. 120). Rapprochement, as Mahler and her colleagues clinically observed, vividly recorded on film, and described in lucid psychoanalytic writings, is the time when the toddler has achieved a sense of separateness and individuality sufficient to enjoy true sharing. Mastery of walking and the beginning acquisition of words mark a qualitative difference in the toddler's sense of the world—actually, of his perception of the two worlds of inner and outer experience. Bridging and boundary setting are important: the toddler continues to mend separation anxiety and build mastery through increasingly symbolic play, while he also becomes more aware of his possessions and surrounding space, defending these against the encroachments of other toddlers. The term *rapprochement* refers specifically to the toddler's seeking out the mother to share his growingly pleasurable sense of difference. What Mahler designates as the *rapprochement crisis* (commonly referred to as "the terrible two's") is the developing ambivalence of the infant as to whether it is more desirable to have mother do it or to "do it *myself*," at a time when the infantile sense of grandiosity and omnipotence are fading. It is also a time when emotions are more differentiated and developed, especially the feelings of sadness and longing (Mahler, 1972a, pp. 119-130; 1972b, pp. 131-148; 1974, pp. 149-165; 1984).

The Pathological Model

Maternal libidinal unavailability, or mother's inappropriate, excessive, or inadequate response during the rapprochement crisis, may create a developmental arrest at this maturational crossroads. Masterson describes the nature of this arrest in detail, adding that not only "nurture" but also "nature and fate" must be considered in assessing the causes of such early sorrow.

On the level of object relations, the inner perceptions of self and other are still divided according to emotional states, requiring maintenance of the split self and other part units. However, within these part units, the self and other representations are no longer fused. Now there is a rewarding part unit, containing representations of a compliant self and beneficent other linked by a common feeling of gratification, and a withdrawing unit, containing representations of a lost self and a rejecting other linked by a common feeling of despair.

The ego can form pathological alliances with either part unit, to maintain a transferential defense against the memories and affects—especially abandonment depression—associated with the real self. But, since the ego itself is split, and retains its strongest allegiance to the infantile pleasure principle, it tends to ally with the rewarding unit, to maintain transient, fantasy-based good feeling (Masterson, 1981, pp. 133–135). A false defensive self can be formed on the basis of this pathological ego/rewarding unit alliance, which gives the semblance of normal (even exceptional) functioning at the expense of great inner stress to the individual (Masterson, 1985, pp. 32-42).

The Clinical Picture

Masterson first defined his concept of transference acting out when describing the clinical manifestations of the borderline personality disorder:

> The borderline transference is not simply transference but transference acting-out, which consists of the alternate activation and projection upon the therapist of each of the split object relations part-units . . . Both, however, represent forms of transference acting-out—an instant re-play—in which the therapist is treated not as a real object upon whom infantile feelings are displaced, but as if he actually were the infantile object. It differs from a transference psychosis in that the patient has the capacity to distinguish between his projection and the reality of the therapist when it is brought to his attention. (1981, p. 149)

The technique of confrontation. The therapist brings the discrepancy between projection and reality to the patient's attention by means of confrontation. Confrontation, as defined by Masterson, is an intervention directed to the part of the ego that is allied with reality and has the capacity to make reality-based observations. The confrontation juxtaposes a more complete view of reality against the distorted and limited view created and sustained by the splitting defense. For instance, a confrontation might point out that the patient's words indicate motivation whereas the patient's actions (lateness, absence) represent reluctance to participate in the process.

The confrontation is integrated when the patient observes this discrepancy between words and action, tolerates the ambivalence connected with this state of mind, and is able to verbalize a negative as well as a positive attitude toward therapy. As treatment progresses, the patient integrates the confrontational process itself, and begins to make his own confrontations.

Confrontation is specifically used when the pathological ego deploys maladaptive defenses to ward off abandonment depression. This leads to Masterson's concept of the borderline triad, a formula which helps the clinician identify the primary level of resistance, as a basis for intervention. The borderline triad can be expressed as "Individuation leads to depression, which leads to defense," or, translated into a clinical pattern, "Confrontation leads to individuation, which leads to depression, which leads to defense and further confrontation." Borderline patients resort mainly to seven primitive defenses: splitting, acting out, avoidance, denial, projection, projective identification, and clinging. The therapist intervenes specifically to confront the first line of resistance, which is represented by one or more of these maladaptively used defenses. At first, this has the effect of bringing the defensive activity as exclusively as possible into the sessions themselves, so that the working through of the transference acting out can begin.

Then, the therapist focuses more exclusively on the rewarding and withdrawing units, which are defensively projected on the therapeutic interaction as a resistance to self-understanding. Usually, it is the rewarding unit that is confronted more persistently, as the patient tries to inveigle the therapist into taking an overly supportive or directive role. The patient does this to stave off the withdrawing unit with its depressive affect.

When the therapist confronts this maneuver, the patient shifts to the withdrawing unit and begins to experience the negative feelings it contains. However, the withdrawing unit is also used defensively, as the patient tries to project it on the therapist and act it out rather than understand it. What follows is the borderline temper tantrum (in either its passive-aggressive or tempestuous manifestation), as the patient tries to recreate the scenario of the withdrawing unit by seeing the therapist as abandoning, and by trying to coerce the therapist into taking on the rejecting behavior of the mother.

This is the point at which many clinicians, in countertransferential despair and disgust, give up and throw the patient out. However, if this maneuver can be confronted (even at the top of one's lungs) as the patient's need to fight with the therapist rather than face internal conflict, the patient begins to investigate the withdrawing unit, tolerate the feelings associated with it, and, in time, to experience it as ego dystonic (Masterson, 1981, pp. 140–145).

Oscillating part units. The borderline patient, very differently from the one with a narcissistic personality disorder and dramatically differently from the schizophrenic patient, shows great lability in interchanging the object relations part units. In the borderline, the sense of self is not so existentially tied to the positive side of the split, so that the possibility of perceiving the self and the other as mixtures of good and bad is imminently attainable.

The therapist is able, I think, to attain a glimpse of true self-and-object formation as the part units are therapeutically acknowledged, brought into line with the reality principle, and adapted to each other through the acquisition of ambivalence. The oscillation of the part units, when not understood, leads to therapeutic confusion (even rout) in work with the borderline; but, when conceptualized, the patient's vacillation allows us a view of the unfinished and distorted developmental process at work.

It seems (extrapolating from the pathological point of view) that the normal infant achieves object constancy by means of a rapid interchange of positive and negative states, until the two blend in one view of the world. This phenomenon seems to be at the root of the rapprochement crisis, of the concept of anal ambivalence, and of the universally acknowledged phenomenon of the "terrible two's." It is a time when the individual's perception of the world fundamentally redefines itself, and, in the pathological parallel, patient and therapist alike have to hold on as definitions of reality swing wildly, emotional states lose their old anchorage, and the self, standing alone from the other, aligns itself with reality reluctantly, hesitating to relinquish the terrifying but golden world of fantasy for something untried and historically untrustworthy.

As this therapeutic crisis attenuates, the borderline patient begins to delineate concepts of inner and outer worlds, a sense of whole self and other, and mixed and differentiated emotions that allow himself a belief in his congruence with consensus reality. This permits him to build higher-level defenses based upon multiple levels of perception. The most important of these defenses is repression, which brings with it the capacity for insight and integration of the self through an analog sense of time, and conscious memory. At this point, the therapist is using interpretation as a major intervention. The distinction between the borderline patient and the neurotic patient here is that the borderline will repeatedly regress under the stress of feeling and will have to be supported by confrontation in order to return to the level of insight therapy.

The technique of communicative matching. Masterson uses the concept of "communicative matching" to describe a particular intervention that he uses with the borderline patient in the working-through phase. The patient at this point is growing increasingly eager to exercise an ability to share—to try out a new kind of communication that is genuinely interrelated, that enjoys mutuality discovered out of an accepted sense of difference. Here is the true, interpersonal sharing across interpersonal space that eventually makes symbiosis seem like a faded rose. In this type of therapeutic communication, therapist and patient draw closer to Greenson's "real relationship," where the therapist can share a few words of wisdom with the patient (who is still trying to fill in a missing sense of "how to") and can even make some personally revealing statements (assuming these are carefully monitored; the goal here is not to be pals, but to provide a realistic experience of sharing for the patient, the appropriate response for the patient who has never had a sufficient experience of maturational sharing).

Communicative matching, in particular, raises the question of how much the therapist's job parallels the parent's task. Alexander raised this (insoluble) question when he spoke of the "corrective emotional experience," and the argument has raged ever since. Therapists *are not parents*, but, like extended family, teachers and friends, therapists are "second chance" people, who provide others with a new relationship within which to grow. We cannot grow except within a relationship—as Freud indicated, we do not simply mature by means of a genetically-determined unfolding program—but the complicatedness of human interrelatedness is still something we acknowledge but cannot conclusively define.

Case Illustration

I have discussed Annie's case in depth elsewhere (see Chapter 13). I will refer to her progress here in a briefer way, but, I hope, without minimizing the trials undergone by both patient and therapist in this demanding work, and the commensurate rewards to be experienced when the two are able to "go the distance" together.

Annie Moore (a pseudonym), now 35 and a successful businesswoman, was referred to the Masterson Group six years ago, following her sixth hospitalization in five years. Her hospitalizations had taken place when significant relationships with men had dissolved. She could not hold a job and remained largely dependent on her parents, alternately sparring with them and throwing herself on their mercy. She challenged all her therapists to tolerate her, and then tested them with amazing energy. She was a veteran of psychotherapy, but had defeated all her therapists (and herself) prior to applying to the Masterson Group. She warned me not to let her con me, saying, "Either I make it this time, or I'm ten feet under."

At first, Annie was seen by Dr. Jacinta Lu Costello, who took the initial impact of Annie's testing in the form of endless phone calls (some in rapid sequence), personal baiting, and precipitant hospitalizations combined with suicidal threats. My contact with Annie has taken place over the past three years, and owes a great deal to Dr. Costello's capacity to set firm limits in the beginning phase.

From my first session with her, Annie threw down a typical borderline challenge: she wanted to have it both ways. She expected to gain from therapy while acting in an untherapeutic manner. Her dress was casual to eccentric; her attitude was loud, provocative, and demanding; she missed sessions and telephoned many times between sessions. When I failed to help her reenact the rewarding part unit by permissively accepting her approach, she rapidly shifted to the withdrawing part unit. If I told her she seemed to want to have her cake and eat it too, she would become alternately guilty and furious: she was a "mental patient," but I was "making" her feel that way by limiting her expression of "freedom." She would shout, slam out of my office, make attacking phone calls and hang up on me, and top things off with another trip to the emergency room.

However, when I continued to consistently confront her magical expectations of gratification ("I get the impression you want therapy without having to do the work it requires"), and when I equally confronted her distorted perception that I was deliberately frustrating her ("I don't think you've caught on that threatening to kill yourself puts me in a position where I can no longer work effectively with you"), she eventually grew calm and introspective. These periods were momentary at first, but over time they have lengthened and deepened into therapeutic engagements with abandonment depression. As I have held the confrontational line—and the switching back and forth of confrontations of the rewarding and withdrawing part units can be exasperating or even disorienting—I have gradually been meeting Annie's real self. She has faced the need of her false, defensive self to be "Sick Annie," to scapegoat for her family, and this at first allowed the impaired real self to come forward ("I always knew I could be great at managing an office, and now I'm going to go for it!").

Annie's emerging real self was a pleasure to meet, even though the appearances were sporadic at first. Annie's real self was a fighter, perceptive, and had a pragmatic quick-mindedness. She developed a knack for self-confrontation that she generalized expertly to the work situation, and unevenly to the on-and-off relationship with her boyfriend.

As Annie relied less on acting out and projection to avoid abandonment depression, the borderline triad became more discernible. As Annie had warned me: "When I do well, I trip myself up." Now, as she began to hold a job longer than she ever had before, and as she began to develop a sense of her real self, she experienced "boredom," which became depression and which led to a need to stir up excitement to stave off a deepening sense of insecurity.

Without the "sick" false self, she was not always sure who she was. Annie then avoided her feelings with drinking, binge eating, shoplifting, and wild fights with her boyfriend (upon whom she alternately projected her conflicts through narcissistic rescue or narcissistic attack). When this phase escalated, she would jeopardize her job and her apartment lease, and would have to rely on the police as the ultimate limit setters. As time went on, this behavior outside the sessions became a manifest defense against the feelings and insights evoked by her sessions, and I adapted the context of my confrontations accordingly. This is the characteristic rhythm of the working-through period with the borderline patient. The acquisition of insight, with the retrieval of memories and accompanying feeling, evokes temporary regressions to primitive defenses, which must be confronted.

It is primarily through confrontation that the ego of the borderline develops its observing stance and is able to perceive the old ways of defense as alien. Psychic structure is built from this process, and in time the ego develops the capacity to repress, and no longer needs to flee back to archaic defensive maneuvers.

During the last year of Annie's treatment, she has been able to manage her relationships with others in a new way, since she has less need to use them for defense. In particular, her relationships with men have changed significantly. Inability to manage relationships with men had been the cause of her many hospitalizations.

During this year, Annie has made peace with her father, stopped feuding with her brother ("It's good to have a brother again"), and, after much turmoil, parted company with her boyfriend in such a way that they have been able to preserve their respect for each other while acknowledging their mutual overdependence.

She also confronted her boss of two years, who, in classic borderline parental fashion, championed her when she was vulnerable (just out of the hospital) and undermined her as she showed increasing self-assuredness. Annie realized he was playing out his "script" with her and decided to forgo her starring role. With professional smoothness, she left the job (for the first time, by her own choice) and secured a new and better position immediately. Her perception of the entire changeover, and her resulting actions, were reality centered and assertive.

Annie is still working through her understanding of her problems, but we have reached the point where communicative matching has become an important part of the therapeutic interchange. In the past, I confronted Annie on the discrepancy between who she wanted to be and how she presented herself. Over time, my comments have been more on the level of shared communication: "Most jobs have a dress code—why don't you check it out?" I have also expressed interest and pleasure when she has discussed improving her wardrobe, or wanted to show me her new purchases (this is an intentional act, illustrative of healthy spoken communication and therefore supportive of it; the developmental parallel is the child of the rapprochement subphase piling toys in mother's lap in the discovery of interpersonal sharing). Annie's desire to share has extended to returning the favor. Just as her early comments on her therapists' appearance used to be as attacking as her comments on herself, now she takes pleasure in giving me fashion pointers while she develops her flair for dressing well. (Interestingly, this began at a time when I was taking a renewed interest in my own appearance, and Annie contributed constructively to the situation, knew it, and used it to support her growing sense of self.)

Inevitably, as Annie has curtailed her acting out and has brought her relationships into alignment with reality, she is entering into a stage of insight regarding her feelings about men. She is making a trial use of the couch, "Where I can take my mind wherever I want to go," and is seeing if she can use a deeper level of insight therapy to reach a still more fulfilling destination in reality.

SUMMARY

Margaret Mahler's developmental scheme of healthy infant psychic maturation can be used to suggest that the developmental arrests seen in the primary adult preoedipal disorders represent frozen steps in a normally flowing sequence (like individual frames in a strip of moving-picture film), and that the interventions used in their treatment shift likewise in a progressive sequence, paralleling the healthy developmental paradigm.

In elaborating and synthesizing the work of Mahler and Masterson, I have drawn heavily on Mahler's psychoanalytic theory and treatment of the "symbiotic psychotic" child and, to a lesser degree, of the borderline child and the borderline disorder generally. And I have been guided by Masterson's conceptualizations as the keystone for a major body of writing on the personality disorders, especially the borderline personality disorder in the adolescent and the adult.

Following both Mahler and Masterson, I have placed emphasis on internalized object relations. First, they contain the individual's view of the world, which can become psychically fossilized and form the basis for a developmental arrest. Second, these inner-world views evolve through the establishment of a coherent sense of good and bad feelings to the beginning of a realistic perception of the self and other—of two separate views of people, defined by positive and negative states.

The inner world of the mature psyche is divided adaptively into two separate views of people, categorized as self and other: the sense of whole personhood predominates over affect and becomes the primary organizer. How the inner world is rearranged from the primacy of affect states to the ascendancy of person states must mark one of the most profound psychic events we experience. It is probably an event that peaks at the time of the rapprochement crisis in the child, and, in the clinical parallel, is at the center of the stormy irresolution of the borderline patient, who cannot decide whether to cling or to bolt, and pours out confusion upon the therapist. I have introduced a hypothesis of oscillating states to attempt to conceptualize how the growing infant—or the patient resolving a developmental arrest—makes this critical changeover.

Borderline storms are matched or exceeded by the sometimes violent protests of the schizophrenic, who is contending with an even more global inner transformation: the disruption of a sense of symbiotic oneness by the formation of opposed good and bad feelings that threaten to split the entire inner world (a process that probably completes itself in the pathological equivalent of the differentiation subphase that initiates the phase of separation-individuation).

The schizophrenic patient associates existential anxiety with the establishment of positive and negative internalized states; to begin to tolerate these states and their minimal alternation shows therapeutic progress. The narcissistic personality disorder is better able to contain this shift but experiences it as perilous and humiliating, and reinstates the positive side as quickly as possible. The borderline personality switches internalized states like an amateur driver overreacting at the controls of a powerful vehicle set in motion: panic subverts mastery. In each case, the core problem seems to be that the sense of person (actually, the sense of a real self) will be swamped by affect.

The challenge for the clinician is to assess and intervene with preoedipal states, and correctly, at a time when therapeutic training emphasizes treatment of the oedipal states. In addition, preoedipal states are often blurred as they defend against each other, or even regress from one level to another (the issue of multiple fixation points is a question for consideration in its own right).

The schizophrenic patient requires minimal intervention on the part of the therapist in order to reinstate an unfinished need for containment, holding, joining—whatever the term may be for a necessary validating sense of merger with another.

The narcissistic patient requires a similar feeling of confirmation, but also requires support for a cogent need to express and understand the self in a rational as well as emotional way. So the therapist supports the schizophrenic and the narcissist by joining and mirroring, but adds an ego-syntonic form of interpretation for the narcissistic patient.

The borderline patient is chaotically engaged in sorting out internalized objects from feelings, differentiating feelings, and accepting objects as ambivalent in nature, as well as separating the world of fantasy from reality and forgoing magic for symbols and action for language. Through confrontation, the therapist must help the patient bring this ricocheting energy into alignment with consensus reality. Except in regressed moments of intense abandonment depression, the borderline patient denounces mirroring as too permissive or as holding out a false promise of a world that is unattainable in reality. (Similarly, the narcissistic patient experiences an uninterrupted dose of mirroring as infantilizing.)

The clinician's assessment of the patient's response to different interventions is diagnostic. Presenting problem and history provide us with important clues to the intrapsychic world of our patients. But the true diagnostic test is in the clinical situation itself, where the patient's problem is repeated transferentially, and consistent responses to the major interventions of mirroring, confrontation, and interpretation tell the story. In addition, when the therapist must change the type of intervention from that which has basically been established in work with the patient, this serves as a diagnostic indicator of significant regressions or of "developmental" progress to a higher level of psychic organization.

The dynamics of preoedipal patients allow us a fascinating glimpse into the formation of the early psyche—an insight strongly supported by the psychoanalytically oriented studies of children themselves. As Mahler states:

> It is a generally accepted hypothesis among psychoanalysts that unless the child successfully traverses the symbiotic phase, and that first subphase of separation-individuation termed *differentiation*, psychosis will ensue. . .
>
> Milder conditions than psychotic disturbances, I believe, occur in children who, though they have passed through a separation-individuation process, have shown ominous deviations from the orderly progression of the subphases. If there is too much overlapping, or other serious disturbances in the differentiation or practicing subphases, and if the rapprochement crises were extreme and did not give way to any degree of object constancy . . . fixation points are created. What may thus ensue is: narcissistic character formation and/or borderline pathology (with splitting mechanisms of the self and of the object world).
>
> . . .
>
> We are still underestimating the pathogenicity, but also the character-building, the personality-integrative role of preverbal levels of development. . . (1974, pp. 162–165)

REFERENCES

Mahler, M. (1952). On child psychosis and schizophrenia: Autistic and symbiotic infantile psychoses. In *The Selected Papers of Margaret S. Mahler, M.D.*, Vol. 1. New York: Jason Aronson, 1979.

Mahler, M. (1961). On sadness and grief in infancy and childhood: Loss and restoration of the symbiotic love object. *Selected Papers*, Vol. 1.

Mahler, M. (1965). On early infantile psychosis: The symbiotic and autistic syndrome. *Selected Papers*, Vol. 1.

Mahler, M. (1966). Notes on the development of basic moods: The depressive affect. *Selected Papers*, Vol. 2.

Mahler, M. (1967). On human symbiosis and the vicissitudes of individuation. *Selected Papers*, Vol. 2.

Mahler, M. (1972a). On the first three subphases of the separation-individuation process. *Selected Papers*, Vol. 2.

Mahler, M. (1972b). Rapprochement subphase of the separation-individuation process. *Selected Papers*, Vol. 2.

Mahler, M. (1974). Symbiosis and individuation: The psychological birth of the human infant. *Selected Papers*, Vol. 2.

Mahler, M. (1984). *The psychological birth of the human infant.* Franklin Lakes, NJ: The Mahler Research Foundation Film Library.

Mahler, M., & Furer, M. (1960). Observations on research regarding the "symbiotic syndrome" of infantile psychosis. *Selected Papers*, Vol. 1.

Mahler, M., & Gosliner, B.J. (1955). On symbiotic child psychosis: Genetic, dynamic, and restitutive aspects. *Selected Papers*, Vol. 1.

Margolis, B. (1986). Joining, mirroring, psychological reflection: Terminology, definitions, theoretical considerations. *Modern Psychoanalysis, 11*, 19–35.

Masterson, J. F. (1976). *Psychotherapy of the borderline adult.* New York: Brunner/Mazel.

Masterson, J. F. (1981). *The Narcissistic and borderline disorders.* New York: Brunner/Mazel.

Masterson, J. F. (1985). *The real self.* New York: Brunner/Mazel.

Searles, H. F. (1965). *Collected papers on schizophrenia and related subjects.* New York: International Universities Press.

Spotnitz, H. (1969). *Modern psychoanalysis of the schizophrenic patient.* New York: Grune & Stratton.

Watzlawick, P. (1978). *The language of change.* New York: Basic Books.

Winnicott, D. W. (1958). Anxiety associated with insecurity. In *Through paediatrics to psycho-analysis.* New York: Basic Books, 1975.

Chapter 8

Diagnosis and Treatment of the Lower-Level Borderline Patient

Ralph Klein, M.D.

The concept of a range of borderline psychopathology is central to the developmental, object relations view of the borderline personality disorder. In contrast to the rather narrow descriptive picture provided by DSM-III-R, the actual range of manifest symptomatology that may overlay a borderline intrapsychic structure is extensive.

Higher-level borderline patients can and often do function fairly well. Lower-level borderline patients generally function poorly. They can, in fact, have so little ability to cope with the demands of living that they have been confined, often on multiple occasions, to an inpatient psychiatric ward. These lower-level patients, who would have been diagnosed as latent schizophrenics using DSM-II criteria, present unique treatment and management problems in both the inpatient setting and the outpatient clinic. These problems arise from the severity and scope of the acting out behavior as well as from the very real gaps in the patients' support systems (such as lack of food, shelter, and medical care).

This chapter presents an in-depth discussion of the lower-level patient, including: (1) a description of the psychopathology of the lower-level patient, which will serve to guide the therapist's interventions; (2) guidelines for inpatient treatment; and (3) guidelines for outpatient treatment.

DESCRIPTION OF THE LOWER-LEVEL PATIENT

The description can accurately begin with DSM-III-R. The impulsive, self-destructive behavior, interpersonal chaos, mood lability, identity diffusion, other- and self-directed anger, and pervasive feelings of emptiness and boredom identified by DSM-III-R all serve to describe, and correctly capture, the quality of behavior and interaction that one can anticipate from the lower-level borderline patient. Among these, a tendency toward self-destructive behavior is the clinical symptom that probably comes closest to being a pathognomonic behavioral criterion for the lower-level borderline disorder.

The presenting picture with these patients is often psychotic-like rather than neurotic-like. Primitive ego defenses are coupled with defects in ego functioning. The result is poorer adaptive functioning and at times the appearance of frank, albeit transient, psychotic-like episodes characterized by infantile regressions, paranoid ideation, hostility, depersonalization and derealization, ideas of reference, illusions, obsessive-compulsive symptoms, and panic-like anxiety. These features may be evidenced as a consequence of separation stress.

More narrowly defined psychotic symptoms, such as hallucinations, delusions, loose and incoherent or illogical thinking, and loss of ego boundaries, usually appear only in association with drug or alcohol abuse or as component features of an associated major affective disorder. These symptoms are unlikely to appear as a consequence of separation stress alone.

The clinical description based on DSM-III-R can be more fully and precisely understood and integrated into a treatment approach if it is coordinated with a developmental, self and object relations approach. Using this model, the manifest psychopathology just described can be seen as arising from an early developmental arrest in the separation-individuation process, and the range of borderline pathology can be understood as corresponding to the time of the underlying developmental arrest, which may begin as early as 14 or 15 months in the life of the child, or as late as the beginning of the third year of life—the time period encompassed generally by the rapprochement subphase of separation-individuation.

As a rule, the earlier the onset of the developmental arrest (which is precipitated by the failure of the primary caretaker to support and encourage through optimal libidinal availability and optimal frustration the child's efforts at psychological growth), the more severe will be the manifestations of the borderline personality disorder. This is the case for several reasons.

First, the earlier the onset of the arrest, the less intrapsychic structure there is in place, and, as the term *arrest* implies, no further growth takes place. As an example, an important milestone—the achievement of stable object permanence—is not reached until about 15 to 18 months of age. The child who does not accomplish this developmental work lacks a critical prerequisite in the building of his internal, "representational" world. Therefore he will never have a stable intrapsychic representation of the parenting figure. Hence, the earlier the onset of the developmental arrest, the greater the vulnerability to separation stress.

Second, the child early in rapprochement has only recently emerged from the more or less absolute dependence on the "self-regulating" functions of the "other." Primative fear of loss of an emerging self through loss of recently acquired capacities for internalized self/object differentiation is much more threatening to the child early in this process. And, if development stops, this fear will be carried into adulthood as part of the emotional baggage of the lower-level borderline disorder.

Third, in the lower-level borderline adult—who suffers from an early-onset developmental arrest—projection, projective identification, splitting (primitive, immature defenses), and withdrawal and distancing (defenses against the dread of absolute dependence engulfment) are common. In contrast, the defenses against abandonment, such as denial, avoidance, and clinging, characterize the defensive structure of the higher-level borderline patient. Splitting still predominates in the higher-level patient, but steps toward integration have generally begun.

The nature of the defenses utilized by the borderline personality disorder has important ramifications in the therapeutic relationship and in the nature of the transference acting out. The higher-level patient—more fearful of abandonment than engulfment—is more likely to rely on denial of the destructiveness of his behavior, while clinging to the therapist and attempting to project the rewarding object relations part unit. The lower-level patient is more likely to utilize projective mechanisms and to view the therapist as potentially harmful, threatening, and dangerous. This is manifested typically as a "hostile dependency," which mixes clinging with withdrawal, distancing, and passive-aggressive behavior.

In addition to the characteristic clinical picture and intrapsychic structure noted, the lower-level borderline patient frequently presents with two historical patterns that correlate with the severity of developmental arrest and the degree of structural damage. First, there are likely to have been periods of marked separation stress and trauma characterized by overt parental unavailability and/or physical separation due to illness, death, neglect, or abuse. Multiple placements in foster homes or institutions, or with members of the extended family, are not uncommon. Second, the lower-level patient is unlikely to have had the benefit of a close nurturing relationship with someone other than the unavailable primary caretaker in the earliest years. The emotional availability of a healthy "other"—be it sibling, grandparent, or foster parent—may modify and limit the pathological effect of the primary parent's unavailability.

TREATMENT STRATEGIES

The treatment strategy for the lower-level borderline patient is based on the unique intrapsychic structure discussed in the previous section. For this type of patient, whatever the therapeutic setting, either confrontive psychotherapy or counseling is indicated.

Confrontive Psychotherapy

All but the most severe lower-level borderline patients will benefit from confrontive therapy. Confrontive therapy is a treatment process that assists the patient in learning to adapt to life rather than defending against impulse. The specific goals are internalization of task mastery and social competence. The treatment process involves confronting those resistances that maintain maladaptive behaviors until these behaviors become ego dystonic. During the course of treatment a therapeutic alliance is achieved between the patient and the therapist. The therapeutic alliance takes the place of transference acting out. No longer does the patient project the rewarding or withdrawing units into the therapist; rather, this alliance represents a new object relations unit for the borderline patient, one in which the self and object reach a consensus that it is the patient's responsibility to identify painful affects, self-limit acting out, and verbalize the affects in the therapeutic hour. The final component of treatment involves the implementation of adaptive modes of dealing with the underlying affects. New behaviors and defenses emerge that lead to improved life adaptation through realistic self-acknowledgment, activation, and assertion. This pattern replaces previous self-destructive behaviors and defenses.

Unlike intensive analytic treatment, confrontive therapy does not give the patient the opportunity to work through the abandonment depression which is at the core of the borderline psychopathology.

To oversimplify for clarity, the therapist is satisfied in treatment with the lower-level borderline patient if the patient is capable of work, let alone working through, and of consistency in relationships, let alone the capacity for full intimacy achieved through freedom from the twin fears of loss of self and loss of the object.

The therapist's neutrality (and objectivity) is of key importance to the success of confrontive therapy with the borderline patient. The therapist must avoid resonating with the patient's various projections. Maintaining therapeutic neutrality with the lower-level borderline patient is no easy task. There is a constant risk that the intense emotions and conflicts and needs operating within the borderline patient will uncover and set into motion vulnerabilities within the therapist.

It is at times extremely difficult to manage these powerful and intense emotions and pathological defenses within the relatively structured setting of the private outpatient office—with a single therapist and a relatively better functioning, higher-level borderline patient. It is even more difficult working with the lower-level patient in either the inpatient ward or the outpatient clinic, where the patient can probe the emotional vulnerabilities and countertransference weaknesses of not just one therapist but of a host of others—including therapists, mental health workers, patients, and the system itself—in order to find relief from dysphoric feelings.

Counseling

There are a number of borderline patients for whom counseling is the treatment of choice. Counseling is not psychotherapy. The concept and practice of psychotherapy imply a belief on the part of the therapist that the patient has the capacity for change and growth, a capacity which the patient has the responsibility to monitor, direct, and sustain.

Counseling makes no such assumptions about the patient's eventual capacity to internalize the capacities to monitor, direct, and sustain in important areas of ego functioning. Counseling, in fact, assumes that a patient's ability to "take in," internalize, or build intrapsychic structure is transient and fragile at best—nonexistent at worst. The good counselor accepts an on-going role in helping the patient to identify and monitor feelings, direct actions, and sustain adaptive functions and defenses. The counselor is an auxiliary ego for the patient as long as the patient has need of such ego support.

The goals and objectives of counseling, therefore, are to reduce anxiety, depression, anger, and any other dysphoric affect or combination of dysphoric affects that are chronically interfering with the patient's capacity to function in the most adaptive and realistic manner possible.

The techniques of counseling include a combination of:

Reality testing: "If you do X, the consequence will be Y"; "If you treat a person in such a fashion, she will most likely treat you in a similar manner"; "If Mr. A is angry, his anger may have nothing to do with you."

Encouragement: "There is no success without some failure"; "Give it your best try—that is all anyone can do."

Direction: "I think you should consider getting a new roommate"; "I think you should apologize to Miss B."

Problem solving: "What are the pros and cons, the advantages and disadvantages of this course of action?"

Medication to reduce dysphoria and relieve symptoms as much as possible.

The profile of the lower-level borderline patient, for whom counseling might be the treatment of choice, includes some or all of the following: (1) repeated, real abuse, neglect, or separation trauma early in life; (2) repeated, severe, prolonged psychotic-like regressive episodes that are secondary to minimal stress or anxiety; (3) a history of repeated serious (life-threatening) suicide attempts or serious homicidal or violent intent or actions.

Generally these features present as a "cluster" in patients with severe, pervasive, and chronic ego defects. Any single feature must be judged in the context of the patient's entire personality organization and of the totality of the patient's strengths and weaknesses. When in doubt, a trial of confrontive treatment is usually indicated initially, for two reasons. First, it is easier to shift from confrontive therapy to counseling than the reverse, because once having consistently and willingly stepped into the rewarding unit projection, the therapist will find it very difficult to switch roles and introduce a new therapeutic frame without producing confusion and a prolonged period of testing in the patient. When a therapist feels that a patient with whom he has been doing counseling might benefit from confrontive treatment, it would be better to refer the patient to another therapist. Second, a decision for counseling will inevitably delimit and preclude in many areas the capacity to build autonomous adaptive functioning.

Once the decision to do counseling is made, however, the therapist can feel free to step in as frequently and repeatedly as necessary to function as an ancillary ego with the above-mentioned interventions, to control either the life-threatening behavior, the psychotic-like symptoms, or the overwhelming and impairing stress and vulnerability to regression.

The following case of Z.N. demonstrates the failure of a trial of confrontive therapy and the subsequent shift to counseling, with resulting clear benefits to the patient.

The Case of Z.N.

The patient was a 39-year-old woman who was referred following the most recent of a series of hospitalizations. The hospital staff had recommended to the family that the patient be transferred for long-term treatment in the state psychiatric hospital.

The patient was an only child. She had always lived at home except for a period of one year after her marriage at age 33. Under the protective umbrella of her parents' constant concern and attention, she had managed always to function adequately—finishing college, teaching, dating occasionally and finally marrying.

Nonetheless, there had been, since adolescence, pervasive feelings of inadequacy, anxiety, obsessive thoughts, compulsive behaviors, and periods of depersonalization and derealization. Her condition was chronic, with no essential change in the symptomatic, psychopathological picture for twenty years. Minimal stress seemed to lead rapidly to severe regressive episodes and hospitalization. Twice she had made a serious, life-threatening suicide attempt. It was following the second suicide attempt that she had separated from her husband and moved back home. In that setting she was able to function marginally but adequately.

It was initially decided to give the patient a trial of confrontive psychotherapy. Although the history of psychopathology argued in favor of a counseling approach, the real life successes she had achieved (her academic and work history) pointed to ego strengths and a reality ego that might be responsive to confrontive therapy.

Over approximately a six-month period, the therapist confronted her maladaptive and regressive behavior consistently and tenaciously. After some brief initial improvement, Z.N. responded to the confrontations with increasing helplessness, mounting anxiety, and exacerbation of symptoms. Her overall functioning worsened. At this point, feeling that an adequate trial of confrontive treatment had been attempted, the decision was made to change the mode of treatment to counseling, with several alterations.

First, the parents were brought in for weekly family counseling in addition to the patient's weekly counseling sessions. The focus of the family sessions was on behavioral change, utilizing behavior therapy principles. The areas discussed and for which a treatment plan was devised included work, socialization, and contribution to self-management and family living.

Second, a series of medication trials was begun for the management of the anxiety, obsessive-compulsive features, depression, and psychotic-like features, with some eventual, albeit limited, benefits.

Third, interventions were focused solely on reality testing, direction, encouragement, and problem solving.

These efforts gradually enabled the patient to restabilize. She was able to remain outside the hospital and to resume part-time work while taking greater responsibility for self-management at home.

Three years later she was still attending monthly counseling sessions while continuing to work and live at home. There had been no further suicide attempts or hospitalizations during this period.

GUIDELINES FOR INPATIENT TREATMENT

Hospitalization is often utilized in the treatment of the lower-level borderline patient, and the inpatient setting magnifies and therefore highlights the problems that can be encountered in the treatment of these patients.

The inpatient unit, in the performance of its work, takes over vital and basic caretaking responsibilities and functions for the borderline patient. This aspect of the system itself encourages each member of the treatment team to resonate with the borderline patient's projections of the rewarding unit. It is the rare hospital ward that does not promote compliance, passivity, and regression in the service of keeping the ward functioning smoothly.

For the medical patient, regression may at times be "in the service of the ego"—necessary for, and compatible with, treatment and recovery. For the psychiatric patient, especially the borderline patient, regression is inevitably countertherapeutic.

The situation is further complicated because the therapeutic needs of the borderline patient differ dramatically from the needs of other patients. On most inpatient units there are many schizophrenic, organic, and mood disorder patients, many of whom respond well to a basic counseling, or directive and supportive, approach. Because most staff are accustomed to this kind of patient–therapist interaction, they find it very difficult to rapidly change approaches from one patient to the next, and to "shift gears" from one moment to the next in order to provide for the unique confrontive needs of the borderline patient. Often a staff member cannot believe that interventions that work so well with some patients are anathema to others.

Given these problems, the place of hospitalization in the treatment of the borderline patient must be carefully considered and the disadvantages weighed against the benefits.

The inpatient treatment of borderline adolescents differs significantly from that of adults. The adolescent is still at a stage of the life cycle in which dependency and shared responsibility for certain functions fall within a realistic age-appropriate norm. Thus the inpatient staff on an adolescent ward may step into parental roles and perform certain parental functions without in so doing damaging their therapeutic objectivity. Most of the comments in this chapter specifically refer to the inpatient treatment of the borderline adult.

In spite of the inherent regressive features of the inpatient setting, there are times when inpatient treatment of the lower-level borderline patient is indicated. Hospitalization should be considered when the patient presents with: (1) genuine inability to function in a less restrictive or regressive setting, (2) behavior that could pose a danger to others, or (3) behavior that is suicidal. Decisions as to whether a patient meets any one of these criteria are often difficult but are inevitably so when they must be made in the context of the psychopathology of the lower-level borderline patient. Let us examine each of these criteria in some more detail.

Inability to Function

The leitmotif of the lower-level borderline patient's life is manifested in the false, defensive self representation as someone who is helpless, out of control, and unable to function without the ministrations of a primary "other." The distortions inherent in such a self representation must be the object of the therapist's intense scrutiny and confrontations. The therapist evaluating a patient who presents as helpless and unable to function must be able to maintain an objective, neutral perspective and to step back and judge dispassionately whether the patient is so seriously impaired as to justify hospitalization. With the borderline patient, more often than not the therapist's judgment will differ from that of the patient. To hospitalize a borderline patient when it is not absolutely necessary will convey a message about the therapist's expectations of the patient that will undermine future confrontations and, therefore, may undermine the very possibility of therapeutic success.

The Danger to Others

Behavior is a reflection of intrapsychic structure. The borderline patient is not prone to violence toward the object, because there is a desperate felt need for the object or "other." It is, therefore, rarely necessary to hospitalize a lower-level borderline patient because of a threat of violence. Hospitalization should, however, be considered when a threat is made under two unique circumstances that in fact alter the psychodynamic picture. The first of these is when a threat is made while the patient is abusing drugs and is intoxicated, delirious, or psychotic as a result. Second, serious attention should be paid when a threat occurs in the context of an attempt by the "other" (lover or spouse, usually) to end a relationship that has been intense and symbiotic. The separation stress is here so great and the panic it generates so intense that the patient is unable to allow the "other" to separate and essentially acts out the admonition "If I can't have you, then no one can."

The Danger to Self

The lower-level borderline patient's conscious and unconscious need to coerce, control, and manipulate the object into assuming a primary caretaking role is so intense that gratification of this need is often pursued despite the destructive cost to the self. In the therapeutic relationship—as part of the transference acting out—the patient may at times escalate the level of acting out to include self-destructive and self-mutilating acts designed to arouse the therapist's concern, alarm, and rescue fantasies. This type of behavior is so common that it is included among the *DSM-III-R* criteria for borderline personality disorder. It serves the patient not only by forcing the therapist into the rewarding role, but also by allowing the patient to manage and defend against anxiety and other painful and dysphoric affects through primitive defensive operations involving somatization, depersonalization, turning against the self, and identification with the aggressor. In order to avoid hospitalization in the face of suicidal threats, and to maintain treatment in an outpatient setting (which is clearly most adaptive and least regressive), the therapist must understand that self-destructive behaviors are usually not serious suicide attempts but, rather, manifestations of the patient's core psychodynamic psychopathology with the associated pathology of self and ego structures. Once this is understood, the therapist must be willing to maintain a firm, consistent therapeutic stance in the face of the pressure created by the patient's suicidal threats.

The following case dramatizes the manipulative, destructive, and defensive use of suicidal gestures to sabotage treatment, control others, maintain a position and self-image of helpless dependence, and relieve tension.

M.A. was a 30-year-old divorced Hispanic woman living with her three children. When she was 16 years old, she had become pregnant and dropped out of school to marry the child's father, an alcoholic and compulsive gambler. The marriage dissolved after three years.

She returned home, married, and had two more children in close succession. That marriage dissolved after three years. In the five years between the end of her marriage and the time she was presented to me for discussion at a clinical case conference, the patient had been hospitalized fifteen times (with an average length of stay of two to three months) for suicide attempts. The attempts usually involved cutting her wrists or overdosing on pills.

When questioned by me she was able to articulate that any stress or demand for her to function autonomously precipitated overwhelming feelings of helplessness, depression, and anxiety, and that the suicide gestures were a way to get hospitalized and "get away from the bad feelings and the pressure."

The patient herself stated that her suicide gestures were just that— gestures. They were dramatic attempts to manage any and every conflictual and anxiety-provoking life situation. M.A.'s history illustrates the endless repetition of self-destructive and treatment-destructive behaviors promoted by the failure of the therapist to confront, set limits, and maintain an objective, neutral therapeutic stance.

Time after time her outpatient therapists succumbed to threat and manipulation. The situation was exacerbated by inpatient therapists whose reactions had meshed with those of their outpatient counterparts, and who had therefore reinforced M.A.'s feelings of helplessness and self-destructive behaviors by permitting repeated prolonged hospital stays.

When hospitalization must be resorted to, several strategies may be followed to minimize both regression and damage to the treatment. First, hospitalization should be for as brief a period as possible. The briefer the hospitalization, the less opportunity for regression and for reinforcing maladaptive behaviors or "solutions."

Second, medication, if used at all, should be given to treat specific target symptoms associated with co-morbid psychiatric illnesses.

Third, continuity of treatment from outpatient to inpatient setting should be a priority. When possible, the outpatient therapist should be the treating therapist during the hospitalization. Such continuity clearly helps to keep the hospitalization brief and focused, and limits the opportunity for splitting and manipulation. When, as is often the case, this arrangement is not possible, communication between the outpatient therapist and the inpatient therapist or treatment team is imperative.

Fourth, treatment must be focused on the immediate causes and consequences of hospitalization. The specific destructive, regressive, or maladaptive behavior or defense that precipitated the need for hospitalization should be explored and confronted. Straying from this issue only reinforces the patient's psychopathology.

Fifth, staff interventions should be confrontive, rather than directive or interpretive. Directive interventions cast the therapist (or other staff members) into the rewarding unit role. Direction, advice, or verbal expressions of sympathy or caring—all, for example, appropriate at times in dealing with regressed schizophrenic patients—are totally countertherapeutic for the borderline patient. Interpretive interventions made early in the course of treatment—regardless of where the patient resides—encourage the patient to avoid and defend against feelings by intellectualization and by isolation of affect.

Sixth and finally, the staff must function as a team. A treatment team is composed of a group of individuals, each with his or her own unique vulnerabilities, strengths, and weaknesses. Each staff member must be made consciously aware that the borderline patient will probe the staff to find the "weak link in the therapeutic chain," the person willing to don the mantle of the rewarding unit object. It is each staff member's responsibility to help maintain the therapeutic structure. Therefore, each member of the team must have some understanding of the meaning of the patient's behavior and of the technique of confrontation and how it is used.

These guidelines were used in the treatment of M.A. at the time of her sixteenth hospitalization following a suicide gesture. Upon admission, the patient immediately found herself questioned by her inpatient therapist about the feelings that her suicidal behavior was intended to express, and confronted about the destructiveness and maladaptiveness of the behavior she used to express those feelings. The patient quickly and openly acknowledged the manipulative and defensive aspects of the suicidal gesture.

At the initial staff conference, M.A. was informed that the staff could not condone the flight from responsibility to manage her own life and, moreover, felt that her treatment could and should be conducted in the outpatient clinic. Further, it was explicitly stated to the patient that she—and no one else—was ultimately responsible for her actions and her life and that everyone else's life would go on—after briefly pausing to reflect, "How sad"—should the patient actually succeed in killing herself, probably accidentally. These statements were specifically designed to counter and confront the patient's distortions in her false, defensive self (helpless, victimized), as well as the manipulative and coercive aspects of the behavior. At the same time, the suggestion was strongly made that learning to verbalize and manage her feelings in an outpatient setting was both preferable and possible.

The patient was discharged after three days and referred back to the outpatient clinic.

GUIDELINES FOR OUTPATIENT TREATMENT

Before we follow M.A. into the outpatient clinic, I will make some general comments about the problems of managing the lower-level borderline patient in this setting.

The outpatient setting is optimum for the psychotherapy of the borderline patient. Here, as in the inpatient setting, the single most common cause for the lack of progress in treatment is the therapist who, by moving in and taking over essential functions and responsibilities from the patient, steps into the projections of the rewarding unit and becomes the rewarding object. The borderline patient often goes from clinic to clinic, from staff member to staff member, or from one private therapist to another in order to seek out the one who is vulnerable to stepping into the rewarding unit.

The lower-level borderline patient presents in the outpatient setting with somewhat different clinical needs and problems than his higher-level counterpart. These are associated with the greater number of problems generated by the lower-level patient's perceived inability or simple unwillingness to cope effectively with his environment.

Confrontive therapy is based on the assumption—at first proposed by the therapist, but later shared by the patient—that the patient is capable of, and responsible for, functioning at all times in a healthy, adaptive manner. The therapist's definition of healthy behavior may not be the same as the patient's, especially the lower-level borderline patient. The practical application of this positive therapeutic expectation is made concrete by the notion of a "therapeutic frame." The frame refers to all the rules of behavior that the therapist takes for granted, and that fill the gap between the therapist's definition of coping maturely and the patient's definition.

For the higher-level borderline patient, the therapeutic frame generally includes such items as responsibility for payment of sessions on time, keeping regular appointments, payment for missed sessions, and not extending the length of sessions for lateness. For the lower-level borderline patient, the therapeutic frame is far more encompassing because of the greater ego defects, distortions in reality perception, and capacity for regression and acting out. Therefore, basic areas such as where the patient lives, with whom he associates, how he spends his time away from therapy, and what he does to manage his life need to be included in the frame and made the basis for the initial (and ongoing, if necessary) confrontations.

If these basic areas of daily living are not included within the therapeutic frame, the lower-level patient will have more than ample opportunity to discharge any and every painful affect in self-defeating acting out. For the lower-level patient, the conduct of daily life is where the therapeutic action must take place. As a rule, the lower the level of borderline functioning, the more clearly stated and the more far-reaching must be the therapeutic frame. Such a clear, and stated, frame helps to maintain the therapist's neutrality and objectivity in the face of the borderline patient's often ceaseless efforts to bend and distort reality—and the definition of adaptation—to meet his own defensive and regressive needs.

Specifically, the following are important to the maintenance of the frame and, therefore, to the successful outpatient treatment of the lower-level patient.

1. A living situation that promotes responsibility and independent functioning
2. A structured day organized around healthy, adaptive objectives

3. An ongoing therapeutic relationship anchored by the therapeutic frame

4. The availability of brief, focused hospitalization should the need for inpatient treatment arise

We will now examine each of these guidelines in greater detail.

The patient should be encouraged to secure the most appropriate and least regressive living situation possible, given his capacities and resources. Such encouragement should come in the form of a confrontation rather than a suggestion or direction. As an example, the therapist would not say, "Don't you think it is time for you to look for your own apartment?" but instead might ask, "Why do you continue to choose to stay in an environment where you are treated like a child?"

Appropriate living situations encompass a spectrum of possibilities including independent living, supervised apartment living, and halfway houses. In general, the less time spent with the family of origin, the better. Typically, the families of borderline patients are unwilling or unable to support efforts at separation and individuation, either because they helped create the problem, because the patient plays a necessary part in the family's pathological structure, or simply because they are overwhelmed at having to deal with the problems and turmoil generated by the patient's pathology.

The structure of the patient's day is another basic consideration in outpatient treatment. The time spent in a structured milieu organized around achieving clear objectives provides the patient with both the need and opportunity to deal with the demands of reality.

The nature of the structure will vary depending on the capacity of the patient and the stage of treatment, but it could involve work for pay, volunteer work, participation in a therapeutic community, or attendance at a continuing treatment program. Consistency and structure provided by each of these settings is critical in providing a framework upon which to build the patient's reality ego and real self identity.

To the extent possible, the nature of the therapeutic relationship should be matched to the presenting defensive style, which will be primarily either clinging or distancing. For many borderline patients, a dyadic, one-to-one therapy is the treatment of choice, because it provides the patient with the opportunity to become intensely involved with another person and to build a new, healthy object relations unit, which offers the patient an alternative to the pathological split object relations part units that have characterized his relationship to internal and external objects. The lower-level border-line patient with clinging defenses is especially suitable for individual treatment.

For the distancing lower-level patient who is uniformly and consistently projecting the withdrawing object relations unit, individual treatment may be intolerable initially and a milieu treatment may be more appropriate. A "programmatic alliance" that emphasizes group participation rather than a one-to-one relationship is often helpful. This can provide the patient with a consistent, real, and healthy interpersonal model without an intense one-to-one relationship, which would generate intense fears of engulfment, danger, deprivation, and devaluation. Such a programmatic alliance functions as a kind of transitional therapeutic relationship until a primary dyadic relationship can be introduced, tolerated, and used by the patient.

The availability of brief, focused hospitalization when necessary has been discussed.

These guidelines were followed with M.A., who returned to outpatient treatment following a three-day hospitalization.

The patient was living in her own apartment with her three children. Her mother, however, was a frequent visitor who essentially took over the tasks of cooking, cleaning, and child care, including caring for the patient. The patient was confronted with the regressive impact upon her of the dependent relationship with her mother. She was able to integrate this idea gradually, and finally to decide to apply for part-time homemaker services so that she no longer had to rely on the mother.

M.A.'s history of poor functioning and almost reflexive therapeutic distancing were indicators that she could not yet function in a work environment. She therefore entered a day treatment program where a step-wise approach to mastering the tasks and social skills required for successful daily living was utilized within the therapeutic structure of an intensive, confrontive group therapy approach.

After three months of regular attendance in the day program, M.A. was offered twice-weekly individual therapy. It was decided by the treatment team that if hospitalization became necessary, the outpatient therapist would retain responsibility for the treatment on the inpatient unit. This arrangement was possible because of the close relationship between the inpatient unit and the outpatient department.

Two years after first appearing in the outpatient department, the patient had achieved a stable therapeutic alliance with her therapist, whom she continue to see regularly. She had had two short hospitalizations during that period, each lasting less than one week. She was now working full time as a salesperson and attending social functions at the clinic two nights a week. She was more consistently available emotionally to her children and able to resist major regressive pulls. She had, in brief, become a functioning, productive individual.

M.A. presented with the most common defensive structure: an alternation of clinging and distancing defenses. In contrast, the cases that follow demonstrate treatment of a predominantly clinging lower-level borderline patient (R.T.) and a predominantly distancing lower-level patient (J.B.).

The Case of R.T.

R.T., a 24-year-old man, complained of inability to function, poor self-esteem, and chronic depression. He was the third of eight children. His father was an alcoholic who had left the family when the patient was 4 years old. His mother had been hospitalized for "mental illness" when the patient was 5. R.T. spent the 6 years following his mother's hospitalization in several institutional and foster care homes. He returned to live with his mother when he was 11. This history of separation trauma beginning at least at age 4 and continuing through age 11 suggested to the treatment planning staff that the patient's fear of loss and abandonment would be great.

By age 14 the patient was heavily involved with drugs. His girlfriend became pregnant when he was 15 and, following her abortion, he verbalized suicidal ideation and was hospitalized briefly. He dropped out of school when he was 17 and spent much of his time aimlessly at home or with friends in his neighborhood. He had particularly stormy relationships with his mother's boyfriends, with whom he would constantly argue. These arguments often ended in his making suicidal threats or gestures. He was admitted to an outpatient clinic day treatment program following his release from his third psychiatric hospitalization, during which he had received a course of electroconvulsive therapy with questionable clinical response. (After a review of the records, it appeared to me that the lack of a positive response to the ECT could have been predicted, since the patient only questionably met criteria for a major depressive illness.)

In his initial months in the program (which he attended quite regularly), R.T. behaved in a manner which the staff characterized as extremely manipulative and clinging. He would constantly go from one staff member to another, seeking to talk about how bad, hopeless, and helpless he felt and requesting advice about everything and anything. He monopolized group discussions with his problems and complaints.

This clinging, demanding, self-preoccupied, helpless behavior seemed to serve to manage, avoid, and contain his enormous underlying depression and fear of loss and abandonment.

R.T. had been in the program for several months when a staff member of whom the patient was particularly fond left. The patient took an overdose of pills in response to this, and was brought by his mother to the hospital, where he was admitted. The next day, a joint inpatient-outpatient conference was held at which it was decided that he should be discharged immediately to interrupt any further regressive acting out of his feelings. Further, the decision was made to discharge him from the day treatment program with the goal of eliminating his opportunity to act out his unremitting search among staff and patients for someone to step into the rewarding unit. Finally, it was agreed that he be assigned to a clinic therapist, who would see him initially three times a week.

The rationale for the new treatment strategy was based on the necessity for channeling all of the clinging behavior into the one-to-one therapeutic relationship, which would promote work on limiting and contain acting out through uniform and consistent confrontation. The day treatment program, it was felt, had encouraged regressive and indiscriminate clinging to essentially nameless, faceless objects.

The patient initially responded to the revised treatment plan with a series of manipulations geared to activate the rewarding unit and, with it, achieve either rehospitalization or readmission to the day treatment program. R.T. spoke constantly of suicidal depression, while devaluing his therapist to other staff and patients. Such acting out was uniformly handled by confrontation and referral back to the primary therapist.

The intensive, dyadic therapeutic relationship which evolved with this clinging borderline patient gave the therapist tremendous leverage in his confrontations with the patient. These confrontations were aimed at all areas of dysfunction in the patient's life, as exemplified by the following:

"Why are you acting so helpless/destructive/passive/inadequate by oversleeping/missing work/taking that drug/hanging around with that friend who is always 'stoned'/living at home, where your mother either ignores you or treats you like a baby?"

One year after individual treatment began, the patient had a shaky but clearly evolving therapeutic alliance. He had moved out of his mother's house and was living with an older brother in their own apartment. He was working in a fast food restaurant and contributing his share to the room and board. He was attending his sessions regularly.

The Case of J.B.

With the primarily clinging lower-level borderline patient, treatment will grind to a halt if the patient is able to find a therapist who will step into the rewarding unit projection. With the distancing, patient treatment will more likely be jeopardized by the patient removing himself from treatment or coercing the treatment staff or therapist into removing him.

The wish to be taken care of is as great for the lower-level distancing borderline patient as for the clinging patient. However, the fear of engulfment (or loss of self) in the distancing patient is so intense that clinging is precluded and feelings of helplessness, inadequacy, and passivity must be dealt with by utilizing other behaviors. The distancing defensive operations which are activated by the fear of engulfment and destruction range from subtle passive-aggressive maneuvers such as disagreeableness and obstinacy to more frank and undisguised aggressive (hostile and angry) or avoidant (withdrawal) behaviors. In this latter group one finds at the extreme the borderline patient who alternates between the hospital and jail. One way or another, this kind of lower-level patient ends up being taken care of.

A typical example of a distancing lower-level borderline patient was J.B., who was referred for outpatient treatment from an inpatient unit where he had been for several months following admission for extreme agitation and psychosis associated with acute drug delirium. After the psychosis had resolved, the patient appeared avoidant and aloof, participating passively in activities or simply refusing to participate.

During the initial outpatient interview, the patient stated that he had no problems except that he was tired from the medication he was taking. Little additional information was forthcoming from him, and he frankly ignored half the questions and responded with one or two words to the other half. He did state that he had no plans for the future and was content to stay home with his mother.

The history obtained from the hospital and family revealed that J.B. was one of four sons born to a depressed, overwhelmed mother. All four boys had different fathers. The patient had been a "hyperactive" child who frequently got into fights at school. He left school at age 16 and worked briefly at odd jobs. There was a history of mild drug abuse, but no history of antisocial behavior.

J.B. maintained himself in a basically passive, dependent position. Intrapsychically, he seemed to be more fearful of losing himself (engulfment and destruction) than of losing the object (abandonment). Clinically, he appeared to continuously activate and project the withdrawn object relations unit: people were seen and experienced as potentially critical, aggressive, or withholding, and he needed to maintain a wary closeness.

J.B. was admitted to the day treatment program, where his attendance was good from the start. It was noted initially that he socialized minimally with his peers but rarely with staff members. However, he did tend to follow staff without speaking.

Several weeks after he entered the program, I was asked to interview him at a case conference. I began the interview by requesting that he tell me about himself. He said he didn't want to. I attempted several confrontations, all of which focused on the potential benefit to him of having me and the staff understand him better and the potential harm to himself of not allowing others to understand him or his problems. He said nothing. We looked at each other for several minutes until, convinced that he was not about to budge, I ended the interview. Confrontation—not coercion or control—is the key to opening up the treatment process with the lower-level patient. Although I wanted J.B. to understand that I expected him to act in a self-interested manner, I also wanted him to know that the final responsibility for doing so was his.

Several times during the first year at the outpatient clinic, the patient was asked if he wished to have individual psychotherapy, to which he would reply, simply, "No, I'm not ready."

J.B. could not allow others to get too close—or too far away. Thus he would follow staff, but not talk to them. He would come to the case conference, but refuse to participate. Rather than forcing the patient into a one-to-one relationship which he felt he was "not ready" for and could not use, he was continued in the day treatment program. Such a program offered a "programmatic alliance" in the place of a dyadic therapeutic alliance.

During the first year in the program, J.B. attended regularly while continuing to live at home. The medication was discontinued soon after he began the program, and no further medication was required.

He began taking classes in pursuit of his high school equivalency diploma. After approximately 18 months he began individual sessions, and shortly thereafter decided to move away from his mother and into a supervised, independent living setting. This was now possible because he had been willing, and was now able, to transfer his need to be close away from the regressive relationship with his mother and toward the healthier relationship with his therapist. Moreover, he was now able to allow himself to be closer without immediately activating fears of entrapment, control, destruction, or engulfment. He completed a vocational rehabilitation training program as a computer programmer and is now working full time while continuing to attend therapy regularly. He is living totally independently in a small one-bedroom apartment, which he shares with another young man.

At one time, M.A., R.T., and J.B. would have been considered untreatable. The advances in developmental, object relations theory and its clinical application over the past twenty years have dramatically improved the chances for them and others like them to lead relatively healthy, adaptive lives. These patients demonstrate well the kind of goals and objectives that the therapist can reasonably expect to achieve with seriously—functionally and interpersonally—impaired patients. Confrontive psychotherapy that operates within the limits of an appropriately realistic therapeutic frame can:

1. Enable the lower-level borderline patient to make an investment in the capacities and functions of his developing reality ego and to reap benefits in terms of degrees of self-acknowledgment, activation, and assertion.

2. Enable the lower-level borderline patient to practice in an ongoing fashion with a new, healthy object relationship the difficult task of building a stable self and object representational capacity. For the lower-level patient in confrontive therapy this achievement remains a goal that can be achieved only partially. However, the greater the borderline patient's capacity to coordinate different perceptions and experiences of himself and others, the more likely the patient will be to have the opportunity to experience himself as stable, and to be able to enjoy being with others rather than being dependent upon

others. Sharing and continuity in relationships become
achievable goals to be struggled with and for.

3. Enable the lower-level borderline patient's reality ego and
developing real self to use more adaptive defenses while
avoiding—or circumventing—still existent ego defects.

These achievements are all possible to some extent as a result of
confrontive treatment with the lower-level borderline patient. New
functions, capacities, and defenses are introduced that can accomplish
for these patients the goals of treatment that apply to all patients: to
love and to work successfully.

Chapter 9

Clinical Manifestations of Separation-Individuation in the Treatment of the Borderline Adult

Karla Clark, Ph.D.

Completion of the processes of separation-individuation, and achievement of the state of being on the way to object constancy, is the crucial developmental step allowing for the consolidation and expression of the real self (Mahler, 1975; Masterson, 1985). The borderline has not accomplished this developmental task. The clinician's job is to attend closely to the rekindling of the separation-individuation process, assisting the patient to separate and individuate. Effective treatment rests upon the patient's improved ability to express the real self, that is, to manage the processes of self activation, and to develop the capacity to distinguish self from other with increasing clarity and effectiveness.

The author thanks Patricia Sax, Ph.D., for her extensive and valuable critique of this manuscript. The author retains sole responsibility, however, for its contents.

It is often difficult to identify the patient's efforts at renewed self activation and separation of self from object. Often, particularly in the early phases of therapy, signs of the activation of the real self are subtle, fleeting, and rapidly obscured. Additionally, authentic indications of separation-individuation may be confused with defensive maneuvers, such as compliance with what the patient perceives as the therapist's desires. If the therapist effectively supports separation-individuation and also intervenes to help the patient stop defensive avoidance of the unpleasant affects that accompany separation-individuation, a climate conducive to success in psychotherapy is maintained. If these interventions do not occur, therapeutic progress will be severely impeded or even destroyed. Clinicians must therefore be able to identify separation-individuation moves in patients as rapidly and accurately as possible. This chapter will describe the clinical context of separation-individuation, providing the clinician with a method for assessing its presence or absence in the psychotherapy of the borderline patient.

The following case vignette will illustrate some of the problems that can occur if the process of separation-individuation is misunderstood. This misunderstanding led at the time to problems in recognizing signs of the emergence of the real self in treatment. This in turn impeded the therapeutic process until the problem was identified and rectified, after which the patient's progress resumed.

CASE ILLUSTRATION: MRS. A

Mrs. A, a borderline woman in her early forties, came into treatment with many problems in her relationship with her family, which completely preoccupied her. This preoccupation with others rather than the self is common among borderline patients. They give the impression that there is no room to think about themselves at all. This inability to consider the self supports deficits in self definition and decreases the clarity of the differentiation between self and object.

Eventually, many of the presenting problems that brought the patient into therapy came under better control. Mrs. A began to pay increased attention to herself during her therapy hours. She had originally planned to enter nurse's training but at this point began to realize that she disliked the physical demands nursing placed upon her and, in addition, lacked real interest in the vocation. She began to wrestle with the problem of which vocational training alternatives to pursue. This illustrates the beginning disinvestment of the object and investment of the self, which, for the borderline patient, represents a giant developmental leap forward.

Masterson describes the process he calls the borderline triad, by which the difficulties in self definition and self activation are maintained: individuation leads to depression and anxiety, which lead in turn to defense. In other words, when attempts to separate and individuate bring up the terrifying affects of depression and anxiety, the patient, rather than persevering, moves into a defense against the affects, in the process defeating his own earlier efforts at self activation. This process is what supports the continuance of the developmental arrest, as the same self-defeating pattern recurs inevitably in response to each effort to separate or individuate (Masterson, 1981).

Mrs. A was no exception. As she began to wrestle with the problem of what alternatives to pursue (in other words, as she began to activate her real self), she defended, became subtly helpless in the transference, and pulled for me to take over.

At that time, I was just beginning to work with this method and, mistakenly thinking that I was supporting the patient's individuation by "communicative matching," I suggested that she consider occupational therapy as a career, since I knew of an interest she had in arts and crafts. She leaped at my suggestion, unconsciously knowing that by so doing she could avoid further self activation. She could now follow my plan rather than devise her own. She began to find out about graduate programs in occupational therapy. Naturally, because Mrs. A was no longer activating herself but instead was in defense (i.e., complying with an object), work in treatment ground to a halt and was replaced by sterile, repetitive, and regressive sessions.

I did not know what was wrong. Finally, she got up enough courage to tell me that as she had found out more about the field, she realized that, for her, a career in occupational therapy would simply be a defensive continuation of her old pattern of doing for others rather than for herself. Then, following this piece of self activation, she defended again—this time by projecting onto me the withdrawing unit part object. She continued: she had had difficulty in telling me about her thoughts because I had been responsible for the original suggestion and she feared my anger, disapproval, and withdrawal of interest if she didn't do as I had suggested.

This revelation allowed for a discussion and clarification of the impasse. She became aware of how easily she "gave herself away," how afraid she was to stand up for herself. She understood that she had projected onto me her image of a mother who withdrew at signs of independence. She saw for the first time that her reaction of compliance was something generated from inside herself, rather than in response to an external source.

The cessation of the acting out of the withdrawing part unit in the transference, and the consequent return of her attention to herself and to her own internal processes, precipitated aspects of the abandonment depression. She was then increasingly able to sustain and explore these affects. She described a kind of deadness, iciness, and emptiness as her abandonment depression deepened.

The real self began to emerge in a more sustained way. She mentioned offhandedly that this mood was affecting her painting. Until then, I had not known that she painted. She revealed that all through the years she had loved to paint and to draw, but that she had always hidden and depreciated her own efforts. She recalled giving her mother a painting for Christmas that her mother had hung in a dark hall, behind a door. She came to understand that, metaphorically, she had done the same thing to her own work and talent. Gradually, as the investment in her self became stronger, she revealed the depth of her passion for creative work. Sessions alternated between that passion and more discussion of her depression and its origins. Eventually, she went to art school, where her difficulties in self activation manifested themselves in periodic impoverishment of her creativity, particularly under separation stress. This in turn became the focus of her work on herself, leading to ever-increasing self activation and sustained efforts in her own behalf as time went on.

Fortunately, this patient and I had been able to resolve her therapeutic impasse, and she could go on to develop her own real self. The experience had, however, brought forcibly to my attention the need for caution in regard to the recognition and technical management of the emergence of aspects of the real self. I felt fortunate that the patient had had sufficient ego strength to resist her own effort to comply with me at a cost to herself. I realized that other patients, less well endowed, might have indeed complied with what they thought I wanted in such an effective way that neither I nor they would ever have known the cost of that compliance. This danger focused my attention on how to recognize the beginnings of real self activation through separation and individuation, and distinguish it from defensive phenomena.

How does one recognize separation-individuation or real self activation? It is my thesis that separation-individuation moves are more easily identifiable if they are viewed not as discrete phenomena but, rather, as part of the context in which they appear. Particularly in the early phases of treatment, one can reliably assess a given move by a patient as truly representing a new level of separation-individuation only when two conditions are met. One views new efforts at separation-individuation in the light of (1) evidences of change from a prior mode of behavior, and (2) the affective climate in which such movement occurs. In the borderline patient, a move toward separation-individuation is always followed by or accompanied by anxiety and depression and/or defenses against them until the abandonment depression has itself been worked through in psychotherapy.

Successful treatment occurs when the patient tolerates, manages, and works through anxiety and depression rather than retreats from efforts at separation-individuation in order to avoid the unpleasant abandonment feelings. The therapist must therefore be able to identify signs of separation-individuation in the clinical situation. This is crucial if one is to track the outcome of such moves and intervene correctly so that the patient's efforts are supported. The question one must always have uppermost is: Does the patient move into his feelings and deal with these feelings following an effort to separate and individuate, or does he defend and move away from them, and in the process abandon his efforts? Specific interventions, such as confrontation (Masterson, 1976) and communicative matching (Masterson, 1985), are based upon this assessment.

The following examples will illustrate some specific ways that separation-individuation phenomena appear in the treatment situation. They are divided into manifestations that occur in daily life and are reported by the patient, and those which the therapist can observe directly during the course of the treatment hour.

EXAMPLES OF CLINICAL MANIFESTATIONS OF SEPARATION-INDIVIDUATION

Efforts at Separation-Individuation Reported to the Therapist by the Patient

It should be self-evident that people who have small investment in the self as opposed to object, and difficulty in identifying their own unique thoughts, feelings, and wishes, will have a hard time standing up for themselves effectively in encounters with others. Therefore, therapists are bound to hear of many encounters between the patient and others in his life in which the patient feels misunderstood, abused, victimized, and helpless. Often in these encounters, the patient's defenses are such that he does not even know what it is that he feels. Separation-individuation occurs when the patient shows increasing awareness of his affective reactions to the behavior of other people, and the effects of his own actions on himself and them. Based upon his improved clarity of feeling, he begins to activate and assert his real self. This in turn leads to an improved sense of the quality of his own participation in these events. In short, he develops a sense of himself as an active force in his own life.

Case illustration: *Mrs. B.* Married for the second time, in her late thirties, Mrs. B reflected on changes she had observed in herself over two-and-a-half years of psychotherapy, first two and then three times a week. Through this sequence, one can see the slow emergence of the real self: (1) the increased ability to control her behavior; (2) the ability to distinguish self from other; and (3) the ability to distinguish intrapsychic conflict from external event.

She recalled how, at the start of therapy, she had regularly collapsed when her husband had thrown tantrums and attacked her mentally and physically. She would cry uncontrollably, bang her head against the wall, and threaten or attempt suicide when faced with these situations. First, she began to control her behavior and to activate and assert herself. She learned to utilize language to show her husband the inappropriateness of his behavior and to set limits to it. Second, she began to distinguish the self from the object. She began to identify times when she provoked him, and she could distinguish between these occasions and those when the provocation seemed to come from him. Then, in a tumultuous climate of depression and defense, she identified a propensity to resist changing things for the better, e.g., dragging her heels in confronting him, and provoking him by her hostile and implacable manner.

This patient had been sent to a series of boarding schools, starting at about age 3. For the first time, as she controlled her acting out with her husband and observed her resistance to changes for the better, she began to question why she had never openly rebelled as a youngster. She saw that instead she victimized herself, suffering and provoking attacks. Mrs. B went on to link her earlier feelings and behavior to her current functioning, where she saw that she did the same thing.

Another indication of separation-individuation is persistence—that is, the increased capacity of patients to sustain efforts at projects to which they have committed themselves. Frequently, the underinvestment in the self (and thus avoidance of the depression) expresses itself as projects undertaken and dropped—hard things avoided altogether. As patients become aware of how destructive such avoidance is, they persevere in spite of intense desires to stop. Separation-individuation is being demonstrated when acting out, avoidance, and complaints are replaced by efforts to be proud of perseverance and conscious efforts to manage or work through the accompanying abandonment affects.

Standing up for themselves better, identifying and expressing their own wants and needs, developing the capacity to express interest and sustain effort reflect increased individuation. Borderline persons will also report changes in the nature of their attachments to others. These changes reflect development of the capacity to separate. They may drop existing relationships that have served defensive, acting-out purposes (for example, clinging or distancing) and substitute new relationships that reflect their growing capacities for self-assertion, intimacy, and empathy.

Caution should be observed in assessing relationships when, particularly during the beginning phase of treatment, the patient reports a total change in the kind and quality of his relationships. Borderline people defensively seek out others who will collude with them in avoiding separation-individuation. These partners can be induced to act out part self or object representations with the patient. The patient himself is unconscious of the destructive potential of these interactions as well as of their defensive nature. Under the sway of his splitting mechanisms, he will genuinely feel that this relationship represents a new and better beginning, warding off all information that would alert him that he is once more headed for disappointment or disaster. His reports of his interactions are colored by his defenses and are therefore difficult for the therapist to evaluate. The clinician must avoid the trap of trying to decide whether a given relationship is "good for" the patient, and remain focused on the clinical task: the furtherance of the development of the real self and the removal of obstacles to that end. In order to evaluate the meaning of a new relationship to a patient, and therefore its relevance to his psychotherapy, the clinician observes the feelings that accompany reports of the new relationship and the level and quality of the work the patient is doing during therapy hours. This information will be more helpful than the patient's verbal report about the new relationship.

Case illustration: Miss C. Miss C had begun therapy while in a relationship with a married man, who alternately told Miss C that he loved her and, as Miss C put it, "dumped" her. This lover offered powerful reinforcement of both Miss C's rewarding and withdrawing unit fantasies. A wealthy married man, he would promise to buy her a home where she could live and never have to worry about supporting herself again. Then he would abruptly dismiss her, avowing his fidelity to his wife, and ignore Miss C's feelings of disappointment and betrayal. He would attack her for being temperamental and selfish when she protested against his indecision and sudden rejecting behavior. During the phase of treatment when Miss C was intensely involved with this lover, very little substantive work occurred. Miss C was much more interested in using her therapist as a back-up rewarding unit, should she be abandoned, than in examining and relinquishing her fantasy about her lover. Through repeated experiences of being disappointed and manipulated, Miss C, over time, was able to face the incredible destructiveness of the relationship. She eventually brought herself to end the liaison. She became depressed and overwhelmed. Before this time, she had no awarenesses that her relationship had functioned as a defense against feelings of depression. She seemed to think that her emotional problems were a reaction to external circumstances. Now she noted that when she began to explore her feelings and activate herself, she became more depressed.

The question was whether or not she would defensively develop the same kind of relationship in order to stop the depression. Indeed, she did flirt with doing exactly that. When she became involved with a more suitable person, she tried to convert the relationship into the old, rewarding unit fantasy. She stopped working on herself and began defining herself solely in terms of the relationship. This time, however, it was obvious to her that when she did that, the work in treatment ground to a halt and her self-esteem plummeted. As she put it to herself, "bells" now went off in her head to warn her that something was amiss. She began exercising caution, tracking her own wish to turn her relationship into a fairy tale. She was then able to control her fantasy and see her partner realistically. Thereafter, she could continue to work on herself and develop the relationship in a healthier way. Finally, when she behaved realistically, she saw that she came to trust her own capacity to exercise good judgment. Thus, slowly, the patient demonstrated a growing capacity for self activation. Concurrently she could involve herself in relationships for realistic gratification rather than for defensive purposes.

The implications of this are clear for the therapist seeking to evaluate a patient's relationships in terms of its destructive or constructive potential. A relationship undertaken under the sway of the false, defensive self will result in a work stoppage in therapy and a halt in activation of the self outside of therapy. This is what occurred during Miss C's first, disastrous liaison, and in her brief attempt to repeat the process with her second relationship. As this case illustration demonstrates, a relationship undertaken by the real self will do neither of these things.

The borderline patient's relationship to his parents inevitably becomes a focus in therapy. An important aspect of growing separation-individuation is reflected interpersonally in the capacity to alter relationships with the family of origin. The following vignette illustrates some of the effects of dealing with living parents in a different way.

Case illustration: Miss D. Miss D, aged 40, had been severely obese since childhood and had entered treatment, once and then twice a week, for help with her weight problem and with a crippling agoraphobia. She initially offered very minimal data about her family, discussing their characteristics globally and superficially. She also avoided meaningful references to her feelings about her relationships with them. In the meantime, there was plenty of objective evidence of the extreme intensity of her attachment to her mother and the cost to herself. She lived alone but saw her mother (who lived 100 miles away) two or three times a week, had all of her most important social contacts with her family, vacationed with her mother, and the like.

It was hard for Miss D to talk about this, much less to recognize the meaning of her behavior. However, she finally began to understand that she felt perpetually controlled through what she perceived as her mother's hostile, self-effacing martyrdom. She felt under constant pressure to perform in order to avoid guilt and underlying feelings of emptiness and void.

After two years of treatment, this patient, for the first time, told her mother that she didn't want to come to visit her. When the mother totally ignored her and pressed the invitation, the patient was able to tell her that she found being ignored intolerable.

Miss D described having feelings of panic and agony when she got off the phone. She said that she wanted to shred her flesh, that she felt so worthless that she couldn't even crawl, much less stand or walk— she wanted to scream and to beg forgiveness for being such a loathsome creature. As I evaluated her effort with her mother, it appeared clear that her response of defending against her efforts at self assertion by activating the false defensive self (withdrawing unit) confirmed the important nature of the effort she had just made. The intensity of internal punishment in response to self activation is indicative of the significance of the individuative move.

All of these examples deal with relationships between the patient and other people. Additionally, growing separation-individuation is reflected intrapsychically in changes in the patient's ability to identify and define introjects. As patients learn to confront and deal more effectively with family members externally, the focus shifts to the parental introjects within and the relationship of these introjects to part self representations. Gradually, the focus turns from a preoccupation with the dealings of others on a day-to-day basis to the effects upon one of internal representations of important figures. This shift reflects greatly improved capacities to distinguish internal from external reality. The following vignette illustrates one patient's efforts to recognize and come to terms with the intrapsychic representations of family members. In this vignette, one can note the progressive evidences of separation-individuation as the patient moves from first identifying his part self and object representations, to distinguishing them from his real parents, to finally recognizing the internal, defensive functions of his introjects.

Case illustration: Mr. E. Mr. E, 41, described in detail in Chapter 4, is in treatment three times a week for problems including chronic feelings of depression, social isolation, underachievement, and substance abuse.

Despite all of this evidence of tragedy in his family and the destructiveness of his family atmosphere, Mr. E initially denied the severity of the pathology in his family and the effects of such an atmosphere on his own development. He was also unable to recognize the complex motivations for his parents' behavior. Instead, he employed splitting, i.e., he alternated between seeing his father as a bad guy and his mother as martyred and victimized, and seeing his mother as a monster and his father as a good man, a hero brought down by illness and despair. Attached to the two object representations—of a monster (whom he came to call the Bad Nun) and of a martyr—were corresponding part self representations: the part self representation attached to the martyred part object was what he came to call the Good Catholic Boy—self-effacing, compliant, obedient, and passive. In this state he felt good. Attached to the withdrawing unit part object representation (the Bad Nun) was a part self representation which he called the Sleaze. This part unit had murderous rage and feelings of terrible badness attached to it.

The first awareness Mr. E developed of his split occurred as he identified the two self representations: Sleaze and Good Catholic Boy. The second came as he identified the nature of the two internal objects. First, he recognized that in reality he had been scapegoated by both of his parents. Later, he came to begin to appreciate some of the tragedy of their lives as well without denying the destructive effects upon himself and his siblings. Once he no longer could characterize them in "reality" as having been martyr and Bad Nun, the door was open for him to understand that these were intrapsychic representations that he had kept separate in order to avoid facing the conflicting feelings of murderous rage, guilt, compassion and (ultimately) feelings of terrible aloneness associated with coming to terms with his past. He was then in the position to notice that the worst part of it was that he knew that he continued to carry these projections and to reenact them over and over in his life, and that he had great reluctance to give them up.

This vignette not only describes signs of separation-individuation that the patient reported from his life, but indicates some of the interweaving of his reports of these events with things occurring within the therapeutic interaction. The following section will specifically discuss experiences of separation-individuation that appear in the therapeutic relationship.

Separation-Individuation Reflected in the Therapeutic Session Itself

In the therapeutic encounter, signs of separation-individuation are found in: (1) the increased ability of the patient to identify and express a range of affects; (2) the freedom to bring in for discussion whatever is on the patient's mind—not only his problematic feelings and encounters, but his interests and enthusiasms as well; (3) signs of improved self-observation, identification of feelings, and assumptions of responsibility for treatment; and (4) the patient's ability to distinguish himself from you; that is, his internal objects from you, his self representations from you, and eventually to see himself and you as whole and separate people.

It is axiomatic that the capacity to distinguish, feel, and discuss a range of emotions is basic to the work of psychotherapy with patients of all sorts. For the borderline patient, it is a central goal of psychotherapy. It is through the development of such abilities, linked with self activation, that the sense of self develops and consolidates. The borderline patient impedes that process, as did Mr. E, with massive projections of aspects of his part self and object relations units onto the therapist. He then acts as if the therapist is this projected part object rather than discussing these aspects of his own feelings and intrapsychic life. Increasing one's capacity to contain, observe, acknowledge, and discuss feelings rather than externalize and act them out is one of the major goals of the psychotherapy and signs of improved capacity for separation-individuation.

Another sign of improved separation-individuation is the growing freedom the patient then feels to bring to whatever he judges to be important for discussion. Often, borderline individuals assume that, like the parental introject, the therapist is only interested in their problems and inabilities to cope. They voice the feeling that their interests and joys have no place in therapy. As therapy progresses, increased individuation is demonstrated by the patient's lively discussions of particular interests and concerns along with consideration of problems and work on aspects of the abandonment depression. For example, in addition to developing her interest in art, Mrs. A had to be able to talk about it in therapy. She had to stop behaving as though it had no place in treatment, and that it had to be hidden. There is separation-individuation in the patient's capacity to discuss her newly defined interests as well as in the interest itself. As the case of Mr. E also illustrates, the power of this shift in the direction of separation-individuation is demonstrated by the feelings of loss and anxiety (i.e., abandonment depression) that accompany the experience of sharing thoughts, joys, excitement, and accomplishment.

A third evidence of increased separation-individuation is the patient's assumption of responsibility for the management of therapy. Progress in this area is indicated by the patient's containment of inappropriate behavior within the therapeutic setting, and the conversion of the impulse toward that behavior into feelings and words. For example, patients may wait for the therapist to start sessions and choose topics. They may "reference off the therapist," taking their cues from her and trying to respond as they think they "should". Mr. E did this when he converted his own interest in painting into a task which he fancied he did for me. Patients may forget material from hour to hour, but expect one to do the remembering for them. They try to get the therapist to resonate with their internal self and object representations by attempting to get one to take care of them, attack them, control them, or reject them. For example, they may avoid paying their bills, arrive late for sessions, or miss appointments entirely and make excuses. They then accuse the therapist of coldness or of lack of interest or investment in their welfare if she bills them for missed sessions, takes notes, or does not allow herself to be manipulated in these or other ways.

Considerable progress in investing in the self is evidenced by the patient's moving toward fuller assumption of his responsibilities. It is also evidenced by the capacity to discuss feelings rather than to act on them. An important axiom of the Masterson Approach is that therapist interventions are always designed to further autonomous functioning. The therapist takes great pains to avoid doing the work for patients. This is one of the reasons behind the therapist's reluctance to give interpretations to borderline patients except under carefully thought through circumstances. Consequently, insights come from the patients themselves. The power of these insights is derived both from the insight itself and from the very act of accomplishing it by oneself. Genuine insight is therefore an important sign of individuation.

How can one distinguish such insight from intellectualization, or from insight used as an excuse to continue behaving destructively? Again, by the company such insights keep: self activation, depression, and defense. For example:

Case illustration: *Mrs. F.* An extremely bright, psychologically minded young woman, Mrs. F began treatment impressively. By the third session, she had pulled together and identified for herself the implication of several major themes in her life. She figured out that she had organized her whole life to avoid rejection, and that she feared rejection because she experienced this as abandonment. She was bright, used intellectual defenses, and skimmed the surface of things in order to avoid her feelings.

How then, could one tell whether she was presenting meaningful insight? First, by the brief appearance of affects of the abandonment depression that immediately followed her insight. She described panicking, felt overwhelmed, and became furious at having to deal with this issue. Then she defended, acting out the wish for reunion by calling her husband at work and having him come home to take care of her.

In the next hour, I pointed out that she had run for cover into her husband's pocket, and that he had a job to do that was put in jeopardy by her call. I inquired as to why she had needed to do this.

She replied, "I felt stripped of my defenses. I felt like when I was a child and my parents briefly got their act together and I felt deposed. They were not using me. I have a hole now—if I am not doing everything to avoid rejection I have to look at myself. What I want. There are no more excuses. If I pull my husband in, I feel less alone. I don't want to go back, but why am I so frightened? I feel so alone and worthless—what if I don't measure up?" The genuineness of the move toward separation-individuation is confirmed by the defense and the feelings which stimulated its employment.

All of these efforts at separation in the therapeutic relationship lead to a situation in which the patient demonstrates his ability to distinguish himself from the therapist, to distinguish between his internalized objects and himself, and finally to see himself and therapist as whole people, with separate complex mixtures of attributes. At this point, the borderline patient has moved from a developmental arrest established during the rapprochement subphase, to the developmental stage of being on the way to self and object constancy. He is in the position to fully implement the activation and development of the real self, a life-long task accompanied by joy, vigor, and courage. This last accomplishment occurs to its fullest extent only at the successful termination of intensive psychotherapy, when taking leave from therapy and therapist.

Although the task of separating fully from the therapist is on center stage only at the end of therapy, and only for some patients, the process of distinguishing oneself from the therapist, which is a precondition for such mourning and ending, is incremental. The incremental steps leading to the formation of this ability are taken in all successful treatment, at least to some extent. All of these efforts, though they fall short of the ideal state of whole self and object representations, represent progress. For example, Mr. E in describing his rage at me for not behaving in a way that conformed with his internal object relations part units, demonstrated his increasing ability to separate self from object and to distinguish internal from external phenomena. Over time, such capacities may, in some individuals, develop into the full-fledged capacity to mourn psychotherapy and to end it.

A final example will further illustrate the development of this crucial capacity.

Case illustration: Miss G. Miss G is a high-level borderline patient in therapy three times a week. In this hour she confronted a major defense: acting out of the withdrawing unit in the transference, reversed so she projected the self representation onto me while in the main she retained the object representation for herself. In this session, she identified this defense. She thus demonstrated a powerful new capacity to self observe, to distinguish self from other and reality from fantasy.

She said to me, after two-and-a-half years of therapy, "I think that what I have been doing all of this time—well, not always, but a *lot* of the time—is to, like, be my mother and make you the daughter. Like, I've not been really present a lot—or I act clumsy and incompetent— or my drinking before I come here—or making it so that you can't win if you talk or if you stay silent. Like—if you talk I get mad and defy you, and if you are silent I am resentful and shut you out. I treat you exactly the way that she treated me."

This patient's insight represented a whole new level of self and object differentiation: a capacity to self observe, develop her own insight, control her acting out, and take responsibility for the work. Following this observation, she was able to control her impulse to continue the behavior. As could have been predicted, as the patient's focus shifted from transference acting out to an exploration of the internal, her insight and the subsequent efforts at controlling herself were followed by a period of rage and depression, with the emergence of genetic material. Thus, as always, the validity of the move toward separation-individuation was confirmed by the context of additional depression and working through.

CONCLUSIONS

Separation-individuation refers to a process within an individual of increasing capacity to identify his own thoughts, feelings, interests, and capabilities, to distinguish between self and other, and to articulate internal experience. When treatment is successful, these capacities begin to emerge in the therapy in a gradual and incremental fashion. The therapist needs to monitor three attributes of this process: (1) the affects, (2) the strengths of the efforts, and (3) the shift from investing in the object to investing in the self.

Clinical manifestations of progress toward the activation of the real self are found in patients' reports of gradual, incremental, improved capacities to identify thoughts and feelings, support the self, pursue genuine interests, and engage in realistic relationships for purposes of intimacy rather than defense. Within the therapeutic context, progress is marked by the developing capacity to express feelings and to discuss interests and concerns, improved ability to manage the responsibility for the conduct of therapy, the capacity to achieve and utilize meaningful insight, the ability to self observe and to distinguish the self from that of the therapist, and the ability to view both increasingly realistically. The result of these efforts is that the patient's real self emerges and is strengthened. The individual then terminates therapy with the increased ability to face and live life and negotiate relationships for realistic and sustaining purposes.

REFERENCES

Guntrip, H. (1986). My experience of analysis with Fairbairn and Winnicott (How complete a result does psycho-analytic therapy achieve?). In P. Buckley (Ed.), *Essential papers on object relations*. New York: New York University Press.

Jacobson, E. (1964). *The self and the object world*. New York: International Universities Press.

Kohut, H. (1977). *The restoration of the self*. New York: International Universities Press.

Mahler, M. (1975). *The psychological birth of the human infant*. New York: Basic Books.

Masterson, J. (1976). *Psychotherapy of the borderline adult: A developmental approach*. New York: Brunner/Mazel.

Masterson, J. (1981). *Narcissistic and borderline disorders: An integrated developmental approach*. New York: Brunner/Mazel.

Masterson, J. (1983). *Countertransference and psychotherapeutic technique*. New York: Brunner/Mazel.

Masterson, J. (1985). *The real self: A developmental, self, and object relations approach*. New York: Brunner/Mazel.

Winnicott, D. (1965). *The maturational processes and the facilitating environment*. New York: International Universities Press.

Chapter 10

Psychotherapy with a Borderline Adolescent: From Clinical Crisis to Emancipation

Candace Orcutt, Ph.D.

INITIAL TREATMENT

Gerda, 15½ years old, came to her first regularly scheduled appointment with her hand in a cast. She had punched a wall during a frustrating discharge process from a psychiatric inpatient unit. It also occurred to her that she might have needed to create a crisis to relieve the anxiety she felt upon leaving the unit.

A month before, while leaving a party alone at night, she had been forced off the street and raped. Subsequently she overdosed twice and was admitted to the hospital.

Gerda, a sophomore in high school, was a well-groomed, overweight girl with long, Alice-in-Wonderland hair. Her manner was engaging, although she described herself as "untrusting." She was intelligent and perceptive; her speech was articulate and fluid except for periodic

185

silences. The silences occurred when she felt sad. She said she didn't like to talk about sadness but, rather, would wait until it was "over." She believed that her problem had to do with "character," which she thought was not such a bad thing, since character could be changed.

I had already spoken separately with Gerda's mother, an author of children's books who constantly traveled in search of ethnic source materials. The mother was attractive, thin, and dressed like a fashionable bohemian. She was quick, intelligent, and intellectualized. She told me she felt as if her life had been "knocked out from under her" by her daughter's hospitalization.

It occurred to me that Gerda seemed like one of her mother's fictional creations—even her name had a storybook quality. "I hate my name," said Gerda. "It isn't a real name, and nobody ever pronounces it right."

Gerda's childhood was described to me by her mother. Gerda was the more reliable historian about her own adolescence.

Gerda had been a healthy baby who was weaned at 9 months and had loved to eat. Her developmental milestones were achieved early, and apparently she toilet trained herself. She developed asthma at about 2½ to 3 years of age, a year before her parents were divorced. When Gerda was 4, her mother decided to move to Quebec to allow herself "time to think." Gerda, uprooted from her home and friends, began to withdraw. Her mother sent her out to buy bread and milk so that she would have to deal with people and learn French Canadian, and somehow Gerda managed. A year later, they moved again to New York City, and the mother's career took priority. At 7, Gerda was a latchkey child, with the door key on a string around her neck so that she could come and go by herself. When her mother arrived home from work exhausted, Gerda tucked her into bed. Gerda used to have "intricate, beautiful dreams" for her mother's benefit, and would recount them in the morning to cheer her mother up.

Gerda's latency period was fragmented by multiple moves, the mother's changing romantic attachments, and extensive trips abroad.

She was the clearest about her early adolescence. At 11, she had begun what she called her "symbolic year," a period of expressing her anger at her mother in all possible indirect ways. For instance, she wrote "I hate you" in tiny letters on the walls in back of the furniture. By age 12 she had declared open war, and she and her mother fought constantly.

By the time therapy started, Gerda had had one surrogate father as well as a series of surrogate mothers who took over her care when her own mother traveled. In school, she was maintaining an A average despite her troubles. Her compliance, social skills, energy, and humor helped her to keep up the appearance of a model, outgoing, all-around student. Actually, she was constantly surprised to find that others perceived her this way. Her sense of herself was tenuous, and she told me that she had hid under her desk during her earlier school experience. Her relationships with both girls and boys had an intense, dyadic quality. She was offended at the idea of discussing her sexual activities with anyone of my generation, but she said that she believed intercourse should be saved for a deeply committed relationship.

On the night of the rape, she had left the party early when a girlfriend had unreasonably grown angry at her and had ordered her to leave. Gerda, upset, was searching for a cab when she was caught from behind by a man with a knife, who forced her into an empty lot and raped her. She walked home in shock, and found that her mother was out. The phone rang, and it was an obscene phone call. Overwhelmed, she swallowed No-Doz washed down with rum, and eventually began to vomit. Her mother arrived home and called the police, but Gerda locked herself in her room and refused to come out. Later, her mother took Gerda to the gynecologist for persistent vaginal bleeding. Gerda then overdosed again on flurazepan (Dalmane) and left a suicide note. This time, her mother got her to the hospital, where her stomach was pumped and she was admitted to the psychiatric unit.

COURSE OF TREATMENT

The treatment—shorter term and crisis oriented—was of 2½ years' duration. For the first nine months, Gerda was seen individually twice a week and with her mother once a week. After that, she was seen individually three times a week for a year, then twice a week for the last nine months. Treatment ended when, at age 18, she graduated from high school and went away to college. From the outset, it was understood that her treatment would probably be time-limited by her college plans.

The first phase of treatment focused on the crisis in Gerda's individual and family life. Although the work was heavily confrontational, it became increasingly insight oriented—especially when the family sessions ended and Gerda took increasing responsibility for her therapy.

In the family sessions the mother and daughter argued, and they could be verbally devastating. At home these arguments escalated into dramatic scenes with screaming and slamming of doors. Enmeshed in each other's anger, they could go on endlessly over such matters as the care of the cat's litter box.

I pointed out that, although they were both concerned with the issue of responsibility, neither was taking it. I labeled the arguments phony and nonproductive, and wondered what it was they would have to face if they stopped arguing. Gerda agreed that the fights were useless and would surely put her "in her grave." Her mother said she feared there would no longer be any communication between them if the fights stopped. The theme of separation emerged (and, of course, the fighting had started when Gerda had begun to move toward adolescent independence). My job, then, was to promote constructive communication and confront phony litter-box talk until, one day, Gerda exclaimed: "We're running the session without you!" With a workable-enough truce declared on the home scene, it was possible to end the family sessions and give Gerda full attention and responsibility for her therapy.

In her individual sessions, Gerda avoided her feelings by chattering entertainingly, more or less nonstop. I confronted this by asking how keeping me entertained was going to be helpful to her. In response, she told me about her "Pollyanna routine," which she had invented to minimize painful feelings in her social interactions. I said I was receptive to all her thoughts and feelings, and that she would be maintaining herself at an impasse by leaving part of herself out of therapy. She then told me that she had always felt safer keeping her feelings "in little boxes," and was afraid of losing control if she didn't.

My confrontations then focused on the silences that increasingly interrupted the "Pollyanna routine"—and each of these silences turned out to be "a little box" containing an unexpressed feeling. Gerda began to see how she inhibited her spontaneity by these silences. I began to realize how sensitive she had learned to become to meet her mother's need for constant cheering up.

Once Gerda began to observe her patterns of avoidance, she began to cautiously test how I would receive her expression of feeling. Anger came first, but obliquely. She began to criticize my office in fine detail. I responded to this in a light way, saying, "How can I help you get it together when I can't even put together my own office?" She became a little more direct, noting that I was from the suburbs, with "all those little polyester people living in little polyester houses." I asked if she was worried about my being synthetic—a fake therapist. She then expressed her annoyance more directly, saying ruefully that I left her to take the initiative and have painful thoughts and feelings when she talked about herself. She also resented not having a choice about being in therapy. I pointed out that she had made a kind of choice through her suicide attempts, and that she could make it easier for herself in the long run if she would learn to say what she wanted instead of doing it.

She told me she would rather feel angry than feel "betrayed." It seemed that the feeling of betrayal related to separation, since she immediately spoke of her discharge from the hospital. The night before her discharge, she was both angry and afraid of her anger. She had dreamed that she was taken from the hospital in a coffin, although she wasn't dead. She sat up in her coffin with her eyes burning "like a character in a horror film." In her dream, she fell through to Hell, where she searched endlessly through dark caves. That night she woke up terrified, with no one to comfort her, and felt as she had when she had had nightmares at 6 years of age.

She next began to bring in her poems and short stories, which she read to me. One story had been written between the time of the rape and her second suicide attempt. It told about a grotesque circus— which was really the world—in which a woman behind a curtain of white silk was "the main attraction." In the story, the curtain is drawn aside, she "makes her one plea to the crowd," and then "a razor-sharp knife descends upon her." Gerda said she was frightened by the feelings in the story and of the feelings aroused in therapy. She was afraid she might be crazy and that, if she told me too much about herself, I would hospitalize her. This was more of a conviction than a fantasy, and let me know how persuasively she had been taught the unacceptability of her feelings.

At this time, she grudgingly admitted that the family sessions were going well, and sadly remarked, "My mother is not a grown-up." She spoke of finding it difficult to have her mother lean on her emotionally, and then began to feel guilty. She then wandered off the subject. I confronted her avoidance, wondering why she chose to create a diversion rather than accept her own feelings (a repetition of pleasing her mother rather than expressing herself). She got mad at me, saying she did not want to get depressed again, as she had after the rape— that she wouldn't be able to put the feelings away and would be stuck with them. I said, "You're stuck with them anyway; why not learn to manage them?" She got mad at me again, and I asked her why she was angry at me for believing she could handle her own feelings.

She next brought in an article on child molestation that stressed the importance of the child's being able to talk about what had happened. This was followed by an attack of laryngitis (the first of many), but she was able to whisper to me that she had had a "flashback" and recalled the face of the man who had raped her.

The borderline triad (individuation leads to depression, which leads to defense) was getting clearer: when Gerda began to express her feelings, she would become depressed and anxious and would defend against these feelings by reverting to the "Pollyanna routine," or an angry outburst, or a physical illness.

On the other hand, the more she was able to tolerate her feelings, the more she was able to remember, and to integrate a sense of continuity of herself. She noticed how discontinuous her memory was and began to mend the gaps, reviewing her life back to age 3, where she had vivid memories, happy and unhappy, of her parents.

She was looking forward to celebrating her sixteenth birthday.

She told me that she was beginning, for the first time, to cry about the rape. She reported having nightmares and difficulty concentrating, and began to cry painfully in sessions. Then she told me of a family "secret" she had forgotten. When she was 7, she had gone camping with her father and his current girlfriend with her 14-year-old son. The teenager sexually molested her, and persuaded her not to tell her father, because their parents would not then be married. Eventually, she did tell her mother, but the matter never went beyond that.

She allowed herself to express anger toward her mother in my presence. She was "a fake person who liked to play mother." Gerda began a catalog of adults who had let her down, and I was included for going on vacation. She also told me that sometimes she hated me for making her feel. Words increasingly carried the burden of her self-expression.

She began to act more for herself. She completely redecorated her room at home, painting over the little-girl-pink walls with a sophisticated gray, and displaying her collection of crystal objects. Her toys were given away or put in the attic (except for the doll's house, which the mother took off to *her* room).

She began to lose her voice again, but continued to prepare herself to talk about the rape. She said it now seemed only to be a part of her, instead of all of her. But she said she still was not ready to trust me enough to begin.

Then she had a series of cancellations because of an earache, a toothache, a cold, laryngitis, and a strep throat. And when she came in, she came in fighting: she said I was intrusive and made her feel stupid and sick. She said she hated therapy and wanted to be independent. I said she was expecting me to be like her mother, and that she was letting this get in the way of using her therapy to help herself become independent. She then decided to tell me about her "secret criminal life," where she hated her mother and had dreams that she was watching her mother being killed. She decided that she had invested me with the "power" to make her feel sick or criticized, and now realized that I actually had no such control over her.

At this point, I was unexpectedly called away by a family illness. At the same time, Gerda underwent an overdue tonsillectomy. When we both returned, she said she had felt betrayed by my absence, but had also discovered that she missed me and cared about her therapy.

The work had been deepening in intensity since family sessions had ended and Gerda had been coming in three times a week. She had internalized my confrontations, catching herself when she began to avoid her feelings. And she was becoming more observant about the borderline triad, noting: "I'm now going to take one step backward because I've taken two steps forward."

One year into treatment, she began to report her dreams regularly. She dreamed she was watching a bright, cold maze of mirrors, and then she was in the maze, with a giant shouting at her. Next, she had a dream in which she was looking out a window through a white gauze curtain. She watched a girl go down a road that divided into two paths. One path led to a spindly house of ice with a cold light in it; inside was a closed box with a padlock. The other path led to "a plump gingerbread house with bright red geraniums living in window-boxes"; inside was an open box. [What a picture of the withdrawing and rewarding split! Remember, gingerbread houses contain witches who eat little children.] As she stood at the window, she held a key that was so cold it burned her hand, and she dropped it.

She associated the cold of the key and the icy house to the mirror in the maze in her first dream, and to the cold she felt during her tonsillectomy, when she came out of the anesthesia screaming for her mother—or when she woke from her nightmares on the psychiatric unit—or from her nightmares long ago when she was 6. She felt she was in the cold, crying for her mother who wasn't there.

She had a similar dream, and I was in it. She was looking through the same window, and someone drew back her arm, which in turn drew back the curtain. She couldn't remember what she saw, but it was terrifying. She felt I was helping her to remove the curtain that veiled painful memories.

She then picked a phony fight with me. Catching herself, she regained her perspective and began to joke about "feeling like a killer." She told me: "Go to your corner and die!"

She said that she had picked the fight because she had made up her mind to talk about the rape but was avoiding getting started.

She reflected that she was experiencing "a new sadness" beyond terror and anger. The sensation of "coldness" she had been describing to me had something to do with the rape but perhaps had been there even before. It was a feeling of coldness inside—an emptiness. She thought of all the times she had set aside her needs to care for her mother, and of the cold house in the dream. She said: "Dreams really do have a meaning!"

She began to reconstruct the memory of the rape. At first she did this by drawing fragmentary, half-symbolic pictures which she brought to her sessions. The drawings contained certain repeated elements: malevolent eyes, a religious medal on a chain, a knife, a stuffed bear being torn apart, dissociated gears and mechanical parts. The paper the drawings were done on was cut in an elongated, hexagonal shape.

She said that the drawings had to do with evil and the destruction of innocence. The rape was "the ultimate deceit that confirmed all other deceits." She said, "These are pictures of my head, filled with broken gears." She felt "fragmented, in pieces that don't fit together." It occurred to her that the paper was cut in the shape of a coffin.

She had more nightmares and a fear of being overwhelmed by a sense of guilt; she said that was why she had attempted suicide. She said she wished she had been beaten, because people didn't believe she had wanted to resist. I said, "Your life was in danger. If you had resisted, you might have been killed." She said she recalled being grabbed from the back. When she started to run away, her sweater was torn off, and she experienced a brief amnesia—perhaps when she saw the knife. She next remembered being in the empty lot and gagged with her own sweater. She thought she was going to be killed and just wanted it to be over. At that point she gave up.

Her recollections of the rape itself were fragmentary, "like pieces of a jigsaw puzzle that don't match." She began to recall the empty lot: a discarded automobile tire, a license plate. She fixed on her assailant's religious medal—how it turned, and how the light fell on the gold (afterward, she often felt panic when she spoke with a man wearing a gold neck-chain). She thought the medal had a mother and child on it.

She was aware of how cold she felt. She said, "His breath was hot, and his pendant was cold."

More nightmares followed. In one dream, she was observing herself in the form of a transparent doll. An arm kept putting gears inside her. Finally, the arm produced a key and wound up the gears. Then she dreamed she was on fire.

In another dream, she was in a glass case locked with a key. She tried to smash the glass, but instead of breaking, it burst into flame.

She began talking about the rape again, saying that her recollections had a feeling of coldness, deadness, like a glass wall or ice. She told me that she never felt angry about the rape—just cold. In the hospital, she had made lists of reasons why she deserved the rape. However, she had felt angry at God.

Gradually, she also became angry about the rape and at her assailant. She said her pictures did not have enough anger in them. At home, she concentrated on drawing the rapist's face over and over.

Her seventeenth birthday passed. She went up to visit her dolls in the attic, but they were no longer a comfort, and she felt all alone.

Recollection of the rape evoked one further memory (probably a screen memory, because it also seemed dreamlike to her). She said that the feeling of cold went back to her early childhood, when her parents were still married and living together with her in the country. She thought she remembered looking out the window on "a shining day." It was the window of her dreams, and it was closed and curtained because it was winter, with the cold snow shining outside. Her father entered, filling the doorway "like a great bear." She could not get hold of the "other half" of the memory, which involved "something frightening." However, this persistent theme of lifting a veil ended here; its implications went beyond the scope of our time-limited work together.

She began for the first time to discuss dating. At first, she felt embarrassed and uncomfortable: "Things are getting out of their boxes . . . things are in messes." I commented that she had felt freer about talking about dating since she had decided to talk about the rape. She agreed there was a connection, in that she now felt better about the dating itself. She said she had gone through a period of having "flashbacks" while dating, but these experiences had lessened the more she was able to talk about the rape.

She completed her junior year with flying colors. She had maintained her high average, scored high on her Scholastic Achievement Tests, was busy in school activities, and enjoyed being a 17-year-old.

As she approached her senior year in high school, her appearance changed as well. Her hair was trimmed to shoulder length, and her dress was more tailored. Her poise seemed to come from an inner balance rather than from a defensively imposed manner. She agreed that she had changed, and that she felt "seventeen, not two or thirty-two."

At the beginning of the school year, she decided to reduce her sessions to twice a week. She said she felt she could get on without the "security" of so many sessions, and that she needed a little more time to be "a teenager with other teenagers" after school. I saw reality in this, especially with termination drawing closer, and with the stepped-up activities and responsibilities of her senior year. So I said it was her choice. She had been prepared to fight me or be directed by me, and said that taking responsibility for making her own choice was much more difficult. She did decide to reduce her sessions to twice a week, with the result that she felt for the first time that her therapy was fully her own choice and responsibility.

She also regressed somewhat in the beginning of this brief but important phase of treatment. Her increased independence (and probably the impending termination) led her to perceive me as withdrawing from her. She accused me of growing distant: I didn't talk like a person; my face was painted on; I had been transformed from a human being to a Pod Person (disguised alien). She was going to retaliate and stop coming, because there were no problems left to discuss, anyway. I asked her how she could say this when, as yet, she had no steady boyfriend. This confrontation evoked the angriest response I experienced from her. It also put the last phase of therapy on the track.

The next session she came in, very poised, and said that it was true she gets into an argument with me when she is resisting a turning point in therapy. Actually, she said, she no longer experienced the rape or suicide attempts as so important, and needed to talk about her present life.

She said she had had a steady boyfriend for the past three weeks, and, although she cared very much for him, she was worried whether or not to have intercourse with him. She was still concerned about flashbacks, and wanted to be sure not to do such an important thing perhaps out of peer pressure in the senior year. She also spoke about fears of maturing sexually: the shift in the attitude of boys toward her, and feelings of disgust about her own body that she had tried to hide in being overweight. She was bewildered, then resentful of her mother's reaction to her increasing attractiveness: her mother kept creating scenes about Gerda's clothing being too provocative (it wasn't so at all).

But now she had internalized confrontation to the point where she remained self-activating while experiencing whatever feelings were being evoked. Consequently, she became increasingly depressed and, I believe, was able to work through the first layer of her abandonment depression.

She felt very alone, without a family, and realized she had always felt this way. She began to weep because she felt that no one in her family had ever cared for her as a person, only as an extension of themselves. She felt cheated that she couldn't even mourn the loss of a family, because there had been no family to begin with (what family there was, was geographically scattered as well as emotionally distant). She said she believed she must be utterly worthless to have driven them all away. Her guilt helped her to maintain the illusion that she could have some effect on their feelings. As long as she could indulge in self-blame, she would not have to relinquish some hope of changing the situation. I said that she must have felt helpless indeed to believe the only way she could get her mother's attention was to attempt suicide, but wouldn't it make more sense to acknowledge the feeling than let it take the form of such a desperate action? Gerda said, "I really feel great hate for you for pointing out what I already know."

The depression that was expressed in her sessions was also contained by them. Outside, her life was increasingly stable, and she made dramatic improvements in assertion and communication.

One day she announced that she and her boyfriend had become lovers. No flashbacks, she said, but no fireworks or roses, either. Just real lovemaking, and she was in a good mood about it.

She even came to the conclusion that her mother wasn't so bad after all—a decent person, though scattered.

TERMINATION

Just before her eighteenth birthday, Gerda had one more fit of anger at me. She said I did not understand her, and that she felt like putting her fist through the wall. When I reminded her that this was what she had actually done when she left the inpatient unit, she realized she was having a reaction to the impending close of treatment.

She used the remaining time well, calling upon her increased capacity to observe, to make responsible decisions, and to follow through despite difficult feelings. Her last accomplishment was to face up to the illnesses she used as an avoidance. She confronted herself, observed her actions, and saw that she exhausted herself by overwork or overplay in order to get sick and avoid feelings.

Her individuation, as well as her integration of confrontation and management of separation feelings, was exemplified in her final sessions. The next-to-last session had been so right—such a healthy balance of sadness, happiness, direct expression of feeling for me, and thoughtful anticipation of her future—that I worried she might waver and miss the last session. With great effort, I said nothing and left it up to her. To my relief (and joy), she came in, and told me that she was proud of herself because she had foreseen that she would try to do something to miss the session, and when the impulse came, she contained it and faced the separation.

EPILOGUE

When Gerda reviewed this account of her early history, she felt that more needed to be said. The following is her reflection on the work she did and still continues to do:

> I am 21 now, and it is six years since I was raped. My initial treatment, which was time-limited and crisis-oriented, succeeded in that it taught me how to survive. Recently I returned to therapy with Dr. Orcutt, but my goals have changed. I am now willing to make a commitment to become whole, not pieced together. It is time to find out why I am so filled with self-hatred and why my answer to difficult events in my life has been to try to kill myself. I have resumed my therapy because surviving is no longer enough. I want to learn how to live.

Chapter 11

Marital Co-therapy of a Narcissistic Couple

James F. Masterson, M.D.,
and Candace Orcutt, Ph.D.

The individual conflicts of husband and wife are often projected onto their relationship and acted out within the context of the marriage. In these situations marital therapy can have a catalytic effect when combined with individual psychotherapy of the two partners.

Ongoing, intensive therapy of the individual is a slowly evolving process, and its effects unfold gradually from the intrapsychic, via the transference, to the interpersonal. For the neurotic patient, who is basically in charge of his or her external world, including relationships, this process focuses on the conflict in the patient's inner world that produces symptomatology. But for the patient with a personality disorder, who externalizes inner conflict through outer actions and interactions, exclusive therapeutic focus on the intrapsychic—especially on such higher-level defenses as repression—not only is premature, but also fails to provide the therapeutic containment which makes such a focus eventually possible.

Therapeutic containment of personality disorder focuses on such lower-level defenses as splitting, acting out, externalization, projection, projective identification, avoidance, denial, clinging, and devaluation. The therapist must help the patient to become aware of these defenses, to learn to observe and control them until they become ego alien, and to understand that they represent a denial on the patient's part to acknowledge and manage what is, after all, intrapsychic conflict.

Extension of intrapsychic conflict onto the stage of the outer world often manifests itself in interactions with others that cannot strictly be called interpersonal, because they are essentially extensions of the individual's problems from the past. These problems are played out using another, not for his or her real self, but as an involuntary actor cast in a role from a scenario the patient repeats in the present, in order to avoid past memories and feelings. This evasion of the patient's real self is possible because consolidation of object relations and structuring of the ego are still in a formative state. As a result, another can be perceived as an extension of the self, and the ego splits reality to support this illusion and mollify the pleasure principle. Truly interpersonal relationships can only be achieved when the patient is able to take back rejected aspects of the self that have been put off onto the other, tolerate his or her internal conflicts *as* internal conflicts, and approach the other as an integrated self, able to be separate and ready to share.

When the therapist helps the patient deal with these extensions of self into interaction with another, it is not precisely accurate to say that this is relating the therapy to the interpersonal sphere. Actually, the work is still with the inner world of the individual, but with its conflicts transposed to the area of social interaction. One might say this represents therapy of extrapsychic issues, which must be met if the patient is to establish a real self capable of real interpersonal relationship.

The narcissistic couple can be described as maintaining a wall between them that is built from a double-sided mirror: each individual sets up (unknowingly) a mirror in front of the partner that imposes a reflection of the self's expectations on the object. Each individual reacts to the reflection of his or her inner self, believing that this is a genuine response to the other, and wonders why the sense of profound loneliness persists.

When a patient with a personality disorder enters therapy with a complaint of marital difficulty, the process of identifying and containing the patient's projections onto the partner (and vice versa) is cumbersome from an individual therapeutic approach. The patient's distortions and deletions in presenting one side of the story handicap the therapist's judgment, especially when the marital problem is so central that it crowds out other sources of information about the patient. The credulity of the therapist is lessened as well, because interventions are heavily reliant on the patient's point of view. In time, enough parallels can be gathered (especially those based on the patient's interaction with the therapist) for the therapist to make an accurate assessment of the patient's stance and intervene appropriately. But the obvious question is: if the marital interaction can be observed live, why settle for hearsay evidence?

If the couple comes in for marital therapy, not only are the self-defeating aspects of their interaction available for immediate study, but also the therapist's comments can be directed to the interaction as it happens, and can be more readily recognized (and less easily denied) by the couple. (Ian Alger's use of freeze-frame video, through which crucial interactions can be captured and reviewed, takes this process still another step. Similarly, Virginia Satir dramatizes these moments by posing family members in a living tableau.) In addition, the couple has a protected place in which to practice new ways of interacting. (Nathan Ackerman, who pioneered in couples' therapy, spoke of "orchestrating" family communication to encourage new ways of relating. He also stressed that the family has its own dynamic that is more than a multiplication of individual dynamics.) Working directly with the couple also facilitates recognition of the malignant pattern that is formed as the individuals' projections inevitably mesh and intensify the repetition compulsion into a vicious cycle.

Just as marital treatment serves as a catalyst for individual treatment, individual therapy supports and deepens the marital work. Individual treatment creates the therapeutic alliance, incorporates information and spill-over from marital sessions into the working-through process, and provides a context for the transition to insight therapy.

The case of Mr. and Mrs. Spiegel (a pseudonym) illustrates the effectiveness of introducing marital therapy concurrently with individual therapy.

Mr. Spiegel, a successful, well-to-do attorney in his forties, came to the Masterson Group after his first wife left him. The separation appalled him, and he struggled with his depression, pushing it away with protests of humiliation and rage. Although he acknowledged the reality by saying, "She doesn't want to be abused any more," still he remained incredulous: "It's like my hand leaving my wrist! How can my hand leave my wrist? It's part of me!" He had always treated his wife as a narcissistic object, and, after 20 years, she had had enough. When he was able to give voice to his depression, he was despairing: "It seems I have this great need to be loved, but I can't love. I take and take. I'm selfish, and there's something horrible inside of me."

THE INDIVIDUALS

His work was brilliant, and free of conflict except in his relationships with his colleagues, where he was impatient and overbearing. In the courtroom, he took center stage and drew in narcissistic sustenance from his audience.

In his marriage, he had expected the same absorbed admiration he received in the courtroom. He said, "Now I see I treated my wife like an audience. I wasn't really interested in her needs, and I'm just the same with everyone else. You know, I charm them, but I won't let myself get involved. Out of sight, out of mind! I can't open up and be me. I'm really a little boy afraid of being mauled and rejected. I'm hiding behind this invincible armor."

Mr. Spiegel came from a poor family. Income was always uncertain because of his father's emotional instability. His mother turned to him as a means of emotional escape, idealizing his intellectual abilities and expecting him to fulfill her unmet needs for attention and prosperity. He described his schooling as follows:

I plugged into education in order to avoid feeling. I became a kind of fact-gathering machine. As I got more and more successful, I became a more and more perfect machine. Being perfect made me feel in control and good about myself. When I think back, I remember, as a kid, I wanted to invent this intricate, airtight Entitlement Machine so I wouldn't feel humiliated and dependent like my parents. I think I knew early on my wife as a person wouldn't fit this Big E, so I ignored her.

Without the armor of his Entitlement Machine, he felt alone and terrified, and he required another person in order to maintain his façade. He recognized this as repetition of his childhood situation: "The bargain was, you take care of me, and I won't become me." Separation made him feel "empty and depleted," and he was faced with his impaired real self, which he experienced as "shy, unworthy, and dependent."

Mr. Spiegel had been coming to the Masterson Group for four years when he decided to remarry. Although he conceded that "when I'm interested in a woman, I expect her to accommodate her life to mine," he did not act upon his insight. Before long, he and his new wife were locked in spectacular fights that caused anguish to both and resolved nothing. Again experiencing himself out of control in a marriage, he conferred with his wife and then requested that she also be seen at the Masterson Group.

Mrs. Spiegel, a mercurial woman in her late thirties and formerly a successful choreographer, came into treatment at the Masterson Group one year ago. She felt she was "severely depressed and in deep trouble." She took more medication than she should, drove too fast, wept uncontrollably and felt like dying. She was a veteran of psychotherapy, but seemed to have persuaded her last therapist that she was too vulnerable and weak to tolerate the process. He placated her with alprazolam (Xanax) and lorazepam (Ativan).

At home, she was in crisis. She sacrificed her individuality to mirror her husband and win his attention. But inevitably she would fail to do this perfectly and would be horrified as he became angry or distant. She would then go into a frenzy, dramatizing herself as a victim. During the consultation, she reported she had locked herself in the bathroom, taken 6 milligrams of Ativan, and had lain mute on the floor while her husband pounded on the door and demanded she answer him. The vengeful element in this did not escape her, as she noted: "Part of me gets frightened, and part of me wants to get back."

There is a labile, tempestuous, clinging quality about Mrs. Spiegel that at first suggested a diagnosis of borderline personality disorder. A closer look at her dynamics shows her to be what we have called a "hidden" or "closet" narcissist. This type of narcissistic personality disorder idealizes a "perfect" object, and so presents the self as subordinate, inferior, and even fragmented. The closer the "closet narcissist" comes to perceiving the other as real (as distinguished from projections from memory and fantasy), the more vehemently she or he reacts to separation from the internalized "ideal" image of the other.

Mrs. Spiegel characterized herself as a "fighter," and she pursued her treatment with determination, despite many setbacks. She was easily swamped by feeling, especially when her husband ignored her or became pompous with her, and often wrote down her thoughts and feelings to help herself achieve observing distance. Her own account of her childhood was written under these circumstances:

> The family scene, bluntly, was a sick show of outbursts, screaming, crazy behaviors, departures and manipulations. My father was a workaholic,

self-made man, who was at once devoted to his children, but always rigid, and usually tyrannical. At his worst, he had an explosive temper, and resorted to verbally and physically abusive punishments. My mother was and is emotionally and intellectually infantilized. Their marriage was basically loveless, friendless, and was without communication or understanding. They abused each other and their children, and were unavailable as parents.

My father died lonely and despairing and in terrible pain. He lost his friends and his fortune and left my mother unprotected. My mother, who befriended no one, is without friends today. She has always played out "victim"—and the relationship she has with her children is empty or angry, which contributed to our self-esteem problems. The message was that no one cared all that much—if they did, it was because we were bad. So we believed the message that we were bad and without value—why else would we be so ignored, punished, and threatened?

At sixteen I separated from my family and began my struggle to correct the past. My brother, however, lacked the strength to overcome the pain; instead, he chose to be ill—chronically, acutely, perpetually ill.

After a month of individual treatment, it was Mrs. Spiegel who requested marital therapy. This seemed appropriate; both partners focused on the marriage in their individual sessions, and the marriage was clearly in crisis. Reality testing became increasingly desirable, but also grew more and more beyond the scope of both husband and wife as the marital conflict escalated.

As the marital sessions ran concurrently with Mrs. Spiegel's individual therapy, she became more observant and was able to begin to set limits to her behavior. She became more responsible: she put aside her medication, drove more conscientiously, and became active in the training and promotion of a local dance company.

She was learning to value herself, but was afraid that self-assertion would drive away love. She realized she longed for a child, but the marriage had been founded on his decision to have no more children, a decision to which she had agreed initially. This dilemma highlighted their conflict and became a nonnegotiable resistance to looking at the marriage itself.

In a recent session, Mrs. Spiegel dared to begin facing her central conflict. She realized that objective scrutiny of the marriage involved the risk of considering that it might not be viable. If she faced this possibility, she would have to face profound separation anxiety, which she perceived as self-annihilating. She was not ready to understand separateness as a healthy stance and the only basis for true intimacy.

MARITAL CO-THERAPY

Whenever a family or a couple is seen at the Masterson Group, the individual therapists involved become co-therapists. This minimizes distortion of content, provides support for the individuals, and offers a role model for improved communication. As it happened in this case, there were male and female co-therapists, which reinforced the opportunity for the couple to identify constructively with the therapists.

Our primary interventions were confrontation of acting out, interpretation, and mirroring. We also clarified interactions, and helped the couple to reconstruct their communication in a more positive way. Our goal was always to facilitate individual assumption of responsibility. We supported the emergence of new insights in the individual sessions, once maladaptive, defensive activity diminished in the marital process. (The use of specific strategies, or structuring of the sessions in the manner of Haley or Minuchin, was not done. The Masterson Approach is predominantly verbal and insight oriented, which distinguishes it from more task-related and directive models.)

THE MARITAL TREATMENT

The pattern of the marital sessions has taken shape over a period of eleven months. During this time, both husband and wife have learned to give up a measure of narcissism in order to begin to love altruistically. For them to do this, their concept of love has had to change. For him, now, love is less defined by his need for control; for her, love is less limited by the belief that it can be won only through self-sacrifice.

In effect, the introduction of marital sessions was our first intervention, aimed at containment of the couple's escalating acting out. Our second line of intervention was directed to their mutual use of projection.

In the first marital session, the two sat on the office couch, clinging to each other like children united by a common fear. They were concerned that their therapists would see no hope in their marriage. This putting of their doubts onto us was the first of their projective maneuvers. Singly and as a couple, they would project bad, depressive ideas and feelings outward instead of owning them.

Customarily, they used these projective maneuvers against each other. It was our job to repeatedly remind them that each was expertly focused on the shortcomings of the other, to the neglect of unresolved problems in the self. We identified the projective defense, and interpreted to the couple how they brought about the distance they feared by attacking each other.

The dread of loss, the splitting off and projection of the fear of humiliation and abandonment, constituted the primary threat to the marriage, as it did to their individual integrity. However, their mutual goal required the capacity for separateness. Each step toward real relationship activated a sense of separation from an internalized, idealized sense of the other based on unresolved attachments to inner representations of long-ago parental relationships. Whenever the other failed to conform to this fantasy, the frustration would begin— for to live with another in the real present means relinquishing the hope of changing the past. Unconditional love, which is most nearly experienced in early childhood, if not found there is not to be found again. This understanding is difficult to accept and contain, and so the couple began their marital sessions by endlessly projecting their insecurity and finding a concrete source of grievance in the other.

They also had found a nonnegotiable issue to argue over: she wanted a child and he did not. When they first married, she set aside the idea of having a child in order to have her husband, but as time passed, she realized she had undervalued her maternal wish. However, she dramatized her feelings in a way that acted as a defense against an intimate marital relationship; her lamentations severely distanced him. This impasse rubbed raw the couple's narcissistic vulnerability. She overidealized the idea of having a child, splitting off her good feelings about herself, projecting them onto the idea of a child, and so experiencing herself as fragmented and empty. He, in turn, feared he would be controlled and drained financially by a child, and would lose his wife's affection to a competitor. The child impasse could always be hauled into their arguments to avoid doing the hard work and managing the painful feelings so as to make the marriage viable.

It was essential to identify the "red flag" issue of the child as a way the couple had of avoiding marital closeness and creating pain for themselves. So far, we were seeing little responsible communication between the two. Either she would nuzzle him and he would stroke her like a pet, or they would viciously attack each other (he with robot-like, relentless rationalization, she with wild and reckless self-righteousness; it was like watching an encounter between Darth Vader and Princess Leah). Each was so immersed in the projections of emotionally charged issues that there was no room (or inclination) to see the other's point of view. Without the capacity to acknowledge a valid difference of opinion, they lacked a foundation for marital negotiation.

The metaphorical wall that divides a narcissistic couple is of a special nature. As we described, it is like a double-sided mirror. They face each other but see only the reflection of their own expectations. As the dilemma continues, each finds the basic fear of being misunderstood and overlooked is coming true. In an attempt to call attention to this, they also reinforce each other's fear of being dominated. So intense is the need to find the source of these anxieties outside the self that highly intelligent and perceptive individuals, such as Mr. and Mrs. Spiegel, cannot distinguish between the real self of the other and their own projections (in individual therapy this same phenomenon appears as transference acting out).

We persistently identified the couple's mutual projections (including additional projections onto us) and interpreted their need (amounting to a basic assumption) that the other person be identical with the self. The price for this, we pointed out, was painful misunderstanding expressed in endless recriminations ("Why can't you experience this exactly as I do?").

They took this in and became more responsible and observant, so that it was possible to carry interpretation further. We noted that dropping the projections and moving closer to separating from inner fantasy brought out predictable defensive patterns in each. He would become arrogant and devaluing, whereas she would become helpless and guilt making, and these persistent patterns meshed to intensify each other.

Because they remained receptive, we took the interpretation further (we would always advance interpretation until we encountered a narcissistic recoil; then we would mirror to repair the sense of empathic fusion). We said that their need to be psychic twins was the real threat to the marriage. True intimacy, we continued, requires separateness, which is fundamental to the capacity to share.

The couple integrated this interpretation enough to begin to experience depression. Rapidly, this led to a splitting defense characteristic of couples enmeshed in personality disorder. When a couple uses this tactic, one partner verbalizes the depression while the other counters with the resistance. The aim is to fend off healthy ambivalence (i.e., "I am depressed and miserable and do not wish to face

this"). This elusive defense is difficult to identify, because each side of
the split is carried by a different person.

At this point, the wife voiced the depression. She recalled experiences of betrayal and loss, and realized that she tended to spoil things
through emotional confusion evoked by fear of losing her husband.

The husband's response was to maneuver her into an argument over
having a child. The wife responded explosively, and the tenuous gains
of the earlier sessions were temporarily swept away as both lost
observing distance. We came to refer to this type of escalation as the
"bonfire," and repeatedly questioned why they chose to add fuel to it
when it destroyed their mutual goal (since the "bonfire" was a form of
acting out, we used confrontation to contain it). We asked: Why did
they hesitate to collaborate to support the marital unit rather than
savage it? Why did they allow their sensitivity to rule them, at such
personal cost, rather than find a way back to a shared path?

The splitting defense took another form, as well, which complicated
reality testing with the couple. When they recounted an event, each
would present a point of view irreconcilable with the other's. The
clearest form of this came to be described as his "facts and figures"
approach, as contrasted to her "feeling" approach. They really
presented two halves of a whole. And it was not his intellectuality nor
her emotionality that was the issue here—they were quite capable of
arbitrarily reversing this split, so that he emphasized feeling and she
logic. The overriding function of the split was to deflect agreement
and keep the bonfire burning out of control.

Again, it was interpreted to the couple how they suffered because of
reluctance to consider each other's point of view.

Responding to ego-syntonic interpretation, the husband then held
steady. He actively supported his wife outside the sessions, and in the
sessions conceded that—whether he faced his responsibilities or
avoided them—he could not escape from his essential depression.

The wife, who had been voicing the depression up to this point, then
switched to the defensive. She reacted with massive denial. She
literally did not hear what her husband said (this had to be pointed out
to her, and his statement had to be repeated). She even attacked him
for his lack of feeling. It was called to her attention that she tended to
push her husband away just as he needed her to reinforce his risking
his vulnerability. She began to see that she was closing him out
whenever his expression of his true self threatened her projections.
Again, it was stressed that each tended to deny the other's separate-

ness, and so maintained an ongoing sense of individual rejection and marital discord.

This defensive shifting predominated until recently, when both at last held steady at once. They began to encourage and question each other and often to carry the major part of the session themselves. She reduced her attacking and started to draw him out. He, in turn, let down his shield more often, and spoke candidly. He described himself as "a little boy with a sword, striking at shadows," and spoke of his concern that he tended to combat shadows rather than confront the tasks of the real world.

The couple had completed a critical therapeutic cycle, and they were perceiving bits and pieces of each other's real self through the defensive grid that blocked their intimacy (instead of a double-sided mirror, the barrier between them had become more permeable and required a new metaphor).

They increasingly searched each other to discover and support authentic self-expression. As they did so, they appeared very different to us. It was easier to spontaneously experience them as a couple. At this time, they also found it helpful to incorporate our statement that the marital unit itself had to take priority if a marriage was to succeed, and that this required that the husband and wife be able to transcend individual issues to effect necessary compromises.

The couple had run through a course of primitive defenses—acting out, projection, and splitting—that they would no doubt repeat, but in a diminishing spiral. They had reached the critical point at which they had begun to identify their problem and cope with it differently. This is a psychic point of no return, where the old defenses are recognized as impediments rather than protections. The couple has the essential information necessary for change, and can implement that change on the basis of increasingly conscious choice.

OUTCOME

Mr. and Mrs. Spiegel have begun the hard work of building a marriage together. The work is based on three essential realizations: (1) Their marital problems are extensions and magnifications of their individual problems. (2) The manifestations of these problems in the marriage can only be handled co-operatively—each must be clear about her or his point of view, understand the other's position, and be willing to compromise to support the marital unit as their priority. (3) They cannot rely upon the models of marriage provided within their families of origin (indeed, this is a major source of anxiety) but, rather, must create their own workable mutuality, based on respect for the self and other, and a willingness to share and compromise.

The marital sessions have had a catalytic effect on the individual sessions. The struggle with depression in the marital therapy has brought out the terror of loss that is at the center of the individual process and undermines attempts at closeness. Mr. Spiegel has shown over and over that he pumps up his grandiose self and devalues her concerns in order to avoid feelings of loss. She has repeatedly demonstrated how she basks in the false radiance of his grandiose self in order to deny her fears of abandonment, and, when this defense falters, she attacks herself by acting out the disappointed, empty self, or attacks him by activating her own aggressive unit through righteous accusations.

In the marital sessions, they have had to see how their narcissistic defenses mesh to bring them perilously close to the destruction of their relationship—a self-fulfilling prophecy. For instance, they learned to observe the following pattern of interaction: When he starts to relax and get close, he begins to experience his feelings, and so he distances. She is so sensitive to any move of his that suggests rejection, that she anticipates he is about to leave her, and displays despair or anger. Because he is already on the run from feeling, he accelerates his withdrawal under the pressure of her emotional outbursts. Increasingly convinced her worst fears are coming to pass, she grows still more frantic. The vicious cycle intensifies until the situation ends in another "bonfire."

As it has become clearer that their marital disturbance is an extension of their individual struggles with narcissistic vulnerability to loss, each has come to realize that this issue is unavoidable in their individual sessions. The marital sessions allowed us to intervene at the moment of crisis—the "bonfire"—and to keep this moment alive as a motivational force. (The family therapists, Salvador Minuchin in particular, stress the function of crisis in interrupting the almost impenetrable homeostasis of families entrenched in this kind of pathology.)

Finally, the marital sessions have provided a place to learn marital skills. As Mrs. Spiegel once said: "We don't know *how* to be married!" Clarification of communication and educational statements have been specifically helpful in promoting this level of coping. Equally important, the ability of the co-therapists to work together, to balance their different personalities and skills in the service of the therapeutic task, has provided a model of teamwork that parallels the couple's task. We have not tried to present a seamless façade that would collude with the couple's need for perfectionism (not to mention any inclination we might have in that direction!). We try to present ourselves as two separate people mutually focused on a priority process. We do not "mathematically" divide the therapeutic task, but share it to make the best use of our individual strengths: one takes more responsibility for the consistent maintenance of observing distance and the clarity of the interpretations; the other risks a degree of immersion in the couple's interaction, in order to provide auxiliary ego support in their struggles to communicate. The co-operative use of these styles creates a self-balancing process that is another advantage of the co-therapy approach.

It seems likely that this case would have reached an impasse if managed through individual treatment alone. At best, it would have presented a nearly interminable task. Introduction of adjunctive marital therapy has unquestionably clarified and shortened the work. The grip of narcissistic pathology on the patient is especially tenacious, and the therapeutic task is elusive and protracted. So there is much satisfaction in finding a way to help a couple draw closer to fulfillment in marriage in less time, which is precious and irreplaceable.

EPILOGUE

The effectiveness of psychotherapy is evidenced in the extent to which patients make the process their own. Mr. and Mrs. Spiegel discontinued their marital sessions when they felt they understood how to remove the barriers that blocked their intimacy. They then carried the process beyond the "nonnegotiable" issue and decided to adopt a child. We were moved by this flowering of their relationship, and reminded each other that it is the patient who determines how far growth can go, after the therapist has helped to open the way to the possibility of new growing.

As the couple describe it, they have become healthier individuals, no longer anxiously focused on the possible dissolution of their mutual goals. As they have continued to experience a "worthier" sense of self, they have come closer to true mutuality and have felt safer in relinquishing their old, defensive attitudes.

Problems remain (as they must), but a profound change in the marriage has occurred. Through a combination of individual and conjoint therapy, the couple has come to understand that concern for the self allows for altruistic concern, and that the opening of the self to another leads to generativity. The more the self is valued, the more the self expands, reaching outward to others in the present and future.

Mrs. Spiegel often clarifies her thoughts by writing them down. Simply, on behalf of them both, she has noted: "Our decision to adopt a child is the full expression of our deep love for one another."

PART III

The Art of Confrontation with the Borderline Personality Disorder of the Self

The borderline patient's need to transference act out—to replay the past in the present—in order not to feel and remember, indicates that a vital element in the conduct of psychotherapy is the therapist's responsibility for maintaining the reality of the therapeutic frame. This provides the necessary context over time within which the patient's projections can be identified, measured and worked through.

Confrontation is the specific therapeutic technique, indeed the critical technique, that helps the therapist maintain the reality of the therapeutic frame and, therefore, that helps the borderline patient to convert transference acting out into therapeutic alliance and transference. Without confrontation, the psychotherapy of the borderline personality disorder would be impossible.

It is imperative, therefore, that the concept of confrontation be sharply defined and understood and its clinical application clearly demonstrated. However, there continues to exist confusion about the term confrontation.

Some authors synonymously use the term clarification, *which seems inaccurate; clarification refers to a cognitive issue about which there is intellectual confusion that is then clarified by an explanation. This is not the case with the borderline patient in the initial stage of treatment. It is not intellectual confusion but the need for defense that is the issue. The confrontation does not* clarify; *rather, it* opposes *defense, thereby creating conflict, which when integrated enables anxiety and depression to emerge.*

Other authors have seen confrontation as being punitive because they are unaware that the borderline patient has little ego capacity to discriminate, select, and control his responses, so that his experience of life is like a cork in the ocean; he moves with the tide and the wind. Confrontation does for him what he cannot do for himself. If his ego structure were adequate so that he could perform these functions, then confrontation would indeed be punitive and inappropriate. Beyond that, those who see it as punitive often have been raised by parents who used

213

confrontation as a punitive measure, and they therefore project this attitude onto a therapeutic technique.

Although the theory of confrontation is simple, its application is an art. The following five chapters apply this art to a wide range of psychopathology ranging from dramatic, overt, aggressive hysterical acting out through passive-aggressive and avoidant acting out to more subtle expressions of helplessness, hopelessness, and clinging.

Throughout all the chapters runs the constant theme of the therapist's task: to be a servant of the process evolving in the patient's psyche and to reflect this process back to the patient rather than react to it: Reflection rather than reaction. The reader can observe how these constant, neutral, informed, reflective, and confrontive therapeutic responses provide the vital frame the patients require.

J.F.M.

Chapter 12

The Art of Confrontation

Ralph Klein, M.D.

In this discussion of confrontation, the choice of a title that emphasizes the "art" of confrontation over "science" or "technique" highlights a fundamental concept concerning the application of this psychotherapeutic intervention.

The notion of confrontation as "technique" carries with it the idea of a rather stereotyped, routinized, even mechanical or impersonal intervention. Indeed, those unfamiliar with its proper practice can find confrontation to be limited in scope, narrow in range and diversity, and, at worst, monotonous, oppositional, and hostile.

A successful confrontation is none of these. It is the catalyst that sets the psychotherapy of the borderline patient in motion and maintains it on its course to its final destination. The proper use of confrontation to accomplish these goals in the treatment of the borderline personality disorder calls forth the therapist's capacity for empathy, introspection, creativity—and understanding and knowledge.

Empathy enables the therapist to use confrontation to acknowledge and address the particular needs of a patient at any given moment, for far from being static and impersonal, each confrontation is unique in that it must optimally take into account the particular patient, and the nature and strength of a resistance or defense at a particular moment, as well as the stage of treatment with its own delimited goals and objectives. If empathy in the psychotherapeutic situation involves the ability of the therapist to identify vicariously with the patient's psychological needs, then the most empathic intervention available to the therapist working with the borderline patient is confrontation.

The use of confrontation also requires that the therapist use introspection to constantly monitor his own feelings as well as the progress of the therapy. A confrontation must not be an effort to direct, manipulate, or pressure the patient because of the therapist's own frustration, anger, needs, or vulnerabilities. Such a confrontation will be ineffective and may well promote greater mistrust, resistance, and acting out.

Creativity in the form of imagination, humor, metaphor, and symbols is of great importance. The successful use of confrontation must take into account the style, language, and imagination of the particular therapist. The art of confrontation is not an act of imitation or repetition. Rarely will I find myself using the same form and content in my confrontations with any two patients. The therapist who attempts to reproduce the technique of confrontation used by others rather than drawing on his own imagination will experience confrontation as a therapeutic straitjacket rather than a crucial tool.

Finally and most important, the successful practice of confrontation requires that the therapist be knowledgeable not only in the "do's and don'ts" of its usage, but also in the theoretical concepts that underlie and define the therapeutic process. Like any art, the art of confrontation is based on a sound understanding of theory and principle. The remainder of this chapter will be devoted to an in-depth analysis of these areas.

CONFRONTATION DEFINED

A confrontation is a therapeutic intervention that demonstrates to the patient a resistance or defense against the operation and expression of the healthy ego or the emerging real self. Defined in this manner, the use of confrontation is not limited to therapy with the borderline personality disorder. What is different, however, is that its role with the borderline patient is one of primary and unparalleled importance. It is the primacy of confrontation in the treatment of the borderline patient that must be emphasized. Such an emphatic statement evokes three questions that must be satisfactorily addressed to justify giving primacy to confrontation: Why does the therapist need to confront the borderline patient? What does the therapist confront in the psychopathology of the patient? How does the therapist confront in order to achieve the therapeutic objectives?

Why Does the Therapist Confront?

Historically, success in the treatment of the borderline personality disorder was long delayed. Chief among the many reasons was a failure to realize that, for the most part, the borderline patient does not come into treatment in order to "get better." Rather, he or she enters treatment primarily to "feel better." Feeling better generally entails one or both of two scenarios: (1) the borderline patient seeks a therapist who will function as a primary and significant other and who will take over in the role of a necessary caretaker, and (2) he seeks a therapeutic situation and a therapist onto whom he can externalize and get rid of, or project, his painful feelings that accompany the withdrawing object relations part unit and the underlying abandonment depression.

If this desire to feel better at any cost was the sole motivation for entering treatment, then individuals with borderline personality disorder could not be helped by psychotherapy. However, experience has shown that most often there is a part of the borderline patient—albeit what seems at times to be a very small part—that does want to "get better." This small part—the patient's impaired real self and reality ego—is developmentally arrested, underinvested, and embattled. Its call for help may appear only infrequently and may manifest itself as a faint, helpless, and anguished whisper at one extreme or a dramatic, self-destructive or self-mutilative act or scream at the other.

It is the therapist's task to ally himself with the impaired real self or healthy ego of the borderline patient. The therapeutic frame—the structure of the therapeutic setting generally—and confrontation more specifically function as a kind of therapeutic "echo chamber" to magnify and clarify the expression of the patient's beleaguered real self. Confrontation enables the therapist to bore through the veritable "garbage heap" of the patient's false, defensive self to make contact with the embattled and impaired real self and to pass the crucial tests and answer the important questions posed by the impaired real self early in treatment: "Can I be helped? Can you help me? Do you take me seriously? Can I trust that you will allow, insist, and expect me to be responsible for my own feelings, thoughts, and actions?"

The answer to all these questions can be communicated to the borderline personality disorder only through the use of confrontation. Statements such as "I can help you" or "I really understand and care" or "You can trust me" will not be believed, because the patient has no reason from his past experience to believe them. Rather, critically needed support for healthy psychological development has been repeatedly withdrawn or unavailable.

The answer to all these questions that the borderline patient must ask during the initial, or testing, phase of treatment determines for patient and therapist the ability to forge a therapeutic alliance. The therapist who passes this initial test offers the patient the hope that the past will not be endlessly repeated in the present, and, therefore, the patient need not endlessly repeat the past in the present (transference acting out). A therapeutic alliance implies the potential for a wholly new relationship in the borderline patient's life, one unlike any that he or she has ever consistently experienced or been able to consistently rely upon. It is a model for a new object relations unit, one that acknowledges and expects and in that way encourages the patient's efforts to build a healthy real self structure. In short, confrontation is a precondition to building a therapeutic alliance with the borderline patient.

The therapist who believes, "I can't confront the borderline patient until I have a therapeutic alliance" or who states, "I must first prove my capacity to be a container or receptacle to 'hold' the patient's rage of feelings of helplessness and dependency" will forgo the therapeutic goal of helping the patient "get better" from the start. The therapist will have to settle for colluding with the patient's false, defensive self and helping the patient to "feel better." The patient's impaired real self will continue to be the victim of this collusion.

What Does the Therapist Confront?

In working with the borderline patient, the therapist must be prepared to confront the pathological defenses and resistances of the patient as these manifest themselves both outside and within the treatment setting. All of the borderline patient's attempts at reality distortion and maladaption through flight from responsibility for thoughts, feelings, and actions must be responded to. They represent the activation of and operations of the patient's false, defensive self. This is of crucial importance, because these attempts at defense and resistance hold sway over the borderline patient, who identifies with the false, defensive self and views it as the real self.

The patient's defenses and resistances uniformly serve to distort his perception of his self-destructiveness and to permit the false self to function through the pathological ego structure without excessive intrapsychic conflict. A confrontation disrupts the defensive operations of the borderline patient. When integrated, it creates conflict—feelings of upset, discomfort, and anxiety—which repeatedly displaces the defensive operation being employed by the patient. For the most part, these defensive operations have enabled the borderline patient to feel good, or taken care of, or at least unconflicted while paying a tremendous cost in terms of adaptation and maturation. The borderline patient can, of course, feel bad. But such bad feelings—often manifested as extensive dysphoria—are associated with the withdrawing object relations part unit and reflect the patient's concern with what he contains and what kind of person he is rather than being associated with intrapsychic conflict.

The borderline patient believes and conveys the notion that he is incapable of containing painful feelings, self-limiting the tendency to act out, and behaving in a mature, adaptive, and realistic manner. He believes and conveys the idea that without the caretaking ministrations of another he cannot manage his life. He believes and conveys the idea that the external world—and those who populate it—are and should be the repository for all the painful and angry feelings and frustrations that make up the patient's life.

Confrontation is the therapist's way, and the only way with the borderline patient, of addressing and challenging these notions and ideas. It is only a patient's conflicts, verbalized rather than acted out, that can become grist for the therapeutic mill.

How Does the Therapist Confront?

In addressing the question "how to?" the therapist must remember that, basically, confrontation is the technical arm of therapeutic neutrality. In working with the borderline patient, "therapeutic neutrality" does not mean that the therapist is a blank screen or operates without a clear therapeutic frame of reference. In fact, the therapist working with the borderline patient must believe, and convey the belief, that the patient is responsible for identifying and containing feelings, verbalizing them in the sessions, and behaving in an adaptive and realistic manner. When a patient fails to do so, the therapist must respond with confrontation. The tactics the therapist employs in confrontation generally fall into four categories, which overlap clinically and can seldom be sharply differentiated. They are:

1. Limit setting
2. Reality testing
3. Clarifying the consequences of maladaptive thoughts, feelings, or behaviors
4. Questioning the motivation for maladaptive thoughts, feelings, or behaviors

Whatever the form of the confrontation, the task of the therapist is to ally himself with the patient's impaired real self and reality ego by stripping away layer upon layer of distortion created by the patient's false, defensive self and pathological ego structure.

In the examples that follow, the tactics just mentioned are usually used in combination to challenge the false, defensive self:

A patient picks up an object to throw in the therapist's office. The therapist would immediately say, "Put that down. I do not allow things to be thrown in the office" (limit setting). This would be followed by asking, "I wonder why you would choose to express yourself by throwing things rather than by talking about how you feel" (questioning the motivation for pathological behavior and inviting exploration).

A patient, about to leave the office after an initial evaluation, suddenly turns to hug the therapist. The therapist might respond with a statement such as, "I do not hug my patients and I do not expect them to hug me" (limit setting). "It is important that whatever feelings you have that you wish to express in the hug, or any other behavior in here, be put into words." This statement is an implicit form of reality testing. It conveys the notion that the therapeutic situation has certain rules and structure; that feelings expressed in words—not behavior or impulsive action—are the vehicles of communication; that the therapist's job is not to be a friend and to make the patient feel better but, rather, to understand the patient's feelings in a way that helps the patient ultimately to modify his behavior.

The patient whose hug is rejected is now likely to respond that the therapist is cold and uncaring—not at all like he or she expected or was led to believe. At this point, the therapist could use an array of clarifications and questions that would confront the patient's pathological defenses, such as:

"It is surprising to me how quickly you perceive me as going from caring to uncaring, from good to bad—like I am two different people" (confrontation of the maladaptive consequences of splitting).

"You act as if 'holding on' to me is easier than 'holding on' to your feelings until the next session" (confrontation of the motivation for clinging).

"I wonder why you get angry when I point out how you put your feelings into action rather than words when this is precisely what has been getting you into trouble in your life and has resulted in your seeking help here" (confrontation of the maladaptive consequences of acting out).

"I wonder why you get so angry when I do my job and expect you to do your part" (confrontation by reality testing of the projection of the rewarding object relations part unit—in other words, the wish/fantasy that the therapist will reward the patient's compliant, infantile, regressed behavior).

"You seem to be trying to make me feel guilty and bad for doing my job as I understand it. Since you have described this as the kind of feeling that has troubled you so often now and in the past, I wonder why this is happening" (confrontation by reality testing, by pointing out the consequences of maladaptive behavior, and by questioning the motivation for the maladaptive behavior of defending the projective identification of the withdrawing object relations part unit—in other words, the wish/fantasy of repeating the past while reversing the roles, wherein now the patient is identified with the powerful, controlling object/parent while the therapist receives the disowned, "bad" part-self representations and feels bad, helpless, and guilty).

The point must be emphasized again that the variety of confrontational interventions is manifold. Each situation of defense and of reality distortion must be confronted by the therapist, but the form and content of the confrontation must take into account the unique patient, therapist, and situation.

At times the most effective confrontation will take the form of the therapist's silence. This is especially true with a patient who is all too eager to let the therapist take over, direct, and do the work of assuming the responsibility for the session, the treatment, and the patient's life.

Learning the tactics (the "how") of confrontation involves patience and determination. The therapist may set appropriate limits in terms of conditions for payment, telephone calls, vacations, and the like, but such expectations must be maintained repeatedly in action and not just in words.

The therapist must learn to constantly monitor the patient's behavior in response to confrontation. The therapist may appropriately reality test a patient's attempt to blur the distinction between feeling helpless and being helpless in an effort to coerce the therapist into directing or managing. However, the therapist may then fail to carry through the confrontation by expecting the patient to act in a more self-activating, self-assertive manner.

The therapist must have a willingness to persevere. The therapist may point out and clarify the consequences of maladaptive activities most of the time but fail to do so some of the time. A therapist's level of confrontation may at times be very high. Failure to confront all pathological or maladaptive activities will not destroy the treatment, but it will slow it down. The therapist and patient will feel as if they are involved in a "therapeutic cha-cha-cha," constantly taking two steps forward and one step back.

Finally, the use of questions is a crucial and central tactic in the art of confrontation. Implicit in this tactic is the expectation that the patient is capable of introspection, insight, and understanding of the roots of his pathology. In addition, the use of questions conveys the message that pathological behavior has meaning that can be understood. It conveys a sense of the patient's ultimate ability to manage the causes as well as the effects of personality disorganization.

SOME OBSTACLES TO EFFECTIVE CONFRONTATION

The therapist who falls prey to the borderline patient's projective defenses will be less able to confront effectively. These patients have available an array of projective techniques that are utilized to organize their representational world and to defend against conflict and painful affects.

When treating a borderline patient, the therapist must avoid stepping into the projection of either the rewarding or the withdrawing object relations part unit. Otherwise the therapist will be unable to maintain a neutral, equidistant stance between the patient's wishes and fears. Specifically, the therapist must avoid projections stemming from the patient's wish and perceived need for a significant, caretaking other and for a receptacle for his abandonment depression, as well as from the patient's fear of abandonment and engulfment.

The following case summary exemplifies the appropriate practice of confrontation as well as potential traps that can undermine treatment.

A therapist in supervision reported that during the course of treatment, the patient had gotten drunk and engaged in dangerous, drug-related acting out. The therapist confronted the patient with the danger that she had put herself in and proceeded to stress that such behavior simply could not continue (an example of limit setting). Because the patient had related her behavior to her feeling that the therapist did not care, the therapist pointed out the necessity of working with her feeling that the therapist did not care rather than acting out the rage.

To this point the therapist had been consistent in his confrontations. His suggestion to the patient that the way to avoid the danger was to work with her feelings continued the process of reality testing (feeling state versus actual state), and suggested that verbalizing these feelings was preferable to acting on them.

At this point, however, the therapist chose to deal with the patient's feeling that the therapist did not exist at those moments of rage not by encouraging exploration of this feeling but, rather, by making the following intervention:

". . . Whenever you approach believing I don't care and feel the intense rage which naturally follows, call me up. Find out I really do care and exist and that I am not gone." By intervening in this manner the therapist has run the risk of stepping into the rewarding unit projection of the patient and, therefore, relieved the patient of the responsibility for containing and exploring his feelings. The notion is also conveyed that the therapist feels the patient is unable to contain the affect and manage his behavior. Further, on a cognitive plane, the therapist has potentially created greater confusion and distortion by accepting that the patient's problem is one of failure in reality testing—specifically, in maintaining object permanence, rather than in failing to achieve object constancy. It is doubtful that the patient was unable to conceive of the therapist's independent existence; it is far more likely that the patient was feeling that he was unable to maintain adaptive functioning without the therapist's presence. In the concluding comments, the therapist was affirming this notion not as a feeling state but, rather, as the actual state of affairs. Finally, the therapist runs the risk of implicitly suggesting that the more out of control, regressed and destructive the patient feels, the more likely he will be to command the therapist's attention and caring—any time, any place.

The therapist would have maintained a more neutral and realistic therapeutic stance had he, for example, stated:

"You seem to be trying to make me responsible for being on call and available to you 24 hours a day to take care of you. I wonder why you are trying so hard to convince me you can't take care of yourself."

Let us look at one additional example of the pitfalls created for the therapist by the patient's use of projective defenses. In the following

description of a supervisory hour, a theme emerges that is one I have
heard countless times.

> I had been pointing out to a resident psychiatrist the need to confront his
> borderline patient with the reality of her self-destructive behavior. The
> resident's initial reaction was, "If I confront the patient with her acting
> out, she will accuse me of being uncaring and critical and trying to
> deflate whatever little self-esteem she has. I will feel that I am not being
> empathic."
>
> I responded that in essence the problem stemmed from his feelings
> and not from the patient's comments—which one must expect from the
> borderline patient. The problem was that he was accepting her
> description of him as being uncaring and critical. In fact, what he should
> now say to the patient was something along the lines of, "Why is it that
> whenever I point out the reality of the mess you have gotten into, you
> feel that I am being critical and uncaring?"

In order to work effectively with the borderline patient, the
therapist must remember that the patient presents in a state of
defense and with a false, defensive self. This is the permanent state of
the patient's life and will become the state of the treatment unless the
necessary interventions are made. Confrontation interrupts the state
of defense only temporarily while propelling the patient into the
borderline triad. Without further and continued confrontation, treatment would again stop and the patient resume his state of defense.
With further confrontation, the process of psychotherapy will
continue.

THE CASE OF A.P.

The following example will demonstrate in greater detail the use of
confrontation during a four-year course of intensive therapy.

The patient was a 22-year-old woman who was first referred by her
therapist of several months, who conveyed two quite different
impressions of the patient when making the referral. While he stated
that the patient needed "analysis" and this was the primary reason for
the referral, he also stated that the patient was being referred because
she had repeatedly damaged his office by throwing things and "the
landlord insisted that I get rid of the patient or that I leave."

As soon as she entered my office for her first appointment, the
patient stood by the door and stated that she had three needs that had
to be met for her to be able to enter into treatment with me: (1) she
needed to know that I would still see her even if she broke something

in my office, because at times she could not control herself; (2) she needed to know that she could call me anytime day or night and that sessions would not be strictly limited to 50 minutes (in fact, she later told me that her previous therapist had always arranged for her to be his last patient of the day so that she might stay in the waiting room as long as she felt she needed to and then would lock up when she left); and (3) she needed to know that she could walk around my office and did not have to stay seated; she insisted that when seated she became too anxious to talk.

It is important to understand the true meaning of these questions or demands. Put into action, these feelings would be a simple expression of the patient's false, defensive self. Put into words, these questions are at one and the same time arising from both the false, defensive self and the impaired real self. Both are asking, "Will you give me what I want and need?" Only one will be satisfied with the answer. If it is the false self, then the treatment will most likely fail. If it is the impaired real self, then treatment will be possible and the first link in the chain of the therapeutic alliance will have been forged.

A.P.'s questions were her way of asking if I could set limits, unlike her former therapist (and her parents before that). Could she rely on me to be any different? Also, was I willing to hold her responsible for acting in an appropriate and adaptive manner? Would I respond to her false, defensive self—a helpless, impulsive child who needed to be excused and tolerated because she was basically unable to care for herself? Her stated need to walk around my office, and her refusal to stay seated, can be viewed as an assertion that acting out was her principal means of expressing her feelings. She rationalized this by stating that it enabled her to think better. In general terms, the patient's tests were geared to determine whether I would step into the rewarding unit, dismantle the therapeutic frame, forgo therapeutic neutrality, and conspire with her false, defensive self.

I replied to A.P. (who was still standing by the door) in the following manner: First, I, and not the landlord, would not tolerate her breaking things in my office. Further, I could not understand why she would use that method of communication rather than telling me her feelings. Second, although she could call me any time, I would not return calls that I felt could wait until the next session. I emphasized that I did not feel useful therapy could take place over the phone. I further questioned her conviction that her problems, which were long standing, needed or could be dealt with in such an immediate and erratic fashion. Finally, I remarked that it was unacceptable for her to constantly walk around the office, because this was a way to dispel her anxieties by converting feelings, literally, into "leaps and bounds" rather than by clarifying and understanding these feelings.

I concluded by stating that if she could live with these answers then therapy might well be able to help her with her problems.

She responded that she didn't like me and that I was cold and distant—not at all like her former therapist—and that I could not help her. (I was not surprised by her response; I knew that the initial volley was not the end of the testing period but, rather, only the beginning.) She went on to request immediate hospitalization. She had been hospitalized twice previously, according to her former therapist, and had been treated with a wide range of medications, none of which seemed helpful. At the very least, she concluded, I must make the hospital arrangements as soon as possible.

Her response to my confrontation seemed to me to have two meanings: one related to the false, defensive self and the other to the impaired real self. First, my refusal to step into the rewarding unit and resonate with her false self had led to the immediate activation of the withdrawing object relations part unit and the object representation associated with it—cold, rejecting, attacking, and potentially abandoning. On the other hand, from the impaired real self came her need to test me further and to determine whether I cared enough to persevere.

I replied that I needed to know more about her before I could possibly determine whether hospitalization was necessary. I wondered what kind of person she was and what she found intolerable about her life that was causing her to seek treatment—beyond the obvious feeling that she was someone who could not care for and control herself.

She responded by sitting down and providing me with some minimal initial information about her present and past life. She described herself as a frustrated writer who had dropped out of college to take an unsatisfying job. She had also recently been rejected by her boyfriend, and this had resulted in a great deal of depression and rage. It was, in fact, this event that had led to her most recent angry outburst in the former therapist's office. She further described herself as a person who could not control her behavior and who needed a great deal of overt affection and evidence of caring. Finally she began to talk about growing up with her parents and about the rage and guilt that accompanied her during much of that time.

During the 20 minutes or so that she spent providing this information, she grew progressively less restless and more depressed. However, when she began to switch from talking about her "needs" and acting out to talking about her feelings and fears, I anticipated the activation of the third arm of the borderline triad: defense. This was in fact the case.

As the session grew to a close, she again requested that I hospitalize her. I stated that I saw no reason to do so based on what I now knew of her, and I felt that she could work in treatment as an outpatient. But, I added, if she felt between now and the next session that she needed hospitalization for reasons not at all clear to me she could present herself at any emergency room. In order to emphasize my refusal to conspire with her false, defensive self, I added that she did not need my permission, agreement, or help in order to get hospitalized.

She exploded in anger and insisted that she would not leave my office until I had arranged for hospitalization. I responded that while she seemed to be making quite an effort to convince me that she was out of control, I felt that she could control herself, and I would hold her responsible for her behavior now and throughout the course of her therapy.

She dropped the subject of hospitalization but stated that she needed more time and did not want to leave the office yet. I responded that we could talk about those feelings next time and that the session was over. She responded by stating that she could not and would not leave. I only repeated that the session was over. She repeated that she would not leave.

At this point I became aware of feeling helpless, trapped, and increasingly angry—all of which alerted me to the projective identification that was taking place. A.P. was projecting into me her false, defensive self representation as helpless, trapped, and enraged while identifying with the object representation that was perceived as powerful, controlling, and sadistic. Knowledge of the dynamics involved enabled me to gain control over the feelings being generated and to make the necessary therapeutic interventions.

Realizing that I was not helpless or trapped—and therefore had no reason to "fight"—I simply arose and stated that I would not conduct therapy in an atmosphere of duress or coercion or emotional blackmail of any sort. If she did not leave immediately, I would be forced to throw her out myself or call the police if necessary. In either case, treatment could not then continue.

She stormed out of my office. I wasn't certain that she would return, but I was certain that I had acted therapeutically.

A.P. did in fact enter into treatment, during the course of which she returned over and over to the questions and issues she had raised in the first minutes of her initial session. The need for confrontation continues throughout the course of treatment, although, as was the case with A.P., the relative time spent on confrontation becomes less and less. Over time in A.P.'s treatment, action still replaced words on occasion, but acting out became more predictable and less frequent. Further, the intensity and amount of confrontation required to bring the acting out to the patient's awareness lessened as A.P. was able to self-limit herself. As an example, she might feel impelled to quit her job, but she would now be able to pause long enough to confront herself with the questions I formerly had to ask: "Is this self-destructive?" and "How will my bills get paid?"

A.P. was increasingly able to experience false, defensive, and self-destructive aspects of her behavior as dystonic. She had previously considered such actions to be part of her basic identity, but she now came to feel real frustration with the false self when she acted against her own best interests.

The following excerpt from a session one year into treatment demonstrates the continued role of confrontation in the circular process of therapy. Although there is a growing therapeutic alliance and the beginning of working through, the need for confrontation has resurfaced. In this instance, A.P. had been contacted by her former boyfriend, who, although involved with someone else whom he indicated he would never give up, was acting seductively toward the patient and stimulating her reunion fantasies.

A.P.: Well, do I fight for him again?

R.K.: I think you mean, do you fight for you again?

A.P.: I guess you're right. It's tough though. I need to accept the end. I have to really recognize it as the end, as just my wanting to hold on—to cling. I don't want to keep repeating the past over and over. Each time I have to work that much harder and it's taking such a long time. . . (she paused and I waited to see whether she would continue to activate herself or whether she would defend). . . I think I have to go with my instincts and call him (she had defended, and this necessitated a confrontation).

R.K.: Are you sure you can distinguish your instincts from a withdrawal symptom?

A.P.: What do you mean?

R.K.: You haven't been opting for your old fixes for a while and you have been feeling uncomfortable and more depressed. Pick up the phone to call your friend and, like magic, you will feel better *and* be right back where you started.

A.P.: Why do you insist on calling it a fix?

R.K.: Because that is what it is.

A.P.: Well, it seems stupid to me. . . (again she paused, was silent, and I waited to see if the confrontation had been integrated or whether there would be more defense). . .The worst part is losing a friend. But I couldn't be a friend to him now. I couldn't give him a commitment. My life isn't together yet; not going in the right direction. I have to get my head together first. How real was the feeling for him anyhow? I guess some people hook up out of need, not choice. I guess it's wrong to hold on to the past when it keeps you from growing up. Oh God, all the time that has been wasted in my life. These patterns from when I was such a little kid. It's scary. It hurts.

Over the ensuing months her depression deepened, and she reported feeling depressed much of the time. However, she was functioning better than ever. In the following vignette from the working through phase, the patient is dealing with guilt toward her parents, another component part of the abandonment depression. At this stage the need for confrontation is infrequent and quickly integrated.

A.P.: I feel so guilty when I don't visit her even though I know I'm a good daughter. I see her when I can, and I'm more sensitive to her needs than my father, who is there all the time. I think I feel guilty when I don't act the part of the child she still wants me to be and still sees me as. What if I am myself? Am I afraid she will die and I will feel guilty forever over what I didn't do for her? Why can't I make her understand? Why can't she care about me?

R.K.: You mean, why can't she be a different person?

A.P.: (sobbing) Why can't she just change?

R.K.: The real question, I think, is why you continue to insist that she give you something that she doesn't have and therefore can't give.

A.P.: (still crying) You're right. It's stupid. I keep expecting her to change and I keep going back and trying to get it. I remember growing up, always expecting and hoping and never getting anything from her. The only person who seemed to understand what I needed was my grandmother. (She went on to recall cold winter mornings when her grandmother would make hot chocolate for her. She loved those mornings and her

grandmother, who died when she was 12.) I still can't understand why
Mother never stands up for me.

R.K.: You still hope to get hot chocolate from her?

A.P.: You're right. I know it. I hate it. But what should I do. How do I stop it.
Tell me!

R.K.: Now you're asking *me* for a recipe for hot chocolate?

A.P.: (laughing) I know better than to ask you for anything.

Later in the working through stage, suicidal depression and homicidal rage emerged in tandem as the full extent of the abandonment
depression was worked through. For A.P., as for most borderline
patients, the abandonment depression was most intense and expressed
most clearly in the feeling, remembered and relived, that if she
separated and individuated and built a real self structure, she would
die or her mother would die. Defenses at this point in her treatment
were largely shorn away, and during the later stages of the working
through phase and the final stage of separation, confrontation gave
way largely to interpretation and communicative matching.

It is, however, confrontation—the art of confrontation—that is at the
center of the treatment of the borderline patient. Confrontation is the
catalyst that makes the therapeutic process work and propels it to its
final goal.

Chapter 13

Confrontation of Hysterical Transference Acting Out

Candace Orcutt, Ph.D.

This chapter describes the first two years of my work with Annie (a pseudonym), a hysterical borderline personality of the most chaotic and colorful sort. She was tyrannical, frantic, quick-minded, seductive, alarming, and always changing. Annie had been the picture of the clinically baffling hysterical patient who drove therapists to despair and recurrently maneuvered herself into the limbo of chronic hospitalization.

However, with the appropriate therapeutic support, Annie is now getting better. Her capacity to change is as dramatic as her personality. Recently, she told me: "I could have been 'Sick Annie' all my life if I hadn't found the right therapy. I could be locked up somewhere. My God, there must be a lot of people like me who are still in hospitals, who are letting their lives go down the drain because they don't know any better—and their therapists are letting them get away with it!"

I had been working with Annie for over two years in twice-a-week confrontive psychotherapy, but her treatment really began six years ago, when she first applied to the Masterson Group and was seen by Dr. Jacinta Lu Costello. Dr. Costello made the diagnostic assessment and set the boundaries for treatment that established the foundation of all subsequent psychotherapy for Annie.

This is Dr. Costello's description of Annie, of her history and the nature of beginning treatment:

Annie, age 29, was referred to the Masterson Group immediately prior to her release from the psychiatric inpatient service. This hospitalization was her fifth in six years and had been precipitated by severe regression following the separation from her husband. The previous hospitalizations were precipitated by suicidal gestures following the break-ups of other relationships.

Although a complete history was not available at the time of the referral, it was known that Annie had had functional difficulties from the onset of puberty. Although she had completed high school and a one-year business school program, her performance and attendance throughout were erratic. From puberty on, her weight vacillated by as much as 50 to 75 pounds, she was picked up repeatedly for shoplifting, and she made multiple aborted efforts at outpatient treatment. In almost every therapeutic effort, Annie would improve functionally within the first month and then deteriorate. Her subsequent demands upon the therapist would then escalate, and, when they were not complied with, she would either threaten to take, or actually would take, an overdose of pills. In two cases, her therapists refused to see her again after discharge.

The most recent hospitalization followed the break-up of her four-year marriage. Although the first years were described as idyllic, the relationship deteriorated as Annie became more dependent and demanding. Her husband finally left. Annie remained out of the hospital for four months following the break-up by moving home, entering treatment, and gradually demanding more and more from her parents and therapist. She insisted one parent remain with her at all times. Her parents finally requested hospitalization for Annie when she insisted on sleeping with them.

This time, Annie had been hospitalized for 15 months. During her stay, she was described by staff as "bright, articulate, demanding, pushy, and manipulative." She was diagnosed as having a Borderline Personality Disorder with hysterical features. At the time of her discharge, staff was angry and frustrated with her. They felt that, while Annie expressed a desire to be more self-sufficient and responsible, she thwarted every effort to realize it.

Before I met Annie, I knew the following: her track record since puberty, and perhaps before, was poor; separations precipitated all hospitalizations; she had frustrated her husband, parents, therapists, and hospital staff to the point where they had fled. And, finally, she was impulsive.

From a positive point of view, I knew she was articulate and bright, seemed to have been successful in engaging people, and on occasion demonstrated the capacity to take initiative and responsibility on her own.

I began seeing Annie four times a week. The primary aim of the treatment was to foster more behavioral control and to alter Annie's self-destructive pattern of managing her life and feelings. Although Annie articulated her agreement with these goals, her behavior suggested that she viewed therapy as a place where you come to *feel* better. Each time Annie actually considered behaving responsibly, she became extremely anxious, and in order to dissipate the painful affects associated with autonomy, she would avoid, act out, or look to me to take over her life.

While the dynamics were clear from the outset, Annie's potential for control was not. Annie was not convinced she was capable, was scared to death to even try, and used every available opportunity to demonstrate to me that I was asking for something she couldn't deliver. I wasn't sure that Annie had the wherewithal to control her behavior. But I also knew that, if I varied my stance by giving in to her regressive demands, I would lose all therapeutic leverage.

Dr. Costello held the line while Annie threatened and maneuvered to be taken care of; when thwarted, she called Dr. Costello a "cold bitch," phoned endlessly, traveled repeatedly to emergency rooms, twice was hospitalized, and frequently persuaded doctors and family members to contact Dr. Costello and question the competency of her treatment approach. But in time, Dr. Costello's professional stamina brought results:

> Luckily, Annie demonstrated increasing strength. Instead of throwing them, Annie began to describe how she would have temper tantrums to get her own way. She felt that often therapists had complied with her demands when they should not have. She warned me that this demandingness would probably continue, and she hoped I was strong enough to take it.

Through confrontation and clinical consistency, Dr. Costello established a therapeutic frame or "holding environment" for Annie, and Annie began to use her energies for (instead of against) herself.

Unfortunately, circumstances intervened when Dr. Costello left the Masterson Group. Annie resumed with another practitioner who was familiar with the Masterson Approach, helped Annie through the separation from Dr. Costello, and then determined that Annie could benefit from a maintenance dosage of phenelzine sulfate (Nardil); however, under the impact of Annie's behavior, the new clinician began to slip from the therapeutic stance.

I began to work with Annie when her current therapy had reached a crisis point.

Annie had her therapist on the run, along with an entire day care center. Her therapist had cut Annie's sessions to once a week, and had referred her to day care for the balance of treatment. Probably reacting to the growing tenuousness of treatment (and, of course, testing as usual), Annie began to act out with a vengeance: stealing, getting drunk, running around in public semi-dressed, telephoning her therapists with frantic persistence (at their home phones when she could), and generally carrying on in such a way as to expose the vulnerability and fray the patience of all those involved in trying to help her.

Individual and day care therapists met with Annie and her family and said that Annie would have to go into residential treatment. Annie, to her credit, said she would be damned if she would give up the gains she had made: her own apartment and her household of four cats. She returned to the Masterson Group with the blessings of the individual therapist and the day care center.

In her initial session with me, Annie presented herself as aggressive, incisively intelligent, emotionally sensitive and labile, and a slob. A veteran of psychotherapy, she had come to look me over, and told me she needed a therapist she couldn't con, who would hold the line. She said that she tended to trip herself up, especially when she started to feel better, and thought that her sickness somehow held her family together. Over the next few weeks, she repeated that I hadn't seen her at her worst, and was worried whether I could tolerate her. Over the next few weeks, as she had done with Dr. Costello, she gave us both a chance to find out just how much the traffic would bear.

Annie came into my office licking an ice cream cone, and attired in something like a mini-negligee. She faced me through impenetrable sunglasses, and petulantly dumped responsibility for the session on me. This was testing elevated to the level of a challenge, and I had my colleague's experience to build on. I began my verbal confrontation on the same level as Annie's nonverbal communication: "Is this your idea of how you build your self-respect here? What's the ice cream? You tell me you're here to stop kidding yourself, but you act like you're at a party! And that dress—if that's what you're wearing—are you telling me you expect to be taken seriously when you come out in public as if you're sleepwalking?"

In response to this confrontation, which had matched the level of her challenge, she pulled herself together in a dignified, introspective way, and I had my first impression of Annie as she could be. That weekend she controlled her drinking, and told me later that modifying her behavior had brought her in touch with fundamental feelings of rebelliousness (feelings she could not be aware of while she was channeling them into behavior).

These first sessions were to set the tone for the first year of therapy. Essentially, this year was devoted to the reestablishment of the therapeutic frame, or holding environment. Annie strove to maintain her gains—to keep her apartment and hold her new job. Persistently, she sidetracked these priorities with momentary crises, but confrontation held her to the presenting problem: she wanted to keep her apartment, her autonomy, and to do so she would have to observe and alter how she stood in the way of her own goals.

Only by contrasting her maladaptive behavior with her chosen goals could I begin to provide a frame of reference within which she could start to perceive the borderline triad in operation. Otherwise, the emotional and behavioral chaos swamped reason and observing distance.

Repeatedly, I returned to her initial statement that she undermines her own progress—for instance, makes a statement of positive intent, then almost at once does something self-destructive—and so avoids the feelings attached to a responsible attitude toward herself. Unfortunately, I would point out, avoidance of the feeling means avoidance of change, as well.

By the end of the year, as Annie began to curtail her acting out and increasingly tolerated her emerging feelings, she began to allow her real self freer expression.

During this first year, Annie began to be aware of, and let go of, a false self she named "Sick Annie." Whenever she began to get her life in order, she would complain of feeling "empty" or "bored"—the beginning of feelings of abandonment depression—and would start to act out. She claimed that shoplifting provided her with a sense of excitement, and that she was uncomfortable feeling "normal."

I asked why she seemed to prefer setting herself up as a mental case and a victim. She replied that it was the only identity she knew. This insight was reinforced by a dream (curtailing of acting out leads to internalizing phenomena, such as insight and dreaming). In her dream, all her relatives surrounded her and called her schizophrenic. The dream expressed not a criticism, but a command.

Annie began to realize that her family had needed her to act crazy to create a diversion from problems not of her making. She then expressed profound sadness over the years wasted in acting crazy. She said that she knew Dr. Costello had understood that the craziness was an act (a manifestation of the false self), and she expressed bitterness over the time lost with therapists who had bought into it.

Annie became increasingly able to experience abandonment depression—to give up the frenetic, "crazy" self that satisfied the needs of her family (and herself) to pass the buck, and so avoid individual responsibility. Part of the time she struggled with an "empty feeling" that marked this psychic transition, and felt bewildered, as though she found herself in an unfamiliar place. Then she would maladaptively ward off growing depression and ambivalence by creating another diversionary crisis: by jeopardizing her lease and her job with on-stage battles with her boyfriend, and by acting out in her treatment with repeated phone calls between sessions.

Annie would call me from a bar, between sessions or during the time of her sessions, drunk, enraged, and despairing. I, in turn, would point out that she was diluting the effect of her sessions by calling instead of coming in on schedule to talk, as was her agreement. I pointed out that these calls were often followed by silent sessions. I said she was avoiding or sabotaging her sessions in order to avoid direct expression of her feelings to me, and ultimately to herself (this type of here-and-now interpretation adds effectiveness to confrontations that have become familiar to the patient and are partially integrated).

By the end of the year, she had built enough confidence in her sessions to try out her feelings on me directly (once the initial line of confrontation has been absorbed by the patient, the resistance shifts increasingly from the external world to the therapeutic sphere of the sessions and the transference). She first practiced on her boss, creating such a scene at work that he called the police and she was taken to the emergency room of a nearby hospital. Once there, she realized she had outgrown that particular game, and used her manipulative skills to get herself discharged. She returned to work to face the music, and was moved that her co-workers stood up for her, and that her boss took her back. She then focused her feelings on me.

Annie came in smoking, eating, yelling, slamming the door. She cut off my attempts to intervene and drowned out my voice. I escalated my confrontations to verbally match her actions—that is, to a point where I could be heard. I shouted her full name, and inquired whether she was interested at all in hearing any feedback from me, whom she was paying. I reminded her (at full volume) that she was throwing away her therapy as she had lamented throwing away her life. Finally, I asserted that therapy could not be conducted at a shouting level, that this was another way of avoiding the work, and I refused to be a part of it. Once again, I was only speaking in a tone of voice she could hear—I think, from her point of view, I was not shouting at all, but using the tone of voice the family used (only, for once, using it to set limits).

She began to compose herself and speak more quietly, and the depression began to come through. She said she fought me because I made her face her feelings of hopelessness and craziness. It was easier to go on the warpath than to become aware of deep anxiety and loneliness.

As long as she continued to report her feelings, I simply listened. Once she began to attack herself (instead of me) and tried to manipulate me into scapegoating her, I confronted her attempt to recreate her family role as "Sick Annie" ("You tell me you regret the time wasted conforming to your family's need to blame someone for their problems, but now you want me to treat you as they do!").

When she began to build a panic around the notion her mind was playing tricks on her, I commented: "You are escalating your anxiety. You are not psychotic, but you would rather drive yourself crazy than be yourself and face your own feelings." She pulled together and told me the source of her anxiety: everyone lately was telling her how much better she seemed, and it was difficult to relinquish her sick, family identity. She was still trying to trip herself up, to distract herself from knowing she was better and did not need to remain a dependent child.

This first year of treatment reestablished the therapeutic frame in two essential ways. First, I helped Annie set firm limits for herself, much as one would contain a child in a temper tantrum until the child can take hold of itself again. Second, I systematically confronted the contradictory goals of Annie's reality ego and pleasure ego, questioning her maladaptive splitting defense—for instance, how she expected to keep a job if she did what she pleased and not what she was hired to do, or how she thought she could get the benefits of therapy while missing sessions when the feelings got difficult. In effect, I refused to be the rewarding unit: the overly permissive mother who let her run wild and run the show. She subsequently saw me as the withdrawing unit—as someone who refused to let her have her cake and eat it too— and she flew into a rage. When I confronted her rage, pointing out that it was serving to defeat her own goals, she began to allow depression to come through. With some toleration of depression came insight into her crazy act—"Sick Annie"—a false self that she used to evade responsibility and to defend against a deeper feeling of real depression and craziness.

Annie realized after her first year of work that her chaotic behavior, promiscuity, rages, drinking, and shoplifting were all ways to avoid the responsibility of growing up, because growing up was associated with feelings of hopelessness, emptiness, loneliness, self-loathing, and craziness. As she began to catch on, she internalized my limit setting, and confronted her own maneuverings. A pattern of shifting behavior began, in which she would activate herself positively, then plunge into chaos, then pull out again.

This pattern still continues but is approaching a more realistic level. She seems to have satisfactorily tested her ability (like a child) to run, fall, pick herself up and run again, while depending on my continuous presence for support in a rapprochement-like way. As her own ego strengthens, she provides her own sense of continuity. This sense of continuity derives from the knowledge of my being there and the discovery that life is not a choice between running free and falling down but, rather, is mastery over a process that includes both.

Then and now, Annie continues her maintenance dosage of Nardil. Annie firmly believes that the Nardil helps her to keep her anxiety level under control, so that she is less likely to work herself into a panic. She has allowed herself an experience of mourning in relation to the medication, as well, for it represents a delimitation of herself—a point at which her conscious will has to give way to biological processes.

The second year of therapy saw two significant advances in Annie's treatment: within the sessions, she began to show more insight and experience more feelings and memories. Outside the sessions, she functioned on a consistently higher level, and tolerated both success and separation in a way she never had before.

Margaret Mahler stresses that the phase of development critical to the psychic maturation of patients like Annie runs on a double track:

separation *and* individuation. For the patient like Annie, whose defenses (acting out, splitting, projection) operate on the more primitive level, I believe the issue of separation, laden with feelings of panic and persecution, represents the most challenging aspect of the abandonment depression. Annie, as she individuates, has been able to anticipate the resurgence of depression, and no longer catastrophizes over it for more than a day or so at a time—her recoveries are quicker, and the depressive descent is shallower. The separation issue—terror of nonbeing, of reprisal and eradication from some omnipotent source—is gradually becoming an issue she is willing to face. This not only relates to the interpersonal experience of gaining confidence from healthy emotional support; it also depends on the building of an inner sense of encouragement, or self-worth.

After Annie was able to be angry at me directly (and no longer needed to apologize at the end of the session, or call back after the session to say she was sorry), she then began to express positive feelings for me and for her therapy. She said: "I don't know what to call this relationship we have. You aren't my friend, but you're more than a friend. This is like a kind of love." And, as she found me both hateful and lovable, she began to see how both qualities could exist and coexist in herself, as well. She began to dress consistently well, with enthusiasm and with flair. She lost 30 pounds. She completed two years at her job, and told me with satisfaction about her raise: "$25,000 a year! How's that for an ex-loonie?"

As she experienced herself as more competent and whole, she was able to face deeper, more symbiotic anxieties, and to then experience the consolidation of a strong and good inner sense, a positive introject. Annie noticed that when she was aware of feelings, she didn't need to steal. So, she reasoned, she stole as a substitute for feeling. She decided to experiment by not stealing, and subsequently reported a strange event. Alone in her apartment, she had sensed "evil forces in the room, trying to suck me up." It was "like a nightmare." She impulsively telephoned her mother (it was three o'clock in the morning), and then "felt something I had never felt before." The feeling was that her mother was *"really there."* She associated this experience to similar (but unresolved) terrible feelings she had endured in the course of her acute hospitalizations. I asked her if she had had nightmares as a child (I was remembering her insistence on sleeping with her parents prior to the last hospitalization). She said yes, and that, after the nightmares, she would cry for her mother. So this strange experience simply became a child's cry in the night that had waited thirty years to be answered, as Annie at last learned to believe in the reliability of her own existence.

So Annie was making progress on the individuative track, and was building inner structure that would support her progress in healthy separation. This was confirmed by a "first" (as she said): Annie threw out her boyfriend, and felt stronger for the separation, for which she took full responsibility.

Annie had clung to George the entire time she had been in treatment with me. In many ways George's personality paralleled Annie's, and, like a typical borderline couple, they alternately rescued and undermined each other. When one was up, the other was down, they always kept a crisis going, and, in short, neither took consistent responsibility for their individual selves. But, finally, Annie had had enough. The separation was not easy, and Annie regressed. I received drunken phone calls from bars, there were missed sessions, and Annie brought George along on one occasion (this was not altogether impulsive, as we had discussed the possibility; Annie seemed to need to bring George in as a transitional device to help her to anchor better in reality). For awhile, Annie could not clearly differentiate her feelings from George's. She could not decide whether he was a victim or a user, and was afraid of misjudging him until she was able to get beyond her guilt and see *herself* as *both* victim and user. Then it was easier to deal with him realistically: as a con artist she had to protect herself from, but also as a confused human being deserving of her forgiveness.

In the process, the break-up took epic proportions. Annie was alternately strong and devastated, and appeared for her sessions acting accordingly. And then it was over. For the first time, Annie had set a limit in an intense personal relationship and felt as though the ground was still solid under her feet.

Delighted with her accomplishment, Annie decided to try another "first," and went on vacation, out of the country, and without her parents. She came through with flying colors and brought me photographs so that I could share her pleasure. The rapprochement-like quality of such moments is unmistakable, and they provide an additional source of satisfaction for the therapist, who always hoped such a turning point was attainable but knew that only the patient could take the decisive step.

Chapter 14

Confrontation of Passive-Aggressive Transference Acting Out

Richard Fischer, Ph.D.

Confrontation of a passive-aggressive borderline patient requires patience, persistence, and a refusal to be drawn into directive procedures or to use confrontation as an angry retaliation to the patient's provocations. This type of patient will use passive-avoidant maneuvers to avoid self-activation and the abandonment depression that accompanies all self-directed initiative. The therapist's refusal to be drawn off course will be rewarded as his patient becomes more involved, improves his ability to manage affect, and to function.

CASE HISTORY: MR. D.B.

Identifying data. The patient is a 45-year-old Catholic single man who lives by himself in New York City. He was employed as an architect in a prestigious firm, but his career had stagnated over the years.

Chief complaint. Mr. D.B. was referred to the Masterson Group by a friend. He had seen several therapists over the past ten years with little improvement or satisfaction. He felt depressed, dissatisfied with his interpersonal relationships and his lack of occupational progress, and suspicious about people (claiming that they used him for their own ulterior motives), and had developed what was an excessive drinking problem over the years in order "to avoid feeling things." He felt generally out of control, passive, and unable to assert himself.

History of Present Illness

Mr. D.B. sought treatment after he changed jobs and discovered that he was still unhappy, unable to manage his subordinates at work, and chronically disappointed because people never reliably met his needs and would desert him if he moved out of his submissive roles. He accused therapists of being exploitive, judgmental, and irresponsible. He tried to form various "contracts" with therapists under which he would pay them only if they produced results and made him happy. He would cite various articles on the ineffectiveness of psychotherapy.

He said that all his life he looked for "partners" in parents, friends, girlfriends, and therapists who would support his interests. He always felt used by the "partner," disappointed and abandoned. He claimed that no partner had ever protected or supported his interests. Although he supervised staff members at work, he felt angry that they did not do their jobs automatically. He felt unable to assert himself and would cover for them and not hold them responsible. He felt overwhelmed by his administrative responsibilities at work. Throughout his life, he had moved from one intense intimate relationship to another. He felt unable to be by himself and needed women to create an "emotional equilibrium." He felt the incessant need to fit into a woman's demands and expectations of him, and felt deserted when he refused to comply. He said abandonment left him feeling terrified. To make matters worse, he usually chose married or unavailable woman who were abusive and provocative. His verbalizations sounded like an endless rationalized litany as to why people should be responsible for his life.

Relevant Past History and Family History

The patient was born and raised in Florida. His parents divorced when he was 8 years old.

He described his mother as selfish, manipulative, and never serving his needs. She reinforced his sense of badness and was intolerant of aggressiveness. He said that his mother "kept him off balance" throughout his childhood. After the divorce he lived with his mother until he was 14, when he withdrew and became sullen and unhappy. He said his mother refused to be accountable and only used him for her own selfish interests.

He felt more positive about his father. However, as a teenager while living with his father he realized that his father had left him with his mother because he could not tolerate the responsibilities of adult life. His father told the patient to get women to care for him. Although the father was more supportive than the mother, his concern would terminate as soon as the patient disagreed with him. The patient accused his father of being judgmental and disinterested in his "real self." His feelings were similar to his father's in that both passively surrendered to women's needs and then felt engulfed.

He described his childhood as being lonely and isolated with an inner sense of badness.

The Course of Treatment

The patient began treatment three times a week demanding to make a "contract." He said that all therapists had refused to be responsible for treatment. He insisted that I should get paid if I produced results and forfeit payment if results were not forthcoming. He said that psychotherapy research had shown that I was providing a service of dubious value. He said that he felt very angry at the women in his life. They had made various promises and he was always left feeling rejected, abandoned, disappointed, and enraged. He said he kept his end of the bargain but they broke theirs.

As I sat and listened he became angry and provocative, claiming that he paid me to do something. He said that he had many good ideas in his work but they never got off the ground because people did not keep their end of the contract. He insisted that I make a deal with him about payment for my services. When I refused he became more angry and demanding.

I slowly took hold of my shock, dismay, and anger about his provocative demandingness. I told him that all his contracts had failed and left him feeling disappointed and enraged. Why should we start this relationship on the same footing? He said, "You are just like all other therapists—refusing to be accountable." He said all his contracts were fair. He kept his end of the bargain but the women began to withdraw, express anger, and eventually left him.

That response immediately seemed familiar because I already had one foot out the door. I became silent and used my withdrawal as an impotent weapon. His demands became more insistent. He claimed that he would not continue in therapy unless I made "a deal." I was secretly hoping that he would stick to his word and terminate treatment.

His assaults and demands would escalate; he would sit silently refusing; he said he would not produce his thoughts because this was a one-way contract. We had reached a stalemate. I became aware that his demand for a contract was prototypical of the dilemma of his life. He refused to activate himself, made demands that others be responsible for his life, and drifted into a state of impotent despair and rage. His life had become a perpetual acting out of symbiotic relatedness in order to preserve the illusion of an omnipotent caretaker. This continuous externalization of internal conflict would enable him to conceal and mask depression and painful affect.

In order to facilitate the therapeutic task of containment of affect, I had to confront the externalization and acting out that were supported by his intellectualization and rationalizations. During the next session I was ready to face the issues. He said he would not speak until I gave a guarantee of success.

I told him that it was unfortunate that he was so bent on destroying any chance he had for treatment. He said, "You'll never be responsible." I said that I was puzzled by his repetitive reaction. He always seemed to let his ideas fall by the wayside whenever he couldn't get someone to sign his contracts. He said that was a problem with others. I said, "Not if it is your life that is getting nowhere."

He looked puzzled. He saw that I meant business. The party was over and treatment began. He tried once again, by saying, "Maybe if I talk and you respond we can get started." I said, "You don't seem to understand; it is your job to present your thoughts and feelings, and if you don't it will be your treatment that will founder." He grinned and gave a coy smirk. He said, "I guess you got my number." This was a successful passing of the first major test of treatment.

The patient's demand for an acting out of symbiotic relatedness had been challenged—the "contract" had become the metaphor for his symbiotic demands. This misconception of a sharing partnership had been confronted and presented for the destructive element that it was in his life. The patient responded positively to this confrontation, which was a sign of his ability to control defense and contain acting out.

The picture shifted within the first six months of treatment. The patient reported feeling passive and nonproductive in his work, unable to assert himself in any area of his life. He felt immobilized and helpless. He began to drink heavily, and used women to fight off feelings of loneliness. He had moved his demands for a rewarding unit to the external environment.

He came to session complaining that his work was not progressing. He had no control over his relationships. He felt invaded by his girlfriends and would passively submit to their wishes. He felt unable to protect his interests and felt enraged that they used him for their own ends. He complained that his work was at a standstill and going nowhere.

I said, "How can anything change, if you are sitting and waiting for it to happen with your work, with your girlfriends, and with me." He became angry: "I'm trying to do a lot." I told him that he was sitting and hoping that it would be done for him, but waiting for Godot wouldn't do a thing for the situation.

The "contract" and its manifestations were once again challenged. He became thoughtful and produced memories about his narcissistic mother using him for her own interests. He sat passively waiting for her to change and she never did. He felt that his father, although more supportive, abandoned him to fend for himself with his mother. He saw his father as weak and unable to assert himself with women. He said that he and his father both used women to bolster weak self-esteem. His father told him to have several women and not put all his eggs in one basket; that way he would be less vulnerable. He said that his father's philosophy made sense.

I said it was unfortunate that he gave up so easily on himself, which left him vulnerable on all fronts. He said, "That makes me very sad. It is up to me to manage everything. I think it is beyond me. I get this feeling of inner badness and I feel like I can't handle it." I told him that his army of support could never do it for him. The idea of containment of affect had been planted, as well as the attempt to seat the conflict in his head.

This patient presented an enormous problem with self-activation. He managed to avoid all personal responsibility by forming contracts and making demands that other people take over for him. When that was confronted his abandonment depression emerged more clearly.

After a year of treatment, he came to his session feeling panicked and desperate. He had a ritual with his girlfriend in which he was to tell her how he was feeling and she had to acknowledge and confirm his experience. His girlfriend refused to listen and withdrew, and he felt panicked and enraged. He said she was unwilling "to share" in a relationship "and that was why he was feeling so bad."

I told him that this was not sharing but, rather, dumping himself on his girlfriend. He became furious. He said if she wasn't available for him in this way then he could not handle his emotions—his anger, his jealousy, and his depression—and that's what a relationship was for. I told him that his relationships would fail as long as he insisted that a woman handle his emotions for him.

He began to feel panic and rage. He said that his father said he should never expose himself to these feelings and should have many women to protect him from this inner turmoil. I told him that he and his father had the same problem in that they both glorified dependency and had developed it into an art form. He said that his father had given him an illusion that through childhood had protected him from his mother's assaults on his personality. He was afraid that, if treatment took away that illusion, he would be left with feelings of inner badness.

The confrontations of the acting out and the demands for a rewarding unit left the patient more depressed. His adaptive functioning improved, and his relationships with women were still characterized by clinging but were less chaotic.

Although this patient's father gave him an illusion of protection, both parents treated his real self with contempt and devaluation. Thus, any urge to activate the self led to agitation, depression, and a retreat toward dependent clinging. The combination of maternal contempt for the real self and paternal advice to avoid self-activation led to the present dilemma: a man who was constantly struggling to avoid personal responsibility and the depression that accompanied any self-expression and initiative. The end product was stagnation in his work and turbulent relationships.

During the next phase of treatment, the patient began to move more deeply into dreams, feelings, memories, and fantasies that centered on homicidal rage toward caretakers and reparative motives. His dreams focused on people dying in tidal waves and volcanic eruptions. They became less disguised when he dreamed of knifing pigs and then feeling a need to stop the blood flow. He also dreamed of running over bodies in his automobile and turning back to see the damage that was left behind. He then recalled early memories of trying to kill a childhood friend for a minor humiliation and being restrained only by external force by his parents. He became aware of how angry he was, how his parents had failed him, and his rage at being on his own. His sessions were more self-directed, and his demands for my direction had disappeared. The patient was now working on his own and was affectively involved in the treatment.

Acting out and affective reexperiencing of the self are mutually exclusive, as was demonstrated in the work with this patient. The patient began to feel fear over his anger and experienced a sense of loneliness and isolation. He began to drink and to cling to women, and his work suffered. I had to confront the patient and connect these behaviors to his discomfort with his affect and especially his rage. The patient became angry and said, "You don't have to feel it—I do." I said, "Once again your 'partner' is called in to help you avoid your feelings and your self." He sat silently, withdrew, and refused to work. He said that he could not face these feelings and I lacked compassion since I was unwilling to help him. I told him that I was different from him and his father. I believed that he could manage these feelings and that unless he was willing to commit himself to this, his treatment would stagnate. He left angrily and slammed the door.

He continued to have trouble activating himself, and felt unable to manage his employees. He said he could not master this. I told him that there was a difference between *would* not and *could* not, and focused on his enormous resistance to managing his work and his feelings in treatment. He realized he equated self-assertion with violence. He remembered that his mother required passivity from him and was too depressed to deal with a young, energetic boy. "She always confirmed my badness. It is very difficult for me to think of my own interests and pursue them. I don't feel deserving or worthwhile. It is as if I have to legitimize my place on earth and then I give up on my self. It all seems so hopeless."

From the beginning of treatment, Mr. B. was relying on others to support his treatment financially. When his father was no longer able to provide some extra money, he relied on a small trust fund left to him by his grandfather. He realized that he had to supplement his income through private consulting to continue in his treatment. He felt stuck, immobilized, and unable to pursue any work. He bemoaned the fact that a larger trust fund was not left to him. I said, "You don't even let the dead off the hook." He smiled and gave various rationalizations as to why he could not pursue extra work since it would interfere with his job. I told him that the only thing that interfered with his job was his refusal to pursue his interests. He began to express anger at his co-workers, his girlfriends, his parents, and me for not doing a better job. I pointed out how enraged he was that the job was now his and only he could make it or break it.

This need to activate himself to support himself financially resulted in a major impasse. He began to fall asleep in sessions, was unable to organize his work, and felt a general inertia in his life.

I confronted his refusal to move himself to help support his treatment. I told him this behavior could only destroy his treatment as it had undermined so many previous projects. He laughed or became angry, telling me he would do what he wanted to. He insisted that I was controlling his life, and he withdrew and remained sullen and oppositional. His job had become threatened, and his financial condition had deteriorated. At this point, I felt perhaps the patient was not capable of self-activation and a thorough working through of his abandonment depression. Perhaps his rage was so great that it required excessive defense and regressive retreat. I broached the subject of changing the course of treatment with the patient. I told him that he seemed unable or unwilling to move further and perhaps it would be more appropriate and economical to switch to once-a-week sessions with the goal of maintaining any symptomatic improvement. The patient became furious, telling me I was judgmental like his mother, and wanted to undermine him like his father. He knew what was best for him and he wanted intensive analytic treatment.

During one session, I focused on a behavior he had of picking his pimples during the session. He told me that it was a very old habit and he would often make knife punctures in his skin. He then remembered trying to stab a boy in his childhood, and how sensitive his mother's skin was. He began to have murderous dreams and panic when he had a dream of knifing his mother. He felt rage every day. He said, "I feel an explosion inside of me. It is like a volcano about to erupt." Meanwhile, his sleeping and drinking began to diminish.

He said, "I realize now my father lied to me and my mother did not want me. I've been hurting myself all along because that was the way to survive. I swallowed my mother's anger and pushed it down with a lot of booze. If I didn't do that I would really want to kill her." At times this rage would result in feelings of panic. He would say, "I want to leave this session. I'm scared of the explosion inside of me. I hate everyone. I hate them for screwing me. I would have done better as an orphan. I hate you for showing me this."

Then he sat and did not talk. I told him that after he expressed his hate for me, he retreated. Did he really have to deal with his feelings in this way? This patient was now moving from his childhood dilemma of submitting to his mother and internalizing her hatred or of being and identifying with his narcissistic father. The identification with his father had been a major defense against being engulfed by a destructive and hateful mother.

Although his material in the sessions was evidence of forward movement, he did not speak about his work or any attempts to financially support himself. When I questioned him, he refused to answer. He told me that his boss (like his father) was envious of him and wanted to undermine his success.

I gave him an interpretation at this point. I told him that he acted in a self-destructive way to keep his father, and that he refused to share his progress with me because of his fear that I would be angry and attack any efforts he made toward self-development and growth. He said, "You are right—it is crazy—sometimes it is hard to believe that anyone can be on my side and support these moves. They hated me but I don't have to hate myself."

He than began to share his improvement on his job: his efforts to support his work, recent publications, and plans to develop some business ideas. I was unable to hide my smile. He said, "You seem to enjoy my success, and that makes me feel good." Clearly, this patient's moves toward self-activation triggered a very harsh, primitive, and attacking withdrawn part unit that required the defense of concealing his behavior. At times, this gave a paranoid and suspicious cast to his character. My interpretation at this point resulted in a new level of relating. Instead of repressing and demanding care or withdrawing and guarding himself, he learned how to work and share.

The patient now contains his drinking, sleeping, and avoidant and regressive behavior. He works steadily and consistently. He recently established a relationship with a woman that has many problematic conflicts. He is now trying to contain his fears of being hurt by his girlfriend's anger and problems. Further work in the area of intimacy is still required before termination can be considered.

SUMMARY

This chapter illustrates the use of confrontation with an acting-out passive-aggressive borderline personality. The patient's acting out, externalization of conflict, and rationalizations became an ingrained life pattern that served to avoid underlying feelings of abandonment, rage, and disappointment with infantile objects. The process clearly illustrates how confrontation of transference acting out is used to redirect affect and conflict from the external world to the intrapsychic realm. The decrease in acting out and heightened affect are clear signs that treatment is moving in the proper direction.

On the other hand, intellectualization, rationalizations, acting out, and absence of affect indicate the activity of defense and the need for escalating confrontation.

By maintaining a neutral therapeutic stance, the therapist also serves as an identificatory model for containment of affect and the management of turbulent cycles during the treatment. The patient can activate himself and face painful affect only after the therapist blocks all avoidant maneuvers through confrontation of acting out.

Chapter 15

Confrontation of the Transference Acting Out of Clinging and Helplessness

Karen Dean Fritts, Ph.D.

Mrs. S., a 45-year-old white woman, was referred by a psychologist who had seen her approximately six years prior for a period of one year.

Her previous therapy had been precipitated by a major loss causing unmanageable separation anxiety. She reported having had "a nervous breakdown" as a result of the ending of her 20-year marriage. Her husband had left her, complaining of her helpless, overly dependent behavior. She described the months after the marriage ended as the worst time in her life. "I felt like I was going to die. I walked around like a zombie for months. I cried endlessly. I could not think straight. I did not know how to cope. Parts of me felt like they were missing. I was becoming confused and panicky. One day I fell apart; something snapped inside of me." She then sought treatment for the first time.

Her reasons for returning to therapy six years later were vague. She complained of depression, a lack of vitality and commitment to life, of floating through life without a purpose. She added that she was often confused and did not understand her thoughts or feelings. Her demeanor changed to pleasure as she described her current marriage, which was the one area in her life that was "perfect" and made her feel whole. Her husband, whom she had met and married only weeks after her divorce, was adoring and made her completely happy. She triumphantly declared that they *never* had "cross words." When he was home and near her, she felt fine. However, when he was at work or out of the home, she moped, felt listless and "empty." She, in passing, noted how horrible it would be to be without a man.

She went on to describe herself as lacking self-assertion; she felt compelled to please and adapt to others' opinions and ideas in order to ensure their approval. Although quite articulate, she described herself as stupid, knowing less than others, and unable to express her thoughts. "When I try to tell others what I am thinking, it always come out a jumbled mess." She complained of having a difficult time making decisions. She turned to others to help her decide what to wear, what to eat, and what to do with her leisure time. In fact, she was quite a beautiful woman; however, she saw herself as only minimally attractive with a great many flaws.

Mrs. S. summarized the impairment of her real self: "I can't seem to find myself. My life is gray and flat. Nothing interests me. I am a grown woman and I fear everything and everybody. I am always concerned with others' opinions of me. I am unable to make heads or tails out of my life and cannot understand what is happening inside of me." She concluded by saying that she was terrified that she was going to have another "nervous breakdown."

As Mrs. S. began therapy, she had sketchy memories of her childhood. Her history slowly began to emerge over months as her defensive system began to yield to confrontation. She was the younger of two children, with a sister 4 years older than she. Her mother and father had divorced when she was 3. She described her father as a nice man, but as very involved with his own life and interests. She saw very little of him and missed him terribly. She was quick to defend his absence in her life. When her parents divorced, he had become an infrequent visitor. However, when he did visit, the parents would spend their time together fighting bitterly. She had felt deeply disappointed when he would depart without a word.

She described the relationship between her mother and father as a chaotic nightmare; "I think she hated him and dedicated her existence to hating him. She punished me for what he did to her." Her mother's accusations of her father's immoral behavior were shared in detail with the patient. She recalled that her mother would talk to her like a friend. Becoming mother's confidante became the basis of their relationship. The patient described her mother as an emotional woman with frightening "black" moods. These black moods were outbursts of rage. Mother would randomly provoke fights. She would scream, name call, and berate the patient verbally and physically. The tirades would continue until Mrs. S. was disoriented and confused and would beg for forgiveness. She rarely understood what initiated these attacks, or what she had done "wrong."

At age 12, Mrs. S. had gone to her father and sister for help. The older sister was immune from the attacks. Mother identified with the older sister while splitting off and projecting the withdrawing unit on the patient, blaming her for her own miserable life. The patient's attempts to get help from those around her were unsuccessful. She was told by the father that it was not as bad as she was making it out to be. If she knew what was good for her, she would never speak about these "upsets" to "outsiders" again. Father's failure to support Mrs. S.'s reality further solidified the defensive self. There were implicit and explicit demands that she deny and distort her reality perceptions and self-expression. Hence, years passed as the little girl became the adult sitting in my office who complained bitterly about her inability to discern reality and express it adequately to others. Expressing her real self, which has been impaired and replaced by a false self, stimulated the early memories. The compliant child, who adapted to her external environment (out of necessity) regardless of its appropriateness, now struggled as an adult with such vital issues as discerning her reality, self-activation, entitlement, self-expression, spontaneity, creativity, and intimacy.

The father's threats and admonitions continued to haunt her each time she made an attempt at activating herself through remembering and putting language to her memories. The smallest emergence of spontaneity was followed by overwhelming guilt, recriminations, and fear of punishment. What she feared most was abandonment. She lived her life in avoidance and denial so as not to trigger these painful memories. Paradoxically, what occurred was the ultimate abandonment of the self through the massive use of primitive defenses. She struggled with expressing what had been forbidden: her reality.

The patient's mother had warned her in overt and covert ways that she was a difficult child and no one liked her. Alternately, her mother would berate and attack Mrs. S., then promise exclusive, undying love for her. Mother reassured her that she was the only one who could understand, love, and protect her. These promises of exclusive, special love were counteracted by the warning that if Mrs. S. wasn't a "good girl," Mother would leave her just as Father had. Mrs. S. struggled to make sense out of such conflicting memories. These cruel overt double messages, threatening loss of love and safety, became the core terror of the patient's life. Mrs. S. came to believe that truth and self expression are linked to abandonment.

There was no history of successful separation-individuation experiences early in life. She remembered elementary school as unpleasant and frightening. She would often feign sickness to stay home with Mother. She avoided activities and relationships that would require leaving her home. She had lived with her mother until she was 19, was her constant companion, and shared a bedroom with her. At that time she had married and moved only three blocks from her mother's home.

She described enjoying learning, although she had never been much of a student. She had dreamed of college but felt it to be "the impossible dream." She had tried several college courses at age 18, only to become anxious and quit weeks before the semester ended.

By late adolescence she was convinced there was only one sure way to survive in life. Her thoughts were devoted to dreams of marriage. Finding a man who could love and take care of her became life's goal. She vowed she would never end up like her mother, alone and bitter. The defensive self was in full operation. She presented herself as a demure, helpless, childlike woman. She was convinced that if she could not find a man to take care of her, she was doomed. She met and quickly married her first husband.

At 19, perhaps feeling reassured by the "safety" of marriage, she once again attempted college. This time, she went as far as completing her academic work, with the exception of finals, before quitting. At that time she reported having her first panic attack and symptoms of claustrophobia.

After ten years of marriage, she went to work briefly as a saleswoman in a department store. Within a few weeks she found it to be overwhelming and unpleasant. "I missed being at home even though I was often bored." She quit and never returned to work.

Her intrapsychic structure was made up of a rewarding part object that was loving, engulfing, and promising "best friendship" and exclusivity in return for complete obedience in the form of regressive and inappropriate behavior. The covert agreement was to keep the expression of the self hidden in return for her survival. The withdrawing part object consisted of an attacking, rageful mother who would hurt her for any kind of deviation from the expected loyalty.

The rewarding part-self representation was that of the good, compliant, sweet child who would put her real self on the shelf in order to please and adapt to those around her. Mrs. S. put great value on being seen as a "special, sweet, valued woman." She displayed this seductive aspect of the self especially well with men. The withdrawing self representation was that of a stupid, unattractive fool who could not do the simplest tasks. The intrapsychic picture explains the patient's exemplary helplessness.

The real self was underdeveloped and fragile at best. She displayed stunted capacities in self-expression, activation, and entitlement. She continually struggled with the ability to self soothe and to make and maintain adult commitments in relationships.

These deficits resulted in the evident overall difficulties in managing her life. The defensive self functioned in such a way as to guarantee her intrapsychic equilibrium and safety through clinging behavior to all those around her at the cost of her own individuation.

The psychotherapy was initially characterized by the presentation of her defensive self in the form of helplessness and confusion in managing herself during the sessions. I, gently yet consistently, asked her why she felt she could not, in the safety of her therapeutic sessions, express her thoughts, ideas, and feelings as they pertained to her life today.

As she struggled in her sessions to do this, she became flooded with memories of experiences and feelings that had been split off and forgotten. She began to remember situations in her young life in which her reality had been forfeited to her mother's sense of reality. She battled with the desire to express herself in her sessions while describing how dangerous it felt. In describing her memories of childhood, she tried to minimize and find excuses for her mother's behavior. I confronted her each time, wondering about her need to do this. I told her that, although she said it made her feel better to defend her mother, her willingness to throw out her own perceptions of reality in order to protect her *beliefs* about her mother resulted in her lifelong problem and current complaints, such as her inability to know what or how she felt today, and her chronic feelings of anger at the friends she chose.

From the very beginning of therapy, Mrs. S. waited for me to direct her sessions. When I sat quietly, she asked me many questions and looked frightened when she was unable to "read me." When I didn't respond to her questions directly but, rather, investigated the meaning of her questions, she would almost always say, "I just don't know." She continued by asking whether I knew what was wrong.

I was supposed to ask the questions and supply the answers. With the Masterson Approach in mind, the similarities of the patient's responses at this point in the therapy were predictable. I wondered whether or not she was, in fact, through her helpless behavior with me summarizing the real issues in her life. She seemed determined to look to others around her to direct and choreograph her life, rather than using her capacities to do that for herself. If she felt as if she could not run her own life, then *that* seemed to warrant investigation. My silences early in the therapy were always seen and felt as a withdrawal, similar to her mother's. My support and persistence in encouraging her own investigation by confronting her projections helped her to differentiate the therapeutic process from her mother's behavior.

She continued to accuse me of not caring about her because I was not, in fact, taking over for her. I repeatedly confronted this by wondering why she would want me to do for her what she could do so well for herself. Her response was, "I can't." The investigations that ensued concerning my quiet listening and her feelings of helplessness gave way to small steps toward defining her thoughts and putting them into language.

As feelings began to surface, she would quickly move away through various defenses: avoidance, denial, projection, or clinging. She would frequently look to me after she had made any kind of statement that expressed an authentic or spontaneous feeling or thought. She would either ask me a question or want me to reply to her response. Slowly, as the therapy deepened, I would confront her by questioning this process. "Why is it that after you express yourself and feel good, you quickly look to me for verification and validation?" Tears flowed as she began to understand how painful even simple communication had become. We began to understand her impulse to "check back" as a desire to obtain the longed-for support of her self-expression. She recognized that she was expecting to be verbally attacked any time she expressed herself.

Through my confrontations, which supported her capacity to activate herself, she cautiously began to take over her sessions. She complained about how uncomfortable this type of therapy was for her, yet she also said that something was beginning to change inside of her. She was identifying and exploring her internal world. She more readily experimented with talking aloud and listening to herself in her sessions. She began to confront herself when she was avoiding, denying, or projecting. Hearing her own thoughts without constant internal intrusion and attack was something foreign to her.

Several months into treatment, she introduced material regarding her first husband that was remarkably similar to that regarding her mother. For instance, he would berate and embarrass her. He threw tantrums that she would apologize for. As she remembered her first marriage she began to cry, saying that she missed him terribly. She felt lost without him even though her current husband was kinder and far more considerate. The desire to repair her relationship with her mother was reenacted in the twenty-year marriage. I wondered why she missed her abusive first husband and seemed relatively disinterested in her current husband, whom she described as kinder and more loving. At that time she made no connection to her early life. I, although tempted, resisted the desire to furnish her with the link.

It was not easy to keep quiet. Using the Masterson Approach as a theoretical structure allowed me to examine my impulses before stepping in. Her helpless and hopeless picture consistently evoked my unresolved caretaking and rescue fantasies. If left unchecked, these fantasies would be acted out in the session. The patient's wish to obtain the lost or missing supplies from the therapist is another attempt to avoid facing the past and the associated pain. The subtlety of the patient's wish and the traumatic early history can make it difficult to resist becoming directive and caretaking. Once again, managing my countertransference so as to not interfere with the patient's work became of central importance.

My vigilance paid off. One day after a long period of silence, as I wrestled with my countertransference, she hesitantly began to speak. She said that just hearing my words in the session, no matter what I said, was a way for her to "feel plugged in." She described herself as a socket looking for a plug—any plug. She felt "happier, lighter" (taken care of) even though she herself noticed that the intensity of the therapeutic session dwindled. I asked her if she thought that it was a good trade-off for her. She examined her "feel better" response and her desire to get me to participate more actively.

Little by little as months passed she experimented with and expressed her thoughts and feelings more readily. She less frequently wanted me to jump in or take over for her. She began to reality test and manage her feelings concerning the attack that she feared. She was less concerned that I would undermine her thoughts or feelings in her sessions. The therapeutic alliance was solidifying. My confrontations mainly focused on the resistance to, and defenses against, expressing her real self. I continually pointed out the tremendous cost and destruction to her healthy self. Her willingness to let others do her thinking and feeling for her was finally being integrated and understood as the major issue in her life. She was beginning to test her newfound capacities in the external world by making slow, gradual individuative moves, expressing herself with friends, family, and especially her husband. She occasionally expressed opinions that differed from his and was delighted when he listened to her views.

As fate would have it, about eight months into the therapy her second husband became seriously ill. This experience created massive anxiety, clinging, hopelessness, and helplessness.

I once again found myself confronted with countertransference. I was stepping in with greater frequency, thereby resonating with her helplessness and hopelessness. I was too active, succumbing to my need to give suggestions and directions. She would immediately "perk up" and say she felt better. I began to contain my countertransference as well as point out the pattern of "feeling good" as a result of my caretaking. Although it provided her with "warm fuzzies," as she called them, I thought it was a tenuous way to feel better. She was relying on others' responses to her as her emotional barometer. I gathered my therapeutic equilibrium once again, and she returned to working. Memories emerged with affect that she was able to express.

After several intense sessions, a question arose about fees. She was testing the frame, as she had done early in therapy. She had canceled her session without adequate notice. She was delighted with the fact that she made a decision on her own. She had decided that the other appointment was very important. Her decision to keep the other appointment seemed valid. However, because she canceled with such short notice, I assumed she would be financially responsible for her interview.

When I told her at her next appointment she was furious. She told me angrily she thought that she had better look for another therapist. I asked her why. She replied, "Because you're not nurturing, not sweet enough, and that if you were an 'understanding' human being, you would not charge me." Mrs. S. was requesting more than understanding. She was, in fact, demanding that I take care of her and the situation.

I disagreed with her and said, "Why would you want me to take the responsibility for your decision?" I continued by wondering why she was confusing being responsible with the emotional component of caring. "Why would you be angry at me for expecting you to be responsible by keeping our initial agreement?"

For the moment she ignored my confrontation and continued to attack me. She had heard that other therapists held, cuddled, and hugged their patients. Some gave them a hello or goodbye kiss. At the very least, they asked lots of questions and provided many answers. She wondered whether she would be better off finding such a therapist.

I responded, "I suppose you can do that if you want to, but I think your *wish* to be cuddled and 'made to feel better' has stood in the way of your growth and development. Why would you want to continue to find people who will 'take away' your feelings and take care of you in ways that undermine your own ability to think and feel?" I added that I did not see that as my role; rather, I saw therapy as a partnership (therapeutic alliance) to assist *her* in better understanding herself and her life. She calmed down a bit and started to speculate about her relationships with other people. She hesitantly agreed that most of her relationships were based on the quality and quantity of caretaking that she could extract from them.

I also wondered why she was so quick to leave therapy rather than stay and work this out. When faced with her own self-expression, which at the moment was anger, she was eager to run. Rather than to feel, express, and work these issues out in her treatment, her impulse was to trade one therapeutic relationship for another. She was looking for a quick fix—this time a "sweeter" therapist. She admitted her commitment to therapy was shaky. She did not like to feel so angry; therefore, she was ready to pick up her marbles and go home.

That confrontation with Mrs. S. hit a nerve. She connected "our fight," as she called it, to old patterns and feelings. Her anger or strong feelings have frequently been followed by running from the situation or replacing people. Tears followed as she said, with sadness in her voice, "I can't even imagine how many times I have run away from myself and my feelings, never giving myself the opportunity to work this out." The session ended by her saying that leaving therapy was obviously not the solution, although she laughed and said, "I still *wish* I had a 'sweeter' therapist! Actually, if I were truthful about it, I would not want to hug or kiss my therapist. It is easier to have others take care of me even if I'm beginning to know it's not good for me. I need to face me and you help me do that. Sometimes I don't like you because you won't do my therapy for me. Oh well, I'll be back."

When she did come back, however, she was fifteen minutes late. I wondered whether her tardiness had anything to do with our previous session. She quickly said, "No." I was quiet. She sat silently then said, "I lied. Of course it had to do with the last session. I was still angry at you." I wondered why missing part of her session was punishment to me . . . rather than hurting herself.

That opened up many sessions in which she began to wonder about her expectations and demands to be taken care of. "When people don't take care of me the way I want them to, I notice that I feel angry. I then want to get even, so I become more demanding. I want it all done for me. Then I never have to risk exposing myself, yet that puts me in this constant bind. I feel helpless, yet I encourage others to keep me that way." She was realizing the extent to which she colluded with her own problems. "Under all this mess, I have no idea who I am. I am a shiny, well-polished robot; a furious robot, mother's robot."

She came in the next week and said she had had a very frightening day. Daily events had seemed to trigger the emergence of early memories. "I was detached all day. I had woozy feelings; kind of like my mind leaving my body, but I went with the feelings and they passed and I was okay. I have had these kinds of feelings all my life. . . I recognize them. I thought a lot about my life as a little girl and I didn't push it all away." Accompanying her less restricted thoughts and feelings were mild panic attacks and depression followed by resumption of defense.

She went on to say that whenever she remembered frightening or sad events, she needed to soothe and protect herself. She would think either of her therapy sessions or of a religious figure that she felt would protect her while she began to remember and tolerate these disturbing memories. Since she had so little internalized structure to rely on, therapy or religion served as a compromise solution while she was in the neophyte stages of building a real self.

I reflected that, although I understood that these pictures seemed to give her strength, still she really did not think that she could tolerate the memories on her own. She sighed and said, "Oh, I think I can, more each day. But once again it's just easier to hold on, even if it's only to a picture in my head. One day I'd like that picture in my head to be me."

Parallel to her therapy, life outside her sessions was changing. She was reassessing her friendships, deciding that many of the friends she chose were, indeed, controlling and demanding. She wondered aloud why she needed this type of friend.

Approximately one year into treatment, as she continued to own more of her intrapsychic life, she said with a great deal of gusto, "I'm appalled to think that those things have happened to me. I was a little girl who, at that time, could not take care of myself. I realistically had no way to protect myself." She continued with tears and astonishment as she said, "The poor little girl inside of me. I weep for the child that never had a chance to be healthy and strong—until now. All this time I thought I was defective. They were defective, and I became the helpless bystander who was caught in the eye of their tornado. I *was* helpless then; however, I have continued to live as I did then. I *was* so frightened to be me. Why would anybody treat another human being like that? I have had to live with all these secrets. [Long silence.] Sometimes I can't even tell whether they're true or not." She was beginning to slide back into defense as a result of the long, sustained self-expression. Prior to this, I sat quietly as she worked. However, at that point I once again confronted her doubting of her own perceptions. I wondered why she was again discounting her reality, thereby throwing herself away. To demand that she have an "outside affidavit of absolute and perfect truth" was once again denying *her truth*. This confrontation allowed her to continue working.

"Yes. To be held, to be loved, to be touched. I've felt like I would die without it. I've been willing to do almost anything for it. I am starting to see how much I've done that has hurt me. I was 'starved' and betrayed by my mother. Then I betrayed myself. What I did to myself to get those crumbs. I'm in a battle fighting demons. I'm in such a turmoil. I'm afraid of myself [the real self]. I am becoming more capable, yet every time I tried expressing myself back then, I got hurt. Now, I am frightened to feel the healthy part of me. She hated me. He could not protect me. There was nowhere to turn. My only solution was to sacrifice me." The ability to remember, feel the pain, and express it in her sessions was remarkable.

The momentum of treatment resembled a dance. Her being able to manage her sessions and life in a more assertive, self-expressive way was inevitably followed by regressions, confusion, and helpless clinging. My confrontations consistently targeted her defensive self, while supporting through communicative matching any expressions of the real self.

The turbulence in her external life quieted down considerably. She coped with daily activities in a more appropriate way. She made several new friends. Although she continued to cling to her husband, she began making assertive steps in the relationship. She slowly mourned the deep pain associated with her childhood. This was difficult for her, yet she was persistent in her desire to help herself.

As part of testing her own capacities, she returned to school. She found it exciting and stimulating. Surprisingly to her, although not to me, she received A's in her first grading period. She anticipated going to work after graduation. There was a gradual reduction in the feelings of panic. Her achievements in school and better adaptation in daily living, coupled with her deepening commitment to her therapy, provided the momentum and courage needed to face her pain.

She expressed continual delight at herself and found tremendous gratification in her own ability to tolerate her feelings and express them to others. The secrets she kept hidden no longer haunted her daily living. She became able to make decisions based on understanding her healthy needs and desires, and to act on her own thoughts and opinions, relying less on others' approval. There was less clinging and acting out of the wish for excessive caretaking. Her relationships began to have an adult quality to them. The result was a feeling of gratification previously unknown to Mrs. S.

SUMMARY

Mrs. S. slowly explored those areas in her psyche that were inaccessible because of defense. The impaired real self, dormant so long, slowly and cautiously began to emerge. She successfully internalized confrontations aimed primarily at her defensive maneuvers to avoid and deny her "self." As she worked more consistently in therapy, it became possible for me to do communicative matching in support of those ideas, thoughts, and feelings that were unique expressions of the real self. As this aspect of the self got acknowledged, rather than attacked, she continued to forge ahead in what she considered to be the "triumphant reunion with herself."

Chapter 16

Confrontation of the Transference Acting Out of Severe Helplessness and Hopelessness

Candace Orcutt, Ph.D.

INTRODUCTORY DATA

Dr. Danny Michaels (a pseudonym), a 38-year-old economics teacher, applied to the Masterson Group in a crisis, saying, "I'm fighting for my life." It was easy to believe his statement: he was visibly depressed, with dark circles under his eyes, a beaten look, and disheveled appearance. He moved slowly, and his voice was subdued. The presenting problem left no doubt he was in a crisis. After the break-up of a 16-month homosexual relationship, he felt suicidal and was functioning minimally. He had lost a teaching position when federal funding was withdrawn, and was financially reliant on substitute teaching, tutoring, and savings. His recent therapist, feeling treatment was at an impasse, had given him a copy of one of Dr. Masterson's books and had then terminated treatment.

263

Although the crisis was evident, it was less clear how Dr. Michaels was *fighting* for his life. He isolated himself—except when he literally courted danger (the risk of random violence) by going to pornographic movie theaters, where anonymous sexual encounters took place. When alone, he drank quantities of wine, popped Valium, and stayed unconscious as much as possible. In sessions, he spoke incessantly of being "fat, ugly, and unlovable—no one will ever love me." He said, "I might as well climb in a garbage can and pull the lid over my head."

My first intervention was to confront him with the contradiction between his statement that he was fighting for his life, and his self-defeating attitude and behavior. His response told me more about him: he rationalized, and became manipulative and evasive. I then confronted this second line of defense ("Do you notice, when I call something to your attention that might be helpful to you, you find ways to ignore it?"). He then seemed to pull himself together around my confrontations, and I had a brief glimpse of someone with a quick, perceptive intelligence, quite capable of grasping the situation and mobilizing himself to meet it. However, when I eased up on the confrontations, he soon reverted to dismal accounts of his pitiful situation, abject unworthiness, and utter hopelessness. I was certain he would respond to a persistently confrontive approach but that he was well entrenched in his defensive misery.

Even at this early stage of treatment, the conflict surrounding the emergence of Dr. Michaels's real self was evident. The defensive, false self was rampant: stubbornly attached to the withdrawing unit, it adopted a helpless and hopeless pose. The impaired real self was swamped, and became visible only as I persistently questioned the false self through confrontation.

HISTORY

Dr. Michaels is the oldest of three children. His younger brothers have distanced themselves from the parents as much as possible, one by joining the armed forces, the other by marrying and moving to Canada. His father and mother are first-generation Americans and hard working. They had high expectations for their eldest son, who was to be the "all-American boy."

The patient reported that his relationship with his parents was "horrible." He said that the family had lived in an atmosphere of "doom and gloom." It was like "living in a cave," with everybody "going in and out of their separate entrances." At the dinner table, they all read.

He said that his mother had both needed and resented him. He felt that she had been seductive, making him her confidant. He said she possessively "devoured" him but, on the other hand, devalued him, calling him "queer" and saying she couldn't understand why anyone would like him. She repeatedly remarked, "Something is wrong with you." And she would put him in crazy-making situations, asking, "Would you rather go out and play with your friends or clean the bathroom?" When he would answer (hoping to please her) that he chose to clean the bathroom, she would exclaim, "What's the matter with you?" (It seems evident here how the patient's false self is built upon the introjected mother of the withdrawing unit; the accusatory, deprecating tone of voice is unmistakable.)

He thought his mother rewarded him for clinging to her, and attacked him whenever he made an independent move. Generally, he felt "punished for existence." The father offered no parental alternative; he was passive and ineffectual, except when reinforcing the mother's punitive onslaughts.

The patient described himself as a "fat, depressed boy" who had sought refuge at school. Academically, though, he had procrastinated and got through by cramming. Most of his friends had been girls, but he had begun to have secret homosexual encounters in his high school and college years, and gained from them what he variously described as "excitement" and "peace."

He married upon leaving college, and tried to establish his own household. Although the relationship was affectionate, the commitment was tenuous, and Dr. Michaels shored it up with nocturnal cruising for transient sexual contacts with other men. Two children were born of the marriage, and the patient remains close to them (an indication of Dr. Michaels's potential for relationship has been, and remains, his attachment to his children, which is caring and altruistic).

He pursued a doctorate in economics, and had difficulty in completing the program. This brought him into therapy for the first time, and, with its support, he earned his degree.

He began to teach, but financial cutbacks eliminated his job. He felt as if everything were falling apart, and sought psychotherapy again. This time, he found a doctor who gave him "everything [he] wanted" in the form of large quantities of obliterating drugs. His relationships with men became more absorbing, until he felt it necessary to tell his wife. They agreed to a divorce.

After the dissolution of his marriage, Dr. Michaels had several liaisons with men and, eventually, a 16-month relationship that focused his conflict. He met Ed, who would become his lover, at a costume party. Despite the fact that he was dressed as an executioner, Ed indicated he preferred to be the passive partner. Michaels, who preferred the dominant sexual role, responded. In the relationship that followed, the two found themselves caught up in sado-masochistic scenarios: Ed crawled on the floor and Michaels hit him with a belt. But a change was taking place: the more the relationship continued, the more Michaels cared for his lover, and the more he had difficulty with impotence. Ed, put off by the possibility of genuine commitment, drew away in pursuit of distant fantasy. The patient clung to the wish that Ed would return; he preoccupied himself and fed off this possibility long after it had passed from reality to empty illusion.

By the time the patient began therapy with me, he had become a walking catalog of grievances (the reason his previous therapist had lost all patience and had terminated therapy). My impression was that he had delivered himself indiscriminately into my hands, leaving his fate to me.

COURSE OF CONFRONTIVE PSYCHOTHERAPY

This is an account of the first ten months of an analytically oriented treatment that is now in its third year. Without this initial phase of confrontive psychotherapy, the present phase of working through would have been impossible. And for the first ten months, unremitting confrontation was required.

At first, the confrontations centered on Dr. Michaels's maladaptive response to his crisis situation. As I have mentioned, this meant calling attention to the discrepancy between his acknowledgment of the situation and his unwillingness to do anything about it.

Dr. Michaels would slouch into his sessions looking dreadful—needing a haircut, and wearing what I thought of as his "lumberjack outfit": a plaid flannel shirt, corduroy pants, and work shoes. He carried what appeared to be his wordly goods in a large, overstuffed briefcase. Typically, he would begin to weep, saying he was helpless to change his situation, hopeless about himself, unlovable, ugly, and fat. He was preoccupied with thoughts of his ex-lover, Ed—it seemed that every day of the week marked an anniversary of something related to Ed, and he dwelt on this at great length.

I began the first of my basic confrontations: for instance, that he would rather present himself as a victim than take responsibility for himself; that he would rather dwell on the past than face the present;

that he was treating his feelings like facts, and turning them into facts by letting them run his life.

In response, he looked surprised, then expressed resentment at my placing the responsibility on him when he was in such bad shape. I pointed out that this was exactly how he stopped himself whenever he tried to mobilize himself: he entrenched himself out of self-pity and spite.

He pulled together a little and said that his sense of overdependency had been there a long time—much further back than his relationship with Ed. He thought he might be repeating a piece of his childhood, when he demanded attention by getting sick. He used to take refuge in illness when teased by other boys, and his mother would take care of him then. Later, his wife nursed him through graduate school.

After this integration of my confrontation, along with expression of insight that evoked deeper feelings, Dr. Michaels reverted to an almost impenetrable stubbornness. This was a clear expression of the borderline triad, with individuative insight leading to feeling, and a renewal of defense. He began to telephone me almost daily. He complained that his apartment was a mess; he rarely went out, but stayed home miserably overeating, drinking, and thinking about Ed. He stated that he was so depressed he thought he couldn't take it any more.

Repeatedly, I expressed "therapeutic astonishment" that he reported he was in a crisis, yet continued the very behavior that maintained the crisis. When he reiterated that he was too fat and unlovable to help himself, I expressed added amazement at his unwillingness to know what he knew: "This is not the response of someone whose life is at stake!" I added, "You are still trying to get me to take care of you instead of doing it yourself."

He then shifted his resistance to the ground of the treatment itself (a sign that the confrontations were beginning to have some containing effect). He said he couldn't change without insight. I replied that he had had years of insight, and this was the result. I reminded him again that he had said he was in a crisis: "If you were in a burning building, would you try to figure out how the fire got started, or would you try to do something about your situation?" He continued his demands for insight, and I added that he was fighting the treatment as he fought himself. I observed that he was here because he believed this treatment approach would help him, and yet he still wanted to do things the old way. He dug in and became angry as well as tearful, and began to threaten suicide. After thoroughly exploring the issue with him, I said that suicide was certainly the ultimate in self-destructive behavior, if that was his goal, and that it was very final. I reminded him that I had no control over his actions outside of sessions, and if he felt he could not control himself, he would have to go to the nearest emergency room.

All this time, the telephone calls persisted, always with the same theme: he had never felt so awful, was hopeless, fat, unlovable, and could think of nothing but Ed. I said he was reinforcing his sense of helplessness by telephoning between sessions, that this diluted his sessions. I said he was being repetitive and only trying to unload on me instead of managing his own feelings. As soon as I started to hear the same old refrain, I said I would discuss it the next session, and hung up.

In the sessions themselves, I held the confrontational line, saying that his therapy was stuck where he was stuck—at the point of taking responsibility.

I saw that Dr. Michaels was upping the ante whenever I held to confrontation. I was the first therapist who had neither taken over for him nor rejected him, but simply expected him to act on his own behalf. The pathological part of his ego was throwing a temper tantrum of major proportions to coerce me into reenacting the old rewarding or withdrawing parent. At the same time, the healthy part of his ego was testing me—making sure he could rely on my consistency—for he was truly in a crisis and needed to know that therapy could provide a secure place for his vulnerable real self to emerge.

He next left word that he had admitted himself for psychiatric hospitalization. This was certainly a gauge of how profoundly he was at war with himself, and needed to clear away all other issues in order to devote his entire energy to his struggle. Perhaps it was also a last attempt to summon up the rewarding unit before he began to take charge of himself.

He remained in the hospital for one month, until his insurance ran out. The treatment plan provided that he go out on pass to continue his sessions with me. At the same time, he saw a doctor for individual contact, had a trial of antidepressant medication, and attended a group run by two additional doctors. Occasionally, he tried to render his several therapists ineffectual by playing us against one another. Fortunately, we were able to maintain sufficient communication to keep the treatment consistent. The patient's depression was defined as characterological, and his manipulations were confronted by the treatment team.

He came out of the hospital somewhat rested. He got a haircut, had his clothes washed and pressed, and began to experience anger when he thought of Ed. He realized that he preferred to cling to a romanticized memory of Ed than experience the anger that would free him from the past.

The testing began again. During the weekend, he left a message saying he was suicidal. Another associate at the Masterson Group was covering the phones that weekend, and returned his call. When the patient found out he could not speak to me personally, he said that the problem could wait until our Monday appointment. On Monday, I confronted him with his need to involve me in his victim act, and he became thoughtful. He said that the "victim" issue had not been dealt with in his previous treatments, and he could see how it had been acted out, instead, when he had provoked his last therapist into throwing him out.

Then he began telephoning Ed and hanging up as soon as the call went through. I expressed surprise that, once more, he was releasing his anger by acting like a victim instead of channeling his anger to power assertion on his own behalf.

A period of self-activation followed. He reached out to friends, strengthened his relationships with his children, and for the first time began to speak confidently of himself as a professional. Also for the first time he spoke about the future, and thought he could do better with someone other than Ed. He said he realized the phone calls didn't help him, and that he needed to assume more responsibility.

His phone calls took on a clearly maladaptive form. He would call upon a network of "buddies" who supported each other's fantasy life with erotic phone contacts. This method of sex-by-ear had become more important as an outlet since the AIDS epidemic had limited more direct sexual contact.

But by now, treatment was in a phase of relative integration. Dr. Michaels was questioning his avoidance behavior and tolerating much of his emotional pain, and so was able to make some behavioral change, which allowed him to achieve increasing insight and more depth of feeling. He noticed that he tended to pursue unattainable people, or provoke a sense of disrespect in people, which would push them away. He spoke of his parents' inability to meet his emotional needs, and the murderous rage he felt about this. He had constructive interchanges with his parents and with his ex-wife. He made a number of promising job contacts.

He was still indulging in addictive behavior with food, wine, Valium, and erotic phone calls, but the symbolic meaning of this acting out was becoming clearer the more he tried to curtail and observe the behavior. He said he always felt hungry. He could never get enough, or get it directly—he told me he had been sneaking food all his life. (In this context, his earlier plea for insight had been just another indirect demand to be fed.)

He fell silent and sucked on his fingers. I asked what he would have said if he hadn't put something in his mouth. He told me he was thinking of food, and of Ed. I said, "Ed is just a high-class hamburger." Dr. Michaels burst out laughing. He then spoke of how devalued and meaningless he had felt as a child, fat and unassertive: "like a pear . . . like an egg." This time, I laughed, and said: "All these similes are about food!" He then began to describe himself as the object of his mother's emotional hunger. Yes, he said, she had "devoured" him, gobbled him up and left him hungry for love.

The observing capacity of his ego increased. He referred to his complaint of being "fat, ugly, and unlovable" as his "catechism," and saw that it was similar to his use of food, alcohol, drugs, and erotic phone calls as a way to stop himself from experiencing the anger and deprivation he felt at not being taken care of. He saw that when he made a move toward taking care of himself, he experienced immense resentment, and reverted to all these ways to stop the feeling and to stop himself. He was on his way to understanding the borderline triad: that individuation leads to depression (and anxiety and rage), which leads to the renewal of defense.

He had long sieges of crying that assumed a different quality from the complaints that were associated with his "catechism" or "Perils of Pauline" melodrama. This grief had the authentic quality of abandonment depression: it was not stereotyped but, rather, led to new and deeper feeling.

He began to express his anger toward me. He said he felt so angry, he wanted to throw his chair through the wall. He began to pound the arm of his chair, and I said, "This is no California pillow-punching therapy! This therapy is about putting it into words." He said he was fed up with protecting Ed when he really wanted to torture and kill him. And his father. And his mother. "And me," I said. "Oh, no. You're a nice lady." I replied, "That's *my* chair you were beating up, that you wanted to throw through the wall." The session was over, but on his way out the door, he stuck his tongue out at me and gave me the raspberry.

Next session, he said he had been experiencing anxiety as well as anticipation on the way to his sessions, and felt angry at me for not making it easier for him.

All this individuative movement necessarily led to a renewed phase of defense. One weekend he telephoned me, leaving a message that he was suicidal and had all his pills lined up in a row in front of him. He was in a rage when I did not return his call the same day. On Monday, I acknowledged it would have been better if I had returned his call the day he made it. However, I said I felt his anger was related primarily to my not being unconditionally available to him.

I was becoming very aware that the sadistic half of Dr. Michaels's sado-masochistic defense system was beginning to predominate (another way to dilute his anger by eroticizing it). History is a valuable guide in these matters, and I knew that in his scenario with Ed, he took the dominant part. He had ordered Ed to crawl, and to worship him. I knew that sanctification of my patient wasn't my therapeutic task, and resolved to take the fun out of the game of torture-the-object.

I said: "You know, I can't stop you from killing yourself. If you have your heart set on it, you'll do it. All I can do is say, 'What a waste,' and fill your appointment time with someone else." He grew serious, and asked, "Do you *really* mean that?"

The next meeting, he announced he was struggling not to have any more "bullshit sessions." He said he was beginning to make an important distinction in his feelings. "This is the core depression I'm feeling, isn't it—not the defensive depression, like when I'm reciting my catechism?"

Toward the end of this confrontive phase of treatment, I perceived the patient to be avoiding me in a way that suggested repetition of an early behavior. I mentioned he seemed to be running away in words, and he responded that he *had* run away when he was about 8 years old. It seems his mother had gone out, leaving him in the care of his father, who fell asleep on the couch. He decided this was it, and packed his socks and other essentials in a brown paper bag. He then set out into the big city. Very soon he crossed paths with his mother, and ran off down a side street, where he hid behind some garbage cans. His mother found him and took him home, where his father slapped him around. Later, when they asked him why he had run away, he said he felt they didn't care about him. I asked him if he saw any connection between this memory and his early statement to me that he might as well climb into a garbage can and pull the lid over his head. After a moment of startled silence, he said he hadn't thought to make this connection. What did it mean? I said, "You still want me to confirm your worth for you, even as you wanted them to do when you were a child."

PROGRESS OF TREATMENT

In these first ten months of confrontive psychotherapy, the patient learned to face his own maladaptive defenses. He began to set effective limits to his behavior, which allowed his abandonment depression to surface, along with a more adaptive expression of aggression (which was no longer turned as unrelentingly toward the self). Gradually, as he assumed more control over his impulses, Dr. Michaels could allow himself increased insight without a subsequent need to act out.

Since that time, he has secured a steady teaching job, no longer acts on his impulse to indulge in potentially risky erotic behavior, is no longer promiscuous, drinks moderately, has discontinued medication (both the Valium and the antidepressant), and has lost weight.

He is now on the couch, engaged in working through his abandonment depression in intensive psychoanalytic psychotherapy.

Dr. Michaels has over 30 years of confusion to overcome. In ten months, with the help of confrontive therapy, he was able to grasp the essential nature of his problem. The battle is with his *belief* in his worthlessness, in that old, pathological belief system that closes off his abandonment depression but also locks out his basic vitality.

In the present working-through phase, the alliance formed in the confrontive phase is the foundation of the therapy. This therapeutic alliance is the precipitate of the many times the patient and I have made our way past transference acting out and countertransferential hopelessness and helplessness and have been able to acknowledge his real self. These moments, when Dr. Michaels has emerged as a quick-minded, witty, and concerned human being, give the treatment its meaning, its direction—and its reward.

PART IV

Countertransference

The greatest obstacle to treatment of the patient with a personality disorder—second only to lack of knowledge—is the countertransference of the therapist. The term countertransference *is used here not in the strict sense of denoting the activation and projection on the patient of infantile conflicts from the therapist's past, but rather, more broadly, to identify all those emotions stirred in the therapist that interfere with the conduct of the treatment.*

It is perhaps belaboring the obvious to say that countertransference difficulties with personality disorder patients are ubiquitous. Why, then, is it that countertransference is so prevalent with these patients? Borderline and narcissistic patients, when they are working through their abandonment depression and are in touch with memories and affects from childhood, will report that their childhoods were much like living in a concentration camp in which the parents were the guards. The only way to survive in such an environment is to be very alert to the vulnerabilities and limits of the guards, so that these can be played upon to fill the inmate's desperate needs. As a consequence, patients are masters at observing and evoking blind spots in the therapist in order to impel the therapist's collusion in the patient's resistance to depression.

The therapist, on the other hand, whose development has, one hopes, been healthier, begins his career as a therapist as a novice in this process. Beyond that, matters are complicated by the fact that the personality disorder patient does not have a therapeutic alliance when he begins treatment, so that he projects upon the therapist without any awareness of the independent existence of the therapist, thus placing the therapist "in the center of the action," where it is far easier to have his emotions evoked. It is most unlike work with neurotic patients, where there is a basic consensus between therapist and patient that they are working together on the problem "over there." In other words, the therapist is not the center of the action. With personality disorder patients, the therapist is in the front line, on the receiving end of all the incoming artillery, and until he learns to understand and deal with it from an objective therapeutic stance, he will continue to be vulnerable to countertransference reactions.

The following chapters illustrate in graphic clinical detail the therapist's countertransference reactions to suicidal threats, to helplessness, to passive-aggressive acting out, to aggressive acting out, and to the devaluation and acting out shown by the narcissistic disorder.

J.F.M.

Chapter 17

Countertransference with the Borderline Patient

Ralph Klein, M.D.

In the course of treatment, a therapist may experience strong emotional reactions that create anxiety or conflict and therefore interfere with the maintenance of a comfortable, therapeutic neutrality. At times such reactions are appropriate and realistic, such as sorrow evoked by a tragedy in a patient's life. Such feelings require relatively little in the way of introspection or self-appraisal unless they distract attention from the patient's behavior—its motivation and meaning.

When a therapist responds to, or resonates with, the transference acting out of a patient, treatment will be seriously compromised. I would designate such a reaction by the therapist as countertransference-like acting out, to distinguish it from countertransference in the narrow, classical sense.

In countertransference-like acting out, the therapist is responding to something the patient is doing. Moreover, it is a reaction that the patient is consciously or unconsciously attempting to provoke in the therapist. The therapist's reaction is not peculiar to the individual therapist; rather, it is a reaction that one might expect from almost any therapist working with a borderline patient, if the therapist is unaware of the meaning and the proper management of the patient's resistances as well as his own reactions. The feelings evoked in the therapist by the patients' resistances, if not acting out, may often provide valuable clues to understanding the patient. To act out on these countertransference-like feelings will inevitably compromise therapeutic neutrality, the therapeutic frame, and, hence, the treatment itself.

Once the relatively healthy therapist has been made aware of the meaning of the patient's behavior—usually through a combination of increased knowledge, supervision, introspection, and insight—he can generally contain his own reactions, modify them, or use them for understanding, and not act them out.

Countertransference-like acting out is to be distinguished from countertransference proper. Countertransference in the classical sense is a reaction that originates primarily in the therapist, not in the patient. It is a reflection more of unresolved, early developmental and interpersonal conflicts within the therapist than of anything within the therapeutic setting. It is between the therapist and his past primarily, and only secondarily (if at all) between the therapist and his patient. The manifestations of such countertransference reactions include:

- prolonged therapeutic stalemates
- persistent, repetitive ill-timed and misattuned interventions
- inability to contain countertransference acting out despite awareness and understanding of the patient's behavior
- inability to utilize and implement supervisory suggestions
- repetitive problems in similar areas despite the dissimilarity among the patients with whom one is experiencing such reactions

Countertransference, by definition, is relatively inaccessible to consciousness, self-discovery, or educational intervention, including supervision. It is imperative for the therapist who wishes to work with these difficult patients to begin or resume treatment when wishing to resolve such chronic countertransference difficulties.

These various reactions within the therapist are not always easy to separate out as distinct entities. Often the therapist's feelings are multiply determined. However, the distinctions that have been identified can be helpful to the therapist in sorting out his or her reactions and in providing guidelines for managing these reactions.

It is especially the therapist's countertransference acting out which I would like to examine more fully before proceeding with clinical examples that demonstrate the full spectrum of therapeutic responses: real feelings, countertransference acting out, and countertransference.

Knowledge of the borderline patient's intrapsychic structure helps the therapist understand and anticipate the nature of the patient's transference acting out and, therefore, to identify and control his own countertransference acting out.

Figures 1 through 4 schematically represent the most common forms of transference acting out and the resulting countertransference acting out evoked in the therapist by each projective mechanism. The borderline patient must, and will, constantly employ these projective mechanisms, especially early in the treatment. The therapist who is aware of the feelings being evoked will be able to respond to the patient therapeutically rather than resonating with the projective mechanisms.

In clinical practice, the relative frequency of use of the projective mechanisms will vary from moment to moment and from session to session and will be based on the nature of the unique defenses and vulnerabilities of the particular patient and the particular therapist. I will discuss each mechanism separately first, before demonstrating them all in action.

FIGURE 1: PROJECTION OF THE
REWARDING OBJECT RELATIONS UNIT

This projective mechanism is the one most frequently found in borderline patients and the one that most frequently evokes counter-transference acting out by the therapist. Why should this be so?

Most people who decide to become mental health professionals do so because of a desire to heal and to save. This desire resonates with the borderline patient's projection into external reality of the intra-psychic image or representation of a rewarding, nurturing, and caretaking primary object or "other." The borderline patient has an internal image or fantasy of what people are like, based on what he

Figure 1. Projection (RORU)

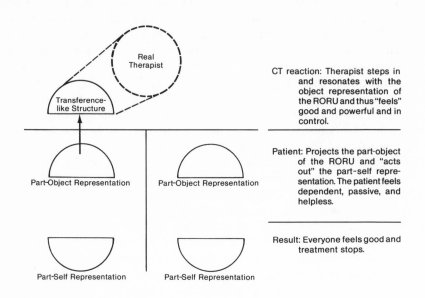

CT reaction: Therapist steps in and resonates with the object representation of the RORU and thus "feels" good and powerful and in control.

Patient: Projects the part-object of the RORU and "acts out" the part-self representation. The patient feels dependent, passive, and helpless.

Result: Everyone feels good and treatment stops.

Part-Object Representation

Part-Object Representation

Part-Self Representation

Part-Self Representation

Transference-like Structure

Real Therapist

perceives as his need and based on his past experience of others. What people are really like in the external world has little opportunity to be perceived by the borderline patient behind the veil created by the projection of the rewarding object relations part-unit. External reality is thus distorted in order to mirror the patient's intrapsychic world.

When projecting the RORU, the borderline patient attempts to get the therapist to take over such essential functions as decision making, nurturing, soothing, anxiety regulation, and self-esteem regulation, while the patient acts or feels as helpless, passive, dependent, or compliant as is necessary to draw the therapist into active participation in, or identification with, that role.

The therapist who steps into the rewarding unit projection does so in order to feel good, powerful, or in control. By becoming the representative in external reality of the intrapsychic rewarding object representation, the therapist gratifies his own unresolved dependency needs and wishes and his own failures in successful internalization of functions and capacities that maintain healthy self-regulation by meeting and gratifying these same needs as they manifest themselves in the patient.

Active participation in the rewarding unit projection is the most common form of countertransference acting out and accounts for the majority of interventions that undermine treatment. When this occurs both the therapist and the patient feel temporary gratification while therapeutic work is halted as the distortions of the past are replayed in the present. The patient will not have the opportunity for intrapsychic change and growth while this process is in effect.

Of course, knowing what is right and doing what is right are separate processes. Success in one area does not guarantee success in the other. Until a therapist understands what is motivating a patient's behavior, it is the therapist's primary task to struggle, first and foremost, to understand the patient—and only secondarily to examine his own behaviors and motivations. However, once the therapist knows what is right but finds himself repeatedly acting in contradiction to this knowledge, he must give primary attention to himself while temporarily placing the patient's behaviors and motivations into a secondary position.

FIGURE 2: PROJECTION OF THE WITHDRAWING OBJECT RELATIONS UNIT

If the projection of the RORU reflects the borderline patient's need to create in external reality a primary other who is felt as necessary for survival, then what motivation underlies the borderline patient's projection of the WORU?

Intense "bad" feelings of anger, rage, guilt, panic, and the like are part of the borderline patient's experience of the abandonment depression. In the conduct of his life, the borderline patient is constantly attempting to "rid" himself of these affects through externalization and projection. These projections tend to be pervasive, massive, and indiscriminately placed into and onto whatever external situation or person is available as a receptacle.

In therapy these projections are likely to fall upon the therapist, most frequently when the therapist fails to actively participate with the projection of the rewarding unit. (This "failure" in the eyes of the patient is in reality a therapeutic success.)

In response to the patient's anger and rage, the therapist must not succumb to, or participate in, the projection of the withdrawing unit. If the therapist is "caught" in this projection, he may be made to feel

Figure 2. Projection (WORU)

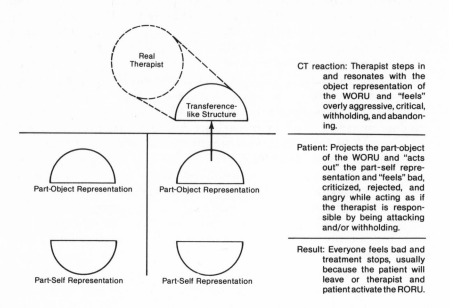

CT reaction: Therapist steps in and resonates with the object representation of the WORU and "feels" overly aggressive, critical, withholding, and abandoning.

Patient: Projects the part-object of the WORU and "acts out" the part-self representation and "feels" bad, criticized, rejected, and angry while acting as if the therapist is responsible by being attacking and/or withholding.

Result: Everyone feels bad and treatment stops, usually because the patient will leave or therapist and patient activate the RORU.

that he is rejecting, withholding, cold, critical, and uncaring, and respond with guilt, fight, or flight reactions.

The therapist who experiences guilt begins to believe that he is indeed critical, cold, and uncaring and attempts to correct the situation by becoming a willing participant in the rewarding unit projection. Anticipation by the therapist of the patient's need to project a withdrawing unit will help to head off the guilt. Also, therapists generally are able to correct the self-distortion transiently created by the patient's projection of the withdrawing unit by comparing such a projection with the reality of their lives—their own stable sense of self-worth as well as the reinforcement and acknowledgment of that self-identity by significant others (friends, family, colleagues) in the therapist's life.

In the "fight" response, the therapist responds to the patient's projection as an attack or assault and retaliates by *becoming* cold, sarcastic, and inappropriately withholding or angry, thus making the patient's projections a reality. When this occurs therapeutic neutrality has been sacrificed and the potential for a therapeutic alliance is interfered with or destroyed.

The therapist who does not explicitly challenge the distortion created by the patient by the projection of the WORU provides the patient with an excuse to leave treatment, or provides himself with an excuse to withdraw either emotionally or in fact from the therapeutic relationship. In either case, "flight" from meaningful treatment is the result.

Thus, the result of stepping in and participating in the projection of the WORU is that both patient and therapist feel "bad" or "angry" and the treatment process is halted, either because the patient or therapist withdraws or because both parties activate and maintain a rewarding unit projection.

FIGURES 3 AND 4: PROJECTIVE IDENTIFICATION INVOLVING THE REWARDING AND WITHDRAWING OBJECT RELATIONS UNITS

The projective mechanisms described in Figures 1 and 2 are the most common employed by the borderline patient, but they are not generally the most difficult for the therapist to manage. A therapist who is knowledgeable about the borderline personality disorder and the Masterson Approach will be alert to the trap of stepping into the rewarding unit projection and can therefore avoid doing so. The therapist who has reasonably good self-identity and object relationships can quickly correct for both the patient and himself the distortion that he is cold and uncaring, and treatment can then proceed.

The process of projective identification is often far more insidious and can be "upon" the therapist before he is prepared for it. Further, the distorted perception of reality which leads to active participation in these projective mechanisms is not easily corrected, as it invokes basic and virtually universal questions about our professional identity as well as our personal self-identity (such as whether the therapist has the ability to help a patient, or if someone else might be far more qualified or able to do so).

In the process of projective identification, the patient projects aspects of the self representation of the rewarding or withdrawing object relations part-unit while simultaneously identifying with aspects of the object representation of the respective rewarding or withdrawing units. When the projective identification involves the rewarding unit (Figure 3), the therapist is made to feel helpless, manipulated, and

Figure 3. Projective Identification (RORU)

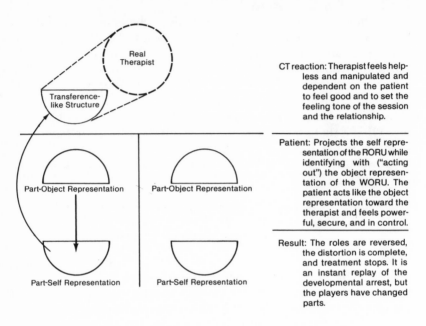

CT reaction: Therapist feels help-less and manipulated and dependent on the patient to feel good and to set the feeling tone of the session and the relationship.

Patient: Projects the self representation of the RORU while identifying with ("acting out") the object representation of the WORU. The patient acts like the object representation toward the therapist and feels powerful, secure, and in control.

Result: The roles are reversed, the distortion is complete, and treatment stops. It is an instant replay of the developmental arrest, but the players have changed parts.

dependent upon the patient for a feeling of well-being and to set the feeling tone of the session. For example, when the therapist finds himself awaiting the arrival of the patient with a sense of diffuse anxiety, which escalates if the patient walks in obviously angry or moody or is dissipated if the patient walks in smiling or bright, he is caught in the projective identification. A related phenomenon also associated with an aspect of the self representation of the rewarding unit is the therapist's felt need to be perfect, which derives from the projection of the patient's felt need to be perfectly compliant or "good." The therapist here feels vulnerable to, and upset by, the patient's criticism or his own self-criticism, usually experienced as guilt.

When the projective identification involves the withdrawing unit (Figure 4), the therapist feels inadequate, inferior, worthless, or bad in response to the patient's explicit or implicit characterization of the therapist as unhelpful, inexperienced, incapable, confused, or simply stupid.

Figure 4. Projective Identification (WORU)

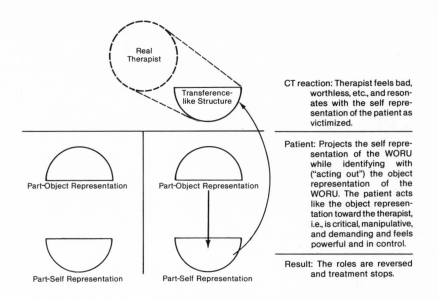

The therapist who is caught up in projective identification involving either the RORU or the WORU will feel victimized and not in control of the therapeutic relationship. Through the mechanism of the projective identification, the historical drama for the borderline patient is being reenacted. Unlike the process of projection, in which the patient is simply repeating, or replaying, the past, the process of projective identification can give the therapist a unique glimpse into the patient's unique and personal past *from the perspective of the feeling state of the patient.* This is because the historical roles are reversed in projective identification, with the therapist experiencing aspects of what it was like for the patient growing up. In addition, the therapist is given a reenactment by the patient of his or her experience of the significant parent or other in the patient's past history. Projective identification, when identified and not reacted to, can be a valuable window into the *patient's* experience of the past. It can take its place along side projection, which is a valuable window into the patient's experience of significant *others* from his past.

Projective defenses should be dealt with in the same manner as the other defense mechanisms used by the borderline patient. The distortions created by the patient's struggle to avoid painful affects must be clarified and confronted. The therapist must push the various projections back into the patient, so that they can be dealt with more appropriately as the patient's fantasies about what he is like and what people are like, rather than as the reality of what he is like and what people are like.

This is accomplished by first identifying what is happening (pointing out the resistance—clarification) and then questioning why it is happening (focusing upon the distortion, faulty perception, contradiction, or maladaptive behavior or response—confrontation). For example, when confronting a projection the therapist might ask:

"Why do you get angry when I don't answer your questions?"

"Why is it that whenever you come up against difficult problems you feel so helpless and look to me to help you out?"

Projective identification would be confronted with interventions such as:

"I wonder why you would rather try to intimidate me than to talk about what is really upsetting you."

"You seem to be trying to make me feel helpless, a feeling that you have told me troubles you so often and was one of the main problems that brought you into treatment. So I wonder why this is happening now with me."

Having now briefly reviewed some major forms of transference acting out by borderline patients utilizing projective mechanisms, and the potential dangers of countertransference acting out by the therapist, we can proceed to case examples that demonstrate these mechanisms in action—from both sides of the therapeutic relationship.

THE CASE OF R.J.

The following case, which I treated as a second-year psychiatric resident, demonstrates all the mechanisms we have reviewed and additionally demonstrates the adage which often applies to work with borderline patients: "Things go from bad to worse and then the cycle repeats itself."

R.J., a 40-year-old woman, recently separated, was working as a freelance writer. Her painful feelings of depression and despair and her desperate felt reliance on me had all proven powerful seducers. Thus, during the first year of her treatment, the patient had successfully manipulated me so that I was an active participant in her various projective, defensive mechanisms.

This was manifested, for example, by my acceding to her request that I let her know when the session had five minutes left. This was necessary, so she felt and stated, so that she could prepare herself for having to leave me and manage her pain on her own. I never questioned why the patient didn't wear a watch, or pointed out her responsibility to manage the time of the sessions and between the sessions, and I only fleetingly wondered whether her growing feelings of dependency on me were good for the treatment or her. I do remember thinking that it made me feel good and in a position to help her. My participation in the rewarding unit projection knew few bounds.

My willingness to step into the rewarding unit evidenced itself even more dramatically when I agreed to have "phone sessions" during my vacation. My participation in the withdrawing unit projection was demonstrated by my feeling that I would be letting her down, failing and abandoning her and my responsibility as her therapist, if I was not always available.

Additionally, I felt exquisitely tuned into R.J.'s every mood and feeling. I experienced relief if the patient was happy and smiling when she walked into a session, and I would feel helpless and depressed if she was angry and attacking. I felt as I if I were being swept along on an emotional tidal wave. I felt I had to be completely, always, and perfectly complaint with her need to be taken care of, and I felt inadequate, guilty, and bad when I saw her experience disappointment in me or feel let down by me.

At those moments when I was participating in her various projections, the patient would feel taken care of, with some relief from her chronic anxiety and depression. But, increasingly, I was becoming aware in the treatment of a sense of frustration, and beginning to realize that although the patient would momentarily feel better, she was not getting better. The sessions and her life moved from one crisis to another, with essentially no evidence of the patient being able to manage herself, or to internalize any of the soothing or caretaking functions I was performing for her.

At this point, I was about a year into her "nontreatment." I was having my initial exposure to the Masterson Approach at that time in my training, and I was eager and determined to begin to treat R.J. correctly.

I began by informing her that I would not, as I had previously promised, have "phone sessions" during my vacation, which was to begin the following week. Of course, I was not just conveying a change in practice to the patient; in my tone and manner I was probably conveying a sense of my shifting understanding of my role and the meaning of the patient's behavior. The patient had no way of understanding what was happening, except to perceive that I was acting "different" and withdrawing from her emotionally, because I did not discuss my "new" perception of my role and my "new" way of understanding her behavior. Rather, I had simply announced my intentions without erecting a new therapeutic frame within which she could judge and understand my actions. Probably, my actions at that time reflected both my lack of knowledge of the consequences of my action, and a countertransference acting out of my growing sense of victimization and loss of control by dramatically seizing control of the therapeutic relationship.

What follows are excerpts from a letter the patient wrote to me and slipped under the door of my office the day before I was to leave on vacation. In it, the patient vividly describes the events of the preceding days and demonstrates the dramatic exacerbation of her projective defenses and, finally, her real confusion over the change in my behavior:

Dear Dr. Klein,
I am so unbearably hurt that I fear angry and hurtful remarks will surface in this letter. Please try to remember and understand their source, and dismiss them as much as possible. [I was beginning to feel uncomfortable and guilty.] . . . What happened this last week seems to be totally incongruent with what I know of you after a year of therapy. My mind is confused and in pieces now. On Wednesday night [the night after our last session before the vacation] I had decided that I was going to move back home with John [her estranged, infantilizing husband. In other words, if I wouldn't take care of her, she would have to return to someone who would, even though she knew how bad he was for her. My discomfort was growing, and so was my guilt.] There seemed no other alternative. Thursday morning I woke with the intention of calling you again and asking you to reconsider. But I knew what the answer would be, and I could not face the unbearable pain [my own discomfort and guilt were rapidly approaching the intensity of pain]. I couldn't hold myself together. The night before I had dreamed that I had found my cat [whom she loved] stretched out on her side, dead. I started losing control [she is describing her fear/fantasy that I feel dead to her and that she, in

turn, will die without the object—me]. Joan [a friend] took me to the hospital emergency room just for sedation. It was when the doctor there told me that you would not speak to me [she had asked the emergency room physician to call me] that I totally lost control. I still know very little of what went on that day. I spent six hours with hospital attendants, in restraints for part of the time. [My refusal to speak to her dashed her hopes of activating the rewarding unit projection, leaving her enraged, frightened, and feeling profoundly rejected. I, at this point, was beginning to wonder what I had gotten myself into with this "new" approach, since I was hardly feeling good but, rather, was feeling alternately bad, uncaring, rejecting, and cruel.]

You worked so hard at developing my trust in you. I can't deal with this hurt. You have hurt me more than anything in life. [I struggled to remember that, in reality, I had merely refused to have phone sessions on my vacation, regardless of the somewhat impersonal tone that must have accompanied my announcement.] It is the frightening situation of a psychiatrist hiding behind a professional pose to justify acting in an inhuman way.

I feel alone and I'm terrified. It seems as if we were involved in some mysterious game, the rules of which were kept from me and were changed without my knowledge. . .

I had changed the rules and failed to let her know how and why. However, I, too, was struggling at that time to understand the "new rules." And struggle I did.

We both survived my vacation. Shortly after my return, however, she unleashed the full intensity of her rage in a session. I withdrew as she ranted on and on, and I became lost in my feelings of helplessness and guilt as she alternately raged and sobbed. I felt totally out of control, and fantasized gaining control by throwing her out of my office window. Instead, I dealt with my feelings of rage by the reaction formation of becoming paralyzed and acting out my feelings of helplessness, worthlessness, and guilt by allowing the session—and her tirade—to go on for 75 minutes instead of the usual 50-minute session.

As could be predicted (since this is a representative example of a common problem), neither this story nor the treatment had a happy ending. The treatment could not be salvaged, for many reasons. I had lost the chance at therapeutic neutrality so necessary for this work by my almost unfailing willingness to resonate with her projections. Too many distortions had been allowed to operate for too long without confrontation. I was too inexperienced to know how to manage the transition from rewarding object to psychotherapist. I had little faith in a new and only barely understood theory. The practice of confrontation seemed to conflict with my feeling that caring and emotional involvement were curative in working with personality disorders. I did not yet understand that caring in psychotherapy means knowing what to do and being willing to do what is right, despite how hard it might seem.

I was in analysis at the time, and it became clear to me that the problems I was having in implementing the new theory and technique could not be totally explained by all these reasons, because I was beginning to apply what understanding I did have to other patients with remarkable success. I realized that beyond the real issue of my relative ignorance, and the countertransference acting out that I was still doing, there were other—deeper and more personal—reasons for my difficulties with this patient. My analyst, realizing this too, initiated one of his rare acts of directive interventions (which demonstrated his concern over a treatment and a countertransference situation that had gotten out of hand) and wondered out loud whether I would succeed in destroying the patient first, or whether she would succeed in destroying me. He firmly suggested that therapy with R.J. be terminated, and the patient referred to someone else.

With great relief, I accepted and implemented his suggestion.

The knowledge gained through reading, experience, supervision, and personal treatment is all invaluable in treating patients like R.J. Although I have learned this over many years, I have continued to appreciate that the intrusion of the therapist's feelings (real, countertransference acting out, and countertransference in the classical sense) all interfere to some degree with the maintenance of therapeutic neutrality, and therefore with the maintenance of the optimal therapeutic relationship in almost all cases. The next case will demonstrate how these feelings must be constantly monitored and assessed regardless of the extent of knowledge, experience, or personal analysis.

THE CASE OF D.W.

The patient, a 27-year-old, divorced Hispanic woman, was referred to me just prior to surgery for the removal of a breast mass. She feared the surgery itself as well as the possibility of a malignancy. In addition, she was concerned about the effects of her emotional turmoil and physical state on her 5-year-old daughter.

She described her early life as having been dominated by her mother and characterized by compliance, submissiveness, and fears of criticism and rejection. She remembered feeling intimidated and helpless at her mother's rages. At the same time, she had felt protected by her mother, whom she perceived as a powerful figure. In latency and early adolescence, her identification with this powerful mother/aggressor manifested itself in a lengthy "tomboy" period. In adolescence, she became an organizer of social protest movements.

The father was a passive, basically absent figure to whom she would occasionally turn for "rescue" from the mother—a response which was never forthcoming.

The patient's marriage had been stormy and had lasted two years. The husband had deserted the family, leaving the patient alone with her daughter. D.W. worked as a hospital administrator, a job at which she was competent and which allowed her financial independence.

After three sessions, which focused primarily on her fears of illness and death and concern for her daughter, D.W. underwent surgery. The breast mass was found to be malignant and was removed.

Following the surgery, she called and requested "phone sessions" while she was hospitalized. Though this was the first time I had done a phone session since years earlier with the patient R.J., I rationalized that it was justified in this situation because I wasn't at all certain that the patient was borderline, and because there were real conflicts that the patient needed to quickly begin to address and manage, such as her concern about her daughter, her job, her capacity to function, and her fear of death. Only in retrospect would I ask myself what was to be lost by such an arrangement and why had I really acted as I had.

When treatment resumed in my office—as soon as the patient had an extra ounce of strength—her acting out and testing began. The diagnosis soon became clearer. Therefore, the acting out and testing became understandable; this was the same clinical course followed by all borderline patients. But I found that with D.W. it was far more difficult than it had been with any other patient for some time for me to respond with therapeutic neutrality to her transference acting out and various projections. I recognized this primarily as a feeling, rather than through any necessity to act it out in my behavior.

The patient would constantly ask for help in managing her illness and her life. After my confrontations around her wish to have me function as her internist, surgeon, and social director, she began to call with "psychiatric" emergencies: depression, anxiety, despair, and fear. After setting limits by pointing out that there were no "quick fixes" for her problems, I further questioned her as to why she felt she could not handle these feelings between sessions. To reinforce these confrontations, I stated that she seemed to want me to function in place of her own self. Following these confrontations, the calls continued, but with decreased frequency. Finally, I told her that I would simply no longer return her calls. At that point, the calls stopped. It seemed to me that the patient had only partially integrated these confrontations and that, rather, she was simply responding compliantly to my setting limits. In retrospect, I should have pointed this out to the patient and confronted her with her attempt to transform me from a therapist to a teacher (actually, a strict teacher/mother). But I didn't.

When she was unable to get me to step into the rewarding unit projection, the WORU would be activated and she would accuse me of being thoughtless, cold, uncaring, and rejecting. When I would insist on being paid on time and would hold her responsible for missed appointments, she would angrily state that I was cheap and "in it" only for the money. I had little trouble dealing with these projections with confrontation. I felt comfortable stripping these distortions from reality and questioning D.W. about the motivation underlying these pathological defenses.

Yet as soon as one defense was confronted and seemingly dealt with, she would invoke another. The impression created was that she was still not integrating the confrontations but simply trying to find what she could "get away with." She would complain that she was not getting better; that my treatment might be great for others but not for her; that I was only concerned about her mind while her body was dying. These projections again proved difficult to handle. They seemingly evoked questions about my professional identity and competence, but I felt challenged by them not only on a professional level but on a personal level. I wondered less about my clinical competence and more about my capacity for empathy and genuine concern. I also was aware of anger, and I questioned whether I was just responding to her projection of the withdrawing unit. I also wondered whether I was responding in unclear ways to the projection of aspects of her self representation when I felt periods of helplessness and questioned my ability to have an impact on her.

The use of projective identification mechanisms seemed even more evident when she would overtly attempt to intimidate me by accusing me of being incompetent, inadequate, and a fool, and she would seek numerous consultations during which she would tell the consultants of my failings. I took no position on the consultations except to confront her about the possible antitherapeutic acting out underlying her seeking these consultations. For example, I would wonder why it was that whenever she was angry at me she would run for a consultation; or, it seemed to me that every time she felt helpless she ran to find someone to tell her what to do; or, why was she trying to make me feel bad and incompetent when these were the very feelings about herself that she hated so and was trying to overcome?

In most of these interactions I felt that I was maintaining the therapeutic frame and my neutrality as well as I could. So I was surprised that the treatment proceeded in fits and starts, with improvement and adaptation reflecting more compliance to, than integration of, confrontations and with periods of defense being prolonged. After a year of sessions, the treatment seemed at a standstill.

At this point, I decided that I had to review the course of treatment in consultation with a colleague who would have a more objective perspective. I systematically went back to examine and look for any holes in the therapeutic frame, breaks in my therapeutic neutrality, evidence of countertransference acting out, and signs of deeper, more hidden, countertransference reactions. Because I had not had so many difficulties with a borderline patient for some time (actually, since R.J.), I suspected that I might find problems in all these areas.

I was right.

Evidence of my participation in various projective defenses employed by the patient came quickly to the surface. After discussion with the consultant, I realized that the prolonged period of phone sessions while D.W. was in the hospital had been a clear example of stepping into the rewarding unit projection, despite my attempts at the time to rationalize this decision. As the consultant pointed out, there was an active and excellent liaison psychiatry department in the hospital where the patient had undergone surgery, and I had seen the patient for only three sessions prior to surgery. There had really been no good or pressing clinical reason for jeopardizing therapeutic neutrality with phone sessions. The explanation was that it was countertransference acting out of my wish to rescue and to take care of the patient. Why had I fallen into the trap? Part of it, I realized, had been my feeling of genuine, real, concern and sadness for the many dilemmas she was facing: her illness and its complications, the anxiety around the malignancy, and her many concerns for her daughter. These real feelings, however, had interfered with treatment by making me vulnerable to stepping into the rewarding unit.

Further review revealed additional evidence of my having broken the frame and my neutrality. I was now able to recognize this reactions, however, as a sure sign of being caught in projective defenses. For example, I was now the one worried about being criticized, attacked, or "scolded" for my behavior, just as she had been throughout her life.

As I began to consistently point out and confront these defenses, she said that she was amazed that it had taken me over a year to figure this out and that I had better examine my countertransference!

There were other, more subtle examples that demonstrated my resonating with her projective identification defenses and my feeling, therefore, alternately helpless and inadequate—clearly split-off aspects of her own impaired self representation. For example, I realized that I had been overly active in using "therapeutic astonishment" as part of my confrontations much of the time with her. I found upon examination that I had been overusing this technique to deal with my feelings that my confrontations were not adequate or skilled enough and that I needed to do more for this patient.

But why was I having so much trouble with this patient and not with so many others, most of whom also had real life problems that could evoke real empathy and feelings but without my having to act out on these feelings? The consultant, responding to my repeated references to the phone sessions many years ago with R.J., asked me if there might not be other similarities either in these patients or in my reactions to these two patients. As I pondered this question, I remember feeling a mixture of anxiety, surprise, and relief. I realized that deeper, more personal aspects of my past that had interfered with my treatment of R.J. were again being tapped into by D.W.

Overall, I realized that I had, under the guise of caring about the patient's improvement, fallen into the role of taking care of her. Although I had been sure that my rewarding unit fantasy had been under control, I now had to acknowledge otherwise. My wish to step into the rewarding unit had been stimulated by my genuine concern for her, my identification with aspects of her past, and my misplaced attempt to deal again with renewed unconscious conflicts from my past. All these feelings, taken together, had become toxic to the treatment. The price of a healthy rewarding unit fantasy in treatment will always be a sick therapeutic alliance.

As a consequence of my awareness of the countertransference acting out and countertransference problems, which could now be consciously contained and further worked on introspectively, I could consistently make repairs on the therapeutic frame and reestablish my therapeutic neutrality. As I began to consistently do my job in the treatment, the patient started to do hers in a more consistent manner. Her acting out gradually ceased over the next three to four months;

she became more depressed, and she started to bring new feelings and memories to the sessions. Fuller and deeper exploration of her feelings of intimidation, helplessness, rejection, and depression as well as other aspects of the abandonment depression was now possible. All of this material had remained partially emotionally walled off because my participation in her transference acting out had continually fueled and activated her wish for the rewarding object, which had consequently kept her from assuming responsibility for her feelings and her actions.

In psychotherapy of the personality disorders, the therapist is faced with a difficult task and an ongoing challenge. The therapist must not only acquire knowledge about the patient and himself; he must also constantly monitor the patient's reactions and his own.

Dynamic psychiatry is just that—personal and always in flux, never static and impersonal. The therapist's feelings are the unspoken half of the therapeutic relationship and therefore of therapeutic failure or success.

Chapter 18

Countertransference with the Passive-Aggressive Transference Acting Out of a Borderline Personality

Candace Orcutt, Ph.D.

Virginia Eliot (a pseudonym) is a woman just entering her forties. She is dignified and sensitive in appearance, but tends to be so self-effacing in manner and understated in dress that she would be easy to overlook in a group. When she does unbend, she shows a quick intelligence and sharp wit. Even at her most anxious (and that is her predominating affect), she is verbally articulate. She is employed full time as an editor, and does freelance work on the side. She lives in an exclusive relationship with her lover, a woman physician.

She applied for treatment because of a deepening depression of four-and-a-half-years' duration. Except for the freelance work, she had been unable to hold a job during that time. She felt that she was in "a dark pit," and feared she might not be able to get out again. Her application to the Masterson Group had been precipitated by the lengthy absence of her lover, who had been out of town completing a research project. Ms. Eliot felt that the separation might be more than she could handle emotionally.

Ms. Eliot is presently terminating her treatment after five years of three-times-a-week sessions. Today she is employed full time, maintains her freelance work, enjoys a social life with her lover, and plans to publish a volume of her own poetry.

This chapter focuses on countertransference issues in the first two years of the treatment, during the period of testing or confrontation that was to develop into the working through of her abandonment depression. During this initial period, Ms. Eliot was entrenched in her resistances, which necessitated a heightened and sustained level of confrontation. These elements combined to make this case especially conducive to countertransference. Add the fact that I was newly learning the Masterson Approach, and my susceptibility to countertransference reactions became still more predictable.

HISTORY

Ms. Eliot is the daughter of intellectual, socially withdrawn parents. Her mother was a violinist, who brought in an income by teaching and giving music lessons. The father is an inventor. Except for a few friends with whom the mother played chamber music, and the father's scientific-minded colleagues, the couple socialized almost entirely within the orbit of the extended family. The father and mother had known each other for many years before they decided to have children. They were so close that Ms. Eliot commented, "Neither needs me." A brother, three years younger than the patient, became a married professional with three children and is depressed, reclusive, and driven.

Her mother was bedridden through much of her pregnancy with her daughter, who expresses intense feelings around these circumstances. She wonders if she might somehow have been damaged by her mother's prolonged inactivity. Conversely, she feels indebted to her mother, saying "I owe her something. She was just lying there, watching this thing grow." Then she adds ambiguously: "She could have grown to hate me."

At about age 3, the patient experienced two traumatic separations from her mother. The mother went into the hospital to give birth to the patient's brother. Ms. Eliot recalls running to the hospital elevator to meet her mother returning with the baby. Terrifying and confusing dreams about elevators, reported by Ms. Eliot during the course of treatment, suggest the emotional importance of this event to her.

Within the year, the patient herself was hospitalized because of acute difficulty in breathing. The problem was compounded because the ward was quarantined, and the mother was unable to visit her daughter, who vividly recalls the loneliness and misery she experienced.

A third separation occurred at this time when she was moved out of her parent's bedroom to sleep alone in the living room. This is the early memory she most often refers to when exploring her feelings of being excluded. After her brother was born, his crib was moved into the parental bedroom, and her cot was moved out. She would sleep in her parents' bed until it was time for them to retire; then they would move her to the living room. She recalls lying awake, missing her mother and crying until she eventually fell asleep.

During Ms. Eliot's childhood, she and her mother were nearly inseparable. When the mother came to teach music and art at her daughter's school, the two shared each other's company at lunchtime and left together at the end of the school day. The daughter's shyness, and the mother's constant availability, kept the patient from forming relationships with other children. In addition, she recalls feeling jealous of the children her mother instructed in the home. She strove to remain at the center of her mother's attention, and her mother welcomed the attachment.

In her adolescence, the patient began to rebel against her mother. She perceived her mother's overpossessiveness as being "spied on," and there were open clashes. This conflict brought out a "crazy" side to the mother, who slapped her daughter, and threw around her belongings when the young woman wanted to move out on her own.

Ms. Eliot's late adolescence and young adulthood were characterized by disappointment and frustration. At college, she was no longer the center of attention, and did not know how to manage school work and socialization by herself. She experienced the first of her depressions, and "stopped trying" and "hid" in her small, cluttered dorm room. She thinks she would not have completed college if a close woman friend hadn't "dragged me out" and mobilized her in her last year. In the same year, she first became aware of her lesbianism.

The battle with the mother recommenced after college. The patient dropped out of graduate school and began the first of several unsatisfying lesbian relationships. She became severely depressed and spent "three months in bed." This time she was able to activate herself, and used the impetus to find her own apartment (she had been living "here and there" to accommodate her need to be with others) and to complete her graduate training. Even though her mother was hospitalized for surgery, the patient, though upset, was able to maintain her self-assertion. For a few years, she had a relatively satisfying lesbian relationship and worked at a publishing house. Then the relationship dissolved, and she developed severe asthma and lost her job.

Ms. Eliot began a steady decline into the depression that would eventually bring her into treatment. During this four-and-a-half-year period, she lived on the remainder of her savings and subsidies from her parents, along with the erratic sum earned from freelancing. Then she began to settle into an intellectually committed relationship with her present lover. However, the relationship was marred by emotional distancing and open fighting. Simultaneously, Ms. Eliot clung to her lover, expecting her to help pay her way and provide constant company. She was unable and basically unwilling to reverse the depression, looking outside herself for sustenance. She did not want to face the loneliness and anger she felt when she had to run her life herself. She was deeply reproachful, and the unresolved anger tied her into a willful knot.

TREATMENT AND COUNTERTRANSFERENCE

Overview

Expression of aggressive feelings has been central to Ms. Eliot's progress. Consequently, my capacity to manage this issue therapeutically has been crucial. It is in this area I have found myself most uncertain and most open to countertransference errors, and also have learned the most. Whenever I have felt ready to permit without interference or obstruction Ms. Eliot's healthy aggressive expression (and this includes my readiness to contain the aggression released), I have found my therapeutic capacity increased, and the patient has grown.

At the outset, I experienced Ms. Eliot as surrounded by a sort of force-field of anxiety. A sense of inhibition, even prohibition, permeated the sessions. In order to avoid stirring up some vague dread, I felt an inclination to be too conciliatory, too permissive (as she said, to treat her as if she were "fragile").

As the expression of anger was facilitated and worked through, Ms. Eliot and I have discussed this atmosphere of anxiety more openly. She has said this was a repetition of her old situation with her mother. She has told me that her mother used to be continually anxious about "losing control" of her image of a good mother, and so tacitly discouraged any show of anger or even self-assertion on her daughter's part. The mother felt any such manifestation would reflect unfavorably on herself. In adolescence, the patient got her "revenge" by turning her mother's worry into a self-fulfilling prophecy: she became openly rebellious, and her mother told her she was afraid to provoke her anger, though they sometimes battled openly.

Ms. Eliot's transference acting out represented her wish to reinstate a maternal caretaking situation. If I would not cooperate, the implication was that she would collapse.

However, beyond the helplessness lay the threat that if I did not cooperate with her wish to be taken care of, she was ready to coerce me into compliance. Still beyond that was the additional threat that she would use me as a target on which to focus her angry projections, and so provide an excuse for a seemingly conflict-free escape into rudimentary independence. And there was always the combined anxiety and wish that the waiting anger would come out in the open, where we would wipe each other out, rather than struggle to gain understanding.

The Learner Countertransference

My countertransference reactions had to be sorted out into two primary categories: the learner countertransference, and countertransference proper—arising as a phenomenon complementary to the patient's transference acting out. (Of course, there is a great deal of overlap between the two categories.)

Masterson has delineated the sequence of countertransference reactions that generally can be anticipated in learning to work with the borderline adult. This can be understood as an eight-step process:

1. *Initial evaluation.* The therapist makes an objective assessment of the patient, which will provide the baseline for later identification of countertransference reactions.
2. *Helplessness.* The therapist experiences the patient's helplessness, and parallels it countertransferentially by adopting a permissive or indulgent stance. Both are in the rewarding part unit.
3. *Overdirectedness.* In an attempt to compensate, the therapist goes to the other extreme, and continues to

parallel the patient's transferential need to be told what to do. Both remain in the rewarding part unit.

4. *Neutrality established.* The therapist begins to take a stance in accordance with reality, but is still unsure. The therapist's insecurity and the patient's inductions lead to a fluctuating pattern of neutrality held, lost, and held.

5. *Confrontation.* The therapist is able to hold a confronting stance consistently. The patient now begins to respond therapeutically, and experiences abandonment depression.

6. *Countertransference guilt.* The therapist reacts to the patient's emotional pain with a countertransferential response that parallels the patient's unwillingness to manage feeling. Both are in the withdrawing part-unit and are likely to reinstate the rewarding part-unit next.

7. *Integration.* The therapist integrates a therapeutic stance and reestablishes neutrality. Once again, the patient begins to align with reality. The therapy is no longer governed by the patient's pathology.

8. *Therapeutic alliance and working through.* The observing, reality-oriented half of the patient's ego allies itself with the therapeutic process, which is maintained by the therapist. Regressions to the previous steps continue, but they become briefer and less intense.

Although my initial evaluation of Ms. Eliot's fundamentally rebellious dependency was intellectually clear to me, I found myself drawn into her muted, protective attitude. Both of us spoke so softly and tentatively, that mutual remarks such as "What?" "Could you say that again?" and "Sorry, I can't hear you" punctuated the first couple of sessions. Encouraged by supervision (and suspicious of my own discomfort), I began to assert myself and practice confrontation ("Are you aware of how very quietly you speak?" "Have you noticed, after you have spoken about feelings, you become silent?"). However, my grasp of confrontation was new and uncertain, and I found breaking through my own inhibition so satisfying that I then veered to overdirectedness with interpretations ("You are silent because you fear that speaking up will bring more loss into your life"). Essentially, I tended to act as though Ms. Eliot couldn't do her own therapy.

If I experienced a sense of awkwardness in the sessions, supervision made the reason for it amply clear. My confrontations improved as I saw that I was duplicating the mother's attitude by managing my patient or by sinking back with her into passivity and resignation. My confrontations also improved as I developed my skill, and so was able to reduce the beginner's anxiety that had made me more susceptible to countertransference reactions. The presence of consistent, sustaining supervision is especially important at this stage of learning, when the therapist is finding her or his balance in the face of the patient's obdurate defenses. Control of the therapeutic process requires a steady, positive self-activation on the therapist's part (a stance that eventually will be integrated by the patient). This control is gained, lost, and regained as the therapist learns to experientially understand both the patient and the process.

There was still the matter of countertransference guilt for me to deal with. In this case, I did not find the emergence of the patient's abandonment depression so difficult to tolerate, but was caught off guard by the aggrieved anger the patient used to try to deflect the abandonment depression. I tended to blame myself, and had to struggle to believe in the efficacy of my confrontive stance. I was tempted to believe (along with my patient) that helping her to correct her distortions of reality was hurting her unnecessarily. Again, supervision offered the objective assessment that I needed.

Integration of my therapeutic stance became easier as I observed how it benefited my patient. Especially as she began to carry her insights into practical action (getting a job, making friends), my approach was validated. The clear evidence of a therapeutic alliance, and Ms. Eliot's assumption of responsibility in working through—in the therapy and in her life—made the treatment increasingly satisfying, and simultaneously reinforced my integration of the therapeutic process.

Countertransference Proper

With the learner countertransference increasingly under my control, I was better able to perceive the countertransference reactions that arose from Ms. Eliot's transference acting out.

My countertransference reactions to Ms. Eliot have taken two main forms, reflecting the split object relations units of the borderline personality disorder and complementing the double nature of her transference reactions to me. Through the countertransference, I have been able to experience how Ms. Eliot, unaware, has tried to shape me into an indulgent, rewarding mother or, on the other hand, into a mother who disregards her individual needs and deep feelings.

Ms. Eliot had been in treatment in the past, and her therapists seem to have stumbled heavily into the rewarding unit first, and then the withdrawing unit—treating her as special, and then dismissing or neglecting her. She commented: "I think I have a frustrating effect on my therapists. I set up false expectations, then don't change much." They seem to have mistaken the intellectual compliance of her false defensive self as a positive sign, and then were discouraged when the "as if" therapy produced no change.

The indulgence of the rewarding unit showed itself clearly when after one month of treatment, I forgot to present Ms. Eliot with her bill. Caught in the act, I decided to explore this oversight with my patient:

Therapist: Maybe I feel you shouldn't have to pay.
Patient: Only my mother feels that way. Why should you?
Th.: Why should she?
Pt.: I think I feel she owes it to me.
Th.: Is there some kind of bargain implicit here?
Pt.: Yes—that I'll agree to remain dependent if she—or you—will take care of me.

On other occasions, the withdrawing unit has predominated, as I have found myself minimizing something of value to her. For example, I provoked her direct show of anger for the first time when I referred to her lover as her "roommate." Examination of my slip led to insight for her. She realized she could be angry with me and still continue her sessions. She also was willing to explore how much her tenuous expression of commitment to her love relationship set me up to undervalue it and, consequently, set herself up to be undervalued.

Once, I incurred greater anger by inadvertently giving away her mid-week appointment. Her schedule had been changed temporarily for the summer. She had switched to a session earlier in the day, and when it came time to revert to the old schedule, I found I had filled the time. This in itself was not so extraordinary, as I could not guarantee to hold the time open for her. But what was unusual was that I had not really discussed this possibility with her, had even implied there would be no problem, and then had taken an attitude that was casual to the point of evasiveness. I was startled into awareness of my error by her tears and recriminations: I was just like her parents, disregarding the importance of her feelings and what belonged to her; I was penalizing her for working; and so forth. She was in a rage, and assumed she had lost her hour forever. She felt unwanted, expendable, replaceable, insignificant. She was afraid she would never want to talk to me again. I acknowledged I had been negligent, but wondered why, instead of taking her anger out on me (and herself), she didn't herself clearly request what she wanted. She was able to assert herself, and, fortunately, I was able to provide a workable session time. This interchange carried over as she learned to assert herself instead of withdrawing out of anger, especially at work.

From a countertransference point of view, it is interesting that this happened just as she had overcome her long-standing ambivalence over maintaining a three-times-a-week schedule. It seemed I had unconsciously engineered a scheduling upset just as she was gaining more confidence (reflecting the influence of the withdrawing unit, when the therapist reenacts the archaic mother's role by withdrawing support for individuation). I also suspect that this may have been an indirect expression of talionic anger on my part: if Ms. Eliot treated her third appointment so inconsequentially, why couldn't I do the same?

Another time, the transference acting out of the "relationship" Ms. Eliot and I were duplicating unaware became clearer as I observed the countertransference derivatives in my actions. The patient often became evasive or apathetic in the face of separation or self-assertion. This was not surprising, considering how her fantasies of retribution had been painfully and repeatedly reinforced by real life happenings. Like the mother, whose denial of separation-individuation focused on her daughter, I became vague and forgetful when the patient was about to go on vacation. Once, I prematurely anticipated her absence and left her in the waiting room for ten minutes into her session time because I was under the impression she was already on vacation. Another time, I forgot that she had gone away, and waited perplexedly for her to show up.

When I shared these experiences with Ms. Eliot, it became clearer that she and I were avoiding direct discussion and acceptance of separation from each other. It seems to me now that I was holding on to her in much the same way that her mother drew her in for company during and after school, for endless mother-daughter confidences that warded off the mother's basic loneliness and depression at the expense of her daughter's emotional growth.

One day, Ms. Eliot hesitantly remarked that she noticed I had been starting late on an increasingly regular basis. I acknowledged her perception, and questioned why she hesitated to confront me. Her response was to describe a vivid mental image of "someone loving and caring holding the hand of a very little girl. I think I'm protecting your image of you! God! This is something entirely new! It's so important for me to reassure my mother that she's a good mother!—to keep up appearances, or what will others think?"

If my countertransference acting out had gone uncorrected, the treatment itself would have recapitulated the developmental arrest, and the process would have stopped, as it had in her previous treatments.

Each time I extricated myself from some manifestation of counter-transference, I found myself up against the same treatment issue: management of aggression (she was having difficulty expressing and differentiating between anger and self-assertion). Each time I attempted to help the patient deal with her resistance to asserting herself, I found myself facing that part of her ego that was allied with her mother's tacit or explicit demand for compliance.

Only repeated confrontation helped her to recognize the extent of that compliance, and eventually to find it ego dystonic. Even after that, she symbolically clung to the mother imago by reversing compliance to open rebellion (both retained the old attachment, so that her reactions still related to past history).

I had to be able to sustain my confrontation of her transference acting out until she could see for herself that she was either inhibiting or dramatizing her aggression because she persistently acted toward me as she had toward her mother. I had to remain steady so that she could observe how repetitiously and inappropriately she behaved toward me and could begin to question and dislike it. If she (and I) could understand I was not like her mother, she could begin to accept her real self: an adult with a variety of choices.

In the ninth month of treatment, there was an important occurrence that had an unexpected outcome. Ms. Eliot came into the office and stated simply: "My mother died yesterday." Her initial reactions were typical of a grieving patient: she felt disbelief but had intermittent bouts of crying and self-recrimination. For me, it was simply a time to be there.

Even then, she was aware that she was struggling with the dual issue of grief and separation. She said she wanted to lean on me to retain the familiar, but also felt that this shielded her from her anxieties and reactions. She needed me to express her grief to, but also knew if she clung to me, she would deny the psychic separation she feared. She was wracked by feelings that she expressed in heightened images: the loss of her mother was as if "a living tree had been pulled up by the roots."

I supported the grief work and confronted avoidance of the separation issue. Still, I experienced a persistent regressive pull. What right did I have to expect her to maintain the same level of effort under the circumstances? Shouldn't I let things coast?

Ironically, life provided a strange parallel when my father became suddenly ill and died. Like my patient, I felt shocked and unprepared to meet realistic demands that required me to rely on untested inner resources. A crisis can mobilize or immobilize us. In this situation, I learned the destructiveness of "protecting" my patient from the work, when therapy could reinforce her capability to manage her loss. Grief, I think, led to a stronger sense of self-trust for us both.

That year, Ms. Eliot found a job, began to manage her own finances, and accepted a deeper degree of commitment to her lover. I consolidated my therapeutic stance.

There are times when with Ms. Eliot I experience an idea, an image that seems unrelated to me, although it has suddenly appeared in my thought process. This is the experience of projective identification. It seems to happen when the patient, completely unaware, "puts into" me some element of her psychic life that she is not yet prepared to integrate. This is a phenomenon commonly experienced in work with patients who are present a preoedipal state of interpersonal "permeability." Because this seems to revive early, dyadic—even symbiotic—psychic states, this occurrence has an eerie, person-less quality. The therapist "becomes" the patient, the patient's mother, or parts of either. It is easy to mistake such perceptions and feelings as one's own, lose the therapeutic stance, and take refuge (usually) in the rewarding unit.

On the week of the anniversary of her mother's death, Ms. Eliot spoke of avoiding her feelings. She made some superficial positive statements about having made progress in her life, and wished her mother could know about them. I became aware of a sudden, intense sensation of hunger. I took advantage of a pause to ask her what she was feeling. In response, she became unexpectedly dependent, resenting that she was obligated to take responsibility for herself the rest of her life. She wanted to think that "soon school will be out, and mother will take care of me again." This could have been taken as an invitation to step into the rewarding unit. Instead, I pointed out that, on the anniversary of her mother's death, she was feeling deprived—hungry, in a sense—but that she was trying to keep this out of awareness. She then remarked that lately she had had some trouble feeding herself, and often arranged it so that she would come to her session hungry. This led to further discussion of how she would like me to feed her and take care of her, and eradicate the painful feelings caused by remembrance of her mother's death.

On other occasions I have "picked up" feelings of anger and sadness, or ridicule, or sudden, almost intolerable hope that she had split off and put into me to "hold" (Winnicott), "contain" (Bion) or "metabolize" (Fliess). Sometimes I have asked her what she is feeling, and sometimes I have speculated on what I am feeling. She has then responded by integrating and expressing the feeling herself.

In dealing with my countertransference reactions, I have seen myself shift from the tendency to become the possessive, dyadic mother to a therapeutic figure who supports the patient's self-expression and growth. The more I have been able to observe, confront, and discuss my countertransference experiences (often directly with the patient), the more I have found myself promoting a secure context for the therapeutic process. Most important, I have learned how to better facilitate the expression of the patient's true self. With good work and the passage of time, Ms. Eliot is emerging from the limitations of the past with a new readiness for self-assertion, creativity, and intimacy.

Chapter 19

Countertransference to Transference Acting Out of Hopelessness

Karla Clark, Ph.D.

The identification and management of countertransference is a crucial aspect in the treatment of borderline patients. In particular, the tendency of these patients to employ the defense of projective identification, which leads the therapist to experience certain strong and unpleasant feelings (which actually originate in the patient) as his own, is an issue frequently encountered in psychotherapy. Problems arise when the therapist (a) fails to identify the source of the unpleasant feeling as within the patient and (b) himself defends against feeling the unpleasant feelings. The solution involves identifying the countertransference, managing it, and then identifying the projective identification beneath and managing that in turn. Using a case presentation, I will demonstrate how this form of countertransference, stimulated by the patient's projective identification, interfered with the therapist's capacity to maintain her neutrality. I shall outline the steps that were taken in order to identify and manage, first, the countertransference and second, the defense of projective identification that had stimulated the countertransference.

THE NATURE OF COUNTERTRANSFERENCE

From the beginning of psychoanalytic theory, management of therapists' feelings has been a source of concern. Freud wrote: "We have become aware of the countertransference which arises in [the physician] as a result of the patient's influence on his unconscious feelings . . . and have nearly come to the point of requiring the physician to recognize and overcome the countertransference in himself" (1957, pp. 144–145). As he suggests, the basic therapeutic task includes the therapist's awareness of, and control of, his own feelings as an important component of the whole conduct of psychotherapy.

A number of therapists, notably Paula Heimann (1950), Heinrich Racker (1968), and Harold Searles (1979), have emphasized the idea that therapists' emotional reactions are natural, inevitable parts of the therapeutic process, and have added the notion that therapists' feelings provide important data for the conduct of psychotherapy.

This way of thinking about countertransference opens up all of the possibilities for the use or misuse of therapists' feelings while engaged in psychotherapy. It also, however, makes the term *countertransference* too broad to be of use as a conceptual tool without further specifying its components. To make use of the concept, it is necessary to make distinctions between aspects of countertransference on several levels: (1) Does it exist at a given moment, and how do you know it does? (2) What is its source? (3) What is its effect upon the psychotherapy? Does it help or hinder the therapeutic process? (4) What mechanisms set it in motion?

The first problem is, how do you know that countertransference is in operation? Therapists' feelings can be felt consciously, be operating preconsciously and thus be relatively readily assessible, or be unconscious. Feelings that are conscious to the therapist are the least problematic; if we know what we feel, we are in a position to make decisions concerning how to use that information. The problem of identifying and managing countertransference becomes more complicated to the degree that the therapist is unaware of his feelings. Little (1951) put it succinctly when she said, "In any case, what is unconscious one cannot easily be aware of (if at all) and to try to observe and interpret something unconscious in oneself is rather like trying to see the back of one's own head—it is a lot easier to see the back of someone else's" (p. 33). The answer to the problem of how to identify something about oneself of which one is unaware lies in part in having a clear picture of what constitutes an appropriate or inappropriate intervention in a given situation. If one then strays from one's conception of the appropriate, this becomes a clear signal that unidentified feelings or reactions are at the heart of the problem.[1]

Having identified the presence of countertransference, the therapist must attempt to identify the source of his feeling. Countertransference may arise from the therapist's past, or unresolved infantile conflicts or neuroses (Reich, 1951, 1973); from the nature of the therapeutic transaction (Jackson, 1956); or from an aspect of the patient's defense, such as the tendency to split off, or disavow and project a part-self or part-object representation or feeling (Kernberg, 1986, p. 230). Identifying the source of one's feelings may not be easy. As the case discussion to follow will demonstrate, it is not unusual for a therapist to have to trace a feeling, or reaction, through several levels before arriving at a relatively comprehensive understanding of the source of the problem.[2]

Third, having identified a countertransference reaction and attempted to identify its source, the therapist must evaluate its effect upon the psychotherapy. One must distinguish between those forms of countertransference that enhance the therapeutic process (henceforth called positive countertransferences) from those that impede it (henceforth called negative countertransferences). I suggest that optimum positive countertransference is in operation when one's feelings are identified, their source is understood, and the affects are under conscious control. This last point implies that one's feelings are used in the service of the intellect and understanding of what would

---

[1]What is held to be effective or ineffective can only be decided when one has a therapeutic framework, or paradigm, which distinguishes what is an appropriate intervention from what is inappropriate. For example, if one were a behavioral therapist, a countertransference reaction might be identified by one's inability to provide a patient with a behavioral prescription where indicated. For a therapist with a developmental, object relations perspective, treating a borderline patient, negative countertransference would be signaled by one's impulse, if acted upon, to provide a patient with a behavioral prescription. The definition of what interferes with treatment is therefore codetermined by the method of treatment itself. The remarks in this chapter are governed by the application of the therapeutic paradigm of the Masterson Approach to the psychotherapy of the borderline adult.

[2]In fact, such an endeavor may prove so complex that it might be better to emphasize the *process of searching* for the source of a given reaction, rather than arriving at a definitive identification of that source, as being essential to the management of countertransference.

be helpful to the patient. Negative countertransference can then be defined as the existence of the converse of any of these conditions to a sufficient degree that the therapy itself is impeded or, worse, destroyed.

Last, when considering aspects of countertransference, one must ask oneself by what mechanisms feelings are generated in the therapist. On the broadest scale, this question involves whatever it is that induces one human being to feel anything whatever about another. One must always ask oneself, even if hoping only for a partial answer, by what means one is stimulated to feel certain feelings or behave in certain ways toward a given patient at a given moment. This chapter will discuss the specific mechanism of projective identification, and how this particular defense mechanism serves as a stimulus to countertransference and/or masquerades as it. This question must be considered within the broader framework of the nature of the borderline personality structure.

COUNTERTRANSFERENCE AND THE DEFENSE OF PROJECTIVE IDENTIFICATION IN THE TREATMENT OF THE BORDERLINE PATIENT

Borderline patients have suffered a developmental arrest at the separation-individuation phase (Masterson, 1976). The borderline individual experiences his survival as resting in the hands of the object. This leads to a characteristic hypervigilance concerning the doings of the internal object, which is reflected in turn in the relationships the borderline patient develops with others in his external world. He becomes a people watcher of extraordinary talent. He puts this talent to work in psychotherapy to understand the therapist. He uses this understanding to further his own ends in psychotherapy, which are to protect himself against the emergence of painful feelings. The patient's antenna are out and scanning with a particular purpose: to avoid experiences that he perceives as threatening to stimulate feelings of either abandonment or engulfment. From the first moment of the first encounter, the borderline is trying to arrange his environment—in this case his psychotherapy—in such a fashion that the affects associated with abandonment or engulfment will not arise. He does this for two reasons. First, he wishes to avoid the experience of these affects in relationship to the therapist (i.e., he fears that that one will engulf or abandon him). Second, he wishes to use the therapeutic encounter defensively in order to avoid the welling up of these feelings inside himself.

In practical terms, he uses his split, intrapsychic structure defensively, and will often attempt to get one to resonate with either his rewarding or withdrawing part object relations unit (Masterson, 1976). Because he is both hypervigilant and intent upon defense, the borderline patient is superb at spotting reactions that will serve his defensive purposes, unaware that if he is successful in this he undermines the treatment. Clearly, therefore, he is on the lookout for one's tendencies toward countertransference in order to exploit them, and the therapist, in turn, must be similarly alert in order that he not succeed in so doing.

What happens when vigilance fails? One form of such failure occurs when, through scanning, the patient locates an emotional vulnerability in the therapist and uses this to induce the therapist to resonate emotionally with a part-self or part-object representation of the patient's own. The therapist experiences the feelings associated with that part-self or part-object representation, and the patient does not. At those times, he is employing the defense of projective identification, in which an unwanted part-self or -object representation is projected by one person, and another person is induced to experience the feelings which are thus projected. When one acts in response to the feelings thus generated in such a way that one interferes with the psychotherapy, one is experiencing a form of negative countertransference in reaction to the patient's projective identification.

When the patient employs projective identification with the therapist, the therapist may confuse the source and feel the feelings which well up inside as her own. For example, a borderline patient may behave in ways calculated to anger the therapist, who responds by feeling angry and by wishing to behave in an attacking fashion (i.e., by assuming the attributes of the withdrawing unit part-object). This is not in itself a problem. However, when negative countertransference occurs, the therapist behaves in an attacking fashion or employs destructive defenses against either feeling the feelings or understanding them. She may, for example, rather than acknowledge her anger and identify the source of the feeling in the patient's behavior, deny that she is angry and, defensively, behave in an overgiving manner. Here, the source of the countertransference is an affective state induced by the patient, but which the therapist misidentifies as originating within herself. The therapist then compounds the problem by employing her own defenses against the affect, and the therapy suffers accordingly.

Resolving the problem involves progressive steps. First, one identifies and analyzes the feelings as if they were one's own, because at that stage one cannot be certain that, in fact, their origin is not within oneself. Second, one is in a position to then understand whether the feeling had its origins in the patient, who then projected it, or whether the feeling is indeed originating inside oneself. Third, one uses the information thus accrued to further the therapy. For example, having isolated the impulse within oneself to attack, covered over by becoming overgiving, one may recognize that one has been provoked to feel and behave as does the internal withdrawing unit part-object. One may then decide to either contain or confront the projection, once it is identified as such. The decision will rest upon the current therapeutic climate and stage of treatment, but will in any case be made from a restored position of therapeutic neutrality.

The following case illustration demonstrates the steps we have outlined in the process of identifying negative countertransference, controlling it, and recognizing the projective identification at its source. It will be shown how only after a lengthy process of identifying and analyzing layers of negative countertransference, could I become aware of the projective identification which was their source. I will discuss the effect my deepening levels of control and awareness had on the therapy, thus demonstrating various aspects of the management of both countertransference and projective identification.

CASE ILLUSTRATION: MRS. B

At the time that Mrs. B started therapy, she was 38 years old, divorced, and had a child. She was engaged to be married for the second time. The wedding was close at hand, and she and her fiancé were fighting constantly and viciously. She said that she felt suicidal, crazy, victimized, and helpless. She attributed her feelings to her relationship, blaming her fiancé, since she thought that she had been healthy and well until they had become involved. Though she blamed him for all of their troubles, she planned to go ahead with the marriage.

Her problems were not confined to her relationship. She was a lawyer with a degree from a top-ranking law school. Despite her obvious intelligence and talent, she functioned poorly at work. She was able to keep herself from getting fired, but her work history included difficulty with superiors around excessive demands for support and guidance and excessive absenteeism. Her difficulties reflected problems more far-reaching than she was ready to admit. Her attention was solely on the crisis presented by her feelings about her upcoming marriage.

Her history revealed the origin and development of her difficulties. It included many separations, losses, and traumas during her childhood. She was raised by her maternal grandmother until she was 2½, when circumstances forced the grandmother to return her to her mother's care. Following this, she lived intermittently with her mother, but spent a large portion of the rest of her childhood in boarding homes and schools.

Desperate to live with her mother, she acted up in school, so that most schools threw her out after two or three years. Rather than respond by keeping her at home, however, the mother simply found a new school or home in which to leave her until the whole pattern repeated itself. In the last years of high school, however, she stopped getting herself into trouble so that she could be returned to her mother's care. She settled into a Catholic boarding school which she loved, and where she felt at home. The nuns at this school made a powerful, positive impression on her. They seemed to offer her the mother's care for which she longed.

She did everything possible, unconsciously, from then on, to avoid further feeling of separation and loss. She completed high school and went on to a college run by the same order of nuns. She completed college and immediately married her first husband. She attended graduate school and had her first child, while she supported her husband during his graduate school education. Then she went on to law school herself and did very well. Her marriage, however, was in trouble by this time. She had become disillusioned with her husband's lack of ability to give her the attention and love she felt that she needed. She consequently decided to divorce him.

Her problems in adaptation did not show up clearly until after she divorced her husband and graduated from law school, both events precipitating abandonment feelings. She defended against the feelings by becoming helpless and non-self-activating. Poor performance at her jobs and a very troubled love life ensued. Retrospectively, she has been able to recognize that, although she had had many interests during school and had received good grades, she had never really managed to live up to her potential. Neither had she allowed herself to feel happy, contented, or accomplished, despite her own considerable talents and the possibilities for fulfillment life had offered her.

This broader awareness of the extent of her problems came much later in therapy. She began therapy with only a very vague awareness that somehow she managed to defeat the potentials for success and happiness which came her way.

With all of the loss and trauma in her early history, her capacity for treatment, particularly intensive psychotherapy, was in doubt. This became an issue with both realistic aspects and countertransference implications. There were, however, many indications that she might well be able to do the work. For example, her history included evidence of a preponderance of clinging defenses over distancing defenses. Her current functioning included the fact that she was deeply attached to and committed to being a good mother to her child (a powerful source of motivation for psychotherapy). Her ability to function well when not under separation stress indicated a degree of ego strength, and the fact that she had many constructive artistic and intellectual activities and interests indicated some probable activation of real self functions (as well as adaptive ego functions), which would help her to manage depression. An early indicator of negative countertransference was that it was difficult to see this evidence. Instead, I was overly concerned about her fragility. I experienced hopelessness about her potential to successfully resolve her problems, which I denied by becoming more eager to be of help to her.

The first eight months of psychotherapy were conducted before I myself started supervision in the Masterson Approach. My feelings of hopelessness about her were aggravated by my inability during these months to find a way of working with her that seemed to help her. Instead, things seemed to be growing worse. She was in great turmoil as, following their marriage, her relationship with her husband deteriorated further. During the holidays there was a major escalation of her symptoms; a particularly bad fight led her to overdose on tranquilizers. I responded to the pressure, compounded by my general fears of her fragility, by feeling anxious and inadequate. I dealt with these feelings by denying the extent to which I felt them, and by redoubling my efforts to give—thereby stepping ever more squarely into the rewarding unit. I became more and more available to her, to try to assuage my feelings of incompetence. Accordingly, she regressed. She spent increasing hours on the telephone with me during weekends and holidays as her "crises" mounted.

Although I was unaware of my negative countertransference and its contribution to the problems that I was having with the case, I knew that there was something wrong with the way things were going. I began searching for a better way to treat her. I turned to Masterson's books on the treatment of the borderline (1976, 1983) and used what I was able to learn there to set some limits with Mrs. B. She responded positively to these limits. The phone calls stopped, and the fights and suicidal threats subsided. I began to feel some sense of her treatability. Because of my sense of her potential, I began to consider increasing her hours to three times a week. The combination of my still fairly pervasive feelings of inadequacy to treat her, the impact of the improvement in the therapy as I began to apply the Masterson Approach, and my wish to attempt intensive therapy with her together solidified my decision to seek supervision.[3]

In the early months of supervision, I was preoccupied with learning the basic techniques of the model, in particular, confrontation. I was also unlearning basic techniques like interpretation and direction, which were part and parcel of a long-established sense of my professional self. Trying to change my ways of doing my job led to feelings of discontinuity and of being off balance. I felt scared, awkward, and defensive. As far as I knew, these reactions had more to do with me and with the new process than with the particular patient or my reactions to her and to her material. I would have to wait until my feelings of newness and strangeness subsided before the overdetermined nature of my feelings of incompetence could become clear to me.[4]

She, meanwhile, was beginning to do much better. Although she and her husband still battled interminably, the suicidal threats, phone calls, and physical violence all subsided. In the therapy, the focus was on the patient's defense of avoidance, which she demonstrated in her daily life primarily by procrastination, and in her therapy by absences and lateness.

As these forms of avoidance came under better control, she began to somatize and began acting out the wish for reunion. She became pregnant and used the pregnancy as an excuse to accept as little responsibility as possible for daily living. She turned to her husband to do all the important work around the house with her older child. Shortly after the birth of her baby, she developed back problems and

---

[3]Adaptive as I believe that decision to have been, it also contained elements of some things later identified as negative countertransference. My concern with competence, and my concern with this patient's fragility, led to my continued defensive unconscious collusion with the rewarding unit—wherein my response to unpleasant feelings of incompetence led me to expect more of myself rather than of her. In a sense, my defense of "doing more" was reflected in my decision to seek supervision. This was the very collusion which the patient had learned to exploit in the months before supervision began, and continued to exploit for some considerable time to come.

[4]This issue is discussed more fully in Chapter 25.

took to her bed for three months, during which time she did not come to therapy, take care of her baby, or fulfill any other responsibilities toward herself or others.

I had the concept of the borderline triad (individuation leads to depression and anxiety, which leads to defense) firmly in my head, but I nonetheless felt disappointed and surprised when Mrs. B interrupted real progress with this return to dramatic self-destructive acting out. I began to doubt the effectiveness of the treatment approach.

She began to pressure me to conduct psychotherapy with her on the telephone, protesting that she could not get out of bed. I was sure that therapy had failed, that she would never return to treatment. Despite my feelings, I managed to take the stance that psychotherapy could not be effective on the telephone, and that she was holding herself back in every way by remaining in bed, despite her back pain. As before, I defensively responded to my feelings of hopelessness and helplessness by wanting to do more. This time, however, I was able to control the impulse, although as yet I did not understand it. I was still at the edge of what was going on: able to identify and control feelings in myself, but without the ability—which developed subsequently—to examine the implications of my feelings.

Eventually, through considerable limit setting by her husband, by the doctors, and by myself, Mrs. B returned to active treatment. Up until this point, I was sustained by two things: (1) my cognitive knowledge that the interventions I felt inclined to make in response to her pressure on me (such as telephone interviews or home visits) were technically incorrect; and (2) weekly supervision. At the time when my patient returned to active treatment, I had begun to integrate my intellectual knowledge and the input from supervision and make it my own. The fact that she responded positively to the therapeutic stance helped in the conversion of that stance from intellectual conviction applied from outside to intellectual commitment applied from inside myself.

It was under these circumstances that my negative countertransference became more available to me for scrutiny as an issue separate from my reaction to learning a new model. I am sure that this came about for two reasons: (1) because the patient's positive response to my having held the line underlined the importance of my continuing to control the nature of my interventions, and (2) because by now I usually had control of the new treatment techniques and theory I was learning, so that the source of my errors could be clearly seen. I had integrated technique to the point where I knew the difference between correct and incorrect interventions. Knowing what I was supposed to be doing helped me see my errors not as happenstances, but as products of negative countertransference issues of my own. I was now in the position to work with myself as well as with her.

This demonstrates the principle that the first criterion for successful identification of negative countertransference is that the therapist must have a model of the psychotherapeutic process that includes a view of correct and incorrect technique. This model must have been internalized to the point that appropriate technique is both understood intellectually and integrated into practice. With this integrated model in hand, one is in a position to notice deviation from appropriate technique. Without it, it is difficult or impossible to distinguish countertransference from ignorance.

First, I noticed that I had a sense of uneasiness. I had the impression that something was wrong with the way the case was going despite the fact that on the surface things looked a lot better. After supervisory sessions, I had the feeling that I was getting away with something, without, of course, consciously trying to do anything of the kind. In preparation for a conference, I had been looking over my process notes in totality. Patterns I might have missed by looking over just a few sessions became clear as they recurred over time. I noticed that every time that the patient began to go beyond her daily life crises and relationships and talk about her feelings, something would happen and she would stop. I couldn't shake a suspicion that I was doing something in collusion with her that was allowing this to happen.

I found myself paying particular attention to errors I made and asked myself whether there was any particular context in which they were likely to occur. Despite powerful wishes to avoid looking closely at the material, I forced myself to see the pattern.

I saw that whenever the patient became uncomfortable, she would, as I experienced it, do or say something that challenged my competence. For example, she might start to ruminate on the fact that she'd been in therapy for over a year and a half and it wasn't getting her anywhere. She wouldn't attack me directly, such as by asking me what I thought I was doing. Rather, she would more typically wonder if she was treatable, or something of that nature. Retrospectively, when she did that, I believe that she was beginning to try to express some of her own feelings of defectiveness and the underlying affect of hopelessness. Each time that occurred, the therapy could have gone two ways: (1) If her externalization of feelings of inadequacy and underlying hopelessness onto the therapy had been confronted, she probably would have taken these feelings into herself and the therapy would have progressed. (2) If I failed to confront the externalization, she might continue to feel as though her inadequacy were a response to aspects of her external life and fail to reach a deeper understanding of her mood.

Each time, my collusion decided the outcome: I did not recognize either her externalization or the underlying projective identification. It was later that I came to recognize that the latter consisted of the projection onto me of a part-self representation of defectiveness, and the associated affects of badness and underlying hopelessness. Instead, I reacted to the feelings stirred up in me, felt the "incompetent" feelings as though they were my own, and defended against them by coming up with some kind of intervention (usually an inappropriately timed interpretation or direction), which warded off my experiencing feelings of incompetence. As soon as I did that, she would stop working completely, waiting for me to continue to do the work. Consequently, treatment was stalemated.

Having observed this, the first thing that I had to do was to learn to control my response, i.e., to keep my feelings to myself when she challenged me. Repeatedly, she would allude to feelings of hopelessness about her treatment and literally stop and wait for me to intervene. It required vigilance on my part to control myself, because she did this again and again even when I thought I had stopped responding.

As a result of my controlling my response, Mrs. B's chronic concerns with daily events gave way to consideration of her own feelings and behavior. The focus began to shift inward. As is the case with many borderline patients, Mrs. B had denied the importance of the events of her own past. She also completely ignored the possibility that she might have an internal life that influenced her perception and conduct of events. She knew that she had had an atypical childhood but had never admitted to herself how truly bleak, deprived, and traumatic it had been. The acknowledgment of these things led her to begin, for the first time, to consider the relationship of her past to her current functioning. This brought with it a diminution of denial of the painful nature of much of her childhood experience, and an increase in her feelings of anger and deprivation—in other words, the beginnings of the abandonment depression.

She turned to a consideration of her relationship with her mother, and began to wonder about its effect on her. She came to see her mother as a manipulator and exploiter whose sole purpose was to get the adult Mrs. B to support her financially. She saw herself as having been compliant and unable to set limits on her mother's demands.

Such progress cannot occur without triggering the abandonment depression, which in turn triggers defense. Mrs. B began to experience internal attack by the withdrawing unit object. Once again, she used projective identification to try to externalize and avoid dealing internally with the defensive activation of the withdrawing unit. I, in turn, did not identify the defense of projective identification, although I continued to make progress in noticing and controlling my feelings. I noticed that, as all of this progress was occurring, rather than feeling good, *I* was feeling bad—incompetent and inadequate in spite of her progress. In the face of the reality of Mrs. B's progress and my obviously improved functioning as a therapist, I now knew the feeling to be countertransference. I therefore asked myself why I felt as I did.

Searching for the source of my feelings, I turned to my own personal life and motivations for clues as to the origin of my response to feelings of incompetence. Like many therapists, a part of what had motivated my career choice had been a rescue fantasy. Over the years, I had come to see more clearly that the ultimate responsibility for the therapy was, although shared, unequally weighted. I had to do my job as well as possible, but it was the patient, not myself, who had to do the essential work of recovery. She, not I, performed her own rescue. At this time I had to give up the residues that remained of the fantasy that I was doing the rescuing in order to do my real job effectively, and thus I had to experience loss. I was still not in a position to recognize my feelings as congruent with hers, but I was working my way through the layers of self-analysis that were precursors to this understanding.

To recapitulate: I first identified a persistent error on my part which was interfering with the psychotherapy. In order to identify this error, I needed some basic tools: I needed a model of what I could reasonably expect from a patient at a given phase of treatment. I needed to know what were appropriate and inappropriate interventions during those phases. I needed detailed process notes so that I could go back over what had happened during an hour with more accuracy than my memory could have provided. Beyond that, I needed the capacity to contain my behavior, identify my feelings, and analyze them myself. *In order to identify and manage negative countertransference, the therapist needs not only an integrated therapeutic paradigm, but also the personal capacities for containment and analysis, where relevant, of unpleasant affects.*

I now knew to be alert when feelings of incompetence rose up in me. In controlling my impulse to act at those times, I now knew that feelings of incompetence, for me, defended against the giving up of residues of rescue fantasy and consequent feelings of loss. I was yet to learn that the feeling which I called "loss" contained the affects of guilt, helplessness, and hopelessness. The deeper layers of my own response were still closed to me, as was, in consequence, an understanding of the patient's defenses and intrapsychic structure. This illustrates the complexity of efforts to identify the source of countertransference.

I thought that I had sufficiently identified the problem. I now sat back and waited to see what would happen. The patient responded by moving more deeply into her feelings and displaying more signs of self-activation in her life. By this time, Mrs. B was up and about, caring for her baby, attending a program that provided physical therapy and helped her learn ways to manage her chronic back pain. Her relationship with her husband was still extremely conflictual, but, for the first time, she began to see that she was not entirely a victim of his irrational concerns and behaviors. She identified the fact that she *played* victim and began to try to assert herself instead. She inquired into the source of her feelings of victimization, and began to admit more clearly to herself how badly she felt she had been treated as a child.

She had a series of confrontations with her father, during which she told him that her childhood had been a nightmare in which he had participated through neglect. She had confrontations with her mother, as she attempted first to get clarification of facts about her past and, later, as she attempted to gain acknowledgment from her mother of the wrongs that had been done her.

These encounters with both parents were fundamentally unsatisfactory to Mrs. B. Neither parent was willing to acknowledge responsibility for contributing to her unhappiness. A long period ensued during which she tried to come to grips with the emotional consequences of their refusal. Interspersed with periods of working through, Mrs. B continued to defend by externalizing manifestations of the withdrawing unit. She continued to battle with her husband, and to interrupt work on internal processes with long stretches in which the hours were filled with complaints about her relationship with him.

Things came to a head when her husband announced that he was leaving her. Mrs. B used his absence to think seriously about his complaints about the relationship. She identified how often she made him feel incompetent and defective with her hostile and critical comments and her cold withdrawals. She knew that she spent a disturbing amount of her time waiting for him to do something wrong so that she could attack him.

This entirely self-generated insight marked an important turning point in the therapy. What had occurred was that the patient had been acting out the withdrawing unit with me by becoming the attacking object, placing me in the role of the beleaguered, inadequate self. When I did not respond, she intensified the same behavior with her husband. She also sometimes reversed this, behaving as if she were under attack and beleaguered, perceiving me (or, more often, her husband, who could be more readily induced to collude in this) as the attacking, selfish, and sadistic other. She oscillated between acting out at home and acting out in the transference, employing projective identification with both her husband and with me.

The acting out continuously interrupted her work on intrapsychic material. She defended against the feeling stirred up by this exploration by activating the withdrawing unit. By externalizing it, she then avoided feeling devalued, inadequate, and hopeless herself.[5] Things had to come to a grave point of crisis—her husband's threat to end the marriage—before she was able to begin to recognize this as a problem within herself rather than between herself and others. Having faced this, she went to him with her insight, acknowledging her attacks and provocations, and he agreed to return home.

She was more successful in containing her wishes to attack him or to provoke him to attack, following this incident. Similarly, I was no longer rising to the bait. The acting out defense was no longer working. For the first time, with acting out contained, Mrs. B began to talk about self-hatred, self-loathing, feelings of being different, defective, a hopeless case. Instead of acting them out, she was feeling the feelings associated with the withdrawing unit.

Simultaneously, she was working actively on her feelings about her mother. She continued to deal with these feelings primarily in terms of her present relationship with the mother, although she also made sporadic attempts to find out more about the reality of her past and to explore her own memories and feelings about it. I expected the

---

[5]Such feelings of hopelessness about the self are still defensive in nature. They conceal the affects of hopelessness about receiving acknowledgment from the internal object for separation and individuation and the need to therefore relinquish that hope and move on. It is these latter affects which are attached to the abandonment depression proper.

abandonment depression to emerge further and to deepen at this point, because the stage seemed set, but instead what occurred were months of dancing around the edges of the feelings, with the patient repeatedly backing off.

Once more, I turned to myself in order to discover what I was doing to contribute to the stalemate. Through supervision it was possible to identify that whenever the patient came close to expressing a particular affect, hopelessness, I would intervene, usually in a way that encouraged the patient to intellectualize. Once more, I handled this by controlling my wishes to intervene, thus slowing down the speed of my response and allowing me to think it through before acting. The following actions were helpful in this endeavor: I asked myself why I wanted to make a certain comment before I made it. Instead of speaking, I wrote down what I wanted to say, focusing on my reasons for wanting to intervene and what I hoped would be accomplished by the intervention.

In the process of doing this, I was able once again to note what feelings came up in me when I did not talk, and I began to do whatever self-analysis I could concerning those feelings. As this was accomplished, I could distinguish my reaction from my patient's, allowing the latter to surface in the therapy hour without interference. Her feelings were anger and hopelessness concerning the profound futility of attempting to get either parent to acknowledge her, even minimally, as a person with wants and needs of her own. She was working through the abandonment depression.

This part of the process illustrates the third factor needed to identify and manage negative countertransference. In addition to the possession of an integrated therapeutic model and the capacity for containment and analysis of unpleasant affects, the therapist should have competent supervision or consultation available.

I was no longer intervening in support of my patient's defense: projective identification. Since it was no longer working as a defense in our relationship, she began to employ other defenses to stop her deepening depression. Because these did not involve me as a participant, I could see them far more easily. I pointed out to her how, in sessions, when she began to refer to feelings of hopelessness, she would change the subject, act out, intellectualize, or otherwise defend. Gradually, her defenses modified.

With countertransference again under control, the patient's depression deepened further. She dealt with memories and feelings, specifically about that period when her mother had placed her in boarding school for what was to be the rest of her childhood. She described vividly the process of giving up hope. She understood her desperate attempts to ward off knowledge of her mother's indifference by accepting her mother's version of the circumstances of Mrs. B's childhood: that is, that she was a wonderful mother who did everything for her child, and that the child herself had to be sent away because she was intractable—or defective.

Her deepening depression frightened the patient, and she employed her unconscious knowledge of me to again try to stop the process. She protested that she did not want to go on with it, that she hated the feelings she was getting. She described feeling something she labeled as a sense of "absurdity" about events, quoted Sylvia Plath, and subtly began to threaten that she was going crazy. She expressed fears of being locked up. She said that she felt suicidal, but that killing herself was out of the question because of the effect that this would have on her children. Then she would grow silent, waiting for me to respond.

I was aware of feelings of anxiety. My feeling was that I had unleashed too much, that she couldn't handle it. I wanted to *do* something. Once more, in response to her feelings of hopelessness, I felt helpless and guilty. I identified that I was feeling "incompetent" again—regressing and wanting to use my old defenses. This time, I saw that these reactions were the attributions I gave to feelings that were originating in the patient. I turned to trying to understand what they meant to her. When I did so, I saw again that she was attempting to get me to resonate with and act out her feelings of hopelessness and inadequacy for her, thus externalizing them and preventing her from feeling them inside. In recognizing that she was employing projective identification to accomplish this, I had converted negative into positive countertransference. I was able to contain the feeling I now knew to originate in her by being very quiet during sessions, intervening only to point out when she diverted herself from exploring her hopeless feelings. I could also confront the externalization. In response, she revealed that she knew that her greatest difficulty was in allowing herself to fully acknowledge the depth of her mother's indifference to her. She spontaneously said that she thought that threats of going crazy were an expression of her fantasy that by this means she could at last wrest acknowledgment from her mother of what she had done to her. She wanted her mother to finally recognize her as a living, sentient, and vulnerable human being who had been gravely injured by indifference, selfishness, and neglect. To acknowledge that her mother would never admit this, she continued, would be to begin to truly break the tie.

She said that her parents' acknowledgment would change nothing—would not make up for the past. It was up to her to go on from here. She recognized that in truth her difficulty was in allowing herself to lead a meaningful and creative life. In a session of great power and emotion, having acknowledged the hopelessness of her wish for acknowledgment from outside in order to effect a cure for herself inside, she was able for the first time to describe the nature of her tie to her internalized mother: "If she was going to have nothing, I sure as hell was going to go down with her." She added that she knew that the worst part of this was that she had continued to abide by this perceived bargain with her mother all on her own, inside herself, throughout her whole life, and that this accounted for her lack of ability to follow through on her successes or to allow herself joy.

SUMMARY AND CONCLUSIONS

I have limited my discussion to the ways in which negative countertransferences interfere with the identification and management of projective identification. Through the induction of affective states within another person that correspond to disavowed part-self or part-object representations, the patient can avoid acknowledging both the existence of the part-self and -object representations and the experience of the affects that accompany them. Mrs. B used projective identification to induce me to act out with her disavowed aspects of her part-self and part-object representations. Because of negative countertransference, I colluded with her induction. Until my collusion was contained, the part-self and part-object representations were not available for scrutiny. When it was contained, I could be objective about my feelings and use them to understand the patient better and to help her more effectively.

Experiencing these feelings is not, in and of itself, a problem. Indeed, one can use the identification of these feelings within oneself to understand what is going on with the patient more deeply. The problem arises when the therapist mistakes the source of the feelings, thinking that the emotions in question are solely her own and have no specific reference to the patient. The problem is compounded if the therapist also employs her own defenses against the affects themselves. Both misidentifying the source of the feeling and defending against it are forms of negative countertransference.

In the case presented, both forms of negative countertransference occurred. Such negative countertransference can be identified only through the recognition of technical errors on the part of the therapist and of the patterns underlying the errors. To rectify the problems, self-supervision, outside supervision, self-control, and self-analysis were employed. All these efforts hinged upon having at one's disposal a model for the conduct of psychotherapy that included clear guidelines for appropriate and inappropriate interventions by the therapist and expected responses from the patient.

In a letter Freud wrote to Ludwig Binswanger in 1913, he spoke of the absolute importance of attending to countertransference:

> It is one of the most difficult [problems] technically in psychoanalysis. I regard it as more easily solvable on the theoretical level. What is given to the patient should indeed never be a spontaneous affect, but always consciously allotted, and then more or less of it as the need may arise. Occasionally, a great deal, but never from one's unconscious. This I should regard as the formula. In other words, one must always recognize one's countertransference and rise above it, only then is one free of oneself. . . All of this is not easy, and perhaps possible only when one is older. (In Binswanger, 1957, p. 50)

This passage certainly demonstrates Freud's growing awareness of the ubiquity of countertransference reactions in psychotherapy, and his appreciation of the need to grapple with this problem in order to succeed with the work. Though the meaning of countertransference has broadened, along with our ideas of its place in the conduct of psychotherapy, the need to recognize and rise above one's countertransference is as great today as it was thirty years ago.

REFERENCES

Binswanger, L. (1957). *Sigmund Freud: Reminiscences of a friendship.* Translated by N. Buterman. New York: Grune & Stratton.

Freud, S. (1957). The future prospects of psychoanalytic therapy. *The standard edition of the complete psychological works of Sigmund Freud* (Vol. 11, pp. 139–151). London: Hogarth Press. (Original work published 1910)

Heimann, P. (1950). On countertransference. *International Journal of Psychoanalysis*, 31, 81–84.

Little, M. (1951). Countertransference and the patient's response to it. *International Journal of Psychoanalysis*, 38, 240-254.

Jackson, D. D. (1956). Countertransference and psychotherapy. *Progress in Psychotherapy*, 4, 234-238.

Kernberg, O. (1984). Countertransference, transference regression, and the incapacity to depend. In O. Kernberg, *Severe personality disorders* (pp. 264–274). New Haven and London: Yale University Press.

Kernberg, O. (1986). Factors in the treatment of narcissistic personalities. In A.P. Morrison (Ed.), *Essential papers on narcissism* (pp. 213-244). New York and London: New York University Press.

Masterson, J. (1976). *The psychotherapy of the borderline adult.* New York: Brunner/Mazel.

Masterson, J. (1983). *Countertransference and psychotherapeutic technique.* New York: Brunner/Mazel.

Racker, H. (1968). *Transference and countertransference.* New York: International Universities Press.

Reich, A. (1951). On countertransference. *International Journal of Psychoanalysis, 32,* 25-31.

Reich, A. (1973). *Psychoanalytic contributions.* New York: International Universities Press.

Sax, P. (1981). *The use of countertransference in therapy with schizophrenic clients.* Unpublished doctoral dissertation, California Institute for Clinical Social Work.

Searles, H. (1979). *Countertransference and related subjects.* New York: International Universities Press.

Chapter 20

Countertransference to Transference Acting Out of Suicidal Threats of a Borderline Personality Disorder

Shelley Barlas Nagel, Ph.D.

Countertransference reactions to suicidal threats, which strike at the heart of the therapeutic relationship, are among the most difficult emotions therapists must manage, and often interfere with and undermine the therapeutic work.

It is important for therapists to recognize their limitations. Suicidal patients are extremely difficult to work with, taxing the therapist's patience and energy. They can be manipulative, demanding, exploitive, negative, and hostile. These factors, in addition to the conscious or unconscious emotional or intellectual attitudes of the therapist toward suicide, may interfere with the therapist's ability to adequately evaluate and assess the patient's real suicidal potential.

Litman (1968) has pointed out that one of the best single indicators for evaluating high suicide risk in patients is the therapists' awareness of their own anxiety, which should not be denied or repressed. A failure to experience anxiety when working with patients who threaten or attempt suicide indicates a therapist with excessively strong defenses against anxiety, or problems with making empathic contact.

Therapists must be able to contain their anxiety in order to keep their perceptions clear, so that they can evaluate patients and their resources accurately. Supervisory consultation is often useful in helping to keep anxiety at levels necessary for effective work, and in keeping countertransference feelings from interfering in the treatment.

However, it must be remembered that no treatment, including psychotherapy, hospitalization, and drugs, can infallibly keep patients from committing suicide. Also, with some patients, there are certain times when a suicidal act is unavoidable. No matter how competent a therapist may be, there are patients who will still take their lives. That ultimate responsibility lies with the patient.

Another way to deal with countertransference problems is to understand the patient's use of the mechanism of projective identification. For example, patients may feel hopeless, but rather than experience this feeling, they project the hopelessness onto the therapist. The therapist identifies with the feeling, unknowingly or knowingly, and begins to feel hopeless and to treat the patient in a rejecting manner. Perhaps, on an unconscious level, the therapist is accepting the patient's fantasies. By this subtle intrapsychic, interpersonal process, patients project their feelings onto therapists and exert pressure for therapists to resonate with the projections. Then therapists identify with the feelings and experience the patients' emotions.

Therapists need to be aware that patients are eliciting their hostile and hopeless feelings. The therapist might say, "I find you are relating to me in a way that makes me feel hopeless or angry." The unconscious identification with the patient's projections is then lessened.

The evaluation of the suicidal patient is crucial to all psychotherapeutic treatment. Beebe (1975 a, b) and Farberow and Shneidman (1961) have discussed the evaluation and treatment process, and pointed out some predisposing factors. A history of a serious suicide attempt is the single most important prognostic indicator of suicidal potential (Weisman, 1974; Tuckman & Youngman, 1968; Dorpat & Ripley, 1967). Patients' developmental histories often include a pattern of deaths, loss, suicide, and trauma among close relatives (Gunderson, 1984).

Suicidal potential is high not only when patients are depressed and expressing hopelessness, but also when they begin to feel better and their depression is improving. Those risk-taking, impulsive patients who communicate their feelings through actions rather than words are at higher risk. Precipitating factors may be loss through divorce, death, separation, or absence of a supportive professional (for example, a therapist's vacation), as well as health problems, social disgrace, or loss of meaning in life.

Although it is true that patients in certain categories, such as those exhibiting multiple, serious suicide attempts and alcohol abuse, have a higher suicide rate (Hatton & Valente, 1984), the suicidal impulse is an important symptom to identify and understand whenever it occurs. It may develop in patients with a variety of emotional problems and has important treatment implications (Pokorny, 1964).

Mintz (1971) reports a variety of motivations for suicide: aggressive impulses turned back upon the self; hostility directed against an introjected lost love object; retaliation, spite, and the wish to punish another by inducing guilt or pain; efforts to force affection or other narcissistic gratification from persons in the social environment; and efforts to rejoin or merge with a dead or lost loved one.

The episodic suicidal impulse may last only a short time—it may be a matter of minutes, hours, or a few days. Prompt recognition and appropriate therapeutic intervention are indicated in order to help the patient get through the crisis. Patients often communicate their suicidal ideas and intentions to others (Robins, Gassner, Kayes, Wilkinson, & Murphy, 1959) and leave clues symbolic of a cry for help (Farberow & Shneidman, 1961). They are often most ambivalent about wanting to be dead and yearning for possible intervention or rescue (Shneidman, 1985). However, in some situations, the patient intends suicide and does not communicate with anyone.

The suicidal plan is important to explore because it provides a bridge between a thought and a definite action. The lethal potential of the plan needs to be evaluated, including the method and the availability of means (Litman & Farberow, 1961; Tabachnick & Farberow, 1961). Specificity needs to be contemplated. A concrete, specific, detailed suicide plan is more serious than an unclear and only fleetingly considered one. The most effective method for reducing the elevated lethality (Shneidman, 1985) is to do so indirectly, by reducing the elevated perturbation, agitation, anguish, or disturbed state.

There is probably not another situation or event during the entire treatment process that requires as much endurance, knowledge, skill, and sensitivity as coping with a suicidal crisis in a patient. During noncrisis treatment, aside from the ever-present need for empathy, quality concentration, and intuitiveness, therapists are constantly faced with evaluating and monitoring patients' responses, in addition to their own countertransference reactions, and with making therapeutic interventions that will be the most help to the patient.

However, when the subject of suicide looms, and active threats begin, there is no time to evaluate and analyze the intricate dynamics and vicissitudes of the treatment. There is an emergency—now. What to do next? What to say? How serious is the impulse? Is hospitalization indicated? Does the patient have pills, a gun, a plan? Are family and friends involved? How best to help the patient work through the crisis? Quick thinking under emotional strain is required to evaluate the intensity of the suicidal urge, and suicidal intent, and the patient's resiliency, history, and ego strengths. The suicidal potential, the quality of rapport between patient and therapist, the diagnosis, and the strength of the therapeutic alliance must all be assessed.

There is no one action that fits every situation. The therapist's task is a difficult one, laden with obstacles and semipermeable barriers. Yet there is courage in the struggle to understand that, while therapists are not responsible for patients' lives, they are responsible for their treatment.

The following case study illustrates the process of management of the patient's suicidal threats, as well as management of the therapist's countertransference reactions.

CASE STUDY: AMY

Presenting Information

Amy was a 34-year-old psychologist, articulate and intelligent. On her first visit, she seemed anxious and despondent. Although she appeared dissipated and disheveled, her attractiveness was apparent. When she began treatment she was out of work, having been fired from a responsible position. She stated she did not like being a psychologist, had not been successful, and wanted to explore another career.

Although she initially denied using drugs, a subsequent session revealed she used them daily, principally amphetamines, in addition to alcohol. She expressed anger toward her family, her former therapists, her former employers, her former lovers, and herself. There was no suicidal ideation present, although she felt depressed, lost, and alone. The last of five suicide attempts had been made two years previously.

History

Her history revealed symptoms of depression as early as age 4. She recalled feelings of loneliness and isolation. She did not do well in school, and was held back in third grade for poor concentration. At 8 she began overeating, and gained twenty-five pounds in three months. In junior high and high school she became a leader. She acquired many friends and developed a vivacious, charming personality, along with an interest in fashion and style, and a knack for funny, quick-witted comments. At the age of 16, she started using drugs and alcohol. Her alcohol and drug use developed into long-term, serious problems.

When she left home and attended college out of state, she had a difficult time managing on her own and flunked out. Returning home to resume her education, she left again in her junior year in order to get away from her family. Over the next few years, she obtained her bachelor's and master's degrees.

Not long afterward, Amy had an abortion. Three weeks after that, she awoke in her apartment one night to find a masked stranger holding a knife to her throat. She described the ensuing rape as the most terrifying event of her life. Over the next two years, she had a few short-term relationships with men, married and unmarried, underwent another abortion, and then lived for several years with a man who was a drug dealer and addict.

She made the first of five suicide attempts at age 21. The most serious attempt followed a session with her psychiatrist. She had not talked about her feelings in the session, but had silently planned to kill herself after the session was over. Amy took an overdose of drugs, ending up in the intensive care unit of a hospital, unconscious for days. She barely survived.

FAMILY HISTORY

Amy was the oldest child in a wealthy family from the East coast. Her father, a successful attorney, had been divorced once before marrying Amy's mother, a former model. Amy described her father as a stranger, remote and unfeeling, who considered her a nonentity. He had no time for her, preferring her sports-minded younger brothers, and always made her feel as if she were incompetent, immature, and irresponsible, both criticizing and ignoring her. The only conversations she had with him were when she asked for money; she felt demeaned when he doled out money, and there were always strings attached. Feeling not only unloved but also hated by him, she described herself as "groveling," always unsuccessfully, to obtain his attention.

Amy described her mother as a domineering and controlling woman who took over Amy's life completely. Amy felt overwhelmed and frightened by her. "My mother ran me. I never learned to think for myself, and to survive, I became manipulative." Her mother told Amy never to show feelings. She would sometimes find her mother hiding in the closet, crying. There was a code of honor Amy felt she must maintain: never discuss the family or her feelings. She had to follow this code to protect the family, but she was furious that she herself was not protected.

Although Amy said her mother was critical and judgmental in her expectations, she also described her as devoted to her family and a lively, charming person. Even though Amy acted helpless, passive, dependent, even stupid at times, she could still present a façade of charm and confidence to the world. She was rewarded for those outward shows by her mother, who did not see Amy as a person with thoughts, feelings, or interests of her own.

Her mother indulged Amy with money and clothes, emphasizing that appearance was everything, setting no limits on Amy's demands for money or on the time Amy spent away from home with friends. Amy resented her mother for not teaching her how to cope, and was afraid of her, too. She was living a split life, presenting a façade to the world of the perfect, upper-class family, with up-to-date chic fashion and charm. Inwardly, she felt devastated. Knowing that something was very wrong with her and with her family, Amy began to feel "crazy."

Treatment

When Amy began treatment with me and I learned of her repeated suicide attempts, and of her bitter refusal to tell her psychiatrist of her impulses, I knew there was a good possibility she would do the same with me. I questioned her capacity to communicate honestly, noting her untruth in the first session when she had denied using drugs, and also her lack of honesty with her previous psychiatrist. I discussed the issue with her immediately, taking a careful history while noting to myself that a background of suicide attempts is the single most important prognosticator of suicidal potential. In addition, I explored in depth over several sessions what she was feeling at the various times, what was behind her most recent serious suicide attempt, and why she had not talked to her psychiatrist about her suicidal thoughts. I gave attention to her methods, the timing, the circumstances of her attempts, her feelings about death, and the problems and pain with which she had been struggling.

During her twice-weekly sessions, I used the therapeutic technique of confrontation to help Amy become aware of the operations of her false defensive self, and the denied, destructive aspects of her behavior and feelings. During the first several months, she showed evidence of integrating the confrontations. She stopped using drugs, made attempts to decrease her drinking, and struggled to control her overeating. Two months after she started treatment, she began a relationship with a man who was unlike her former boyfriends. He was not married, he had a good job, and he treated her well. With the support of therapy, she found a job and began functioning better than she ever had. However, she still had great difficulty seeing herself as intelligent and capable.

Slowly, she came to perceive the relationship between her feelings and her behavior, developing the ability to observe herself. She began living in reality instead of in fantasy, saying, "I don't like what I see. There's no foundation. I have wasted years by not taking myself seriously, by hurting myself with self-destructive behaviors."

For the first time, she began to experience feelings instead of numbing them with drugs; she was learning to contain emotions, tolerate them, and deal with them in her sessions. Intermittently, when she could not manage them any longer she would act out by drinking, compulsively overeating, clinging to her boyfriend, and increasing her sexual activity.

I made it clear to her that drinking and coming to therapy were at odds with each other. I wondered why she had not gone to Alcoholics Anonymous, since she had real problems with alcohol. After five months of treatment and repeated confrontations of the seriousness of her drinking, she began attending AA.

Soon after starting in AA, Amy moved to a new job. That same week, her boyfriend left on a trip and, because I was away from the office, she missed one therapy session.

When I returned, Amy called, sounding cheerful on the phone, and asking, "Hi, did you have a good time?" She wanted to confirm her appointment for the following Friday, and to tell me that the time would not interfere with her new work schedule. Her voice was sweet, high-pitched, and buoyant. She said, "I'm fine; I'm feeling great," and hung up. Three hours later, she took 25 Valium and drank half a bottle of wine. When she awoke the next day, she called, crying, to describe her suicide attempt.

When my shock wore off, I felt helpless, frustrated, and guilty. Was it my fault? Had I missed something in her treatment sessions, or on the phone right before her attempt? Where had I gone wrong? I felt responsible, anxious, and angry. Eventually, I denied these uncomfortable feelings, telling myself I had resolved them.

Amy appeared at the next session pale, lethargic, sick, and depressed. She spoke about being too lazy to live. "It's too much work— to work at it when I feel overwhelmed and stressed. I'd just rather kill myself. I just want to check out. I feel alone. I go so far. I can't keep up the façade of someone who dresses nicely and who has no inside self— none." As if in reproach, she added, "You didn't know what was going on—and you are pretty smart." I replied, "So—you outsmarted me."

Amy remained extremely depressed, angry the pills had not worked. She talked of wanting to slash her wrists. I was angry and nervous, afraid she might kill herself later. Desperately, I found myself talking too much, trying to reach Amy, to pull her away from her suicidal impulses.

Her mood changed during the next three months as she attended Alcoholics Anonymous, stopped drinking completely, and became treasurer of her AA group. She terminated the relationship with her boyfriend and decided not to be with men sexually until she resolved some of her deeper problems. Although she was depressed, she was again able to talk about her feelings in treatment. She threw herself into her work and became the top salesperson of the month for her company.

In spite of Amy's dismal history, including long-term, serious drug abuse, alcohol problems, and suicide attempts, she had now given up using drugs and alcohol. She attended AA regularly, she was not clinging to a man, she was not overeating, and for the first time in her life, she was functioning well on a job. After ten months of treatment and a "trial-by-fire" testing phase, I hoped she was on the verge of moving into the working through of the abandonment depression.

I wanted to see her as healthier than she was, and to believe she had the capacity to work through her depression. I wanted her eventually to have a solid foundation, a healthy self, inner strength, and new capacities for love and for work. I hoped that some day her emotional struggles and her pain would be resolved. However, she appeared to be a lower-level borderline patient, and I was not sure about her capacity for treatment.

At this time I was anticipating a two-and-a-half-week vacation. I informed all my patients when I would be leaving—all except Amy! With her, I was not able to get the words out. Her suicide attempt during my previous absence frightened me, and I had difficulty determining how much of my feelings were due to my fears and how much were due to the reality of her clinical picture.

When finally I told Amy of my vacation plans, she replied with relief she was glad I was going, because she then would not have to come to her sessions. I felt relieved until, in the next breath, she began talking about how very vulnerable she was, how she had tried so many times to kill herself in the past, and how she was proud of being a master at hiding feelings. Then she said, "I'll do it for the last time. I'll get a hundred Valium instead of twenty-five, and my family will think it's your fault. The way to nail you, if I really wanted to get you, would be to commit suicide."

Once again, I felt frustrated and impotent. Although I made some comments, my unacknowledged anger at her manipulative behavior made it difficult to assess all that was going on, or to be certain what to do about it. For the moment I "bought" her projection that I was responsible for her life, and it would be my fault if she killed herself. I had to work to discover how my angry countertransference feelings were inhibiting my ability to see Amy clearly, and to confront her with her own self-destructive anger. Amy continued to talk about "nailing" me, and about how it would be "my fault" if she committed suicide. As I became aware of my countertransference anger, it dissipated, and instead of equivocating as I had done during previous interchanges, I now forcefully confronted her manipulation of me. I said, "Do you think you're not responsible for your own life? Why do you want to hurt yourself to get back at me? You expect me to save you? Whatever your fantasy may be, the lives of those you want to hurt will go on, and you'll be the one who is gone."

Amy reported she was as depressed as ever. My confrontations hit her very hard. She had felt nothing for so long that feeling so much was overwhelming. "You were saying you're not concerned about what my family thinks of you, that you're a professional, and if I kill myself, I'm dead and other people's lives go on. I realize how angry and manipulative I've been. It's ugly to me, being that kind of person. I'm destroying myself. If I don't start talking about this stuff, I won't have a choice. It will only be a matter of time before I start drinking or using drugs again, and I don't want that to happen. I have a choice in this. You said that on an intellectual level I may know I'm responsible for my life, but that on a gut level, I don't. That disgusts me."

She proceeded to talk about her mother and their relationship. She began crying as she confessed, "I wish you weren't going away. It's not like I feel like throwing myself off a bridge, I'm scared, I'm so emotional now." Her crying continued. "I wasted years. I had no coping mechanisms. I was mentally ill, irresponsible. I shut down so young from the pain. I don't like myself. I've got to change or I'm going to die. I can't use anything to make the feelings go away. I have to talk."

In the time remaining before my trip, she did not rely on her defensive self by detaching affect and withdrawing, but instead expressed her despair and sadness. I said very little. My task now was to listen, supporting her ability to do the work herself. Amy was working better in therapy now, and the suicide threat was less imminent. Much of my anxiety, I realized, was due to my own anger at being manipulated, apart from her clinical situation, and I felt less worried.

When I returned from my trip, Amy reported she had done very well in spite of my absence, and in spite of the death of a grandmother whom she loved; however, she had just learned the day before that the division of the company where she was employed was folding and that soon she would be out of a job. She felt tense, worried, and discouraged. Thoughts of suicide returned as she began to job hunt. She said, "I don't have regard for my life. When things get tense, I get suicidal." She emphasized: "You should know this. This is important. I have disregard for my life. What's the point? I don't even want to be alive and I wish I weren't."

Once more I began to feel helpless and preoccupied with her suicidal talk. I tried to reinforce the positive steps she was taking, and interpreted her desire to kill herself as an escape from having to face anxiety. I felt anxiety that she was going to drink, and anger that she was testing me when she threatened to leave AA, saying, "I'm getting turned off to AA. I'm not really impressed. I like being around winners, not losers, and anyway, I'm not convinced I'm an alcoholic, and you should know that."

She spoke of suicide again. "I get so down and I think of suicide." I replied, "Rather than using your own resources, you think about suicide." She talked about feeling suicidal and desperate six months earlier, when both her boyfriend and I had been away at the same time, and she had lost her job.

I was still upset about that suicide attempt. In the following dialogue, I confronted her suicidal impulses.

S.B.N.: You didn't talk about your suicidal feelings to me then.

Amy: I wasn't aware I had them.

S.B.N.: I find that hard to believe. You just said you had them, and when you were with Dr. G., you silently planned in the session to kill yourself. You actually walked out and took a bunch of pills and ended up in the intensive care unit unconscious for days.

Amy: I may not have been aware I was going to try to kill myself before you left, but when I called you, when you came back, I knew; I planned it.

S.B.N.: Why didn't you say something to me?

Amy: I didn't trust you then. To me, telling another human being of my desperateness is vulnerability; it's weak, and dishonorable. If you feel like committing suicide, you do it, you don't talk about it—it's kind of like I still think. If I wanted to do it, I wouldn't call you up and say, "Can you please help me?" Suicide is the ultimate decision. It's not up for discussion.

S.B.N.: That sounds very manipulative and angry.

Amy: What you're saying is, if I wanted to do it, I'm not going to talk about it and screw you. I don't mean it like that.

S.B.N.: Yes, you do. How am I supposed to trust what you say to me, when you say, "If I wanted to go do it, I'll do it, and I won't talk about it"?

Amy: What would be the point of talking about it, so somebody could talk me out of it?

S.B.N.: If I thought you were thinking about suicide, I'd do everything in my power to stop you, including putting you in the hospital.

Amy: I'm telling you I'm not suicidal.

S.B.N.: Yes, but if you were, you wouldn't tell me.

Amy: Yes, that's true. If I ever got to the point where I thought I'd act out, I wouldn't tell you. I haven't told anyone before. That's too bad you think that's manipulative. It's my life!

S.B.N.: It's such an angry, manipulative gesture!

Amy: It is if you're doing it to hurt somebody.

S.B.N.: You're right—that's what it's all about.

Amy: Yes, I suppose.

S.B.N.: Everyone's life goes on, whatever you may think, and you're the one whose life is over.

Amy: I've tried to kill myself a lot of times, in order to hurt people. I was angry. Yes, I guess you're right. One time I was so out of it, I wasn't even thinking. That's right, it is manipulative in that sense, but it's a person's right. We just have a philosophical difference.

Trying to control my own feelings, I felt a rare flash of hate for my work, wondering why I had ever gotten into this field in the first place. I heard her say, "That last time really was serious. I don't know how I ever came out of that." I answered, "It seems to me you're playing Russian roulette." She replied, "The other times I called for help. In June I didn't. I just woke up the next day."

Now I let some of my angry feelings show. I said sarcastically, "One hour after calling me and being sweet and everything . . ." Mimicking her sweet, high-pitched voice on the phone, I continued, "You said, 'I'm fine. I just wanted to check in,' knowing you were going to do it?" She answered, "I was real angry." I responded, "Why couldn't you talk about your anger instead of acting it out?" She said, "It seems bizarre to be that angry just because someone goes away. Big deal. I was out of touch with my feelings. I didn't know what was going on." I answered, "Cop-out! I don't believe you didn't know what was going on." "All right, all right," she said, "I just didn't want to tell you, that's all."

As the session progressed, I was both angry and sad. I thought about the future. As she walked out of my office, I realized how fragile she really was. "*She could go drink and kill herself right now!*" I couldn't trust her to tell me the truth, as I had thought I could.

I did not sleep well that night, thinking about her, feeling despondent. I was enraged, angry at myself for taking her on as a patient in the first place, and feeling oppressed because I was saddled with her. I felt as if I had a noose around my neck and a ten-ton weight on my shoulders.

After another session, in which she was detached and distant, talking about suicide and her fears about showing vulnerability, I realized there was an ego-syntonic quality to her view of suicide. It was my responsibility to make this view ego alien in order for her to overcome this suicidal acting-out defense.

The issue was not simply suicide, but also her commitment to treatment. By keeping the fantasy of suicide alive, as if she were making a decision about which dress to buy, she was avoiding the commitment necessary to make treatment worthwhile. If it got too hot, she always had the option of suicide. As long as she did this, she could not get out of treatment what it offered.

I realized I was not seeing how stubborn Amy's resistance was. She needed more "therapeutic astonishment," more "affect," more intense confrontation from me. Treatment was supposed to be devoted to growth and health, not to suicide. She was acting as if she were taking the contract between us, the essence of the work, and flushing it down the drain. I needed to convey this idea to her.

At the next session, I said, "I've been thinking about our last session and the one before that. You are making a charade and a mockery out of your treatment, and you're doing it with a straight face. You are hanging onto the fantasy of suicide as an option. Doing that keeps you from making a commitment to treatment. Suicide is not an option. It's not a possibility. We're talking about getting well, about managing feelings. We're spending time in treatment dedicated to growth and understanding and healing, but you have the fantasy that you can bail out if it gets too hot."

She agreed. "You're right. I do use suicide as a game and the fantasy as an option. See, my expectation is—what I'm supposed to do is, I'm supposed to come in here and trust you completely, and the more I think about that, the angrier I get. I tell myself if I'm going to get through all this garbage I'm supposed to come here and share feelings, and I'm supposed to call you if I get suicidal, and I think, 'Why should I trust you or anybody?' I do use it as an out."

Toward the end of the session, she said, "You're right. If I don't start trusting you, I'd better kiss this off, because I'm wasting my time and yours." She started to cry, and, perhaps beginning to let go of the suicidal defense, she said, "I've never felt more alone in my life. You really are alone in this life. You hit home when you talked about that suicidal stuff. We're heading into a different stage in our relationship. We're countering each other. I'm not afraid of you any more, and I don't put you on a pedestal. Maybe it's time to start really talking."

For Amy, suicide was a defense against her wish to trust, and also against her fear of disappointment. We were now beneath the defense. Early in childhood she had trusted her mother, only to feel betrayed. Trusting and depending on others seemed hopeless. In her mind, if she could not trust, the only way out was suicide. My interventions were successful because they broke through her defensive denial and acting out, releasing painful affect. She moved deeper into the next level of her treatment.

It was time for interpretations about her fear that I would disappoint her, too. I hoped this would allow her to begin talking about these feelings so she would not have to act them out.

At the next session, Amy was extremely depressed. She was insecure about being out of work. She talked, without feeling, of her fear of my judging her and knifing her in the back, and of her mistrust of people. I suggested that she was worried I was going to disappoint her also, and not follow through. She replied, "I'm worried that you'll judge me. I'll be sorry that I made myself vulnerable—I've been sorry in the past. The more I'll talk, the worse you'll think of me. You'll think I'm crazy." I answered, "You're worried I'm not only going to judge you harshly, but that verbally I'll hurt you, and I'll use what you tell me." She said, "Exactly. That's it." As she talked about her family, I said, "You are afraid I'll let you down, just like everyone else has." She became sad, pensive, saying, "I just appreciate the fact you acknowledge that I've been hurt."

At the end of the session, as Amy was talking about the difficult time—Christmas and no work and no money and depression and anxiety—she demonstrated integration of my confrontations, saying, "You know, you were absolutely right about the suicide stuff. If you hadn't said what you did, I would have been thinking of suicide these last few days." And then she added, "I said to myself, 'That's not an option any more. I'm just going to get through it, no matter what.' I didn't go through and plan out how I'm going to get pills and kill myself. I just thought, 'I'm going to get depressed, and I'll be around when I'm 40. I'm not going to kill myself.' I guess I'm getting less and less self-abusive."

During the next few weeks, Amy functioned well. Although she felt depressed and anxious at times, she contained her feelings, both managing and supporting herself. She obtained a temporary job while she went about exploring various professional possibilities and setting up interviews. She was hopeful about herself and about the future. In addition, she relied more on her own experience, instead of relying solely on the perceptions of others. She was better able to distinguish her inner world of feelings and fantasies from the outer world of action. She had learned that just because she had feelings did not mean she had to automatically act on them.

After seven months of sobriety, Amy was invited to speak at an Alcoholics Anonymous meeting. Feeling proud of her progress, her growth, her choice of the healthy path she was taking, she said to me, "I'm using my own resources and I'm liking who I am today—for the first time in my life."

Soon thereafter, I was about to leave my office for a week's vacation. Glancing at the clock, Amy said, "I feel a bit strange because I know I'm not going to see you for a week. I have bad memories of your going away, the time when I tried to kill myself. I was freaking out all over the place then, and I wasn't even in touch with it. Now, here I am unemployed, but I'm busy. It doesn't matter that you're going away."

After fifteen months of treatment, Amy had less need to sacrifice adaptation to defense. She talked more about her feelings instead of turning to defensive discharge through alcohol and drug abuse. She was not clinging to people as much in order to get them to take care of her or to give her constant reassurance; instead, she derived some gratification from taking care of herself. Her developing real self began to emerge as she made attempts to assert, express, and activate herself.

After I returned from vacation, she said to me, "When you went away, I did great. I had two hours of feeling bad; I started feeling strange, getting a sinking feeling. I said to myself, 'That's O.K., I can handle some feelings. They're only feelings, after all.' I cleaned my apartment, went to an AA meeting, and I was fine. I'm not so shaken by people coming and going. I can take care of myself."

Epilogue

At that point, I thought Amy was doing quite well, and I had no worries about her committing suicide. I thought she was "cured" of any such thoughts. She appeared to have integrated my previous confrontations. In my mind, the suicide problem was solved. However, during the next year, suicidal thoughts and feelings returned. With a history of six suicide attempts, I realized it was naive of me to believe that her thoughts of killing herself had been eradicated. This was a problem she would need to talk about again and again. No matter how calm, stable, or rational she might appear, her difficulties with this problem had not been fully resolved. I had to understand further what problems she was trying to solve by her suicidal thoughts, and to explore more deeply her anguish, despair, and suffering.

During the following year, she expressed suicidal feelings on some occasions related to new work situations, although she did not make any suicidal attempts. She acquired several new jobs, but she remained at each job only a few months before she quit or was fired. She had great difficulty acknowledging her capabilities, identifying her professional interests, and activating herself. She shifted among being unemployed, looking for jobs in fields for which she did not have adequate training, and working in jobs beneath her potential. She avoided making a commitment to any one field, and avoided obtaining any additional training or education.

It became evident again that Amy did not yet have the ego capacity to operate in a demanding job requiring responsibility, self-activation, and autonomous functioning, all of which would trigger separation anxiety. Masterson has discussed how separation anxiety triggers the withdrawing unit, and the abandonment depression with all its components, including rage (1972, 1976, 1981, 1983). It was clear from clinical experience that Amy was not able to accommodate significant separation and self-activation without triggering a depression which might then take over.

It was tempting to believe that she was integrating my confrontations thoroughly. Indeed, sometimes she was. Yet, in her case, I realized I would have to accept the fact that there were limits to what she could do, and that no amount of confrontation was going to enable her to do more. It was important to operate within the range of her capacities. In addition, I wanted to see her as healthier than she was, and I periodically had the illusion that the therapeutic alliance was solid. In truth, the alliance was fragile, and subject to recurrent fluctuations and transference acting out.

Recently, Amy obtained a job that uses her prior professional education, her business skills, and her personal experience. She has also enrolled in additional postgraduate coursework. However, whether Amy will be able to handle the feelings that arise as she activates herself, and will choose to persist at the job despite obstacles, remains to be seen.

Amy's journey continues to be difficult, but despite her setbacks she has exhibited courage and the desire to change, to struggle, and to grow. She wants to be healthy. She has been a member of Alcoholics Anonymous for several years, consistently free of alcohol and drugs. She no longer attempts suicide, but uses her therapy sessions and AA to talk about her feelings and thoughts. She realizes she has spent many years anesthetizing herself with alcohol, drugs, food, and sex, and that she has lost precious time in self-destructive behavior and consequent lack of growth. Acknowledging her progress, Amy recently said, "I'm not where I want to be yet, but I'm not where I once was, and for that I am grateful."

REFERENCES

Beebe, J. (1975a). Treatment of the suicidal patient. In C. Rosenbaum & J. Beebe (Eds.), *Psychiatric treatment: Crisis/clinic/consultation*. San Francisco: McGraw-Hill.

Beebe, J. (1975b). Evaluation of the suicidal patient. In C. Rosenbaum & J. Beebe (Eds.), *Psychiatric treatment: Crisis/clinic/consultation*. San Francisco: McGraw-Hill.

Dorpat, T., & Ripley, H. (1967). The relationship between attempted suicide and committed suicide. *Comprehensive Psychiatry, 8* (2), 74–79.

Farberow, N., & Shneidman, E. (Eds.). (1961). *The cry for help*. New York: McGraw-Hill.

Gunderson, J. (1984). *Borderline personality disorder*. Washington, DC: American Psychiatric Press.

Hatton, C., & Valente, S. (1984). Assessment of suicidal risk. In C. Hatton & S. Valente (Eds.), *Suicide: Assessment and intervention*. East Norwalk, CT: Appleton-Century-Crofts.

Litman, R., & Farberow, N. (1961). Emergency evaluation of self-destructive potentiality. In N. Farberow & E. Shneidman (Eds.), *The cry for help*. New York: McGraw-Hill.

Litman, R. (1968). Psychotherapists' orientations toward suicide. In H. Resnik (Ed.), *Suicidal behaviors: Diagnosis and management*. Boston: Little, Brown.

Masterson, J. (1972). *Treatment of the borderline adolescent: A developmental approach*. New York: Brunner/Mazel, 1985.

Masterson, J. (1976). *Psychotherapy of the borderline adult: A developmental approach*. New York: Brunner/Mazel.

Masterson, J. (1981). *Narcissistic and borderline disorders: An integrated developmental approach*. New York: Brunner/Mazel.

Masterson, J. (1983). *Countertransference and psychotherapeutic technique*. New York: Brunner/Mazel.

Mintz, R. (1971). Basic considerations in the psychotherapy of the depressed suicidal patient. *American Journal of Psychotherapy, 25*, 56-73.

Pokorny, A. (1964). Suicide rates in various psychiatric disorders. *Journal of Nervous and Mental Disease, 139*, 499-506.

Robins, E., Gassner, S., Kayes, J., Wilkinson, R., Jr., & Murphy, G. (1959). The communication of suicidal intent: A study of 134 consecutive cases of successful (completed) suicide. *American Journal of Psychiatry, 115*, 724-733.

Shneidman, E. (1985). *Definition of suicide*. New York: John Wiley & Sons.

Tabachnick, N., & Farberow, N. (1961). The assessment of self-destructive potentiality. In N. Farberow & E. Shneidman (Eds.), *The cry for help*. New York: McGraw-Hill.

Tuckman, J., & Youngman, W. (1968). Assessment of suicide risk in attempted suicides. In H. Resnik (Ed.), *Suicidal behaviors: Diagnosis and management*. Boston: Little, Brown.

Weisman, A. (1974). *The realization of death: A guide for the psychological autopsy*. New York: Jason Aronson.

Chapter 21

Countertransference to Transference Acting Out of a Narcissistic Personality Disorder

Richard Fischer, Ph.D.

The narcissistic personality disorder presents a grandiose façade that pursues admiration and idealization. This seemingly inpenetrable façade defends itself against stimuli that might frustrate the mirroring of the false defensive grandiose self by devaluation and acting out of narcissistic entitlement demands. The narcissistic patient has to continuously preserve an omnipotent and invulnerable perception of the self and will respond to any reality confrontation by the therapist as an assault or as malevolently motivated behavior.

The therapist must make a technical shift when working with the narcissistic disorder. Interpretation of the narcissistic vulnerability and the defensive need for the grandiose self becomes the primary focus of treatment. This interpretation must be done empathically, because the patient's sensitivity will immediately discern any negative intentions from the therapist. Confrontation, the primary tool in the work with the borderline patient, must be used minimally here, to question behavior that is self-destructive or hazardous to the treatment contract and the therapeutic frame. The inevitable disappointments and empathic failures that occur during the course of treatment become the prime focus of interpretive work, along with the defensive reactions such as narcissistic rage and withdrawal, devaluation, arrogance, and contempt.

The therapist does not provide or gratify the request for perfect mirroring, but tries to empathically interpret all reactions to the disruption of mirroring, or idealizing needs. In order to be effective in this task, the therapist must not identify with narcissistic projections by trying to omnipotently supply the valued resource, nor should he be angered by these demands and retaliate with punitive and excessive confrontation.

The empathic interpretive stance is crucial in the work with the narcissistic personality disorder, but many potential countertransference reactions steer the therapist away from a position of technical neutrality.

Some therapists with more fragile self-esteem or unresolved narcissistic sectors in their own personalities may immediately identify with the omnipotent idealized projections of the patient. This will force the therapist to try to gratify narcissistic demands, and both the therapist and the patient will "bask in the glow" of a euphoric narcissistic unity. This will quickly break down as the patient's demands accelerate and the therapist becomes angry at the lack of gratitude for all his efforts. The therapist who reinforces the patient's grandiose wishes is trying to delay the inevitable narcissistic disappointment and rage. The therapist must have a sufficient sense of self-worth and be comfortable in his professional role to avoid being seduced into such a position by his patient.

The second typical response is one of anger and envy of the narcissistic position that "the world is their oyster." Most of us have painfully given up the position of infantile omnipotence, with varying degrees of success. The narcissistic patient who continually acts out this infantile and egocentric position may undermine the therapist's tenuous defenses, making him vulnerable to feelings of envy and anger.

The initial response to this is a retaliation by the therapist, which is manifested by overt anger, withdrawal, contempt, or excessive confrontation. The therapist may justify these retaliatory maneuvers as appropriate technique, and the punitive component may be denied.

Sometimes there is a combination of trying to meet the patient's narcissistic needs and then responding with helplessness and anger as the patient becomes demanding and lacks appropriate gratitude for the provisions by the therapist.

A third type of countertransference is demonstrated by the didactic therapist who tries to persuade the patient to relinquish his narcissistic position. Although this may appear to be sound advice by the therapist, it is perceived as an empathic failure by the patient. Most therapists have an object-related view of the world, in which concern and interest in others is a primary value. The narcissist, on the other hand, with his pursuit of money, fame, and power, comes from an egocentric and self-centered position, in which the use and often the exploitation of others is necessary in the pursuit of narcissistic supplies. If the therapist's world view is disturbed by the egocentric perspective of his patient, then he may want to change him and encourage him to make his behavior more "object related." Such a therapeutic stance will inevitably result in a stalemate, and the patient will withdraw from treatment.

Another countertransference focal point is the therapist's response to chronic devaluation, and narcissistic entitlement demands from the patient. The therapist must be secure enough in his professional identity to understand that this transferential response is a core sector of narcissistic pathology. The patient needs to deny and devalue any stimuli, including reality clarifications by the therapist, that interfere with his invulnerable and omnipotent perception of himself. The narcissistic patient may use entitlement and grandiose perceptions of himself to ward off painful affective states and diminished self-esteem. The therapist must be sensitive to this phenomenon and interpret the patient's driven need to depreciate any stimuli or persons that evoke such painful affects. The narcissistic patient is unable to contain worthless and depreciated aspects of himself. It is necessary for the therapist to contain such painful affects during the course of therapy. The therapist may instead respond with anger and withdrawal and attempt to reason with the patient, while trying to persuade him of the therapist's positive intent. This may place the therapist in the vulnerable position of vacillating from resonating with narcissistic demands to appease the patient, to retaliating angrily and punitively as the patient's rage does not diminish.

The following case presentation details various transfer-ence–countertransference themes that interfered with the establish-ment of a therapeutic alliance and frame, resulting in an inconsistent stance with the patient and the eventual premature termination of treatment.

CASE HISTORY: MR. JOHN KAYE

Identifying Data

The patient was a 48-year-old white Catholic married man who lived in New Jersey with his wife and 18-year-old daughter. His 27-year-old son was attending school in upstate New York. Mr. Kaye was a successful private investor and entrepreneur.

Chief Complaint

Mr. Kaye contacted the Masterson Group after he identified his problem by reading about it in a newspaper article. Mr. Kaye complained that "I never had a real relationship and I feel disturbed by this." He was considering separation from his wife.

History of Present Illness

Mr. Kaye was a successful businessman locked in a long but uninvolved marriage. He had had an extramarital relationship with a woman in another city for the past eight years. He was considering a marital separation because he was "tired of the game" and had enough money to support her in a very comfortable style. Mr. Kaye admitted to having been completely self-centered throughout his life, having no real interest in women except for sexual satisfaction.

Mr. Kaye claimed that his problematic life was the result of a traumatic childhood characterized by rejection, abandonment, and a lack of love. Ten years prior his feeling that his parents consistently lied to him had been reinforced by his accidental discovery of his adoption. At that point, the patient felt lost and enraged. He felt rage toward his mother for this deception and set out to "prove himself" by making a fortune. At the time of coming to therapy, he felt envious of those with relationships and was worried about being alone after his marriage. Mr. Kaye presented two distinct images of himself: "a tiger who can accomplish anything and intimidate anyone and an impotent, enraged, unloved orphan who has no one."

Relevant Past History and Family History

The patient was born and raised in Buffalo, New York. He had been placed in an orphanage for two-and-a-half years, at which time he was adopted. He had had a childhood fear of being left alone. His earliest memories focused on rejection. His mother was described as a rigid, cold, rejecting, and sadistic woman who always used harsh physical discipline. His father was described as gentle and loving, but never around because he worked. The patient had three older brothers and four older sisters. He felt that he was viewed as the "black sheep" of his family.

Early school years were characterized by conflict with teachers and alienation from his work. His academic record was poor, and he dropped out of school in the ninth grade, left home, and became involved in a series of businesses. He married when he was 21; he reported being an interested father.

The Fifth Session

After a clinical evaluation, treatment on a thrice-weekly basis was recommended. The patient said that presently he could come only twice a week because of his exercise schedule and his need to lead his double life and visit his girlfriend. He said that therapy would have to conform to his schedule. This was not confronted at the time by me. The sessions were set up to fit the patient's schedule.

The patient began by devaluing bankers, lawyers, and rigid professionals, saying that they are ignorant and hide behind titles. His grandiose self-image emerged when he spoke about his always getting his way and never being intimidated by anyone. This devaluation and grandiosity constituted a clear reference to his early view of the therapeutic relationship, his fear of domination and being hurt by a treatment contract, and a need for narcissistic leverage in our relationship.

I countered this image of himself with another image of his being a frightened child who was mistreated and pushed aside. The patient began to focus on his wife and girlfriend, saying that he used them merely to cater to his needs and would not allow them to make demands on him. Beyond that, he was never able to give to his wife, who complained bitterly. He said he could never expose himself and allow himself to be torn to shreds again (a clear reference to being destroyed and attacked by the therapist). He needed to maintain a strong front.

I focused on his fear of showing himself and sharing himself in a relationship, thus risking humiliation again, and on his protecting himself by always taking the upper hand in relationships. I did not clarify how he did this in the transference by dictating that sessions revolve around his needs. The patient said that he had managed to keep his wife like a dog—obedient to her master. He would never allow himself to need someone again. I focused on his seeing others as needy and subservient, and how he was unwilling to see those needs in himself.

This confrontation was motivated by irritation at his devaluation and enslavement of those closest to him—including me. The patient superficially agreed but ended the session by saying that he was planning a business trip to Europe for three weeks, and had to do this several times a year. I did not respond to this comment.

Summary. Because I am angry at the patient's devaluation and grandiosity, I confront his impaired self (the two images of himself). I feel attacked and devalued. The patient has already suggested a weapon of choice: "take the upper hand." This confrontation leads to increased grandiosity and defensiveness. When the patient depreciates his wife, I once again confront his avoidance in perceiving his own shortcomings. The patient's transference acting out increases, and he raises a serious obstacle to his treatment: his business trips threaten the continuity of his therapy. I do not take this up with the patient, just as previously I left unexplored his refusal to come three times a week because it interfered with his exercise schedule. My countertransference need is manifested as I respond to the patient's narcissistic demands by trying to please him and avoid his anger and devaluation. If the therapeutic frame had been clearly defined and maintained, then a natural emergence of the impaired self could have been facilitated and examined in response to his reactions to my natural failure to perfectly mirror his narcissistic demands.

The Sixth Session

The patient began by declaring that treatment had to be conducted on his terms. He said that he was tired of his life revolving around the whims of others. He insisted on taking a stand on this issue. He defiantly said, "If I have to go to Europe I'll go and miss my sessions, and that is nonnegotiable."

I told him that he was handling this relationship like all other relationships—on his terms—and that his automatic response was defeating the goals of his treatment. The policy regarding vacations and his responsibility for missed sessions was then explained to him.

The patient responded with narcissistic outrage and defiance and said, "I understand you, but your schedule and your vacation don't mean anything to me." He said that his time and schedule came first and that we would have to negotiate a more reasonable policy regarding his cancelled appointments. He continued by saying that he would consider my treatment contract if it was the only alternative for an effective course of therapy. He then asked about my reasons for having such a rigid policy.

I responded by telling him that the patient had to be responsible for the hours and the treatment. I gave concrete reasons and explanations for this responsibility, and justified my policy, because I was feeling defensive. I tried to convince the patient that my policy was reasonable and not harsh. I was experiencing guilt as I identified with the patient's projections. My response was to rationalize, explain, and justify my treatment contract.

The patient responded by restating his refusal to accept any arbitrary policy. I then said, "Your needs have been so put off that you react with such anger and disappointment even when I am just talking about a policy designed to protect your treatment."

The patient then admitted his anger was excessive, and wondered why he needed an "edge" in all his relationships. He said, "If you don't have an edge, people chew you up and spit you out." This was a clear reference to being attacked and destroyed by the therapist. He continued with the recognition that he was like an animal living in a jungle and that if he did not change he would sacrifice all intimate relationships. However, he insisted that his defensive interpersonal dominance was necessary in the business world.

I told him that treatment was not business, and his same need for dominance was being reenacted in his defiant stance regarding the treatment policy. He continued by telling me that money was of no concern to him, but that the time required of him was a problem. He said, "I always need to dictate terms." I replied, "Even at the expense of your treatment." The patient then spoke about his being mistreated during childhood. He cited incidents of being laughed at and humiliated as peers called him a bastard. He never knew what they meant by such comments. He used these memories to justify his self-righteous stance, saying that he could never accept any arbitrary policy and claiming that we would have to negotiate. I agreed to this and thereby ended the session by colluding with the patient's narcissistic demands.

Summary. The patient continues to present narcissistic demands, claiming that treatment should revolve around his schedule. Although I empathize with his disappointment over my imperfect mirroring, the contract is never fully clarified and accepted. I try to convince the patient of the "rightness" of and necessity for my policy. Thus, I unconsciously identify with the patient's demands and try to please him by explaining my policy rather than interpreting his self-defeating, self-centered response and grandiosity as a defense guarding the impaired self.

This patient will continuously test until it becomes clear that he is responsible for the sessions. This may be a subtle point, but it is essential that the patient does not walk away thinking that the contract is on his terms, where he can maintain perfect mirroring. Although my empathizing was on target, I have colluded with the patient's attempt to see me as a narcissistic object.

The patient has a clear choice; use the therapist as a narcissistic object or face frustrations, wounds, and injuries. To avoid such injury, he devalues treatment and calls me "unreasonable." I have unwittingly identified with these projections and tried to be reasonable with the patient, justifying my position, explaining myself, and eventually I avoid clarifying the contract.

I am feeling guilty and have come to doubt myself. Am I rigid? Is my policy harsh? Am I being sadistic in trying to maintain a therapeutic contract? I feel that the patient has such a difficult life. Why add insult to injury? Perhaps by being flexible and gratifying I can "fix" this patient. I have begun the insidious process of trying to prove my therapeutic merit to the patient. In a sense, he has projected his impaired self into me, while I am unconsciously acting out this inadequate, frightened self representation.

With this patient the therapist must use empathic mirroring responses and must also strictly manage the therapeutic frame through confrontation of transference acting out. The therapist must maintain therapeutic neutrality in opposition to narcissistic demandingness, instead of vacillating between anger and a desire to please the patient.

The patient is saying, "I have been mistreated. Others must be responsible for me so I can avoid repeating those feelings and preserve my grandiosity." The patient is trying to maintain his self-worth. The therapist, by identifying with those demands, is trying to maintain his self-image as a "benign helpful therapist." Could I omnipotently alleviate his painful feelings by gratifying him? Why interfere with his business trips?

The Seventh Session

The patient was twenty minutes late for his appointment. He began by expressing his hatred for New York City because it interfered with the demands of his schedule. He was furious that traffic was so unpredictable and refused to leave earlier and have to *wait* for me. However, he went on to say that being late was a sign of disrespect, and that he would leave if someone was five minutes late for an appointment with him.

I commented that he seemed to act very quickly in dropping a relationship over callous behavior from someone else. I continued by saying, "Perhaps you are concerned that I would have that same insensitive reaction with you."

The patient responded, "Someone has to have sensitivity or I won't work with them." He spoke about his family's callous indifference, their unilateral decisions and restrictive rules and how they never gave reasons for their rules and regulations. He went on to tell me that we could not meet on a frequency of three times a week. He told me that Fridays and Mondays conflicted with *his* schedule and he wasn't willing to change his schedule for anyone.

I told him that he had a fear of accepting my policy blindly, and that he feared being exploited by me as he had been by his family.

The patient just left the session, stating, "Twice a week is fine."

Summary. The patient begins by externalizing responsibility for his lateness. His tendency toward impulsive acting out (i.e., dropping a relationship) is confronted by me. He expands on his fear of being mistreated by arbitrary rules—a clear reference to the treatment contract. The patient follows up by greater demands and acting out, refusing to modify his schedule to permit treatment to begin. Although I empathize with the patient's fear, much greater confrontation is required to deal with these demands, which threaten the fabric of his treatment. I have once again identified with the impaired self projections of the patient. I should have used dramatic technique (i.e., therapeutic astonishment) to confront the escalating acting out. I avoided this to avoid the patient's rage, which was displaced to New York City and would surely have been directed at me if I had confronted properly.

The Eighth Session

The patient began by devaluing therapy as being for "nuts" and said that everyone in the waiting room was embarrassed, like at a V.D. clinic. I asked him if he felt uncomfortable being here. The patient denied his discomfort but said that scheduling was a problem. He could no longer come in in the afternoons because of business, and in another week he had to go to Europe. Similarly, he wouldn't come on some mornings because of his exercise. I wondered if these demands would ever end. I confronted his sabotaging of his treatment through his insistence on having everything on his terms. The patient accused me of being unreasonable and of demanding a lifestyle change for him. I was furious by then. He insisted that he was willing to compromise and that I was rigid. I asked him why he was distorting the treatment arrangement into an intrusive restriction of his life. The patient threatened to leave treatment because he feared that I was trying to dominate him. He refused to consider coming three times a week. He then insisted that I should be responsible for his missed sessions and consider it a business loss. He said that my treatment policy was etched in stone and he could not accept it. He also insisted on taking his European trips without charge. He said that he would not allow himself to be penalized by me. I went into a long explanation about the need for the patient to be responsible for the hour that he missed by paying for the time. The patient then agreed to the policy because I explained it to him rather than forcing him to accept it blindly.

Summary. The patient's acting out and devaluation escalate, with major negotiation around the treatment contract and threats of flight from treatment. My initial confrontations regarding the sabotaging of treatment are on target. The patient then projects the attacking onto me, accusing me of being unreasonable and dominating. I move away from this by being concrete and reasonable and providing detailed rationalizations for my policy. In short, I swallow the hook and bait rather than confront and question the patient about his perception of treatment being an intrusion as opposed to an ally in his life. Furthermore, the patient's priorities needed to be questioned.

This is a person with monumental success in business but dramatic failures in interpersonal relationships. How can business and exercise take priority over his treatment? Accepting his distorted priorities is colluding with the patient. Throughout the session my feelings ranged from anger and outrage over his persistent self-centered demand-ingness to feeling unreasonable, demanding, arbitrary, and rigid. Is the patient right? Am I merely trying to make a schedule that fits my needs? Am I like him? These doubts interfered with a proper confrontive stance.

The Ninth Session

The patient discussed his upcoming business trip to Europe, which would greatly reduce his taxes. He devalued people who pay taxes as being foolish. He expressed anger toward politicians for ignoring the needs of their constituents. He then turned to his wife's dependency and her fears of leaving the marriage. I confronted the patient with his own separation difficulties and difficulty in acknowledging his own dependency. The patient then focused on his financial insecurity and rationalized his separation fears as being economic. He agreed that his fear of dependency on others was enormous and detrimental to his relationships.

The patient said that he viewed his marriage as a cage that needed to be broken. He needed a distant relationship, where the woman was just there to service his needs. He knew he had to leave his marriage. I confronted the patient's plan to act out, and told him that his fear of intimacy was in his head, and flight or avoidance would not resolve it. I also felt angry at his devaluation and haughty arrogance. The patient resisted, saying that he was rich enough to make all his relationships on his own terms. He needed an edge in all relationships, as an insurance policy that he wouldn't be abused—particularly in business. I pointed out that he was sensitive to being dominated, and that was how he has been reacting to the therapeutic contract. I said that this perception of treatment was skewed, and perhaps his image of relationships was similarly distorted, making him respond like a caged animal. The patient said that he used superficial relationships to avoid his fears. He needed a woman who made no demands on him. I pointed out that any demands would upset the apple cart—if he had to respond to her and be involved, then he could be hurt. The patient said that he could never be in a relationship that required something of him. He knew if he left his wife, he could get out of the cage (a reference to treatment). I pointed out that the cage was based on his own intense fears of intimacy, and that he could not avoid these by leaving a marriage. The patient said that I was right, but he would have to leave his wife and find out. He also realized that he would probably lose his girlfriend, since he could never give her what she needed.

Summary. The patient begins by devaluing taxpayers and expressing anger at his wife's dependency. I confront the patient with his own dependency, which is too confrontive an intervention to use with a narcissistic personality disorder. I am motivated by my anger at the patient's contempt. He has called me and other taxpaying citizens fools. Why not strike back and call him on his dependency? It is not I who am feeling inadequate, but the patient who is feeling dependent. The patient defends by externalizing his dependency onto financial issues—a typical externalizing response to confrontation by a narcissistic personality disorder. He then focuses on his restrictive marital cage, which has a transference meaning. His need to reduce a woman to a service-supplier is related to his fear of dominance and involvement in treatment. I confront his avoidance, and flight from the marriage, but avoid calling his attention to the repetition of the same in treatment through his trips, thus accepting his pathological defensiveness.

The patient's focus on dominance is correctly greeted by me with an empathizing comment that links his fear of responsibility in a relationship and the potential to be hurt. The patient recognizes his fears but insists that he will have to leave the marriage (a prediction of his future flight from treatment). Although I was correctly understanding his fears, I should have linked them more directly to his avoidance of treatment, his business trips, and the destructive consequences that such acting out would have on his therapy. I avoided such confrontation, overcompensating for my excessive confrontation earlier in the session. I did not want to appear as a "bad guy". Once again, I vacillated from anger (which resulted in excessive confrontation) to appeasement and evasion of the necessary confrontation of his acting-out avoidance, and the destructive consequences for his treatment. Confrontation with this type of patient should be limited to acting out that threatens the continuity of treatment, and should not be used to force the patient to accept warded-off, depreciated aspects of the self representation, particularly in the treatment.

The Tenth Session

At the beginning of the session, the patient continued to present a grandiose image of himself and talked about his ability to "will away pain." He claimed that his wife was fearful about being on her own. He said he teased his wife by analyzing her problems like the "nutcracker" does to him. He feared hurting his wife if he left her but wondered if that was an excuse for his fear over separation. He claimed that a friend of his left his wife and she committed suicide. He did not want to hurt his wife. I confronted his concern for his wife as an avoidance of facing his own fears regarding the separation. The patient said that he would be all right. He said it wouldn't bother him at all, and laughed at my comments. He said if he got divorced, he would only need a good maid.

The patient said he was afraid that he might never be capable of having a relationship. He said he stayed away from closeness because of his fear. I reassured him that as his fear diminished, so would his problems with closeness. The patient said that his wife wanted a divorce, but he just wanted a trial separation. He liked to keep the door open. He felt that once he left his wife, his excuses would be over. He said that his girlfriend was like him. She couldn't give and she wouldn't make any demands on him. He said that he might not have the guts to leave his wife. He ended by saying he would be back in two weeks after his business trip. He then said that he had better be cured, because he planned to live to 120 and would be sexually active to the end. He predicted he would eventually die at the hands of a jealous husband.

The patient never returned for treatment and did not respond to a letter.

Summary. The patient resumes his grandiose defensiveness, probably as a response to the excessive confrontation of the previous session. In short, he says that "pain does not threaten him" (i.e., nor does confrontation). He continues along these lines by seeing his wife as scared and fearful, whereas he remains untouched. I confront this, and the patient responds by devaluation (i.e., laughing at the therapist) and omnipotent denial of his fears. Although my confrontation is correct, it is unnecessary and seen as a criticism by this patient. This confrontation is motivated by my anger over the patient's self-aggrandizement, and is designed to force the patient to examine his impaired self. The patient then discloses his fear that he can never master his problems. In an uncharacteristic way, I provide the patient with reassurance, and inform the patient that he needs to work on the fear and can then have relationships. This is probably motivated by my guilt for being too confrontive. The patient ends with a grandiose statement about living to 120 and remaining sexually potent, and needing a superficial, nondemanding relationship with his girlfriend.

This probably reflects the patient's fear of being dominated and attacked in a more involved relationship, and his need for narcissistic exploitation of other people (i.e., his wife is just a maid) to avoid such fears. It also can be seen as a predictor of his flight from treatment—"I cannot tolerate an involvement with a therapist. I opt for narcissistic protection." The reference to a fatal attack from a competitor probably indicates that the level of anxiety and hostility in the transference is becoming intolerable.

Conclusion

This patient viewed all relationships in terms of dominance and submission. He avoided his fear of attack through narcissistic retreat, which was demonstrated in treatment by demands for perfect mirroring, and a failure to see the destructiveness of his behavior. Thus, in his view, preoccupation with exercise, traffic, and business took precedence over concern for relationships (i.e., treatment). The patient feared that if he accepted the requirements ("demands") of a relationship (therapeutic contract), then he would lose his unconditionally gratifying mirror. This would expose him to primitive fears, intense rage, and terrifying feelings of helplessness and despair (he would become "the enraged impotent orphan").

In working with this patient, my emotions would radically shift from feeling attacked, criticized, and devalued. I felt inadequate in my role as therapist, and felt the need to prove myself. This resulted in my shifting from a placating, pleasing role, in which I tried to meet the patient's demands, to an angry, "confrontive" role, in which I would "put the patient in his place."

My anger was often the reaction to being treated as an extension of the patient's grandiose self, and feeling that my existence as an autonomous person had been nullified. My devaluation of the patient took the form of a private fantasy in which I saw the patient as too old and too rigid, unable to benefit from psychotherapy. At times I would gloat over his despair over his tragic and empty life. At other times I felt guilty for these thoughts and would try to placate and please the patient, feeling that I could omnipotently repair his emptiness. By identifying with his projections, I had allowed him to successfully project his impaired self into me. I had become the "impotent therapist" who had to "prove himself," and I felt enraged at the patient for not recognizing my skills and therapeutic intentions.

A more consistent approach would have required maintaining a therapeutic frame by confronting destructive acting out, examining the patient's grandiose demands, and interpreting his reactions to the inevitable disappointments and frustrations of those demands. To do this effectively, I would have had to relinquish my fantasy of omnipotence and "become" a therapist.

Narcissistic patients who act out present a number of treatment problems. Acting out combined with the inability to tolerate confrontation creates a treatment dilemma. Whereas confrontation is a most powerful tool with borderline patients, it must be used sparingly with narcissistic patients and confined to destructive acting out and its hazardous effects on the treatment. Furthermore, the patient's reaction to confrontation must be continuously monitored and explored. Excessive confrontation can be used to express the therapist's anger.

Narcissistic demandingness and rationalization forces the therapist to be treated as an extension of the patient, and his own separateness is nullified. This can be experienced as a threat to the therapist's autonomy and separateness. If the therapist resonates with these projections, he may vacillate from attempts to meet those demands to angry withdrawal. Thus, anger and reaction formation on the part of the therapist can be seen as a response to being treated as an extension of the patient's grandiose self.

Narcissistic patients use contempt and devaluation as defenses for various reasons. The therapist can respond with a feeling of injury or diminished self-worth. This can produce an angry response in the therapist or withdrawal and refusal to set a clear therapeutic contract. The therapist can also respond by pleasing the patient and forming a narcissistic alliance, in which they both can "bask in the glow" and avoid the feeling associated with the impaired self. The therapeutic contract is challenged, because it can be seen by the patient as an infringement and a loss of perfect mirroring. It must be maintained, while assessing the patient's reactions.

Thus, the therapist must be cautious that he does not resonate with narcissistic demands, and he must confront acting out that interferes with the treatment, while he continuously examines the patient's reactions to his confrontations. Narcissistic demands and extraordinary sensitivity to disappointment must be repetitively explored. A proper empathic and interpretive stance can be maintained only if the therapist avoids resonating with the demands of the patient.

PART V

New Perspectives

This final section demonstrates how the therapist, incorporating the Masterson Approach, can use this theoretical and clinical knowledge to pursue new avenues of research and practice in the study and treatment of the disorders of the self.

In Chapter 22, Dr. Klein brings a developmental, self and object relations approach to the integration of drug therapy and psychotherapy. In so doing he addresses a question that has increasingly confounded clinicians treating patients with a diagnosis of borderline personality disorder. Dr. Nagel, in Chapter 23, relates the techniques of this approach to the problems of addictive behaviors and, thus, expands the clinician's store of therapeutic strategies.

In Chapter 24, Dr. Orcutt applies the Masterson Approach to a pivotal issue for psychodynamic theorists—the Oedipus legend. She creates an original and exciting clinical narrative by weaving together preoedipal and oedipal themes. Finally, in Chapter 25, Drs. Clark and Orcutt take on the task of applying the Masterson Approach to the complicated field of clinical supervision. In this chapter, the similarities and differences in clinical practice and clinical supervision are examined in detail.

By demonstrating how the Masterson Approach can be applied to a wide spectrum of phenomena—dynamic theory, the process of supervision, and applied clinical practice—this section, it is hoped, will not only provide insight into the topics presented but will also serve as a model to encourage the reader to use the Masterson Approach as the basis for original theoretical contributions and new clinical applications.

J.F.M.

Chapter 22

Pharmacotherapy of the Borderline Personality Disorder

Ralph Klein, M.D.

The question appears simple at first glance: What is the role of pharmacotherapy in the treatment of patients with a borderline personality disorder (BPD)? The question is of equal, and considerable, importance to medical and nonmedical psychotherapists.

In reality, both the question and its answers are enormously complex. This complexity deepens from day to day as the clinical and research literature on both the diagnosis of BPD and the use of various pharmacologic agents increases exponentially.

It is the purpose of this chapter to address some key issues that arise when the use of medication is being contemplated in the treatment of a borderline patient. Four areas will be addressed:

1. A discussion of the importance of a correct diagnosis: both in the evaluation of the literature concerning the efficacy of drug treatment with supposed borderline patients, and in the decision as to whether or not to use medication with a borderline patient.

2. A review and critique of the literature dealing with medication and the borderline patient.

3. Guidelines for the use of medication with the borderline patient within the framework of an object relations, developmental model of personality disorders.

4. Case vignettes that demonstrate the application of the clinical guidelines.

THE PROBLEM OF DIAGNOSIS

Before the role of medication in the treatment of the BPD can be assessed, there should be general agreement concerning the definition to be used for the diagnosis of BPD. Despite the introduction of specific diagnostic criteria in *DSM-III*, the issue of the definition of BPD remains far from resolved. This accounts for much of the confusion, contradictory research findings, and varying clinical recommendations regarding the use of medication.

A basic problem in attempting to define BPD and the role of medication in inherent in the theoretical underpinning of *DSM-III*, which is primarily descriptive or phenomenological (Spitzer, Williams, & Skodol, 1980). At first glance *DSM-III* and *DSM-III-R* seem to be presenting a concept of BPD as a stable personality structure. This impression is conveyed by the explicit statement that BPD begins by adolescence, affects long-term functioning, and causes, as well as reflects, social or occupational dysfunction (*DSM-III-R*).

However, *DSM-III-R* proceeds to focus attention on symptoms, which are the most unstable and changeable diagnostic markers. Further, the focus is most prominently upon symptoms found in inpatient and outpatient hospital and clinic settings and, therefore, upon the lowest-functioning patients in the diagnostic category.

Clearly, there is a range of "borderline pathology" that *DSM-III-R* does not take into account. Masterson (this volume, p. 8) has stated that, if the criteria of *DSM-III-R* were applied to most of the borderline patients he sees in treatment, few would qualify for the diagnosis of borderline personality disorder. Although *DSM-III-R* has the advantage of lending statistical reliability to various clinical studies, it creates questions about validity and the generalizability of the findings from a relatively narrow group of patients to a broader population. This seems of special significance when it involves the choice of therapeutic intervention. As a parallel example, depending upon the severity and presenting picture, a patient with diabetes might be treated with insulin, oral medication, or simply by weight reduction and dietary control.

In addition to the problem of generalizability, a second problem created by diagnosis based primarily on symptoms or symptom cluster is summarized in Figure 1. Whenever primarily descriptive and quantitative criteria are used, the clinician or researcher will inevitably be faced with substantial overlap, which can, in turn, lead to misdiagnosis and confusion. Categories that are substantially different may have many features in common ("men" and "women" is one example that comes immediately to mind). Again, this will have important treatment implications. For example, a patient with an illness that would be responsive to medication might be misdiagnosed as evidencing BPD and fail to receive proper treatment. Conversely, a patient with BPD might be misdiagnosed as having an illness amenable to drug therapy, the use of which could expose the patient and the therapeutic relationship to unnecessary risk and potential damage.

Figure 1 points out the most common areas of clinical overlap. Some researchers suggest that the overlap between the diagnosis of borderline syndrome and the affective syndromes is in the range of 40 to 60% (Gunderson & Elliott, 1985). Others focus their attention on the considerable number of patients who meet diagnostic criteria for both BPD and schizotypal personality disorder (SPD). This overlap is in the range of 25 to 50% in most studies (Frances et al; 1984; Spitzer et al; 1979). Some clinicians focus on the psychotic features of BPD, find significant overlap with the "schizophrenic spectrum," and view the patient with BPD as "borderline schizophrenic" (Kohut, 1971). Finally, there is significant overlap with other diagnostic categories within Axis II; in fact, the percentage of dual diagnosis between BPD and other personality disorders (other than SPD) ranges from 10 to 25% (Kass et al, 1985).

What sense can the clinician make out of these figures? Are we dealing with misdiagnosis, or is the concept of the BPD an unnecessary and useless construct resting on a foundation of covert and dubious theory? Is it a diagnosis, as one eminent psychiatrist suggested, to be found primarily in cities with psychoanalytic institutes and opera

Figure 1

		Other Personality Disorders		
		BPD & Other PD Avoidant Histrionic Passive-dependent Narcissistic Paranoid Antisocial Compulsive Schizoid Overlap: 10-25%		
Schizophrenias	Schizotypal Borderline schizophrenia Schizophrenic spectrum – withdrawal – isolation – anger/hostility – paranoia – derealization – depersonalization – ideas of reference – psychoticism – panic/anxiety – obsessive/compulsive Overlap: 25-50%	BPD (by DSM-III-R criteria)	Affective Illness – mood lability – depression – clinging – acting out – impulsive – self-destructive – emptiness/void – boredom – angry outbursts – panic and anxiety Overlap: 40-60%	Major Affectiv Disorde (with melanch and/o psychos

houses (Vaillant, 1984)? Most important, is it a disappearing diagnosis which can and should be subsumed by other diagnostic categories and treated as they would be treated?

I would argue that BPD is a distinct clinical entity that can and must be separated from other diagnostic categories. The figures and overlap cited by many clinicians and summarized in Figure 1 are invalid, representing misdiagnosis. I will now discuss these common areas of overlap, confusion, and misdiagnosis.

The Overlap Between BPD and Affective Syndromes

The use of broad diagnostic categories or terms such as "affective disorder" or "mood disorder" is inaccurate and confusing. For diagnostic, research, and treatment reasons, a distinction should always be made between the milder dysthymias, atypical and hysteroid depressions, and the more serious major depressive illnesses, with and without melancholic (vegetative) and psychotic features. In many studies these distinctions have not been made, or all types of "depression" have been lumped together, with this contributing significantly to the very high overlap figures (Stone et al., 1981; Carroll et al., 1981; Akiskal, 1981; Pope et al., 1983).

In two of these studies, major depressive disorder was specifically cited as overlapping with BPD. However, it has been my experience that the *DSM-III-R* criteria for major depressive illness are too broad and tend to blur clinically with those present in other mood disorders. A 1985 study by Barasch and colleagues seemed to reach a similar conclusion. In this study, 40% of the borderline patients had an episode of major depression during a three-year follow-up period. However, 40% of the patients in the study who had other personality disorders also experienced episodes of major depression. The authors concluded that either BPD had no special relation to affective disorder, all patients with personality disorders are predisposed to affective disorders, or *DSM-III-R* criteria for major depression are too broad. This third alternative appears most reasonable and consistent with the wide range of variation in the clinical findings across studies. In fact, studies that restrict the definition of affective disorder to either bipolar or melancholic unipolar illness find the range of overlap between BPD and affective disorder to be in the range of 3 to 13% (Frances et al., 1984; Pope et al., 1983; Charney et al., 1981; Gaviria et al., 1982). These figures are only slightly higher than comparable figures estimated for the general population (Weissman et al., 1981). This makes sense if one uses a developmental model, because a borderline patient should be (statistically) as vulnerable to a physiological depression (illness) as anyone else.

The Overlap Between BPD and SPD

The relationship, or overlap, between BPD and SPD is one of great interest and importance. Spitzer and colleagues (1979) spearheaded the effort in the late seventies to separate out from the borderline spectrum a group of patients with phenomenologic and biologic links to schizophrenia (S) but without full psychotic manifestations—the schizotypal personality—and to leave intact a group of individuals with a stable, primitive, but nonpsychotic ego structure—the borderline personality. More recent genetic, biologic, and follow-up studies have added support for the soundness of this distinction (Kendler et al., 1981; Stone, 1983; Baron et al., 1983; Kendler et al., 1984; Torgessen, 1984; Siever et al., 1983, 1984; McGlashan, 1986).

It is a matter of more than just historical or academic interest whether it is justified to separate these two entities, or whether a unified concept should be maintained. This is especially so when selecting patient samples for drug trials and when trying to evaluate study results, because SPD on most outcome measures hovers on the border between the Axis I diagnosis of (S) and the Axis II diagnosis of BPD. Therefore, studies that indiscriminately include SPD with BPD will tend to show poorer outcomes and more significant drug treatment responses, whereas those that eliminate SPD will show better outcomes and less drug response.

The conclusion I have drawn is that it is necessary and clinically useful to distinguish two subcategories within the group of patients who typically satisfy *DSM-III-R* criteria for SPD. One group (designated BPD/spd) displays prominent schizotypal symptoms such as psychoticism, hostility and paranoid ideation, phobic anxiety, ideas of reference, and obsessive-compulsive symptoms as a relatively distinct cluster in the presence of other typical BPD symptoms. A second group (designated S/spd) manifests primarily isolation, poverty of affect, and distant interpersonal relationships as the most prominent schizotypal features and may be more related to the schizophrenic spectrum. The implications of this distinction for pharmacologic and psychotherapeutic intervention will be discussed later.

The Overlap Between BPD and "Borderline Schizophrenia"

The history of the development of the borderline diagnosis began with attempts to distinguish a group of disorders on the "border" of psychosis, but with a stable character structure that would distinguish them from the ranks of the schizophrenias. In keeping with this view, many clinicians have conceptualized psychotic or psychotic-like experiences as a central characteristic of BPD. The Diagnostic Interview for Borderline Patients (DIB), developed by Gunderson and colleagues (1981), included psychosis as one of its five content areas. In *DSM-III-R*, brief psychotic episodes are mentioned as associated features. The inclusion or exclusion of patients with psychotic symptoms will again be important in understanding and evaluating the results of drug studies.

In my clinical experience, psychotic episodes in patients with BPD have almost always been associated with either drug or alcohol abuse or have been a part of a psychotic major depressive illness. Though many clinicians have stated that brief psychotic episodes can be a result of separation stress alone, I have rarely observed this. A study by Pope and colleagues (1985) sheds light on this question. The researchers conducted a systematic study of the nature of psychotic symptoms in patients with BPD. The cases of 33 patients meeting *DSM-III-R* criteria for BPD were reviewed, using both "narrow" (*DSM-III-R*) and "broad" (DIB) definitions of psychosis. Only 8 patients displayed psychotic symptoms meeting the "narrow" *DSM-III-R* definition. In all of these cases, the symptoms appeared to be attributable to either severe drug abuse or major affective disorder, present simultaneously with BPD. The remaining patients displayed only "broadly defined" psychotic symptoms or symptoms that appeared to be under voluntary control. The authors concluded that it was inappropriate to consider psychotic symptoms a feature of BPD itself. On the other hand, "factitious" psychotic symptoms, as defined by *DSM-III-R*, do seem to be a feature of BPD.

The Overlap Between BPD and Other Personality Disorders

The overlap between BPD and other personality disorders varies depending upon which personality disorder BPD is being compared with. This is a general problem for all Axis II diagnoses in *DSM-III-R*, because among outpatients diagnosed as having a personality disorder, two-thirds meet the criteria for two or more diagnoses (Kass et al., 1985). For the purpose of making drug treatment decisions, this problem is not of immediate concern; however, drug therapy trials inevitably will be attempted for symptoms associated with avoidant, histrionic, paranoid, compulsive, and antisocial personalities.

We can now redraw the original diagram and replace it with a more workable and accurate model (Figure 2). This diagram reflects the current state of the art of rigorous differential diagnosis, and from its vantage point one can evaluate the clinical studies and recommendations to be presented.

Figure 2

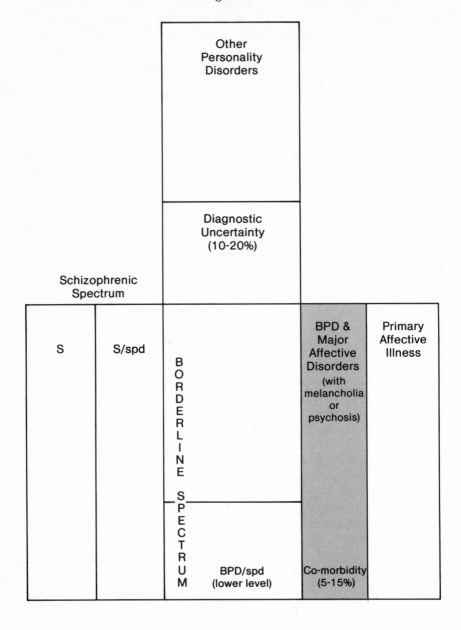

In this schema, the diagnosis of BPD is made when criteria additional to those required by *DSM-III-R* are used. The additional criteria are based on a systematic evaluation of ego strengths, defenses, developmental level, intrapsychic structure, and nature of the transference acting out and transference, as well as the response to therapeutic interventions. This multidimensional, structural diagnostic process has been described elsewhere by Masterson (1976).

The "borderline spectrum" described here includes those patients (BPD/spd) with symptoms or a symptom cluster (psychoticism, ideas of reference, paranoid ideation, etc.) that can be viewed as schizotypal symptoms within the framework of a borderline disorder—what has been often referred to as lower-level borderline.

The interface between the BPD and the affective spectrum of disorders is represented by an overlap or co-morbidity rate of 5 to 15%. This represents patients with a diagnosis of BPD and major depressive illness with melancholia or psychotic features.

The interface between BPD and the schizophrenic spectrum shows no overlap or co-morbidity. Individuals with severe personality disorders with borderline features who present with prominent affective poverty, isolation, and distance in interpersonal relationships, but who do not satisfy criteria for the schizophrenias, represent part of the schizophrenic spectrum and are designated S/spd.

Finally, the interface between BPD and other personality disorders is represented by an area of diagnostic uncertainty that is often resolved only by careful assessment or by a trial of psychotherapy. My experience would place the percentage of diagnostic uncertainty at 10 to 20%.

Thus, the only area where the interface of BPD with other Axis I or Axis II diagnoses shows significant overlap or co-morbidity is with major depressive illness with associated melancholic or psychotic features. Otherwise, careful diagnostic and differential diagnostic practices must be adhered to in order to make the kind of decisions that are critical for correct treatment, whether with psychotherapy or with pharmacotherapy.

REVIEW AND CRITIQUE OF THE LITERATURE

The diagnostic confusion and controversy that result from using the *DSM-III-R* categorical classification system make drug evaluation in clinical practice, and assessment of research, difficult. Additionally, controlled studies have just recently begun, and there is a current paucity of data upon which to base treatment decisions. My review of the existing data includes the following categories of drugs:

1. Antidepressants
2. Neuroleptics (antipsychotics)
3. Anxiolytics
4. Anticonvulsants

Antidepressants

Antidepressants have been used in the treatment of BPD with two different treatment objectives, which corresponded to two different concepts of BPD.

One objective has been to treat the affective symptoms and instability (including depression, emptiness, boredom, and impulsiveness) that are viewed as core features of BPD. In this view, BPD is a variant form of affective disorder, and by treating the affective disorder one is treating the BPD.

A second objective has been to focus on and treat the affective symptoms as features of an affective disorder that is co-morbid with BPD. In this view, BPD and affective disorder are independent entities that may or may not coexist.

Consistent with the view advanced earlier in this discussion, most controlled studies have found, not surprisingly, that patients *with a concurrent affective disorder* were more responsive to medication than were those who had only BPD (Pope et al., 1983; Charney et al., 1981; Cole et al., 1984). In fact, Pope and colleagues (1983) specifically found that none of their patients having only BPD showed a clear treatment response. Gunderson and Elliott (1985), in an extensive review of BPD and affective disorders, concluded that antidepressants appeared to be useful when a *co-morbid* affective disorder was present. They also concluded, however, that even when antidepressants are useful, the response rate is lower than expected, even when treating patients who meet criteria for major affective disorder. This conclusion is consistent with the hypothesis suggested by Barasch and colleagues (1985) and with my clinical experience: that *DSM-III-R* criteria for major depression are too broad. The response to treatment of patients with major affective disorder with associated melancholia, psychotic features, or both is in the range of what one would expect.

Two additional interesting results have emerged from recent studies. First, many researchers (Pope et al., 1983; Cole et al., 1984;

Soloff, 1981; Soloff et al., 1986) find that the drug response to depression in patients with a diagnosis of BPD (*including those patients who meet DSM-III-R criteria for major depressive disorder*) is heterogeneous: some patients' depression responds to antidepressants, whereas others' responds to antipsychotics. In trying to make sense of these findings, Soloff and colleagues (1986) speculate that the treatment response is attributable to relief of the severity of symptoms rather than a fundamental medical effect. I would add that these research findings do not separate out those patients with and without melancholia or psychotic features as part of the major affective disorder. Such a separation, I believe, would enhance therapeutic specificity.

A second interesting, and clinically important, finding is that in some patients antidepressants (especially the tricyclics) seem to facilitate behavioral dyscontrol (Soloff et al., 1986). Thus, the clinical practice of using the response to a trial of medication as a differential diagnostic tool should not be done routinely or undertaken lightly. Along with the more common side effects of antidepressants, the potential for serious behavioral dyscontrol must be considered.

Neuroleptics

Neuroleptics have been used for many years in varying doses in broadly, and often idiosyncratically, defined BPD. Only a handful of recent studies have dealt with criteria-defined borderline patients using double-blind designs and standardized outcome measures (Soloff et al., 1986; Leone, 1982; Serban & Siegel, 1984; Goldberg et al., 1986). Leone and Serban and Siegel reported significant improvement in broadly defined borderline patients using low dosages of neuroleptics in non-placebo-controlled studies.

Goldberg and colleagues reported a placebo-controlled, double-blind trial of neuroleptics in outpatients diagnosed as exhibiting BPD, SPD, or both, according to *DSM-III-R*. Drug–placebo differences favoring the neuroleptic were found on scores of psychoticism, illusion, ideas of reference, phobic-anxiety, and obsessive-compulsivity. The patient sample was clearly biased toward schizotypal features; it not only included patients with pure SPD, but also had among its inclusion criteria the presence of at least one psychotic symptom. Of particular clinical interest was the evidence for a powerful placebo effect:

Another point worth noting was the surprising extent of response while taking placebo to problems that seemed to be relatively enduring personality characteristics. Selected patients in the study showed a level of positive change that made most of us guess that they were treated with active drug, only to discover that they were taking placebo. . . It is noteworthy that change while taking the drug is not the same as change due to the drug, because the former includes a placebo effect. Since the clinician cannot subtract that part of the patient's response while taking drug that was due to placebo he might misinterpret a patient's response while taking drug as being due to the drug. (p. 686)

The evidence for such a powerful placebo effect from clinical research findings should strike a cautionary note for any clinician faced with evaluating anecdotal and non-placebo-controlled reports.

Finally, Soloff and colleagues (1986) conducted a double-blind controlled trial of an antidepressant (amitriptyline) and a neuroleptic (haloperidol) in patients with BPD defined by *DSM-III-R* criteria and a score of 7 or more on the DIB. Haloperidol was superior to both amitriptyline and placebo against anxiety, hostility, paranoid ideation, and psychoticism. In addition, although the patients had symptomatic problems sufficiently severe that pharmacotherapy was considered to be clinically indicated, in 20% of the patients screened, the symptomatic picture had resolved sufficiently within a week after they had sought treatment for pharmacotherapy to be considered unnecessary. Summarizing these findings, Soloff and colleagues state:

We have demonstrated the efficacy of low-dose neuroleptic therapy in a short-term, acute-illness treatment setting. It may be argued that short-term studies address only reactive state disorders in patients with BPD, not their chronic vulnerability to episodic decompensation. At present there are no empiric guidelines or proof of efficacy for the maintenance use of neuroleptics in borderline disorders. (p. 697)

Echoing my own thoughts, Gunderson (1986), commenting on the work of the Soloff and Goldberg groups, concluded:

In my view, a . . . reasonable implication of these studies is not to mistake the real, albeit limited role that neuroleptics appear to have in the treatment of some symptoms that are common in patients with BPD or SPD for treatment of the personality disorder itself. (p. 699)

Anxiolytics

The potential for abuse of benzodiazepines and other so-called minor tranquilizers by the general population and by patients with BPD is enormous. They are drugs that are often subjectively pleasing in their effects and very difficult to discontinue. The profile of action has led to their use in treating specific features of BPD, especially episodes of dysphoria with mixed anxiety, depression, and rage. Consistently, it has been reported that the benzodiazepines, including alprazolam (Xanax), increase the incidence of behavioral dyscontrol, including hostile outbursts, aggressive behavior, and suicidal ideation and acts in a variety of patients (Ryan et al., 1968; Gardos et al., 1968; Gaind & Jacoby, 1978; Gardner and Cowdry, 1985). To my knowledge there have been no double-blind, controlled studies on buspirone (BuSpar) and BPD.

The usefulness of alprazolam for phobic and panic disorders in patients (including patients with BPD) has been strongly demonstrated (Sheehan et al., 1984; Chouinard et al., 1982). In evaluating the presence of phobic and panic disorders as co-morbid conditions in patients with BPD, the clinician must adhere to rigorously defined criteria in order to avoid creating one more "gray area" of diagnostic overlap and confusion between BPD and panic disorders to replace the overlap and confusion between BPD and affective disorders.

Anticonvulsants

One hypothesized mechanism of behavioral dyscontrol in patients with BPD involves epileptoid overactivity of limbic system structures. This has been suggested by the similarity of symptoms between patients with complex partial seizures and those with BPD (Cowdry et al., 1980), and by the findings of increased incidences of head trauma, encephalitis, and seizure disorders in adolescents with BPD (Andrulonis et al., 1981).

In one double-blind crossover trial reported in the literature (Gardner & Cowdry, 1986b) carbamazepine (Tegretol) decreased the severity of behavioral dyscontrol in 11 women with BPD significantly more than did placebo. The authors emphasized the preliminary nature of their findings and the need for large-scale placebo-controlled trials. The same authors subsequently reported that 18% of their study subjects suffered from carbamazepine-induced melancholia (Gardner & Cowdry, 1986a). Clearly, research in this area is in its infancy, and no clinical conclusions can be drawn at this time.

The next section will draw conclusions that may be useful in guiding clinical practice, given the present state of knowledge and research.

GUIDELINES FOR CLINICAL APPLICATION

Drawing upon the results of the studies cited and my own clinical experience, I suggest the following clinical guidelines:

1. Careful attention should be paid to diagnostic precision.
2. The use of medication should be based on objective criteria (signs) rather than solely on subjective reporting (symptoms), whenever possible.
3. There should be an awareness that there are risks to the therapeutic relationship inherent both in giving and in not giving medication.

I would like to review these three guidelines before applying them to actual case histories.

Diagnostic Precision

Correct treatment requires correct diagnosis. As I have stressed in the first section of this discussion, there are many difficulties to overcome in making a correct diagnosis of BPD. Although a comprehensive and careful diagnostic process considers presenting symptoms as formulated by *DSM-III-R*, this information is valuable only as a guidepost that points the differential diagnostic investigation in one direction or another.

The diagnosis of BPD must be multileveled and multidimensional. Evidence of BPD should be discernible throughout the life history of the patient. Of special importance is a history of separation stress. A careful review of the patient's lifelong capacity to separate and attach, individuate and self-regulate, helps assess the level of developmental arrest and the overall ego defenses and defects. Further, a structural interview is critical to validate assumptions made from the historical data. The structural interview assesses the capacity to test reality, the nature of self and object representations, and the capacity to acknowledge and activate the self.

In the structural interview, an important area to attend to in making a differential diagnosis is a patient's response to confrontation. For example, the borderline patient, after momentary surprise, will likely integrate and work with a confrontation; a schizophrenic patient will likely become disorganized and overwhelmed with anxiety to the point of difficulty with, or loss of, reality testing. A narcissistic patient may typically react with cold indifference and devaluation; a paranoid patient with distrustfulness or rage; a schizoid patient with anxious withdrawal or detachment; a psychopathic patient with attack or manipulation.

The diagnostic procedure recommended here cannot be done quickly. Differential diagnosis is a time-consuming process that requires patience and knowledge. Careful diagnostic attention must be paid not only to the diagnosis of BPD, but also to all those Axis I diagnoses that may be present in the borderline patient as they would be in anyone. This is especially true in evaluating those conditions most likely to cause diagnostic confusion because of symptom overlap and the possibility of co-morbidity, such as major affective disorder with melancholia and panic disorder.

Evaluation of Objective Signs

To stress objective observation over subjective reporting in determining when drugs are useful is critical, because to do so will help the clinician to differentiate personal, dynamically determined emotional states, for which medication is usually not indicated, from impersonal, nondynamically determined emotional states, which often will respond to medication. For example, one should not treat a borderline patient for "depression" with the goal of making that patient "feel better." Rather, one should treat the specific symptoms or diagnostic criteria of depression or melancholia (such as weight loss, anorexia, loss of energy, early morning wakening, and marked psychomotor retardation or agitation), with the goal being specific symptomatic, observable relief.

The use of objective criteria should be based on observations of the patient made in sessions as well as on reports of affective, behavioral, and cognitive problems outside of sessions. These two levels of observation should reinforce and support each other. In regard to affect, when behavior and ideas reported in the session are markedly different from those reported outside the session, then medication is rarely useful, because what is being reported is most likely dynamic and conflictual, not adynamic and static.

Another very important "objective sign" in the evaluation of any patient's depressive symptomatology is the presence or absence of a family history of affective illness. Primary affective disorders are familial illnesses (Winokur & Clayton, 1967; Perris, 1982). Moreover, although familial is not synonymous with genetic, many studies have provided impressive evidence to justify attributing a major portion of the increased familial incidence to genetic factors (Mendelewics and Rainer, 1977; Cadoret, 1978; Gershon et al; 1971).

The presence of a positive family history should be a red flag to the clinician evaluating the patient. The greater the frequency of such disorders in a family, the greater should be the weight given to this factor. BPD also tends to run in families for reasons that have little or nothing to do with genetics. Therefore, it is imperative that the clinician assess as accurately as possible the diagnosis made in other family members. Because this is rarely possible by first-hand investigation, it is necessary to get from the patient or other family sources as many details as possible regarding the family members' specific symptoms as well as any treatment, including the response to treatment.

The most objective sign for any diagnosis is a biological marker. At present, there is no independent biological hypothesis or marker for BPD. The clinical tests suggested as markers of depression or schizophrenia are not sensitive or specific enough to be ideal research or clinical tools. Progress is ongoing in the search for such sensitive and specific markers.

Even after the diagnosis of BPD has been made, and criteria for the use of medication have been reported and observed, medication must be used within carefully defined boundaries. We will now examine the appropriate use of the various categories of psychotropic medication.

Neuroleptics. Efficacy has not yet been sufficiently determined to recommend guidelines for the long-term use of antipsychotic medication in BPD.

Short-term use of antipsychotics is justified in patients with BPD for treatment of psychotic episodes or states in order to decrease agitation and to better ensure the safety of the patient and others. Such relatively brief psychotic episodes or states in the BPD patient are usually secondary to either drug abuse or intoxication, or accompany severe major affective disorder, usually with associated melancholia.

Short-term use of antipsychotics may be justified with highly agitated lower-level borderline patients who present with a symptom cluster of "factitious" psychotic-like symptoms: hostility, paranoid ideation, ideas of reference, panic-anxiety, and obsessive-compulsive features that are not transient (state dependent). I have designated these patients as BPD/spd to distinguish them from patients with schizotypal features that likely are part of the schizophrenic spectrum (S/spd). There is usefulness to such a distinction despite the fact that both patient populations may be treated with neuroleptics. In fact, this distinction is crucial to the understanding of the fundamental difference between symptom and personality organization and to the ramifications of this difference for treatment intervention. The BPD/spd patient may benefit from neuroleptics in alleviating certain symptoms, but the Masterson Approach, emphasizing confrontation, would be the psychotherapeutic treatment of choice for the underlying personality disorder. The S/spd patient may benefit from neuroleptics, but the Masterson Approach to treatment would be contraindicated. Instead, reality testing of ego boundaries, advice, direction, counseling, social skills training, and vocational training would be the therapeutic interventions of choice.

Efficacy of long-term use of neuroleptics in the BPD/spd patient has not yet been studied; however, my own clinical experience is that such use *may* be justified.

Antidepressants. Patients with BPD who meet the *DSM-III-R* criteria for major depression with melancholia, psychotic features, or both require medication.

Patients with BPD who meet the *DSM-III-R* criteria for major depression alone are a controversial group, but most likely they do not require medication, because the distinction between chronic characterological depression (as in a patient with BPD) and major depressive disorder appears more quantitative than qualitative. In discussing the diagnostic criteria for chronic characterological depression (dysthymic disorder in *DSM-III-R*), it is pointed out that "the boundaries of Dysthymia with Major Depression are unclear" (p. 230). Patients with chronic characterological depression do not respond well to medication. According to Akiskal (1983):

> Characterological depressions begin early in life and pursue either an intermittent or nonremitting course. Typically, onset is insidious in the vague past of childhood or early adolescence, and the illness pursues a protracted course. . . Two-thirds of our patients with early-onset characterological depressions failed to show appreciable response to clinical trials with tricyclics, MAOIs, and lithium. (p. 17)

Thus, when faced with a borderline patient who seems to have symptoms of a major depression, the therapist should remember that in the absence of melancholia or psychotic features (or a positive family history), and when the symptoms have been chronic (present for more than two years), the likelihood of a response to medication is only one in three. In this case dynamic treatment which addresses the underlying characterological pathology is far more likely to be the treatment of choice. The presence of melancholia, psychotic features, or a positive family history associated with features of a major depressive disorder (present for less than two years) will greatly increase the treatment response. However, even in those cases where BPD and mood disorder coexist, successful medication treatment will not treat the dysphoric (including depressive) affect associated with the underlying borderline personality structure.

Anxiolytics. There is at present no discernible role for anxiolytics in the treatment of BPD. There is growing evidence for the usefulness of alprazolam (Xanax) in the treatment of panic disorder in all patients, including the patient with BPD who also meets rigorous criteria for this disorder.

Anticonvulsants. There is at present no substantial proof of efficacy for anticonvulsants (primarily carbamazepine) in the treatment of BPD.

Drugs and the Therapeutic Relationship

When dealing with a patient with BPD, the therapist must be aware of the risks to the therapeutic relationship both of giving and of withholding medication. For the nonmedical therapist, the issue can be seen as the risk involved in referring the patient for medication as opposed to not making the referral.

The use of medication is frequently perceived by the patient with BPD as a statement that he is not responsible for his behavior or for attempting to manage and contain painful affects. Further, the therapist runs the risk of stepping into the "rewarding unit" and damaging, perhaps permanently, the therapeutic frame. It is a thin therapeutic tightrope to walk when explaining to a patient that medication functions to allow responsibility for feelings and actions to return to the patient, and does not function to relieve the patient of responsibility for those feelings and behaviors. Adhering to the rigorous treatment criteria suggested in this discussion will minimize intrusions into the therapeutic relationship and damage to the therapeutic frame.

The decision not to use medication when in doubt also involves risk for the therapist, who may now be under great pressure to succumb to the patient's inevitable projections of the "withdrawing unit," or to the pressures created by the therapist's wish to do "the right thing." The therapist, in other words, is more vulnerable to thinking, "I wonder if I am being withholding and cruel or wrong in keeping from the patient help that might well relieve the patient's pain." A therapist in this vulnerable position is more likely to step into the rewarding unit in areas not involving the use of medication.

The next and final section of this chapter will discuss cases of patients who presented with complicated, and typical, clinical pictures. I shall apply the guidelines suggested here in assessing the role, if any, of medication in the treatment process.

CLINICAL APPLICATION OF TREATMENT GUIDELINES

The following case vignettes demonstrate the variety of clinical pictures and difficult treatment choices that confront a clinician. Each case will be presented briefly and then discussed within the framework of the three guidelines we have presented.

Case 1: Mr. A

Clinical picture. Mr. A had been referred for treatment during his third hospitalization in a year for suicidal ideation and gestures, and inability to function at his job as an advertising executive.

When first seen, Mr. A stated that he felt that his life had come apart. His second marriage was "on the rocks" and he no longer felt competent or capable at work. He stated he needed some "magical" answers and was hopeful that God, or his therapist, would hear his plea and help him, as he was now totally reliant on others. He further stated that he was helpless and overwhelmed by feelings of depression, shame at being such a lowly creature, and guilt for all his past offenses and insensitivities. The hospital treatment team had decided on a presumptive diagnosis of BPD with associated major depression.

Evaluation by guidelines. Although the patient fulfilled the *DSM-III-R* criteria for BPD, a careful assessment of the history and the results of a structural interview led me to a presumptive diagnosis of narcissistic personality disorder. Despite the diagnosis of major depressive disorder, the staff in the hospital where I first saw him in consultation (for possible ECT) had observed no vegetative (melancholic) symptoms: he had a good appetite and normal sleep pattern and activity level, and he described his depression primarily in terms of loss of self-esteem and helplessness. Thus, there seemed little indication for either ECT or antidepressants. In fact, he had presumably been on large doses of antidepressants for several weeks, but a routine check of the antidepressant blood level had come back as zero—indicating noncompliance. Finally, I assessed a recommendation for further drug treatment or ECT in terms of the effect this would have on the patient's intrapsychic structure. It seemed to me that such a recommendation would be complying with the patient's manipulations and efforts to act out his helplessness, whether by my stepping into the rewarding unit (if he was borderline) or by functioning as a devalued idealized object (if he was narcissistic). My recommendation to the staff and the patient was for discharge from the hospital and psychotherapy, not pharmacotherapy.

Follow-up. The patient was treated over a period of four years. Medication was never given. The diagnosis of narcissistic personality disorder was confirmed. The depressive symptoms were alleviated as the underlying pathological personality structure was dealt with in treatment.

Case 2: Ms. B

Clinical picture. Ms. B was 24 years old when first seen in consultation. She was an inpatient at the time and was scheduled to receive ECT. During my consultation, she stated that her "illness" had begun two years before, coinciding with her graduation from college. Since then, she had felt depressed and overwhelmed with anxiety while living at home with her parents. She manifested increasingly disorganized behavior, characterized by depression, suicidal gestures, and hysterical-violent outbursts. She had been diagnosed as manic-depressive or schizophrenic and had been treated with a variety of medications.

Evaluation by guidelines. Evaluation of the patient's early history revealed much evidence of separation anxiety and stress recalled by the patient from the age of 4 years. Further, upon exploration, it became clear that she had actually been acting out since early adolescence and was a heavy drug user. The latter seemed directly related to the disorganized behavior referred to earlier. The evaluation interviews demonstrated good reality testing, an impaired real self characterized by a self representation as "helpless, stupid, and inadequate." Along with split self and object representations, she showed a capacity to integrate confrontations, and to shift rapidly from silliness to seriousness and from destructiveness to depression.

The theme of the borderline triad ran throughout her life. The diagnosis of BPD was tentatively made. Further evaluation through questions and observations revealed no signs of either melancholia or depression with psychotic features. As an example, although she would lie in bed for days at a time, she would avidly consume the meals her parents would bring her while she was in bed.

She showed no deterioration of function consistent with a schizophrenic picture. Her anxiety, paranoid ideation, and other transient psychotic features seemed clearly induced either by conflict or drugs. Finally, it seemed clear from the history and her interactions with her parents that the use of drug treatment would be to step into the rewarding unit and would serve to further infantilize the patient and damage the therapeutic frame. The diagnosis of BPD was so compelling in this case that there was little internal struggle over whether I was withholding needed medication. Additionally, I had the evidence from past trials of medication that drugs were not effective.

Follow-up. Despite the patient's ability at times to invent new and previously unknown (to me) forms of acting out, medication was never necessary over the four years of treatment, during which the patient confirmed the diagnosis of pure BPD. Though she could not be seen frequently enough to permit working through of her abandonment depression, she was able to use treatment for ego repair and to sustain an adaptive and functioning life. By the end of treatment, she had long stopped her drug use, had completed graduate school, was working as a respected social worker, and was living alone while maintaining relatively stable relationships.

Case 3: Mr. C

Clinical picture. The patient was 19 when he was referred to me. He had been hospitalized most recently following a serious suicide attempt. He had actually been severely symptomatic since age 16, when he had left home for college. Intravenous drug use and antisocial behavior were among the more serious forms of acting out. He had dropped out of college in his sophomore year and had spent the next year living in California with his drug-addicted girlfriend, to whom he had clung tenaciously. The most immediate cause for his suicide attempt and return home had been the death of his girlfriend from an overdose, and his own fears that he was going "crazy"—a fear founded on chronic symptoms of paranoia, ideas of reference, panic-anxiety, derealization and depersonalization, and obsessive-compulsive features, characterized by delusion-like ruminations. He presented himself as overwhelmed and overwhelming, and I found myself faced with a real differential diagnostic dilemma. I was not reassured by the fact

that I was the ninth psychiatrist he had seen since age 9, without a
clear diagnosis and treatment plan having been determined.

Evaluation by guidelines. At first the differential diagnosis included
schizophrenia, BPD, SPD, major depression with psychotic features,
and atypical depression. Clearly I was confused. Over several months,
however, the developmental history, evaluation of ego strengths and
defects, nature of self and object representations, and response to
therapeutic interventions allowed a composite picture of BPD to take
shape.

The borderline triad gradually unfolded, and the patient began to
respond to the Masterson Approach of confrontation by beginning to
self-limit the tendency to act out, to identify feelings and contain them
rather than act them out, and to bring his feelings to the sessions
where they could be worked on. The initial schizotypal features,
however—most prominently the ideas of reference, paranoid ideation,
phobic-anxiety, compulsive ruminations, derealization, and depersonalization—persisted over the initial months constantly and unremittingly and seemed to exist in a parallel plane to the intrapsychic
structure of a typical BPD. The final diagnosis I arrived at was
BPD/spd. The treatment decision in this case was twofold: to treat the
symptom cluster characteristic of SPD with neuroleptics, while
treating the intrapsychic structure characteristic of BPD with the
Masterson Approach.

The cluster of schizotypal features all responded significantly to low
dosages of neuroleptic, leaving the patient and me free to deal with
the impaired real self. Confrontations were focused on the manifestations of distortions in self and object representations (such as splitting)
and the impairments in the real self (such as failures in self-activation).
At times, it was necessary to explicitly clarify what the drugs could be
expected to do and what he was expected to do.

Follow-up. The patient is currently still in treatment. Efforts to
discontinue the neuroleptic on two occasions resulted in a significant
exacerbation of the schizotypal symptoms. On the parallel track, the
patient has made remarkable progress to date in ego repair, adaptation, and building of ego structure. A therapeutic alliance has been
achieved, splitting has diminished, depression and destructive acting
out have significantly lessened, and the patient has now completed
college.

As ego defects continue to be repaired, the schizotypal symptom cluster (as I refer to it), which reflects a pattern of ego defects associated with extremely low-level borderline patients, may no longer require drug treatment. This hypothesis is still to be tested with this patient. Only when ego repair is well advanced can the capacity for working through of the abandonment depression be evaluated.

Case 4: Mr. D

Clinical picture. The patient was a 29-year-old man who presented with the chief complaint that, after two years of psychotherapy, he was still depressed. He reported that, although the treatment had been of great benefit to him in his interpersonal life and had helped him to resolve many difficulties, the depression, as he put it, "was always there waiting for me." His therapist had recently moved away, bringing his treatment to an end; however, he had been ready to stop anyway, since he had felt most of his conflicts had been resolved. He had been reading some of Masterson's work and had wondered if perhaps his depression was really an "abandonment depression" and that that was why it had persisted over all this time.

Evaluation by guidelines. A careful review of the patient's current functioning was not indicative of BPD or, for that matter, any personality disorder. It seemed that his prior treatment had indeed been helpful to him in resolving what appeared to have been clearly oedipal, triadic issues. His work and social functioning indicated the presence of whole self and object representations. This impression was confirmed by the behavior in the evaluation sessions.

During the evaluation, several additional and significant facts emerged. Mr. D insisted that he knew what it was like *not* to be depressed. The feeling which had been present these past two years was different from anything he had experienced earlier in his life—it was not like ordinary sadness, nor was it like mourning. He had known and experienced both.

A bout of depression similar to the depression of the last years had occurred once previously, after his freshman year in college, and he had been forced to leave school for a semester. That depression had seemed to resolve itself spontaneously.

This depression made him feel that he was always dragging himself around. It was, he said, "like a constant feeling of fatigue, a trapped feeling, like pushing against a wall." It was usually worse in the morning, and it cast a pall over everything—even the things he enjoyed most. Finally, he reported that his uncle had suffered from depressions and had been treated successfully with antidepressants.

Though the evidence for a major depression with melancholia was not clear cut, the absence of a distinct personality disorder, combined with the quality of the depression as described by the patient and the positive family history, all led to a diagnosis of affective disorder.

Follow-up. The patient was begun on a trial of antidepressants. Within two weeks he reported that the depression was gone. After a year of being depression free, we agreed to a trial period without medication. The depression returned within one month. Upon resumption of the antidepressant, the depression again was relieved. The patient has continued on the medication for the past three years. I speak to him every three months to monitor any problems with the medication. He is not involved in psychotherapy.

Case 5: Ms. E

Clinical picture. Ms. E first presented to me for treatment when she was 31. She had come at her mother's insistence, following a year of treatment with another therapist during which time the patient's condition had worsened. She had been increasingly isolating herself from work, family, and friends while complaining of boredom. According to her mother, the patient was acting more and more "odd." Ms. E's previous therapist described the mother as extremely intrusive, and stated that there seemed to be a malignant symbiotic relationship between mother and daughter. Her diagnosis of the patient was that of a distancing lower-level borderline.

Evaluation by guidelines. Although in taking a history some degree of retrospective distortion is always present, my overall impression was that the patient seemed to have had a relatively normal childhood, adolescence, and young adulthood. By her mid-twenties, however, she had begun to change. Friendships became difficult to sustain, and her career goals seemed to become diffuse. She had spent much of her adult life moving from job to job, always complaining of boredom or disinterest. She was not especially interested in dating, and instead contented herself with being with her family and maintaining a casual (but fantasized romantic) friendship with a man whom she had known from a previous job.

The assessment of current functioning seemed consistent with a schizotypal picture of psychoticism (magical thinking, odd speech, suspiciousness) along with social anxiety, isolation, interpersonal distance, and poverty of affect. The diagnosis seemed consistent with S/spd—in other words, she seemed to be the type of isolated, affectless patient with SPD that may be related to the schizophrenic spectrum. Therefore, I felt that a trial of neuroleptics was indicated.

My concern about the possible interference of this recommendation with the therapeutic relationship was minimal, since the patient seemed aloof, cold, and distant anyway. I was hopeful, in fact, that the drug would allow me access to her.

Follow-up. The medication worked well. Within two weeks the patient was interacting much more spontaneously, with improved affect and with much more clearly goal-directed speech. Her tendency to digress and be vague and metaphorical improved dramatically. Her social isolation decreased somewhat as she made some effort (albeit with difficulty) to socialize. She resumed work and seemed genuinely happier, although she still complained of boredom and emptiness. During this time, she was seen for weekly counseling sessions, which focused on problem solving.

Against my advice, she discontinued the medication after six months. This was followed by a rapid return of symptoms. Resumption of medication led to improvement once again. One year later, she discontinued the medication again. This time there was a full-blown and prolonged psychotic decompensation, whose duration and features (delusions, loosening of associations, and incoherence) met the criteria for a diagnosis of schizophrenia.

Case 6: Ms. F

Clinical picture. The patient was a 35-year-old woman physician who presented with severe phobic symptoms and hypochondriacal concerns, which had escalated in the aftermath of the recent death of her mother and a miscarriage. She stated that throughout her life separations of all kinds had been difficult and emotionally traumatic. An additional presenting problem was her extreme obesity—she was 100 pounds overweight.

Evaluation by guidelines. Assessment of the past history and present functioning revealed a picture consistent with a diagnosis of upper- to mid-level borderline personality. Though the patient functioned well in her career, her interpersonal relationships were dominated by the borderline patient's twin fears of engulfment and abandonment. This manifested itself on the one hand in problems with intimacy (especially in her marriage) and on the other hand in separation stress and extraordinarily intense, clinging relationships.

Whereas the patient satisfied a multilevel diagnosis of BPD, she also met *DSM-III-R* criteria for panic attacks with associated agoraphobia. Despite her intense, clinging, rewarding unit projections, I was prepared initially to start drug treatment for her phobic and panic disorders. However, her refusal to take any medication because of her hypochondriacal concerns removed this issue from consideration initially.

Follow-up. Treatment over a period of three years using the Masterson Approach was dramatically successful in treating the basic personality disorder, with remarkable improvement in ability to tolerate separation stress, improved interpersonal relationship and capacity for intimacy, and dramatic weight loss (in the first year of treatment, she lost 80 pounds).

Her vulnerability to panic attacks in situations from which flight was difficult (traffic jams, tunnels, theaters, airplanes) was, however, a continued source of distress well into the second year of treatment until she was able and willing to accept medication (in this case a monoamine oxidase inhibitor, phenelzine sulfate—Nardil—was used). Her wish to try the medication at this point in treatment represented her desire to further activate her real self. The medication brought rapid relief from these symptoms.

Case 7: Ms. G

Clinical picture. Ms. G was 23 when I first saw her following her discharge from a psychiatric hospital, where she had been for two months after a psychotic episode. The discharge diagnosis from the hospital was BPD with probably drug-induced psychosis.

The patient dated her psychiatric history back to her first year in college, when she had dropped out of school. The patient returned home, where she lived with her parents until finishing college. She tried various jobs after graduation, but complained of boredom and intermittent depression. She spent most of her salary on a frenetic and promiscuous social life and on drugs. Her relationships were chaotic, and she described herself as "flirtatious, demanding, and easily hurt."

She complained of having no sustained interests, besides men, and of being unable to finish anything she started.

Evaluation by guidelines. Careful assessment of the patient supported the diagnosis of BPD. However, it also became clear that the patient's psychotic episode had been the first frank manifestation of a severe bipolar manic-depressive illness. Over the five years that I treated her, she had many severe manic and depressive episodes, which required repeated hospitalization and which, unhappily, were not responsive to lithium treatment.

The management of her BPD was almost as difficult as the management of her affective disorder. Therapeutic work with her splitting and other pathological defenses would be interrupted at times by the fury of her manic rage or the weight of her profound depressions. At times her helplessness, for example, would be an expression of her underlying personality structure and would respond well to confrontation; at other times it would be an expression of subtle shifts in her underlying biology and would respond only (and dramatically) to changes in medication.

Follow-up. The coexistence of BPD and affective disorder in this patient demonstrates that, rather than simply requiring a two-track treatment plan, such situations may prove doubly difficult to treat. Five years of treatment enabled this patient to achieve a more stable and adaptive interpersonal lifestyle; however, the management of her affective disorder remained elusive. At the conclusion of the treatment she was referred to a university hospital center to take part in a research protocol for management of severe nonresponsive affective disorders.

CONCLUSION

The question of the role of medication for the borderline patient is a complicated one. In a review of the literature and my own clinical experience, it becomes apparent to me that, at times, there are as many answers to this question as there are borderline patients! The therapist should, however, remember that medication treats symptoms. It does not build intrapsychic structure. The therapist should be aware not only of the benefits of medication but also of its limitations.

REFERENCES

Akiskal, H.S. (1981). Subaffective disorders: dysthymic, cyclothymic and bipolar II disorders in the "borderline" realm. *Psychiatric Clinics of North America, 4,* 25-46.

Akiskal, H.S. (1983). Dysthymic disorder: psychopathology of proposed chronic depressed subtypes. *American Journal of Psychiatry, 140,* 11–20.

American Psychiatric Association. (1987). *Diagnostic and statistical manual of mental disorders* (3rd ed., revised). Washington, DC: American Psychiatric Association.

Andrulonis, P.A., Glueck, B.C., Stroebel, C.F., et al. (1981). Organic brain dysfunction and the borderline syndrome. *Psychiatric Clinics of North America, 4,* 47-66.

Barasch, A., Frances, A., Hurt, S., et al. (1985). Stability and distinctness of borderline personality disorder. *American Journal of Psychiatry, 142,* 1484-1486.

Baron, M., Gruen, R., Asnis, L., & Kane, J. (1983). Familial relatedness of schizophrenia and schizotypal states. *American Journal of Psychiatry, 140,* 1437-1442.

Cadoret, R.J. (1978). Psychopathology in adopted-away offspring of biologic parents with antisocial behavior. *Archives of General Psychiatry, 35,* 176-184.

Carroll, B.J., Greden, J.T., Feinberg, M., et al. (1981). Neuroendocrine evaluation of depression in borderline patients. *Psychiatric Clinics of North America, 4,* 89-99.

Charney, D.S., Nelson, J.C., & Quinlan, D.M. (1981). Personality traits disorder in depression. *American Journal of Psychiatry, 138,* 1601–1604.

Chouinard, G., Annable, L., Fontaine, R., et al. (1982). Alprazolam in the treatment of generalized anxiety and panic disorders: a double-blind, placebo-controlled study. *Psychopharmacology, 77,* 229-233.

Cole, J.O., Salomon, M., Gunderson, J.G., et al. (1984). Drug therapy in borderline patients. *Comprehensive Psychiatry, 25,* 249-262.

Cowdry, R.W., Pickar, D., & Davies, R. (1980). Limbic dysfunction in the borderline syndrome. In *New Research Abstracts,* 133rd Annual Meeting of the American Psychiatric Association. Washington, DC.

Frances, A., Clarkin, J.F., Gilmore, M., et al. (1984). Reliability of criteria for borderline personality disorder: a comparison of DSM-III and the diagnostic interview for borderline patients. *American Journal of Psychiatry, 141,* 1080–1083.

Gaind, R., & Jacoby, R. (1978). Benzodiazepines causing aggression. In R. Gaind & B. Hudson (Eds.), *Current Themes in Psychiatry, Vol. 1.* London: Macmillan.

Gardner, D.L., & Cowdry, R.W. (1985). Alprazolam-induced dyscontrol in borderline personality disorder. *American Journal of Psychiatry, 142,* 98-100.

Gardner, D.L., & Cowdry, R.W. (1986a). Development of melancholia during carbamazepine treatment in borderline personality disorder. *Journal of Clinical Psychopharmacology, 6,* 236-239.

Gardner, D.L., & Cowdry, R.W. (1986b). Positive effect of carbamazepine on behavioral dyscontrol in borderline personality disorder. *American Journal of Psychiatry, 143*, 519-522.

Gardos, G., DiMascio, A., Salzman, C., et al. (1968). Differential actions of chlordiazepoxide and oxazepam on hostility. *Archives of General Psychiatry, 18*, 757-760.

Gaviria, M., Flaherty, J., & Val, E. (1982). A comparison of bipolar patients with and without a borderline personality disorder. *Psychiatric Journal of the University of Ottawa, 7*, 190-195.

Gershon, E.S., Dunner, D.L., & Goodwin, F.K. (1971). Toward a biology of affective disorders. *Archives of General Psychiatry, 25*, 1-15.

Goldberg, S.C., Schulz, S.C., Schulz, P.M., et al. (1986). Borderline and schizotypal personality disorders treated with low-dose thiothixene versus placebo. *Archives of General Psychiatry, 43*, 680-690.

Gunderson, J.G. (1986). Pharmacotherapy for patients with borderline personality disorder. *Archives of General Psychiatry, 43*, 698-700.

Gunderson, J.G., & Elliott, G.R. (1985). The interface between borderline personality disorder and affective disorder. *American Journal of Psychiatry, 142*, 277-288.

Gunderson, J.G., Kolb, J.E., & Austin, V. (1981). The diagnostic interview for borderline patients. *American Journal of Psychiatry, 138*, 896–903.

Kass, F., Skodol, A.E., Charles, E., et al. (1985). Scaled ratings of DSM-III personality disorders. *American Journal of Psychiatry, 142*, 627-630.

Kendler, K.S., & Gruenberg, A.M. (1984). An independent analysis of the Danish adoption study of schizophrenia: VI. The relationship between psychiatric disorders as defined by DSM-III in the relatives and adoptees. *Archives of General Psychiatry, 41*, 555-564.

Kendler, K.S., Gruenberg, A.M., & Strauss, J.S. (1981). An independent analysis of the Copenhagen sample of the Davish Adoption study of schizophrenia: II. The relationship between schizotypal personality disorder and schizophrenia. *Archives of General Psychiatry, 38*, 982-984.

Kohut, H. (1971). *The analysis of the self: A systematic approach to the psychoanalytic treatment of the narcissistic disorder.* New York: International Universities Press.

Leone, J.F. (1982). Response of borderline patients to loxapine and chlorpromazine. *Journal of Clinical Psychiatry, 43*, 148-150.

Masterson, J.F. (1976). *Psychotherapy of the borderline adult.* New York: Brunner/Mazel.

McGlashan, T.H. (1986). Schizotypal personality disorder. *Archives of General Psychiatry, 43*, 329-334.

Mendelewics, J., & Rainer, J.D. (1977). Adoption study supporting genetic transmission in manic depressive illness. *Lancet, 268*, 327-328.

Perris, C. (1982). The distinction between bipolar and unipolar affective disorders. In E.S. Paykel (Ed.), *Handbook of affective disorders*, pp. 45-48. New York: Guilford Press.

Pope, H.G., Jonas, J.M., Hudson, J.I., et al. (1983). The validity of DSM-III borderline personality disorder. *Archives of General Psychiatry, 40*, 23–30.

Pope, H.G., Jonas, J.M., Hudson, J.I., et al. (1985). An empirical study of psychosis in borderline personality disorder. *American Journal of Psychiatry, 142,* 1285-1290.

Ryan, H.F., Merril, F.B., Scott, G.E, et al. (1968). Increase in suicidal thoughts and tendencies, association with diazepam therapy. *Journal of the American Medical Association, 203,* 1137-1139.

Serban, G., & Siegel, S. (1984). Response of borderline and schizotypal patients to small doses of thiothixene and haloperidol. *American Journal of Psychiatry, 141,* 1455-1458.

Sheehan, D.V., Coleman, J.H., Greenblatt, D.J., et al. (1984). Some biochemical correlates of panic attacks and their response to a new treatment. *Journal of Clinical Psychopharmacology, 4,* 66-75.

Siever, L.J., Coursey, R.D., Brody, L., et al. (1983, May). Eye tracking and schizotypal personality. Paper presented at the Annual Meeting of the American Psychiatric Association, New York.

Siever, L.J., Klar, H.M., Runden, I.E., et al. (1984, May). Schizotypal and borderline personality. Paper presented at the Annual Meeting of the American Psychiatric Association, Los Angeles.

Soloff, P.H. (1981). Pharmacotherapy of borderline disorders. *Comprehensive Psychiatry, 22,* 535-543.

Soloff, P.H., George, A., Nathan, R.S., et al. (1986). Progress in pharmacotherapy of borderline disorders. *Archives of General Psychiatry, 43,* 691-697.

Spitzer, R.L., Endicott, J., & Gibbon, M. (1979). Crossing the border into the borderline personality and borderline schizophrenia. *Archives of General Psychiatry, 36,* 17-24.

Spitzer, R.L., Williams, J., & Skodol, A. (1980). *DSM-III:* The major achievements and an overview. *American Journal of Psychiatry, 137,* 151-164.

Stone, M.H. (1983, May). Family data and therapy of schizotypal patients. Paper presented at the Annual Meeting of the American Psychiatric Association, New York.

Stone, M.H., Kahn, E., & Flye, B. (1981). Psychiatrically ill relatives of borderline patients: a family study. *Psychiatric Quarterly, 53,* 71–84.

Torgessen, S. (1984). Genetic and nosological aspects of schizotypal and borderline personality disorders: A twin study. *Archives of General Psychiatry, 41,* 546-554.

Vaillant, G.E. (1984). The disadvantages of DSM-III outweigh its advantages. *American Journal of Psychiatry, 141,* 542-545.

Weissman, M.M., Myers, J.K., & Thompson, D. (1981). Depression and its treatment in a US urban community—1975–1976. *Archives of General Psychiatry, 38,* 417-421.

Winokur, G., & Clayton, P. (1967). Family history studies: I. Two types of affective disorder separated according to genetic and clinical factors. In J. Wortis (Ed.), *Recent advances in biological psychiatry.* New York: Plenum Press.

Chapter 23

Addictive Behaviors: Problems in Treatment with Borderline Patients

Shelley Barlas Nagel, Ph.D.

Therapists have few successes and many difficulties in treating borderline patients with addictive behavior problems. Often, therapists do not accurately identify addictive behaviors as such, nor do they fully understand the underlying borderline pathology, or adequately manage the treatment process. It is unfortunate that excessive overeating, compulsive sexual behavior, and alcoholism, for example, are all treated separately in the literature. Few attempts have been made by researchers in these areas to compile and share knowledge, or to formulate general theories of addiction (Miller, 1979). This contributes to the confusion and lack of integration in the field.

This chapter will discuss the addictive behaviors, their underlying psychopathology, and a therapeutic treatment approach. Problems in the treatment of borderline patients with addictive behaviors will be addressed throughout this discussion.

DIFFERING VIEWS OF ADDICTIVE BEHAVIORS:
REVIEW OF THE LITERATURE

One view of addiction is that it can be characterized as a disease, a pathological state with particular signs and symptoms. There is an increasing body of both clinical and research evidence supporting the disease concept of addiction. Smith and colleagues (1985), referring to drugs and alcohol, state that addiction has a predictable prognosis if the addiction-prone individual continues to use them. Smith sees addiction as a composite of compulsion, loss of control, and continued substance abuse in spite of adverse consequences.

Jellinek (1952, 1960) first advanced the concept of addictive disease when he proposed that alcoholism is a progressive and potentially fatal disorder involving loss of control. He described a downward spiral of identifiable symptoms and behavior with certain deteriorative stages. This disease concept has been criticized and remains controversial among professionals (Khantzian, 1980; Szasz, 1974). Some argue that the biological mechanisms are stressed too much, with little attention paid to psychological problems, and that the disease concept minimizes personal and social responsibility in the development of addictive behaviors.

Silber (1974) views alcoholism as a symptom, characterized by persistent or excessive drinking. He states that alcoholism has most generally been regarded as an addiction, and that an alcoholic develops a dependence upon alcohol with the expectation that it will help avoid pain and will bring about a feeling of satisfaction and comfort. Vaillant (1983) points out that alcoholism becomes a disease when loss of voluntary control over alcohol consumption becomes a major factor in much of an individual's social, psychological, and physical deterioration.

Since Jellinek's study, the disease concept has been embraced and promoted by Alcoholics Anonymous, the National Council of Alcoholism, the National Institute on Alcohol Abuse and Alcoholism, and the American Medical Association (Marlatt, 1983). In spite of the controversy surrounding alcoholism, and the need for more conclusive research, the disease model is considered by the majority of addiction specialists to be the best paradigm for understanding the chronic substance abuse patterns that lead to progressive deterioration of social, economic, or health functions (Smith, Milkman, and Sunderwirth, 1985).

I believe the definition of the addictive behaviors can be extended to include not only drugs and alcohol, but also extreme overeating, sexual overindulgence, and excessive gambling, to name just a few behaviors. In addition to dramatic changes in affective states, these excessive behaviors have disease-like characteristics, such as loss of control, compulsion, and continued participation and involvement in the behavior in spite of obvious self-destructive consequences.

There is a fine line between, on the one hand, engaging in activities with greater intensity and frequency, and, on the other, becoming compulsive and out of control. For example, Vaillant (1983, p. 309) explains that "the exact point at which minimal alcohol abuse merits the label of alcoholism . . . will always be as uncertain as where in the spectrum yellow becomes green." Vaillant says it is impossible to locate the trigger point at which the casual drinker becomes physiologically and psychologically addicted to liquor. "You are an alcoholic when you're not always in control of when you begin drinking and when you stop drinking" (O'Reilly, 1983). This same reasoning can also apply to overeating, sexual behavior, gambling, and many other addictive behaviors.

In the literature, drinking and drug taking have been linked, emphasizing the pharmacological basis of behavior. Psychiatrists, social workers, counselors, psychologists, and other mental health professionals have often specialized in the treatment of one addictive behavior; few have extended their therapy and research efforts to cover more than one or two of the disorders. In addition, specialists in these areas have worked in relative isolation from one another, seldom communicating about treatment and research issues. The emergent concept of the addictive behaviors points to possible commonalities among these seemingly diverse problems. Parallels can be drawn between drinking, drug taking, gambling, sexual behavior, overeating, overspending, shoplifting, and addictive relationships.

The addictive behavior can be viewed as a progressive disease, because it develops a life of its own. There is also, however, underlying pathology. Patients with addictive behaviors fall into diverse diagnostic categories. A great many of these patients exhibit a borderline personality disorder as described by Masterson (1972, 1976, 1981) and Kernberg (1975). Although many of the excessive behaviors of borderline patients may differ, the character structure or underlying pathology is the same. Borderline pathology has been implicated in alcoholism by both Masterson (1976) and Kernberg (1975). Earlier, the pioneering work of Otto Fenichel (1945) attempted to define a diagnostic category of the "instinct-ridden characters" who act out their conflicts through alcohol or drug abuse, but who also may suffer from "addictions without drugs" (a group that includes excessive gamblers, kleptomaniacs, overeaters, and "love addicts").

In Vaillant's case material on addictions (1983), he concludes that the sociopathy and related behavioral problems are defensive, symptomatic, and indicative of the enormous difficulties such individuals have tolerating painful affects, particularly depression and anxiety. Khantzian's observations are similar (1974, 1975). He concludes that both the impulsive behavior and the addiction are closely related to problems with aggression, anxiety, and, most emphatically, depression. In describing heroin addicts, he states that deprivation or overindulgence in the mother-child relationship can result in early ego impairments that may later lead to addiction problems. Khantzian continues (1980) that for many, alcohol abuse is one more expression of an ego deficit, with lack of impulse control.

Khantzian (1980) describes Tyndel's study in which 1,000 alcoholic patients were given psychiatric evaluations. He found psychiatric or personality disorders, or both, present in all instances, and concluded that the alcoholism resulted from attempts to deal with long-standing discomfort associated with psychopathologic processes and related social difficulties.

Borderline patients have ego deficits, such as lack of impulse control and poor frustration tolerance, which often are manifested in food addiction. Overeating is an obsessive, compulsive addiction of a highly complex nature. Food can be even more addictive than drugs, alcohol, tobacco, or gambling, and at least as destructive. Because people cannot do without food, each time food addicts eat they are in danger of succumbing to their compulsion.

Overeaters have difficulty with self-hate, hopelessness, and anger, states Rubin (1978). He says the difficulty in handling anger is something overeaters share with alcoholics (1970), both groups being very angry people with remarkably little awareness of their anger or how to handle it. One group uses food, the other alcohol, both trying to anesthetize feeling. Rubin believes repressed anger plays a powerful role in the addiction, and that the roots of the condition can often be traced to early and complicated family relations.

In a discussion of the emotional aspects of obesity, Hamburger (1951) reported four types of overeating. One group overate in response to emotional tensions that were essentially nonspecific, such as loneliness, anxiety, and boredom. Another group reacted by overeating during chronic states of tension and frustration, using food as a substitute gratification in unpleasant or intolerable situations. In a third group, overeating was a symptom of an underlying emotional illness, most frequently depression, and in the fourth group, overeating took on the proportions of an addiction, distinguished by compulsive, intense craving for food.

Stunkard (1959) describes the binge-eating syndrome as characterized by the sudden, compulsive ingestion of large amounts of food in a short time, usually with subsequent agitation and self-condemnation. The conclusion Bruch reaches (1973) is that obesity is associated with, and directly related to, personality and developmental disturbances. She points out that these patients suffer from an abiding sense of loneliness, and that emotional states are cues to begin overeating.

Browning (1985) describes the bulimic patient, and says obsessional symptoms such as binge eating tend to become secondarily autonomous, that is, they become independent of the conflicts for which the symptom was initially a remedy. As with any addictive activity, while the eating binge lasts, the state of consciousness is altered and inner tension abates. The act of eating and the immediate feeling it produces generate an anesthesia. For a short time there is no feeling, only numbness and lethargy. Then the compulsive purge begins—vomiting, starvation, or laxative or diuretic use—only to lead to more discomfort, shame, self-hate, remorse, and possible physiological complications.

When overeating results in obesity, it may be relatively easy to effect short-term weight changes. However, the real problem is whether this represents a lasting improvement. Poor prognosis is mentioned in almost every scholarly work on weight management. One of the most quoted statements in the literature on weight control is the declaration that "most obese persons will not stay in treatment for obesity. Of those who stay in treatment, most will not lose weight, and of those who do lose weight, most will regain it" (Stunkard & McLaren-Hume, 1959, p. 79).

Along with psychotherapy, Bruch (1973) suggests that psychological support is a necessary part of every reducing regimen and has found its best execution in the group approaches, such as Weight Watchers and similar enterprises. Overeaters Anonymous, a self-help group based on the successful principles of Alcoholics Anonymous, views compulsive overeating as a disease, and offers support and hope of recovery (Overeaters Anonymous, 1980).

Excessive, mood-altering sexual behavior, frequently damaging and destructive, is another expression of an ego deficit with lack of impulse control, and is aimed primarily at avoiding and masking unpleasant affect, conflicts, painful memories, and an abandonment depression. In fact, Carnes (1983) states that fear of abandonment is at the core of sexual addiction. He describes these patients as using denial, distorting reality, ignoring problems, and participating in self-destructive, impulsive acts. These descriptions are similar to Masterson's discussion of borderline patients (1976).

As with the other addictive behaviors, the activity becomes autonomous, producing additional problems: interpersonal difficulties, anxiety, depression, and further complications. All types of compulsive behavior, such as gambling, shoplifting, and spending, are frequent counterparts and may be woven into the scenario of sexual addiction (Miller, 1980). Physical violence, too, is a way to release pent-up tension and is reported by Carnes (1983) as a concurrent behavior in sexually abusive families.

For the patient who is using sexual behavior defensively, the ritual, arousal, and excitement of the entire episode—including the sexual interactions and mood-altering experience—may be every bit as intoxicating and addictive as alcohol is to the alcoholic, or heroin to the addict. They seek a "quick fix." The intoxication of the whole experience is what the sexual addict looks for in order to move through the cycle from despair to short-lived exhilaration. The addict wants to connect with another person, to merge, fuse, become one, in order to take away the pain and fill the emptiness of the inner emotional abyss. Peele and Brodsky (1975) discuss addictions with relationships and with love. Interpersonal love, "people addiction," is described as one of the most common yet least-recognized forms of addiction. These patients use relationships as if they were a drug or a "fix." The same needs that drive some patients to drink or to use drugs drive the love addict, often with painful, destructive consequences.

Carnes (1983) reports on those with multiple addictions who go on food binges to avoid depression after a sexual binge. The additional emotions and conflicts precipitated by the sexual acting out can then lead to other forms of addictive behaviors: drugs, food, alcohol, or compulsive spending. The often denied destructive cycle is repeated again and again, fueled by discomfort and distress.

By far the most pervasive combination of addictions is sexual addiction in conjunction with alcohol or drug dependency. Many researchers attribute sexual excesses and even incest to alcoholism.

"Alcoholism was another common characteristic of incestuous informants and has been frequently associated with incestuous behavior" (Herman, 1981, p. 76). The reality is that alcoholism is often an illness concurrent with, rather than the cause of, the addiction. Many alcoholics have discovered that the treatment of one addiction does not cure the other. There is growing documentation (Carnes, 1983) of the interaction between the two addictions. One of the greatest unacknowledged contributors to recidivism in alcoholism and other addictive behaviors is the failure of treatment approaches and programs to treat multiple addictions. As many recovering alcoholics know, when they give up alcohol they often substitute another addiction. Overeating may begin, along with other compulsive activities.

AN UNDERLYING INFLUENCE IN ADDICTIVE BEHAVIORS: THE SPECIAL SIGNIFICANCE OF INCEST

Therapists sometimes overlook an important influence underlying addictive behaviors in borderline patients: the patients' childhood experience with sexual abuse. Frequently, experiences of child molestation and incest have occurred in the lives of borderline patients, further damaging and interfering with their developmental processes. Thus, more wounds, impairments, and painful reinforcing scapegoating experiences are superimposed on the already problematic borderline psychic structure. As Carnes states (1983, p. 77), "The presence of sexual compulsivity of any form has its impact on children and creates vulnerability to addiction."

Numerous studies support the destructive results of early sexual abuse. Butler (1978) concludes that adolescent alcoholism, drug addiction, suicide, and runaway behavior are sometimes symptoms of a deeper and more painful problem. She cites several retrospective studies which indicate that underlying much of adolescent acting out is a source of pain that has been overlooked or ignored. Benward and Densen-Gerber (1975, p. 6) agree, citing a drug program in New York City which reported that 44% of all female addicts in the rehabilitation center had been incestuously assualted. In a study by Weber (1977, p. 65) in Minneapolis, 75% of the women working as prostitutes were found to be victims of incestuous assault.

Herman (1981) describes a study in which 60% of incest victims complained of major depressive symptoms in adult life, and 20% had periods of time when they were alcoholic or drug dependent. Most described their drug abuse episodes as ineffective attempts to cope with feelings of loneliness and depression.

It now appears that sexual abuse of children is much more widespread than was previously believed. Butler (1978, p. 15) reports that Dr. Henry Giarretto, founder of the Child Sexual Abuse Treatment program in San Jose, California, believes sexual abuse of children by immediate family members and other relatives is rising in epidemic proportions. Butler (1978, p. 16) also cites studies by Landis and Peters which support the widespread occurrence of incest. Landis reports that of 1,800 college students responding to a questionnaire, one-third had at some point in their lives been sexually abused, and Peters concludes that over half of all children are victimized by an adult they know and trust.

Although childhood sexual abuse is apparently widespread, all too often therapists do not recognize when this abuse has occurred. Without this recognition, treatment of some addictive borderline patients may be limited. Therapists frequently say they do not see many patients who have experienced incest, molestation, or physical brutality. This is not necessarily because their patients have not had these experiences but, rather, because therapists overlook, deny, or ignore the existence of these problems. Therapists may have uncomfortable feelings about the topic and back away from it, or may be unprepared to help, lacking proper training.

Often they fail to include the topic in taking an initial history. Sometimes they do not recognize clues the patient may be giving, or, as treatment progresses, they are not aware of indications of past incest experiences. Many therapists do not understand the dynamics of the shame, guilt, repression, and denial involved. Nor do they understand that years of secrecy and isolation make the patient unable or unwilling to talk about—or even remember—these experiences and the emotions surrounding them. Unless patients can remember, they may be compelled to repeat the experiences, acting out behaviorally the equivalent of painful recollections.

These experiences of betrayal, suffering, and mistrust are exacerbated when a patient goes to a therapist who does not identify or understand the ramifications of incest. Often, addictive behaviors are vehicles of denial, allowing the patient to look away from painful earlier experiences, and not feel the emotions associated with them. It is important for therapists to question in their own minds whether or not these patients are simultaneously reenacting and denying past sexual trauma through alcohol and drug abuse, overeating, undereating, bulimic purging, or compulsive sexual behavior with one or multiple partners.

Also, in many cases, weight is a central physical manifestation of past incest experiences. During treatment, patients have expressed thoughts such as: "The fat protects me. It separates me from my sexual feelings, memories, fears. I can keep myself fat and unattractive, and I don't have to deal with the pain from the past." For borderline patients with addictive behaviors, the need to defend against feeling and remembering past sexual abuse becomes linked with the need to defend against feeling and remembering an abandonment depression.

Many therapists do not understand that, although actual intercourse may not have occurred, there are still many damaging sexual interactions, behaviors, and subtle patterns that have been experienced by these patients. Butler (1978, p. 5), for example, does not use the dictionary definition of incest as "sexual intercourse between closely related persons where marriage is forbidden," but instead defines it as any sexual activity or experience imposed on a child that results in emotional, physical, or sexual trauma.

These experiences plant malignant seeds that infiltrate the patients' development, self-image, self-esteem, sexuality, and future potential for intimate relationships. The trust between children and their parents is devastatingly, irretrievably lost when adults do not control their impulses and protect their children, but instead impose their sexuality upon a child. At that moment, a scarring imprint is branded on the child's psyche, obscuring and interfering with the development of a healthy self. A complex bond develops between the child and the abuser, resembling the bond between hostage and captor, but more basic, and so more devastating and long-lasting in its effects.

Children are unable to perceive the reality of the betrayal. They are not able to understand or to alter the adult's behavior. The child cannot safely conceptualize and conclude that the trusted abuser may be disturbed, self-serving, exploitative, ruthless, and incapable of love. Instead, to survive emotionally, these children distort reality and believe that they themselves are bad and provoked the abuse. They believe that the fault, blame, and responsibility lie with themselves. The victims are left with unhealed wounds, and with scars of grief, fear, shame, humiliation, and the burden of the secret carried. They are encumbered with self-hate, self-doubt, and self-recrimination.

These patients live in a private inner world filled with tormented questioning: "Why did I let it happen? Did it happen? Am I making it up? Why didn't I say no? It was my fault. I'm bad, defective, different, damaged."

Filled with self-hate, they feel alone and worthless. They are forced to live a double life while keeping silent and hiding the past, thereby feeling incongruent and dishonest in the present. Outer and inner façades begin to develop, splintering off the possibility of the development of a real, authentic self.

The loss of faith in those who betrayed them, the desertion and abandonment by those entrusted to protect them, is too devastating and painful to experience, and conflicted feelings are desperately defended against. Primitive defenses are strengthened, and there is pressure toward acting out, splitting, and living in fantasy rather than in reality. The child's sense of abandonment and betrayal is deepened, and borderline dynamics, when present, are intensified.

For these adult patients, the painful experiences of childhood are woven into the fabric of their lives. Therapists must learn to see the hidden emotional scars and bruises of addictive borderline patients, to hear not only the words spoken, but to listen for the deeper messages unspoken. Only then can therapists help patients express and work through those blurred and buried painful memories and emotions that contribute to the addictive behaviors.

TREATMENT APPROACHES TO ADDICTIVE BEHAVIORS

The ego defects, abandonment depression, and defenses against it—especially denial—are often at the very core of the problem, predisposing borderline patients to addictive behavior problems. Patients with addictive behaviors use denial a great deal, some very convincingly. This is one of the reasons therapists can have difficulty identifying, recognizing, or diagnosing the behaviors. Seldom does the patient seek out the therapist and say, "I am an alcoholic. Can you help me?" Sometimes the patient will complain of symptoms that are actually the result of excessive drinking, such as insomnia, diarrhea, upset stomach, and nervousness, but the therapist may not make the connection between the symptoms and the cause. Therapists, who tend to expect straightforward histories, are often taken in by the evasions. The therapist has to look more deeply at what is presented. These patients deny reality and avoid facing their dysfunctional, maladaptive lifestyle, and their consequent suffering. Therapists need a high degree of alertness and suspiciousness to realize that these patients may not be accurate in reporting, may be lying or denying, and cannot be relied upon to divulge their symptoms freely. Many patients are not aware of painful feelings, because the purpose of the behaviors is to deflect them. The acting-out behavior is their attempt to avoid introspection, feelings, and memories.

Many patients come to treatment with the addictive process not yet full-blown or blatant, and the condition may be difficult to identify and diagnose in the early stages. More than half the alcoholics seen by physicians go undiagnosed (Vaillant, 1983, p. 295). It is likely that alcoholism will not be diagnosed by physicians, psychologists, or other helping professionals (Brown, 1985, p. ix). Many of these professionals recognize only grossly stereotypic alcoholic drinkers, and the therapist's own belief system and patterns of alcohol use may interfere with the appraisal of less obvious alcoholics. Tiebout (1951), having worked exclusively with alcoholics, states that psychiatry has failed dismally with alcohol problems, and that looking to the causes of the symptoms is inappropriate. The only sound therapeutic approach to impulse problems is to focus on the seriousness of the symptoms, with the goal of control through sobriety and abstinence.

All addictive behaviors, although not necessarily full-blown, need to be recognized by therapists as serious, problematic, and destructive. Many therapists naively agree when the patient says, "I only had a few drinks"; "I only took one 'hit' of marijuana"; "I went off my diet a little"; "The Valium really takes the edge off."

Sometimes, in order to relieve the patient's anxiety or depression, psychiatrists prescribe habit-forming drugs to a highly addictable person without enough exploration of drug and alcohol use. Patients may take amphetamines, tranquilizers, or hypnotics, for example, and develop an addiction or exacerbate an already established one. With a patient who is drinking excessively, this produces a superimposed drug addiction, without diminishing alcohol intake. In this way, therapists may support the patient's self-destructive behaviors, denial, and pathology.

Kernberg (1975) points out that any medication influencing the central nervous system is contraindicated in the course of long-term, psychoanalytic psychotherapy. He states that patients, particularly those with alcohol and drug problems, need to learn to control the symptoms on their own, and to take responsibility for managing their level of anxiety or depression, their appropriate responses, and their psychological alertness. In the majority of borderline patients he examined, tranquilizing medication was not necessary.

Acting-out behaviors can be disturbing to therapists, and trigger countertransference feelings. The therapist may act out with the patient by becoming angry, attacking, or withdrawing. With patients who drink excessively, the therapist's aggression can be mobilized to a degree that may become disruptive for the therapy (Silber, 1959). Out of frustration, therapists may use interpretation to deal with their *own* feelings, rather than the more appropriate therapeutic technique of confrontation when patients are acting out.

Some therapists, too, may have their own difficulties with addiction and may deny the destructiveness of their patients' behaviors. Because of their denial about their own excessive behaviors, they may not recognize the destructiveness inherent in these patterns and will collude with the patient's acting out.

These patients will be unable to overcome their problems until they stop the addictive behaviors. Initially in treatment, addictive behaviors need to be the primary focus of concern, with sobriety and abstinence the first goal of the therapeutic process. One of the problems in the field, as mentioned earlier, is the controversy between those who view alcoholism as a disease and the proponents of the psychiatric medical model. The latter group seeks the causes of a symptom and consequently may minimize the seriousness of the symptom itself, such as drinking and drug use.

Many clinicians tend to see this subject in black or white terms and to be on one side or the other. I believe the problem needs to be viewed more in shades of gray, to allow consideration of its full complexity. Alcoholism is an addictive behavior that is a disease with discrete symptoms and a progressive course, which eventually develops a life of its own. It causes depression, marital breakup, and unemployment. However, addictive behavior, such as alcoholism, is also symptomatic of deeper problems, of underlying psychic distress. Evidence indicates that significant ego impairments and other psychopathology predispose patients to alcohol problems. But acknowledging that there is underlying distress does not eliminate the necessity for a sound therapeutic approach to the management of impulse problems. The addictive behavior must be designated as the main focus of concern. One error in the treatment of a borderline patient who uses alcohol excessively, or of any such patient, is the assumption that the alcohol abuse will diminish with treatment of the underlying psychological problems.

The seriousness of the addictive behavior symptoms must not be ignored in order to focus on deeper issues. Troubling, repetitive, excessive behaviors must be faced directly and firmly at the beginning of treatment. Root causes cannot be the initial focus, because until the acting out stops, the patient is unable to explore conflicts on a deeper level. Only then can interventions be considered in response to the other characterologic and symptomatic problems that have previously been masked by the addictive behaviors. For these adult patients, the painful experiences of childhood are woven into the fabric of their lives. In treatment, after the excessive behaviors stop, therapists can then help patients acknowledge and deal with the past experiences and feelings that lie behind the behaviors. As they begin to deal with these feelings, however painful the process may be, patients can then begin to make healthy, conscious choices based on present reality, rather than continuing to reenact the past. Eventually, the patient can learn to appreciate the differences between impulse, thought, and action.

In his treatment approach, Masterson (1972, 1976, 1981) initially gives priority to addressing the defensive behaviors. Empathic and emphatic confrontations are aimed at stopping the behavior. The denied destructiveness is pointed out, as are the past history of problems, the consequences of the actions, and the ways in which patients are endangering themselves. Confrontations and limit setting of destructive expressions of impulses help patients become aware of their rationalizations, denial, and unrecognized destructive patterns.

It is common for borderline patients with addictions to drop out of therapy very early. Many therapists think they have a therapeutic alliance when they do not; others consider it impossible to establish one. And yet there are others who expect these patients to stop their addictions and give up their main defenses in order to demonstrate their motivation and capacity to form a traditional treatment alliance, when the reality is that, at the outset, borderline patients do not have that capacity. These patients have little basic trust, poor object relations, and use splitting as one of their main defenses. One of the most difficult problems, and a major cause of failure in treatment, is that therapists do not understand the process of initiating, establishing, and maintaining a therapeutic alliance (Masterson, 1978, 1981).

Because the therapeutic alliance is at best brittle and fragile at the beginning of therapy, the first as well as continuing goal of psychotherapy is to establish, strengthen, and maintain that alliance (Masterson, 1978, 1981). Masterson has developed a specific psychotherapeutic approach designed to repair the faulty separation-individuation of the borderline patient (1972, 1976, 1980, 1981, 1985). This approach has been tremendously successful in treating borderline patients with addictive behavior problems, in conjunction with participation in AA and similar groups.

Vaillant (1983) suggests that alcoholics usually need some kind of substitute for alcohol, such as a support group like AA. Says Vaillant: "AA is the most effective means of treating alcoholism, and it works for sophisticated, Harvard-educated loners as well as for gregarious blue-collar workers." He argues persuasively that it is not only essential but possible for alcoholics to gain control of their lives.

Many therapists lack in-depth knowledge of AA. They criticize AA as authoritarian, unscientific, superficial, and excessively religious. Hellman (1981) points out that these frequently biased opinions do not reflect the complexity of the AA program, and suggests that devaluing of AA by professionals is a serious problem, because the negative judgments are ultimately communicated to patients. (Objectively, it should be noted that proponents of AA sometimes view psychotherapy with a similar bias. The issue of adequate attention to the alcoholic's problems remains the same either way.)

Within the framework of the AA program, development of responsibility, movement toward autonomy, emotional growth, and adaptation are stressed. In her study on alcoholism, Brown (1985) describes a model of treatment that combines Alcoholics Anonymous and psychotherapy. AA is recommended for anyone who is concerned with drinking and for all who wish to stop, even though she states not everyone will accept referral. Hellman (1981) concludes that there is no inherent antagonism between AA and psychoanalytically oriented therapy. In many cases, the therapist can successfully integrate the lessons AA teaches about alcoholism and addictions to better help patients make gradual modifications in their defenses and to improve their adaptation.

Addictive behaviors need to be viewed in a larger framework, not seen and treated as separate entities. Chronic addictive behavior causes much suffering. The therapist can help stop the destructive acts, encourage participation in a support group when indicated, utilize appropriate treatment methods, and eventually deal with underlying conflicts and depression. All these interventions lead to a potentially hopeful outcome. The treatment journey for borderline patients with addictive problems, although destined to include struggles and victories for both the therapist and the patient, can result in change, growth, and healing.

REFERENCES

Benward, J., & Densen-Gerber, J. (1975). *Incest as a causative factor in anti-social behavior: An exploratory study.* New York: Odyssey Institute.

Boyer, L., & Giovacchini, P. (1967). *Psychoanalytic treatment of characterological and schizophrenic disorders.* New York: Science House.

Brown, S. (1985). *Treating the alcoholic: A developmental model of recovery.* New York: John Wiley.

Browning, W. (1985). Long-term dynamic group therapy with bulimic patients: a clinical discussion. In S. Emmett (Ed.), *Theory and treatment of anorexia nervosa and bulimia.* New York: Brunner/Mazel.

Bruch, H. (1973). *Eating disorders: Obesity, anorexia nervosa, and the person within.* New York: Basic Books.

Butler, S. (1978). *Conspiracy of silence: The trauma of incest.* San Francisco: Volcano Press.

Carnes, P. (1983). *The sexual addiction.* Minnesota: Comp Care Publications.

Fenichel, O. (1945). *The psychoanalytic theory of neurosis.* New York: W.W. Norton.

Frosch, J. (1967). Severe regressive states during analysis. *Journal of the American Psychiatric Association, 15,* 641–685.

Gunderson, J., & Singer, M. (1975). Defining borderline patients: An overview. *American Journal of Psychiatry, 132,* 1-10.

Hamburger, W (1951). Emotional aspects of obesity. *Medical Clinics of North America, 35,* 483-499.

Hellman, J. (1981). Alcohol abuse and the borderline patient. *Psychiatry, 44,* 307-317.

Herman, J. (1981). *Father-daughter incest.* Cambridge, MA: Harvard University Press.

Jellinek, E. (1952). Phases of alcohol addiction. *Quarterly Journal of Studies on Alcohol, 13,* 673-684.

Jellinek, E. (1960). *The disease concept of alcoholism.* New Haven, CT: College and Universities Press.

Kernberg, O. (1967). Borderline personality organization. *Journal of the American Psychiatric Association, 15,* 641-685.

Kernberg, O. (1975). *Borderline conditions and pathological narcissism.* New York: Jason Aronson.

Khantzian, E. (1975). Self-selection and progression in drug dependence. *Psychiatry Digest, 36,* 19.

Khantzian, E. (1980). The alcoholic patient: An overview and perspective. *American Journal of Psychotherapy, 32* (1), 4-19.

Khantzian, E., Mack, J., & Schatzberg, A. (1974). Heroin use as an attempt to cope. *American Journal of Psychiatry, 131,* 160-164.

Mahler, M. (1975). *The psychological birth of the human infant.* New York: Basic Books.

Marlatt, G. (1983, October). The controlled-drinking controversy: A commentary. *American Psychologist,* pp. 1097-1110.

Masterson, J. (1972). *Treatment of the borderline adolescent: A developmental approach.* New York: John Wiley; Brunner/Mazel, 1985.

Masterson, J. (1976). *Psychotherapy of the borderline adult: A developmental approach*. New York: Brunner/Mazel.

Masterson, J. (1978). The borderline adult: Therapeutic alliance and transference. *American Journal of Psychiatry, 135* (4), 437–441.

Masterson, J. with Costello, J. (1980). *From borderline adolescent to functioning adult: The test of time*. New York: Brunner/Mazel.

Masterson, J. (1981). *Narcissistic and borderline disorders: An integrated developmental approach*. New York: Brunner/Mazel.

Masterson, J. (1985). *The real self: A developmental, self, and objects relations approach*. New York: Brunner/Mazel.

Miller, P. (1979). Interactions among addictive behaviors. *British Journal of Addiction, 74,* 211-212.

Miller, W. (1980). *The addictive behaviors*. New York: Pergamon Press.

O'Reilly, J. (1983, April 25). New insights into alcoholism. *Time,* pp. 88-89.

Overeaters Anonymous. (1980). *Overeaters Anonymous*. Torrance, CA: Overeaters Anonymous.

Peele, S., & Brodsky, A. (1975). *Love and addiction*. New York: New American Library.

Rinsley, D. (1965). Intensive psychiatric hospital treatment of adolescents: An object relations view. *Psychiatric Quarterly, 39,* 405-429.

Rubin, T. (1970). *Forever thin*. Berkeley, CA: Berkeley Publishing Corporation.

Rubin, T. (1978). *Alive and fat and thinning in America*. New York: Coward, McCann & Geoghegan.

Sandler, J., Holder, A., & Dare, C. (1970). Basic psychoanalytic concepts. II: The treatment alliance. *British Journal of Psychiatry, 116,* 555-558.

Silber, A. (1959). Psychotherapy with alcoholics. *Journal of Nervous and Mental Disease, 129,* 477–485.

Silber, A. (1974). Rationale for the technique of psychotherapy with alcoholics. *International Journal of Psycho-Analytic Psychotherapy, 3* (1): 28-47.

Smith, D., Milkman, H., & Sunderwirth, S. (1985). Addictive disease: Concept and controversy. In H. Milkman & H. Shaffer (Eds.), *The addictions: Multidisciplinary perspectives and treatments*. Lexington, MA: D.C. Heath.

Stunkard, A. (1959). Eating patterns and obesity. *Psychiatric Quarterly, 33,* 284-292.

Stunkard, A., & McLaren-Hume, M. (1959). The results of treatment of obesity: A review of the literature and report of a series. *Archives of Internal Medicine, 103,* 79-84.

Szasz, T. (1974). *Ceremonial chemistry*. New York: Anchor Press/Doubleday.

Tiebout, H. (1951). The role of psychiatry in the field of alcoholism. *Quarterly Journal of Studies on Alcohol, 12,* 52.

Vaillant, G. (1983). *The natural history of alcoholism: Causes, patterns and paths to recovery*. Cambridge, MA: Harvard University Press.

Weber, E. (1977, April). Incest: Sexual abuse begins at home. *Ms.*

Zetzel, E. (1956). Current concepts of transference. *International Journal of Psycho-Analysis, 37,* 369-378.

Chapter 24

The Separation-Individuation Phase as Symbolized in the Oedipus Legend

Candace Orcutt, Ph.D.

What is that which has one voice and yet becomes four-footed and two-footed and three-footed?

The riddle of the Sphinx obliquely tells us that the central metaphor of psychoanalysis, the Oedipus myth, is a commentary on more than one age of man. I hope to show that a deeper understanding of the myth extends meaning beyond that of Oedipus' meeting with Jocasta—as outlined by Freud—to his encounter with the Sphinx (a mother figure of a different sort), and thereby illuminate still earlier preoedipal infantile psychic life.

This chapter has been adapted from a dissertation written in partial fulfillment of the requirements for the degree of Doctor of Philosophy in Clinical Social Work at International University, St. Christopher, W.I., 1983.

411

It was in *The Interpretation of Dreams* (1900) that Freud first introduced his conceptualization of the myth, believing that the artist, like the dreamer, has direct access to the unconscious:

> While the poet, as he unravels the past, brings to light the guilt of Oedipus, he is at the same time compelling us to recognize our own inner minds, in which those same impulses, though repressed, are still to be found. (p. 263)

Like Schliemann discovering the site of Troy, Freud had the genius to show the way, and those of us who come after can extend the dig to new levels.

My thesis is that Oedipus' meeting with the Sphinx, and his solving of her riddle, is a mythical recapturing of the infantile experience of separation-individuation, of the actualization of a sense of self at the expense of the primitive mother imago. Unless he can get himself past the Sphinx, Oedipus can never have his day with the seductive Jocasta.

Just as the wish to marry the mother is at the core of Oedipus' relationship with Jocasta, so the fantasy of matricide (and the corollary, infanticide) is at the center of his encounter with the Sphinx. If the child cannot "kill off" the primitive perception of the mother and continue his psychic growth, he will be "devoured" by her. This fantasy derives from such fundamental longings as the child's desire to be independent, and the mother's desire to hold onto him. The fantasy also derives from complicated mechanisms such as talionic rage evoked by separation anxiety and the projection of that rage onto the mother imago.

As Freud used the Oedipus legend to show the intensity and universality of the fantasies of destruction and desire associated with the triangular relationship of child, mother, and father, so this earlier part of the legend can be used to demonstrate the similar force and relevancy of primitive destructive fantasies in an aspect of the mother-child dyadic relationship. And each instance demonstrates our conflicting need to both forget and remember our earliest and deepest fantasies. The solution is a metaphor.

Freud himself did not pursue the riddle of the Sphinx with any persistence, although, curiously, it was a youthful daydream of his to be immortalized with a bust bearing Sophocles' description of Oedipus: "Who divined the famed riddle and was a man most mighty" (Jones, 1955, pp. 13–14). Interestingly enough, Jung and Rank, both dedicated to understanding archaic states preceding the Oedipus complex, and both champions of the individuating, creative self, took a passing fancy to the Sphinx. Jung (1911–1912) describes her as a personification of the "terrible" or "devouring" Mother (p. 181), while Rank (1929), noting that her name means "the Strangler," believes she represents birth anxiety that the hero must overcome (pp. 144-145). Neumann (1949), Fromm (1948), and Grotjahn (1949), all recognize the Sphinx as a symbol of the archaic Great Mother Goddess, and interpret her relationship to the hero accordingly. Grotjahn adds:

> Freud was fully aware of the problems posed by the phenomena of matriarchy, feminine deities, the symbol of the Sphinx and man's hostility toward the woman who gave him life. . . Freud preferred to stop at the Oedipus level rather than go further and make the still deeper interpretation that matricide antedated parricide. (p. 307)

SOCIORELIGIOUS CONTEXT OF THE FEMALE GREEK SPHINX

The Sphinx is a symbol of the Great Mother Goddess in her negative aspect. She brings pestilence and despair, devours youths, and is associated with graves. Her dolefulness may have been increased by the fact that she represents the old matricentric society that was out of favor in Sophocles' time. That prehistoric society, bound by tribal ties and a magical sense of oneness with nature, was superseded by patriarchal society, with its emphasis on individual assertiveness, objective justice, and a detached pantheon of Olympic gods with distinct personalities and responsibilities. This social change (which took millennia to accomplish) was perceived by the Greeks as an intensely conflictual transition. This is clearly articulated in such plays as Sophocles' *Antigone*, where failure to resolve the conflict destroys the House of Thebes. In the *Oresteia*, by Aeschylus, the House of Atreus is similarly threatened, and the tragic hero, much like Oedipus, is finally absolved of his crime—in this case, matricide. On a cosmic level, the establishment of a patriarchal society of law is reflected in the myths of the overthrow of the earth-forces by the Olympic gods. Thus, Apollo slays the Python and becomes lord of the Delphic Oracle. In the parallel story of the hero, Oedipus destroys the Sphinx and becomes riddle-master and king.

Typically, fearsome composite beings such as the Sphinx (for example, her half-siblings Cerberus, the Hydra, and the Chimera) were descendants of Gaia, the primordial Earth Mother, and were associated with the old religion. As Greek society evolved, these creatures often came to serve a transitional function, by providing heroes such as Oedipus, Bellerophon, and Heracles formidable means for proving their manhood. These dragon-slayer myths (which have their counterparts worldwide) reflect not only the hero's individuation, but also the shift of culture from dependency on the bonds of kinship to establishment of a society guided by objective laws.

So, it would appear, the Oedipus myth represents cultural as well as psychic evolution. It is no doubt an oversimplification to speak of society individuating from the influence of the Great Goddess, as the self evolves from the mother-child dyad. Like a psychoanalytic reconstruction of one person's past, our theories of history are colored by retrospective fantasy. Nevertheless, the Oedipus myth found its most powerful expression in Greece in the fifth century B.C., that golden era—dedicated to individuality and self-knowledge—which subsequently influenced the entire Western world and the Eastern world as far as India. The Oedipus myth has had an impact on both the art and science of the West, and, I surmise, its potential as a metaphor for the development of the individual and collective psyche is still mostly untouched: "Its roots go down to Hades" (Vergil, IV, line 446).

OEDIPUS AND THE SPHINX

The Sphinx appears early in the legend of Oedipus, as he has only begun his wanderings. Oedipus, uncertain of his origins, consults the Delphic Oracle and is met with the apparently tangential and alarming prophecy that he will kill his father and marry his mother.

Determined not to return to his home in Corinth, he sets out to elude his fate and encounters it almost at once. At a crossroads, he is bullied by a nobleman old enough to be his father, and kills him in a burst of rage. As he continues his journey, Oedipus crosses the plain of Thebes and is halted by the Sphinx, a creature with the body of a lion, wings of an eagle, and face of a woman.

The Sphinx has been terrorizing Thebes by asking a riddle of every traveler who comes by, and by devouring those who, up until this time, have inevitably failed to give her the right answer. To Oedipus, in turn, she puts her question: "What is that which has one voice and yet becomes four-footed and two-footed and three-footed?" (Apollodorus, 1939, pp. 347–348).

Oedipus replies: "Man; for as a babe he is four-footed going on four limbs, as an adult he is two-footed, and as an old man he gets besides a third support in a staff" (p. 349).

The Sphinx acknowledges the correctness of this answer by committing suicide, and Oedipus continues on his way to Thebes. Once he is there, his heroism is crowned with kingship and a royal marriage, for the ruler of Thebes is reported slain by robbers on the road. Never thinking of the nobleman he slew at the crossroads, nor of the Oracle's prophesy, Oedipus fulfils his destiny by accepting Jocasta as his queen.

How does the encounter of Oedipus and the Sphinx recapitulate the infant's separation and individuation from the mother?

The first clue, as I have said, is the figure of the Sphinx herself. She is a symbol of the mother. In addition, she is a symbol of the *early* mother: incompletely perceived, part fantasized, not fully human, but mingled with animal instincts and desires (Jung, 1911–1912, p. 181; Rank, 1929, pp. 144–145). Like the early mother, what are most accessible about her are her face and voice—the rest is magic.

Her riddle is the key to her meaning. The riddle is about human change (infancy, maturity, old age), but, more specifically, it embodies the developmental tasks of the separation-individuation phase. The content of the riddle concerns itself with walking; the form of the riddle is a contest of words; and the answer to the riddle requires a sense of identity. Oedipus meets the Sphinx's challenge by speaking a single word that demonstrates command of verbalization and motility, and the ability to define himself.

In addition, the riddle replaces the usual bloody combat between hero and monster, reducing it to a harmless-seeming word game. Some Greek vase paintings even show Oedipus and the Sphinx gazing introspectively at each other in a way that suggests intimacy rather than antagonism. A peculiar—and significant—aspect of the verbal combat is that it creates an interpersonal (so to speak) relatedness between the hero and the Other. Oedipus and the Sphinx are a dyad, and their enigmatic task is unquestionably shared.

Before going further, I would like briefly to review Margaret Mahler's (1972a) conceptualization of the separation-individuation phase, especially the rapprochement subphase. I will then return to the myth and compare the two.

Mahler (1972a) observed that "the biological birth and the psychological birth of the individual are not coincident in time," for the latter is a "slowly-unfolding intrapsychic process." Although, as she points out, this is a process that "reverberates throughout the life cycle," "the principal psychological achievements in this process" take place from about the fourth or fifth to the 30th or 36th month of age (p. 120).

The earliest subphase of differentiation (in which the infant begins to emerge from the symbiotic orbit with the mother) gives way to the practicing subphase, in which the infant begins to enjoy his autonomy. The child experiences "major periods of exhilaration, or at least of relative elation," seemingly "intoxicated with his own faculties and with the greatness of his world." This elation appears to arise from the acquisition of upright locomotion, as well as from increasing maturation of the ego, and also "escape from absorption into the orbit of the mother" (pp. 126–127).

At the same time the infant is enjoying new freedom, he is also establishing a "specific bond" with the mother, takes pleasure in gazing at her across space, and returns to her for "emotional refueling." The "distance modalities" of seeing and hearing are heightened in importance, and the transitional object makes its first appearance to paradoxically bridge the space between infant and mother and ensure its perpetuation (pp. 124-125).

At the height of separation-individuation, the rapprochement subphase takes place. Mastery of locomotion initiates this phase, and the acquisition of language and symbolic play now begin. At the same time, the sense of physical separateness becomes a mixed blessing, and separation anxiety increases. The "refueling" of the previous subphase becomes "an active approach behavior," as the toddler "seems to have an increased need and wish for his mother to *share with him* every new acquisition on his part of skill and experience." As sense of self and object grows clearer, the child begins to recognize the largeness of the real world, and the smallness of himself, especially as he realizes he must learn to manage the world "more or less 'on his own.'" He can no longer summon up and partake of the old magic of maternal power. At this "crossroad" that Mahler termed the "rapprochement crisis," the child must give up the "delusion of parental omnipotence," and with it his "delusion of his own grandeur." This crisis is frequently marked by "dramatic fights with mother" (pp. 128-130).

The rapprochement subphase gives way to the final but open-ended subphase, which Mahler (1972b) calls *"on the way to object constancy"* (p. 132).

Oedipus leaves what seems to be his home and parents in Corinth to search for his identity. He has heard rumors he is not the true son of the King of Corinth, so he journeys to consult the Delphic Oracle on the matter. From here on, he makes an almost continuous pilgrimage to discover himself and be reconciled with what he finds. Every step of the way touches the influence of the Great Mother: first Delphi (the

Oracle was hers before Apollo usurped it), then the crossroads (sacred to Hecate, her infernal aspect), then the plain of Thebes (guarded by the Sphinx, her negative aspect), then Thebes itself (with Jocasta, the real mother), then Colonnus (with her avengers, the Furies, who become the Beneficent Ones as Oedipus at last resigns himself to his nature). This is a pattern reminiscent of the touching back to the mother figure that Mahler describes in the practicing, but especially the rapprochement, subphase of separation-individuation.

And, as in Mahler's description, each move is propelled by a mixture of longing and aversion. As Mahler wrote of the rapprochement subphase of "searching and sharing" (1984), it is "the mainspring of man's eternal struggle against both fusion and isolation" (1972a, p. 130). Further, the "growing away process" of psychic birth (which reaches its height at rapprochement) initiates "a lifelong mourning process," for *"inherent in every new step of individual functioning is a minimal threat of object loss"* (p. 120). No statement could be truer in describing the fortunes of Oedipus, whose every achievement turns bitter until he is able to turn bitterness to an achievement.

But the encounter with the Sphinx takes place when Oedipus is the young hero at the height of his power, testing himself and drawing new confidence from his mastery of danger. Soon this moment will make him King of Thebes. Because he already knows something about the longing for an identity, he is able to answer the Sphinx's riddle. Because he is still eager and not yet disillusioned, he takes pleasure in playing the riddle-game with her, and believes he has won: he "kills her off" lightly, without the understanding of sorrow and isolation that will be his experience afterward. He does not yet know that "separation" from the Sphinx will lead inevitably to the marriage with Jocasta, and just as inevitably to the insight that he has overvalued his individual will in a world that works by its own laws.

The Oedipus myth presents the Oedipal incestuous wish as fully realized and enjoyed before disillusionment occurs. Similarly, the encounter with the Sphinx represents the wish of the separation-individuation phase of development: to "kill" the mother; to become triumphantly assertive through interplay with a magical entity who has power over one's being and nonbeing. The encounter with the Sphinx occurs in the opening part of Oedipus' journey, which is concerned with the spontaneous gratification of desire. The latter part reveals the inevitable consequences of the human passion for self-knowledge, a harsh but eventually redemptive continuation of the unravelling of the riddle of the self.

   The Sphinx and the Delphic Oracle are related, both historically and
in the Oedipus legend. Briefly, here the Sphinx is a reverse oracle, who
turns Oedipus' question back on himself. So, at the beginning of his
quest, Oedipus looks to external power for self-knowledge, but the
appearance of the Sphinx marks a turning point where he must, under
threat of death, assume responsibility for identifying himself. At the
moment he does so, his magical questioner dies, reflecting the
disappearance of the primitive mother imago into the unconscious
(just as the death of Jocasta will mark the decline of the "oedipal"
mother figure). This turning point can be taken as a metaphor for the
rapprochement crisis, where dramatic interchange with the mother
leads to the child's loss of "the delusion of parental omnipotence," and
leaves him very much aware of the necessity to manage his world "on
his own."

   But, despite these undercurrents, the encounter with the Sphinx
symbolizes an early, often exuberant time of life when a sense of
individuality can be pursued not too far away from the watchfulness of
a magical, omnipotent guardian. Oedipus is the universal hero (the
indomitable child in all of us), mastering the early tasks of traveling
and quick talking and finding himself as he discovers the world. When
he conquers the Sphinx, it is through the interplay of words, and the
hero—like the individuating child—becomes a game-master. The
riddle of the Sphinx represents a special kind of combat which can be
likened to a child's acceptance of individuation through symbolic play.

   The riddle, like the "moment" of rapprochement, represents the
point in the myth at which Oedipus begins his long development of
insight. Up until now, he has been ruled by impulse; from now on,
literally and symbolically, his time to rule begins. Picture in your
mind's eye (as the Greek vase painters did) how the hero and the
Other meet. The young man, with his cloak and distinctive traveler's
hat, has been crossing a great plain, intent on reaching the walls of a
distant city. He rounds a low hill, and abruptly is caught within the
shadow of immense, outspread wings. He looks up from shocked
immobility to make out, against the glare of the sunlight she blocks, a
being like a winged lioness, but whose face, crowned with wild hair, is
that of a serene and beautiful woman. As his sense of reality lurches,
the Apparition begins to sing. At first he can only watch and listen, but,
as she continues her song, the creature furls her wings and settles back
on her haunches. The traveler also—but without taking his gaze away
from her—seats himself, on a convenient rock. The more he watches
and listens, the less he fears, for he understands that she is singing to

him about himself. He is alert and ready as she ends her song, enigmatically smiling, and waits for his answer. The transformation from outward searching to inward discovery has taken place as Oedipus and the Sphinx have been joined by their mutual gaze and the sound of her voice. Then he speaks the answer, "Man," and finds himself alone in the sunlight, facing the gate of Thebes.

A last comment on the riddle rests upon D. W. Winnicott's concept of transitional space. In "The Location of Cultural Experience" (1966), Winnicott describes how play originates from the interpersonal "space" that is created in the process of separation of self and object:

> From the beginning the baby has maximally intense experiences *in the potential space between the subjective object and the object objectively perceived*, between me-extension and the not-me. This potential space is at the interplay between there being nothing but me and there being objects and phenomena outside omnipotent control. (p. 381)

Winnicott and Mahler both describe the importance of the "space" left by the growing separateness of mother and child: first there is the need for intermittent closure of the space, then for occurrences and things to bridge and mend the distance, and then, increasingly, a playfulness with distance that allows the sense of reality to shift about until the new sense of internalized continuity is established.

As Winnicott (1951) points out, this third "spatial" area prefigures the adult cultural experience, which is based on a balance of subjective and objective perceptions:

> The third part of the life of a human being, a part that we cannot ignore, is an intermediate area of *experiencing*, to which inner reality and external life both contribute. It is an area which is not challenged, because no claim is made on its behalf except that it shall exist as a resting-place for the individual engaged in the perpetual human task of keeping inner and outer reality separate yet inter-related. (p. 230)

In the separation-individuation transition, the old, magical, omnipotent ideation gives way to a flexible mastery of simultaneous realities. Winnicott continues: "I am therefore studying the substance of *illusion*, that which is allowed to the infant, and which in adult life is inherent in art and religion" (p. 230).

The Oedipus myth is a continuous commentary on the tension that exists between universal "necessity" and individual pride. It is the interplay between the two that shows the full measure of both and provides illusory moments of unity between them. Such a moment is the riddle-game between Oedipus and the Sphinx. And this life-and-death confrontation is presented in a form that has a quality of play.

The "game" between deity and hero reflects the interpersonal aspect of play. The type of game, the riddle, represents the transformative nature of play.

The riddle of the Sphinx challenges Oedipus to establish and integrate different levels of perception in order to arrive at a new sense of himself. Insight, by definition, is impossible without a multiple perception of reality. The separation-individuation phase brings a decisive sense of inner and outer realities and of a transitional reality to bridge them. The riddle of the Sphinx represents the transitional reality that resolves paradoxes in the experiential moment. Is the riddle about the primitive perception of an indistinct part object (four legs? two? three?), or is it (as Freud intimated) an oblique reference to the whole-object-oriented perception of sexual intercourse and the difference between male and female? Oedipus could have answered the question from either point of view, but then there would have been no experience of insight, no growth. In an inspired moment, he realizes that one answer can contain all the shifting possibilities: Man. Like Oedipus, we recapture this childhood sense of discovery through transformative play—in jokes and riddles, and in unpuzzling the multiple levels of myth.

REFERENCES

Apollodorus. (1939). *The library* (J. G. Frazer, Ed. and Trans.) (Vol. 1). Cambridge: Harvard University Press.

Freud, S. (1900). *The interpretation of dreams* (J. Strachey, Ed. and Trans.). New York: Basic Books, 1953.

Fromm, E. (1948). *The Oedipus complex and the Oedipus myth*. New York: Harper and Brothers.

Grotjahn, M. (1949). The primal crime and the unconscious. In K. Eissler (Ed.), *Searchlights on delinquency*. New York: International Universities Press.

Jones, E. (1955). *The life and works of Sigmund Freud* (Vol. 2). New York: Basic Books.

Jung, C. (1911–1912). *Symbols of transformation* (R. F. C. Hull, Trans). Princeton: Bollingen, 1952.

Mahler, M. (1972a). On the first three subphases of the separation-individuation process. In *The Selected Papers of Margaret S. Mahler* (Vol. 2). New York: Jason Aronson, 1979.

Mahler, M. (1972b). Rapprochement subphase of the separation-individuation process. In *Selected Papers*.

Mahler, M. (1984). *The psychological birth of the human infant.* Franklin Lakes, NJ: The Mahler Research Foundation Film Library.

Neumann, E. (1949). *The origins and history of consciousness* (R. F. C. Hull, Trans.). Princeton: Bollingen, 1954.

Rank, O. (1929). *The trauma of birth.* New York: Harcourt, Brace.

Winnicott, D. W. (1951). Transitional objects and transitional phenomena. In *Through paediatrics to psycho-analysis.* New York: Basic Books, 1958.

Winnicott, D. W. (1966). The location of cultural experience. *International Journal of Psycho-Analysis, 48,* 369–372.

Chapter 25

The Masterson Approach and the Supervisory Process: Stages of Teaching and Learning

Karla Clark, Ph.D.,
and Candace Orcutt, Ph.D.

Therapists learning the Masterson Approach to the treatment of personality disorders encounter a unique set of learning tasks that require a corresponding unique set of supervisory functions. This chapter describes the stages of supervision, and delineates the therapist's primary learning tasks and emotional responses during each stage. These center around the reactivation of the therapist's feelings about his own separation-individuation and his own narcissistic vulnerability.

Why are separation-individuation and narcissistic issues reactivated in supervision? The giving up of old ways and the learning of new ones stirs up latent unresolved aspects of the developmental task of separation-individuation for the psychotherapist, as well as for the patient. This tendency is exacerbated when one is treating personality disorders because separation-individuation issues are core problems of the borderline and narcissistic patient. Since these concerns are at center stage for the patient, they become center stage for the therapist as well, who must be alert to dealing with separation-individuation issues at all times. This constant focus may reactivate any unfinished vestiges of the therapist's separation-individuation process. Beyond that, the patient's use of the defense of projective identification, which evokes emotional response in the therapist, may also stir up counter-transference feelings about separation-individuation.

This reactivation of separation-individuation issues creates problems for the therapist and the supervisor. When things go well, the resolution of unresolved pockets of conflict produces a firmer sense of professional identity, with underpinnings of enhanced competence and creativity. Usually, the supervisee achieves this through an ongoing process with predictable stages and associated learning tasks.

Before describing these stages in detail, it is necessary to discuss how we view the supervisory experience as whole, that is, what we consider our job to be and how we propose to accomplish it. The supervisory process has been described from varying perspectives. Austin (1952), for example, stresses the importance of individuality in the process of learning the practice of social work, and claims that the essential skill in supervision is the selection of a teaching method based on an individualized educational diagnosis. Like those of other important social work educators (see, for example, Towle, 1954) Austin's delineation of supervisory functions is based on the assumption that supervisor and supervisee are involved primarily in furthering the professional growth of the latter. Supervision in their view has as a basic goal the growth and development of the supervisee. Theoreticians writing from this point of view therefore stress the educational and growth-promoting aspects of the supervisory process. In contrast, Eckstein and Wallerstein (1972) focus less on the orderly unfolding of learning processes and stages. They are concerned primarily with impediments to learning, which intrude from external sources, and learning resistances, which have their origin within the learner.

In this chapter we attempt to combine these approaches, describing supervision both in terms of its normal, developmental progression—with expectable learning tasks predominant at different phases in the process—and in terms of the learning resistances or specific problems that may appear during each phase.

We have divided our observations into five sections: the first addresses the general goals of supervision and the nature of the supervisory task; the second through the fifth discuss the specific stages of the supervisory experience.

I. THE PURPOSE OF SUPERVISION

The Context

Supervision occurs in a number of situations and settings for a variety of purposes, ranging from the purely formal fulfillment of administrative requirements to the fully voluntary contracting by one individual for learning from another. Naturally, the context to a great degree determines what occurs in the transaction (Eckstein and Wallerstein, 1972).

Two factors greatly influence the context of the type of supervision discussed here. First, we mostly supervise experienced clinicians who have attended conferences or read literature that has stimulated their interest in learning this approach. These supervisees are mostly learners with considerable clinical experience and a sense of a professional self who have some acknowledged dissatisfaction with the way the work has been going and who want to change it. Second, the supervisory contract is entirely voluntary and may be stopped at any time without adversely affecting the career of the supervisee, because it does not involve administrative or clinical responsibility for the supervisee. The responsibility of the supervisor is entirely to the supervisee to the enhanced development of the professional's sense of competence through learning a specific body of theory and technique that increases his effectiveness with personality disorder patients.

The Goals of Supervision

The Masterson Approach itself can be viewed on two levels. At the more inclusive level, it is a way of thinking about human development and pathology based on two interwoven theories. First, we understand the person based on aspects of his developmental history (developmental theory). Second, we focus on the way in which that history has interwoven with the individual's own internal processes, influencing his internal sense of self, his perceptions of internal objects, and how these self and object representations relate to one another (object relations theory).

This combining of developmental and object relations theory is translated into a theory of how the individual integrates the two levels of experience, his development and his internal interpretation of his development. This personal integration or interpretation, we believe, heavily influences the individual's ways of approaching life's challenges for productivity and intimacy. Productivity and intimacy themselves support the development and expression of the individual's real self (Masterson, 1985). On this broader level, therefore, we have a theory of the activation, development, and psychopathology of the self that potentially can be applied to how one thinks about a wide range of problems encountered in therapy. At this point, we have applied it to the problems of specific groups of patients: the borderline and narcissistically disordered individuals.

The theory is therefore both specific to the treatment of these particular individuals and a metaphor, or example, of how other clinical problems or areas might also be theoretically approached.[1] We hope that over time, the broader potentials of the theory will be explored by us and those whom we teach. In supervision, however, we focus on the imparting of a basic body of knowledge about a specific psychotherapeutic technique applied to the specific clinical populations whom we have already studied extensively: personality disorder patients. Our goals are therefore to prepare the individual to apply the theoretical perspective in broad and creative ways by first teaching him the rigorous specifics of the application of the theory and technique to patients with personality disorders.

Our approach assumes that specific developmental arrests are at the heart of the characterologic problems of the narcissistic or borderline patient, who also has characteristic internal images of self, other, and relationship based on how he has interpreted and internalized relevant experiences. We have developed specific, distinct therapeutic techniques through which to approach him, based on these assumptions. We predict that applying the techniques will have certain short- and long-term effects on the course of the psychotherapy, the development of the patient's sense of self, and the quality of his life. The supervisee is thus confronted with learning not only an approach to human problems, but a body of theory and technique of great specificity and rigor in regard to specific clinical populations. Both theory and technique will differ from that which he has previously acquired. To help him master this new material, we must, as supervisors, teach specific skills.

---

[1] In fact, this chapter serves as an example of the application of the theoretical approach in a new area: the description of a model for the teaching and learning of psychotherapy based upon developmental, self, and object relations concerns.

First among these skills is the capacity to formulate and test hypotheses concerning clinical material through clinical interventions. Second is the ability to modify one's approach based on the outcome of the interventions. When one uses the Masterson Approach, the patient initiates some course of action and the therapist tries to understand whether it furthers self activation, expresses the affects associated with that activation, or reflects defenses against self activation or affects. Whether one intervenes, how, and to what end, is determined by that evaluation. When one makes an intervention, one has an idea of how it will come out, and then watches closely to see whether what happens conforms to the hypothesis. If it does, one proceeds; if it doesn't, one asks oneself why not.

Thus, the clinician must learn to have a clear idea of what to expect: what the patient needs to do in order to improve, what the therapist needs to do to help him do so, and what to do if a given intervention does not get a predictable response. One goal of supervision is to increasingly prepare the clinician to perform the tasks of hypothesis formulation, intervention, observation, and hypothesis modification autonomously, in an integrated, thoughtful, and open-minded way.

There is, however, a more basic goal. It is through a combination of skills and open-minded creativity that patients are best served and knowledge in the field advanced. To work in this way, in addition to technique, the clinician must have developed a secure sense of an evolving, autonomous professional self. This latter point is the crux of the matter: The goal of supervision goes beyond the attainment of good treatment skills. The expression of these skills rests upon the development and enhancement of the professional self. Therefore, our goals are to support the furthering of self-activation processes within the therapist in addition to enhancing skills and knowledge.

By the end of the supervisory process, the therapist should be familiar with the theoretical model and be able to see its application in the clinical material. He should be able to form a diagnosis in structural terms, which includes a view of the patient's introjects, his defenses, his capacity for reality testing, his problems in self-activation, and the way in which his symptoms reflect these aspects of his personality.

When the therapist looks at a given patient at a given moment, he should be able to fit what is going on into the diagnostic picture that he has developed of the patient. He should have the capacity to modify what he has hypothesized based upon what he observes. He should then be able to translate this into specific interventions based on his evolving diagnostic hypotheses.

In addition, he must have the capacity to understand the patient empathically as well as intellectually, and to understand and observe his own reactions and relate these to the clinical material. This implies a highly developed capacity for self-observation. Self-observation involves the development and enhancement of the capacity to observe the therapeutic self objectively, to identify and work with one's errors and understand the general outlines of one's own countertransference inclinations so that these are identified, controlled, and utilized effectively instead of destructively in the therapy.

These two factors—mastery of the model and enhanced capacities for self-observation and self-control—together form the basis of the autonomously functioning self of the therapist, which will place him in the position to use himself creatively in the therapeutic process. This is the goal of supervision. In order to reach these goals, the supervisor must be prepared to perform certain specific tasks.

Functions of the Supervisor

The functions of the supervisor are best defined in terms of the model of psychotherapy being taught. Fleming and Benedek (1966), for example, based their theory for the teaching and learning of psychoanalysis on the development in the learner of the capacity to use the three tools of introspection, empathy, and interpretation, which they see as the basis of the art and science of independent psychoanalytic practice. To this group of three we would add the grasp of a body of specific new theoretical information with which the supervisee in all likelihood is not fully familiar. Further, one must assist in the development of the skills involved in three therapeutic techniques in addition to interpretation: confrontation, mirroring, and communicative matching, all of which, again, are probably either unknown to the supervisee or imperfectly understood. Last, and perhaps most important, it is the supervisor's task to identify major countertransference vulnerabilities in the supervisee and bring these to his awareness so that they do not interfere with his therapeutic effectiveness.

The supervisor must evaluate the adequacy of the supervisee's grasp of the body of knowledge underlying the Masterson Approach. She must provide both objective information (when that is indicated) and be able to suggest sources from which that knowledge can be acquired (such as books and courses). She must also remain alert to the increasing capacity of the supervisee to apply that knowledge himself, test this capacity, and support the development of the capacity for independent use of the model.

She must teach awareness of and the use of therapeutic processes, which involves increasing the supervisee's capacity to look at the context of interventions, what precedes and follows them, and how the supervisee fits this into the general plan for treatment.

She must be able to teach technique and provide, through specific examples and guidance, answers to the specific technical questions of the supervisee.

As with the imparting of information, the intent of these interventions by the supervisor is to provide the supervisee with the groundwork for proceeding on his own. It is therefore as important to know when to stop as when to start teaching this technical material. The supervisor must be alert to the time when such technique teaching is no longer useful to the therapist, and support the creative development of his own unique style of intervention, within the confines of the theoretical framework.

Similarly, the process of drawing the supervisee's attention to countertransference goes through stages. His capacity for and use of self-awareness must be mapped out, and he must be helped to develop this self-awareness as is appropriate. For example, a student who is very aware of his feelings but not of the ways to use these in an objective, intellectual fashion to further therapy must be helped to frame the intellectual component of his reactions; a supervisee who is intellectual must be helped to become aware of his feelings when his intellectualization leads him to collude with the patient to avoid feelings.[2]

As the supervisee masters technique and theory, mistakes in therapy can increasingly be viewed as reflections of countertransference. At

---

[2]An even wider generality might be drawn regarding the learning process as it is applied to skills in which intuition plays a prominent part. Many therapists, to some degree (often to a high degree), perceive their work as an art. Therapists who rely on the feeling/intuitive capabilities of right-hemisphere thinking characteristically resist learning of an explicitly systematic/logical left-hemisphere type. There is concern that the intuitive capacity will be lost. Temporarily, indeed, it seems that it is, while the therapist is engaged in developing and synthesizing functions of both hemispheres. A transitional period of confusion and antipathy toward the learning is often met with. Similarly, therapists who rely basically on a left-hemispheric, intellectual approach often have difficulty engaging right-hemisphere functions. These emotional/intuitive qualities are perceived as wild or irrational, and may be closed out defensively. A fuller synthesis and use of the brain's capacities can only enrich the skills of either the "artist" or "scientist" type of therapist.—C.O.

that point, the supervisor must draw these to the attention of the supervisee in such a way that he gains control over his response, without allowing supervision to convert into therapy. The goal is self-awareness and self-control on the part of the therapist, not the resolution of intrapsychic conflict.

All of these duties are performed within the framework of a supervisory relationship which itself has characteristic stages of development. Our discussion of these stages will include the major learning tasks appropriate to each, which are characterized by certain feelings and behavior on the part of both supervisor and supervisee.

II. THE SUPERVISORY PROCESS

Miller (1977) quotes Bertha Reynolds as having delineated five stages of clinical learning: (1) An acute stage of self-consciousness, during which the student's energies are mobilized against the prospect of danger to himself as a person. The teacher's role at that point, as Reynolds sees it, is to provide security, with the intent of finding some adequacy in the learner's background for negotiating periods of distress. (2) "Sink or swim," during which the student is barely able to keep up and is dependent on the opinion of people in the know for a sense of well-being. At this point, the learner may have the vocabulary of mastery but is without the ability to command it. The teacher here increases security by mobilizing previously acquired knowledge and skills and encouraging some reliance on spontaneity in the student. (3) The stage at which the student has some understanding of the situation without the power to control his own activity in it. There is a shift from preoccupation with the self to concern with the external situation. The learner understands what should be done but is uneven in his ability to do it. The teacher may be tempted to criticize at this stage, but appropriate supervisory technique entails mobilization of the learner's own analysis and self-criticism. (4) The state of relative mastery. At this stage, conscious intelligence and unconscious responses work together with integrated wholeness. The learner thinks of himself in a new way, objectively. At this point, new and continued learning can occur through competition, the initiation of research, the pursuit of relevant knowledge from other fields, and so forth. (5) The stage of learning to teach, which includes the capacity to approach the individual learner as well as to encompass the situation to be mastered by the learner (p. 355).

These observations parallel to a great degree the process of supervision as we have conceptualized it. Because, however, we are dealing with adult supervisees who have been in practice for a time, the process is complicated by the losses and distress involved in the giving up of aspects of learned behavior and of the old sense of the autonomous professional self. While all new learning requires a process of giving up, disintegration, and reintegration, it is particularly acute as an issue with people who have already gone through this process and thought that they found themselves upon the farther shore, only to have to undergo it again. This process interweaves with the process of learning of new material outlined by Miller and gives the supervisory process in the Masterson Approach with experienced practitioners its particular cast.

Stage One: The Establishment of Supervisory Authority

The first stage in the supervision process involves the supervisee's acknowledgment that there is a body of theoretical and practical information to be learned and that he is willing to put in the time and effort to obtain it, along with a simultaneous awareness that the supervisor has the skills necessary to teach the material. The supervisor's focus is to assist the therapist in developing the theoretical and technical skills required to apply the model, through minute scrutiny of the clinical work. The working relationship has to develop in such a way that nonjudgmental scrutiny of the therapist's interventions and thought processes is permissible, and this with an adult learner who in all likelihood has not had such an experience in many years. Issues of authority and autonomy are therefore predominant at this stage. In contrast to Miller's learner in stages one and two, the typical supervisee in the Masterson Approach also has to unlearn previously hard-won material and relinquish equally hard-won professional autonomy. This tends to complicate the beginning stages of supervision.

We have observed that the enthusiasm with which the therapist enters supervision in the Masterson approach is rapidly counterbalanced by at least some degree of unrest. In most settings, supervision of psychotherapists tends to be somewhat lenient and inexact. The work of the therapist is rarely under direct scrutiny. There are good reasons for this, including protection of confidentiality, and the need to transcend content to make the best use of the supervisory hour. Partly as a result of this, most therapists develop a highly personal style, and are accustomed to modifying their interventions based on their own observations and assessments rather than as a result of direct injunction from another person.

However, the Masterson Approach is theoretically and technically exacting. The therapist tracks the borderline triad, for example,[3] and intervenes only to confront a maladaptive use of the ego's defensive capacity. Like all good techniques, this is elegantly simple and open to objective scrutiny—one is either doing it, or one is not.

Since such objective scrutiny of his work often runs counter to the supervisee's experience, it commonly meets with almost as much resistance from the supervisee as its clinical counterpart elicits from the patient. Most clinicians have experienced permissive supervision. The therapist who comes for this advanced instruction has previously been trained in a style of "Don't tell me what to do; just show me how I can use your ideas without your systematic scrutiny of how I apply them." This first problem, then, could be described as a "cultural" one: the therapist must develop the self-discipline to suspend old ways of working in order to try the new, and must accept close review of this change, when this is not the accustomed way of working.

The dynamic issue that appears in this initial stage relates to the sense of self as therapist. The therapist has come to supervision believing the Masterson Approach will be beneficial to learn. The therapist has decided to make a commitment beyond the salad bar of learning opportunities offered by conferences, but usually expects to be able to filter theoretical learning subjectively to the treatment level. The supervisee using the Masterson Approach is immediately required to report from process notes taken during the session, and is held to specific rules for intervention (e.g., he must have an objective in mind when he intervenes).

Few clinicians seek this as their initial training, and those who do may seek it because they are concerned with difficult patients and have already sweated out certain ways of working with them. The requirement that the clinician start anew, and account for it in process recording, tends to challenge the sense of self-as-therapist. Worse, despite creditable work, the experienced clinician feels reduced to the status of a beginner. As Searles (1962) wrote of the analytic candidate: "He feels faced with the threat that he will be forced to exchange a professional identity which he has achieved over years of arduous clinical experience, and which he cherishes . . . for an identity which will be not only very different but, so he is convinced, far more constricting" (p. 274).

---

[3]Individuation leads to depression which leads to defense (Masterson, 1981, pp. 140–145).

Example 1. A supervisee in his fourth supervisory hour referred to an interchange with the supervisor in which she had insisted that he stay with a certain theme and demonstrate that he could recognize it in his process notes rather than move on to a more global discussion of concepts. He said, "I think I have resistance—it's painful—and I think the reason it's painful involves autonomy questions. My attitude in coming into this is there are things I want to know, and I want feedback about what I'm doing. I think that the way that we are doing the process is that there have been a few times that you have said something and I have said I got it and wanted to move on, and you wanted to stay with it. And it makes it like you want to stay with it, and if I stay with it, it is for you instead of for me. That's what I mean about autonomy questions."

The supervisor acknowledged the difficulty this skilled practitioner had with her attitude, which might erroneously imply that he was a beginner rather than an experienced practitioner. She freely acknowledged the possibility of her own overconcern. She pointed out, however, that the supervisee had certain ways of handling the feelings evoked around autonomy that were then interfering with his own learning goals.

For example, rather than staying with and following one case, so that both he and the supervisor could track what happened with his interventions, he was presenting different people every time: this protected his "autonomy" at the expense of his learning. She related this to his apparent thought that his autonomy was best protected by having general global discussions of the patients' major themes rather than detailed discussions of the therapeutic process. She pointed out that this attitude sold him short, in that he thereby avoided scrutiny of his own work and thinking, thus interfering with his own learning objectives in supervision. The supervisee acknowledged that she was correct and began to focus on sticking with one case.

This illustrates one of the more common transactions in the beginning stages of supervision between a competent experienced supervisee and a supervisor in the Masterson Approach, in which the therapist experiences the expectations and rigor of the new model as a threat. This particular supervisee was willing to openly discuss his feelings, which led to their adequate resolution. At this stage, unfortunately, open discussion of this problem is only one of a number of ways in which conflicts about autonomy and the sense of professional self are expressed.

Two sorts of attitudes are common at this stage. One is an eagerness and receptivity to learning the model. The basis of this eagerness may be that a student has genuinely made up his mind to learn the material and is receptive to the process. Sometimes these students go through the task of giving up old ways of operating and learning new material with minimal difficulty and evasiveness. The supervisee in Example 1 is such a learner. He viewed his own reactions as a block to his learning, brought them up for discussion, and acted to improve things following the discussion.

However, openness and apparent receptivity may indicate a kind of idealized, unrealistic, and passive assumption that "teacher knows best," which may show up in a surface compliance and agreeableness. This latter sort of supervisee may show all too few signs of difficulty in subjecting his work to scrutiny, because he is acting out his dependence; his real problem has to do with anxiety about functioning autonomously. His problems surface later, when the focus shifts to the assumption by the therapist of more autonomous responsibility for examining his work critically and taking independent steps to correct it. (See examples 6 and 8.) The supervisor working with a cooperative and enthusiastic supervisee should remain alert either to an undercurrent of evasiveness and difficulty, and recognize it, or to its absence, and be alert to the possibility of a supervisee with a compliant defense.

There is a second group of supervisees who are not so apparently or truly cooperative. They may be openly struggling with autonomy issues, as was the supervisee described earlier, but with more difficulty in resolving them, or they may have a kind of a "prove it" attitude, based on either intellectual or emotional skepticism. Skepticism, like cooperation, can have many meanings. It may be a healthy process of critical thinking in an autonomous adult, or an attempt on the part of the supervisee to avoid giving up his professional autonomy, or the upper edge of a more entrenched problem with learning. Which of these motivations exists can probably be best determined by how open the supervisee is to modifying self-destructive ways of handling his feelings in order to permit himself to learn.

How the supervisor handles this problem is crucial. The supervisor, suddenly facing a supervisee turned evasive or outright hostile, must first understand that the average supervisee is not accustomed to being told what to do, even though that is the contract. The supervisor must consciously recognize the problem with the supervisee, find a way to discuss it, and point out the ways in which the supervisee is interfering with his own learning processes. Only then can the different bases of the uncooperative attitude become clear.

The beleaguered therapist may translate his discomfort, initially, into what he perceives as an interpersonal struggle regarding his autonomous functioning, instead of recognizing the threats to his old sense of autonomy and sense of professional competence that are implied in learning a new model. It is important at this stage that the supervisor recognize both the need to establish supervisory authority, and the equal need not to define that authority in a way that infantilizes the mature therapist. Otherwise the conflict will indeed become interpersonal and the supervision will suffer if not founder.

Authority is mainly functional in the service of growth. As Margaret Mahler said of the rapprochement experience of childhood, sharing and seeking to share characterize the emergence of true autonomy in healthy maturation (1965, p. 39). In the adult, an independent state of mind should transcend issues of power. However, even the healthiest adults strive for this goal more than they achieve it. Ideally, the supervisory experience is essentially a matter of sharing. Two responsible clinicians get together to teach and to learn, and assume the roles necessary to accomplish that task. In reality, in so doing, the two take on a duality which may strike chords reminiscent of the duality of parent and child. It is an opportunity for unresolved issues of autonomy to make an untimely reappearance, and the task of learning may temporarily give way to protestations and assertions of who is in charge.

Example 2. Just as the patient externalizes inner conflict by attacking the therapist, so the therapist may translate therapeutic struggles into supervisory ones. The supervisor begins to hear that the patient being discussed seems to be losing trust in the therapy and even may be harmed by the introduction of the new technique. This intimation may then evolve into a full-scale supervisory conflict.

An experienced and perceptive therapist initially described supervision as a "place of purpose" where she could find a new "grounding for a concept of depression." She presented a patient who had reached a therapeutic stalemate after three-and-a-half years of treatment. She began to confront her patient's desire to seek comfort rather than work through her problems.

The patient at first integrated around the confrontation, and then (since the rewarding unit defense had been disrupted) shifted to the withdrawing unit defense, mentioning in the transition that her mother was distant and cold and didn't show her enough recognition. The therapist then began to experience *herself* as distant and cold, although, simultaneously, she experienced herself as therapeutically "on target."

The patient escalated the testing of the therapist and began to act out, appearing late for sessions and not paying. The therapist began to feel personally responsible for the patient's transference acting out, especially when the patient accused her of lacking empathy. In a countertransferential reaction, the therapist felt a sense of separation when the rewarding unit was interrupted and, in a maneuver parallel to that used by the patient, relocated the conflict from within her own feelings to an externalized dispute with the supervisor.

She said she feared the supervisor's recommendations would "disrupt the confluence" between herself and her patient and force the patient from treatment. The supervisor confronted this counter-transference reaction, with the result that, after an initial seven sessions, the supervisee sent the following letter:

> I am discontinuing supervision.
> It disturbs me that you continue to interpret my complaints in terms of resistance to the work as opposed to statements to you about your supervisory style.
> You don't allow enough for my judgment regarding my patient or for my integrity regarding intent to learn this method.
> The help I need is in learning to identify and prioritize treatment issues, not to be directed to actions I should be taking on vague and undigested understanding of the material. Once I am clear, I know perfectly well how to proceed.

After some soul searching, during which the supervisor struggled with issues paralleling both the patient's and the supervisee's, the following reply was sent:

> I have received your letter informing me that you are discontinuing supervision, and I regret that you did not choose to discuss it with me.
> It seems to me that you shortchange yourself if you focus your concern on my supervisory style rather than on your own reactions. Your patient in supervision responded to your initial use of confrontation. You stopped confronting your patient when she began to test your new style of working with her, and at the same time you began to question the supervisory process.

Every supervisee encounters transference and countertransference problems, which must be resolved for the learning to proceed.

The supervisee had been questioning her own countertransference acting out when the reply arrived, and decided to return. Two sessions later, she reported that her continued self-inquiry into the guilt and anger evoked by her patient's resistance had led to a breakthrough in personal insight.

As this example shows, issues of individuation ("Don't interfere!") dominated this transaction. Only when these were resolved did they give way to issues of separation ("My patient and I are in a new, strange place and are afraid we will lose each other"). In general, during stage one, individuation issues are most prominent. This is reflected in the therapist's perception of himself as having his individuation threatened by a giving up of autonomous control of his practice. It is also threatened by the achievement of new skills and knowledge (which force further individuation).

This is not to imply that separation issues are not also present during this stage of the work. As in Example 2, these are mobilized by separation from fantasies concerning the relationship with the patient (separation from the supervisor is of course not so relevant at this point, when the attachment between supervisor and supervisee is just forming).

Serious supervisees in our experience manage the impact of this first stage. They are professionals who are used to taking psychic "risks" in behalf of their patients, and will continue to do so in order to meet the tough challenge their work provides. As one supervisee reflected: "The issue for the worker is whether to come back after trying it out. This treatment doesn't have the pacifying effect people think therapy should have. Other therapists around you say you're too extreme. You almost have to start all over again. You're really in the mud."

As the therapist accepts the authority of the supervisor, masters the theoretical and clinical material intellectually, and begins to work collaboratively concerning the patient, the field shifts. Although the focus is still primarily on issues of individuation, Stage Two of supervision is ushered in as the therapist sees that the approach works, acknowledges this, and begins to try to apply it in a less ambivalent way.

Stage Two: Loss of the Old Professional Sense of Self

The second stage of the supervisory process emerges as the supervisee acknowledges to himself that the model works and that the supervision is effective. While this realization may bring with it some sense of excitement and satisfaction, characteristically the supervisee is soon more depressed and subdued than otherwise.

At root, the therapist is mourning his prior sense of professional self, which may include defenses that he has activated against his own separation-individuation and acted out in his conduct as a therapist. One typical form that such acting out takes is the tendency of therapists to step into the rewarding unit with patients. They do this for various reasons, among these to defend against abandonment feelings of their own by being "needed"; to avoid giving up the fantasy of "changing" another person, and to exercise grandiosity. Therefore, efforts to contain and control the acting out bring on powerful feelings. As one supervisee put it: "While I held my ground, I came away from the session depressed. . . I wasn't the rewarding unit any longer . . . My interpretation of these feelings was further validated by my subsequently experiencing early, forgotten childhood memories of fear associated with being alone."

A further source of discomfort for the seasoned therapist is to be found in his acknowledgment of prior errors as he compares his present work with his previous efforts. This often evokes painful feelings of loss of self-esteem, shame, guilt, and grief as earlier failures with patients are relived.

The supervisor's stance is to be empathic and supportive of this process, while remaining alert to the possibility that the therapist will convert these feelings into actions or defenses that impede the supervision. The supervisor's task, during this critical period, is to reinforce mastery of the material and the expectation that it is within the capacity of the clinician to do the work. In addition, the supervisor has to draw the therapist's attention to his countertransference so that it does not interfere with the psychotherapy.

This latter task must be done within the context of a supervisory rather than a psychotherapeutic frame. It cannot be overemphasized that the therapist who sees borderline and narcissistic patients does some of the most challenging work in the field. The patient is often under immense emotional stress and tries to pass as much of this as possible along to the therapist. The therapist's job is to contain the feelings, sort them out from his own, and help the patient take responsibility for them. The supervisor's job is to reinforce the work of containment without stepping over the boundary and becoming therapist to the therapist.

Frequently, this runs counter to a wish on the part of the supervisee that the supervisor turn into therapist. This wish in part is an acknowledgment on the part of the supervisee of the stirrings of unresolved conflicts brought to the surface by the patients and the Masterson Approach. It is partly a learning resistance. In contrast to psychotherapy, supervision requires that the individual evaluate and control his responses according to objective performance criteria. Turning supervision into psychotherapy would eliminate the necessity to painfully evaluate and control one's errors. During the second phase, the supervisor must make sure that the distinction remains clear between therapy and supervision, and that the supervisee is assisted in containing his emotional responses in his patient's interests. The feelings of the supervisee are examined to this end alone: to help him identify what feelings in him may impede the psychotherapy, and assist him in converting these feelings to a positive force in the conduct of the psychotherapy.

Example 3. A supervisee who had been working with the Masterson Approach for a considerable period attended a conference on counter-transference. In his next supervisory session, he began talking about his own reactions to his patient's material in a very personal way. Before the supervisor knew it, the supervisee was discussing his own childhood, his mother, and the feelings that his associations evoked.

The supervisor, concerned at the blurring of the supervisory relationship, brought the change to the supervisee's attention and asked him how, specifically, this material was relevant to what was going on with his patient. The supervisee became angry, saying that he had had the impression, from the conference, that his own emotions were supposed to be what was attended to in supervision. The supervisor replied that what was important for the purposes of the supervision was the effect his feelings were having on the work, that the question was whether he, the supervisee, could contain them; it was not their purpose to work these through. The supervisor went on to point out that the supervisee had been having difficulty in presenting material about this patient of late, based on his own expressed wish to "do it himself." She pointed out that discussing his own, rather than his patient's, process was related to this confusion about doing it himself. On the one hand, he was acting as though to discuss his work interfered with his autonomy. On the other hand, to convert the supervision into psychotherapy implied that he could *not* do the work. Both of these attitudes were destructive to his learning goals.

The therapist accepted this comment and returned to a focus on the patient, showing more initiative in assessing his own material and improved integration of theory. He soon understood that his patient was enormously resentful of doing independent, autonomous work and acted out with him by becoming helpless and accusatory. He, in turn, had felt inadequate and had defended against this by becoming clinging and accusatory in supervision. When he controlled this, he understood the patient's projective identification as part of what precipitated his own reaction and used his increased understanding of the process to confront the patient effectively.

This example illustrates a process typical of this phase of supervision. The supervisee feels the depression and anxiety attendant upon loss of the prior autonomous professional self, and often feels corresponding resistance to taking the next steps in the development of renewed professional autonomy based on the integration of the new theoretical model. Additionally, he experiences the onslaught of the patient's projective identifications, which he often confuses with his own responses. Rather than deal directly with these feelings, he may act out in supervision.

Example 4. In example 3, the supervisee tried to convert supervision into psychotherapy. Alternately, the supervisee may assume a sort of false self, rewarding unit stance in which he is overly compliant with the supervisor. This stance is more commonly found among supervisees who have not expressed their negative feelings openly, either during stage one or earlier in stage two. It may require that the supervisor assume a stance which is closer to therapeutic, but, as in the following example, the stance always keeps the nature of the educational contract between supervisor and supervisee at the forefront. The goal is not psychotherapy for the supervisee: it is the furtherance of mastery and professional autonomy.

Supervisees respond to the depression and confusion of this period in various ways. Some are able to identify and control the feelings so that they do not provide a major learning impediment. Others, as in the following example, try to defend by converting supervision to psychotherapy or by other forms of compliant behaviors. By becoming dependent or compliant, they ward off their feelings of loss, inadequacy, and uncertainty, and unwittingly impede the development of new skills.

One supervisee of three years had progressed in a model way: facing his own anger and self-assertion in order to help his patients face theirs; attending conferences; inviting his supervisor to speak at his agency; referring a case to the supervisor; and making the major individuative moves of returning to personal psychotherapy and leaving agency work for private practice. The supervisor was impressed with the increasing professional and personal maturity of the supervisee, but sometimes felt uneasy that all these changes had taken place without disturbing the supervisory field.

Suddenly, the therapist lost two patients (including the one followed in supervision) and concluded that he could no longer afford supervision because of the reduction in income. The supervisor accepted the fact that there were financial realities involved, but questioned whether there might be other motivations. The supervisee, it was pointed out, had been very giving to the supervisor but had been disappointed in certain ways. The supervisor had not yet referred a case to him, for example. The supervisor wondered whether the therapist was experiencing resentment at not being "rewarded" for his giving. The supervisee returned to the next session to say that he had experienced an important insight concerning the need to give and expectation to receive. He was more open and assertive, and the work continued.[4]

The supervisor during this period must be alert to the possibilities for defensive compliance while at the same time offering realistic support and advice concerning case management that will lead to the development of the supervisee's skills. The supervisor must distinguish times when genuine support and assistance are indicated from the sort of clinging designed to ward off feelings and retard autonomous functioning. Because during this phase the therapist has given up his prior sense of professional competence and is by no means confident of his own skills, he will realistically turn to the supervisor in times of

---

[4]Subjective issues on the part of the therapist need not be excluded from the supervisory process. The line between supervision and psychotherapy is sometimes a fine one. The concern is one of priority, which in this case means the enhancement of the therapist's clinical skills, and thus the aligning of the therapist's disclosures to the therapeutic task. Here, the supervisory task was merely to identify the problem and its most immediate source with the supervisee so that the clinical work could resume in an effective way—not to work it through.

stress for direction and help. The supervisor must at these times be prepared to provide them.

Example 5. The following example shows the importance of active advice and support during this phase of supervision.

The patient had rigorously tested the therapist from the start, beginning with a first session in which the patient claimed to have overdosed and demanded to be taken to the hospital.

In a later session, the patient, angry that the hour ended before she wanted it to, locked herself in the therapist's bathroom and refused to come out. The therapist telephoned the supervisor, who pointed out that the patient was escalating demands on therapy to a point where the supervisee had to demonstrate the limits of therapeutic responsibility. Consequently, the supervisee told the patient that he had no choice but to call the police, whereupon the patient resumed responsibility for herself and came out.

Over time, the mourning of the old professional self and the feelings of depression attendant upon giving up whatever defensive gratification the therapist experienced from his old ways of intervening with the patient subside. The therapist feels and acts increasingly in control of the material. He begins to be able to generalize from case to case, no longer feeling that he has to discuss everything with the supervisor. The supervisor, during this phase, needs to be alert to the changing nature of her function: to provide less and less active guidance and advice and to focus increasingly solely on countertransference issues as these obstruct the psychotherapy.

With this shift of attention from the active teaching and acquisition of material to a stance that supports the new autonomy of the supervisee, Stage Three of the process commences. In this stage, countertransference holds center stage and the psychodynamic basis of the supervisory interchange shifts from a concern with matters of individuation to matters of separation.

Stage Three: Focus on Countertransference

When the authors began to outline this discussion, we informally named this stage of the supervision "It's Me!" This designation most accurately reflects both the mood and the tasks of this particular phase. The supervisee now has control of the approach and knows it. When he errs, he knows that it is not from ignorance. He is no longer concerned with the giving up of his prior sense of professional identity. His difficulties with his patients and in supervision at this point have to do with two things: matters in the psychotherapy that stimulate unresolved conflicts of his own, and matters in supervision that concern his feelings about doing things competently.

The supervisory task during this stage is to refrain from offering unnecessary support and advice and to increasingly support autonomous functioning. Supervisory interventions during this period focus on countertransference.

Example 6. A supervisee in the third year of supervision came in with a question concerning how to "handle" the spacing of hours. The patient, who had previously been seen on Tuesday and Thursdays, had had a schedule change and wanted to come on Monday and Tuesday instead. The supervisee wanted to know how the supervisor would handle such a request. Rather than answer the question, the supervisor asked the supervisee what criteria he would use to evaluate such a schedule change. He was further asked what he would expect if he allowed the schedule change to occur. He first answered with a reflexive response, saying that, of course, the patient would regress and defend. The supervisor (who felt that this response was a resistance to really thinking for himself about the clinical material) challenged this and asked him again what he would predict, based on what he knew of this particular patient. He thought about the question further, and reached the decision to permit the schedule change. He thought out for himself both what he would tell the patient and how he would evaluate his decision.

The supervisor in this case had reached the decision, based on knowledge of the particular supervisee, that the problem being presented had to do with the supervisee's difficulties in taking responsibility for autonomous professional decision making, and based her intervention on this decision. Prior to this incident, it had been openly acknowledged between them that this particular therapist resisted acknowledgment of his professional, autonomous self. Consequently, the intervention was understood by the supervisee in the context of his own acknowledged problem and processed as a further piece of work on that particular problem.

Such interchanges are common in Stage Three. Alternately, a persistent or glaring error by the therapist may signal the presence of countertransference to the clinical material, and is dealt with as such.

Example 7. A supervisee responded inappropriately to a comment made by a patient. This patient, a clinging and distancing borderline patient, had made the decision to stay out of an adult offspring's difficulties. This decision was appropriate and, furthermore, was the kind of decision that had always been very difficult for the patient. Typically, she interfered inappropriately, took over, became enraged at her subsequent feeling of being overburdened, and lashed out at the offending offspring. When the patient made the decision to stay out of her son's affairs, the therapist responded by confronting her "avoidance of responsibility" rather than supporting the appropriateness of her decision not to interfere. He was unaware of having made an error. When it was pointed out to him that he had done so, he paused, thought about it, and said that his feeling at the moment had been rage at the patient. His feeling had been: a mother should take care of her child. The supervisory discussion that followed was confined to the need to be careful to control his impulse to intervene when the patient discussed her relationships with her adult children and to observe his own resultant feelings carefully. He did so, and later reported to the supervisor that he had discussed what had come up for him with his own therapist, with important personal results.

Examples 6 and 7 impart some of the flavor typical of interchanges during this phase of supervision. The supervisor and supervisee have a solid working alliance. The bounds of supervision are understood and respected. There is consensus concerning the issues being worked on. The supervisee does so with increasing feelings of mastery, self-esteem, and the capacity to apply the model on his own.

Increasingly, the supervisee begins to be able to articulate his experience and his clinical ideas. The issue begins to arise as to how long ongoing supervision—as opposed to periodic collegial consultation—is appropriate. The final stage of supervision is at hand.

Stage Four: Separation, the Self and Creativity

The goal of supervision is twofold. Primary is the attainment of good patient treatment. But this cannot be genuinely achieved without reaching the ancillary goal: the therapist's reclaiming of professional autonomy that incorporates the new knowledge. Reclaimed professional autonomy, partially relinquished in the service of learning this method, further assumes that the therapist will continue to seek consultation on difficult cases throughout his career, and that this does not conflict with autonomous functioning. Therefore, separation from the supervisor refers to the loss of the roles of teacher and learner, and the assumption of the roles of professional colleagues. The last task of supervision is one of managing the loss to both supervisee and supervisor of the relationship in such a manner that the independent and creative self of each is strengthened. Like all maturational processes, this is at core a grief process, and a sadness accompanies the joy of mastery.

The supervisor's function as the final stage begins is to identify whatever regressive defenses the supervisee develops to deal with this loss, to refrain from entering into the process herself, and to support and encourage mastery.

Example 8. The supervisee in example 6 announced the desire to cut back supervision to every other week. The supervisor commented that the decision belonged to him, but that, from her perspective, there were certain areas of learning that he had not addressed during supervision. Knowing this particular supervisee's commitment to learning, she questioned the decision to cut back rather than to address these particular areas. This supervisee had recently completed certain important individuative moves, such as passing a licensing examination and undertaking further graduate study. The supervisor raised the question, in the light of this particular individual's problems with allowing competence to develop and show, whether the decision to cut back was a function of the wish to avoid dealing directly with the change in status between the two of them, from one in which the supervisee had seen himself as a dependent learner. She added that much could and should be learned in a collegial way, but hazarded the guess that, rather than face the anxiety of acknowledging this, the supervisee was wishing to leave. The supervisee acknowledged this and with great emotion spoke of the feelings of loss attendant on his perception of himself as a learner, and his continuing fear of attack and loss if he openly acknowledged his new skills and used them in supervision. He commented wryly that he had seen himself as walking through a dark wood with the supervisor taking his hand and leading the way, and noted the discomfort he felt at the prospect of walking the path side by side. This led to a relaxation of tension in supervision and change in the tone of the hours to a more equal and collegial atmosphere.

Each of the authors has experienced the pleasure of seeing a supervisee transcend supervisory issues to take credit for mastery of technique and promoting of a patient's progress. Each has experienced both the anticipation and the dislocation of repeatedly assuming the mantles of teacher and leader and giving them up in favor of the development of a collegial relationship. Transcending one's own feelings of loss in favor of the gratification of participating in the professional growth of the supervisee has had to be repeatedly worked through. When both supervisor and supervisee manage this final transition, the work is enhanced for both. At such a juncture, supervisory struggles are beside the point (as they really always were). At the end, our hope is that supervisor and supervisee find themselves separate, individual, and equal. Two adults, who agreed to assume authoritative and dependent roles in the service of learning, relinquish those roles and the fantasy traces attached to them. In the process, the hopes of mending the past through rebellion, conformity, dominance, or permissiveness have had to be given up. Old views of competence and identity have had to be mourned. Uncertainty has had to be endured. New competences and identity have had to be acknowledged. When this goal is achieved, supervisor and supervisee enter into the real satisfaction of finding each other as colleagues in present time, assured of each other's support in the continuing effort to understand our patients and discover ways to help, learn, and teach.

REFERENCES

Arlow, J.A. (1963). The supervisory situation. *Journal of American Psychoanalysis, 11,* 576–594.

Austin, L. (1952). Basic principles of supervision. *Social Casework, 33,* 411-419.

Blitzsten, N. L., & Fleming, J. (1953). What is a supervisory analysis? *Bulletin of the Menninger Clinic, 17,* 117-129.

Eckstein, R., & Wallerstein, R. (1972). *The teaching and learning of psychotherapy.* New York: International Universities Press.

Feldman, Y., Spotnitz, H., & Nagelberg, L. (1953). One aspect of casework teaching through supervision. *Social Casework, 34,* 150-155.

Fleming, J., and Benedek, T. (1966). *Psychoanalytic supervision: A method of clinical teaching.* New York: Grune & Stratton.

Grotjahn, M. (1954). About the relation between psychoanalytic training and psychoanalytic therapy. *International Journal of Psychoanalysis, 35,* 254-262.

Grotjahn, M. (1955). Problems and techniques of supervision. *Psychiatry, 18,* 9-15.

Mahler, M., with La Perrier, K. (1965). Mother-child interaction during separation-individuation. In *Selected Papers of Margaret S. Mahler, Vol. 2.* New York: Jason Aronson.

Masterson, J. (1981). *The narcissistic and borderline disorders: An integrated developmental approach.* New York: Brunner/Mazel.

Masterson, J. (1985). *The real self: A developmental, self, and object relations approach.* New York: Brunner/Mazel.

Miller, R. R. (1977). Clues from the past about clinical learning: Reynolds and Towle revisited. *Clinical Social Work Journal, 5,* 351-362.

Schlessinger, N. (1966). Supervision of psychotherapy: A critical review of the literature. *Archives of General Psychiatry, 15*, 129-134.

Searles, H. (1962). Problems of psychoanalytic supervision. In *Collected Papers*, pp. 257-276. New York: International Universities Press.

Towle, C. (1954). *The learner in education for the professions: As seen in education for social work.* Chicago: The University of Chicago Press.

Zetzel, E.R. (1953). The dynamic basis of supervision. *Social Casework, 34*, 143-149.

Index

447